OFFICIAL REPORT

OF THE

SIXTEENTH INTERNATIONAL

CHRISTIAN ENDEAVOR CONVENTION

HELD IN

MECHANICS', WOODWARDS' PAVILIONS, AND IN MANY

CHURCHES.

SAN FRANCISCO, CAL., JULY 7 – 12, 1897.

First Fruits Press
Wilmore, Kentucky
c2015

First Fruits Press

The Academic Open Press of Asbury Theological Seminary

204 N. Lexington Ave., Wilmore, KY 40390

859-858-2236

first.fruits@asburyseminary.edu

asbury.to/firstfruits

THE "COMMITTEE OF '97" AT WORK AT "HEADQUARTERS" IN THE Y. M. C. A. BUILDING.

OFFICIAL REPORT

OF THE

SIXTEENTH INTERNATIONAL

CHRISTIAN ENDEAVOR CONVENTION,

HELD IN THE

MECHANICS', WOODWARDS' PAVILIONS, AND IN MANY CHURCHES.

SAN FRANCISCO, CAL., JULY 7–12, 1897.

PUBLISHING DEPARTMENT,
UNITED SOCIETY OF CHRISTIAN ENDEAVOR,
646 WASHINGTON ST., BOSTON, MASS., U. S. A.
1897.

ON THE CREST OF THE CONTINENT.

The Christian Endeavor Army in the Mormon Stronghold. — A Picture of the Intermountain Christian Endeavor Convention at Salt Lake City.

ROSSING the continent! What a lesson in patriotism to thousands of young people! We believe that this was one of the chief lessons taught by the great Convention; that in the hearts of thousands of young men and women was born an earnest determination to be better citizens of this that Mr. Moody calls "the best country God ever gave a nation."

Ah, little thought that young pastor up in Maine sixteen years ago that his care for his lads and lassies, and their hearty following, would lead to so mighty issues! that after only three half-decades the railroads of a continent would be taxed to carry to its extreme border the young Christians enlisted under the banner there set up, and that he himself would be present with fresh news of their allied brigades in Europe, Asia, Africa, Australia, and the isles of the sea!

As the trains sped into the evening shadows, the chaplain of each car condensed his company, song leaflets were distributed, and glorious morning and evening prayers were held, that made of every car a Bethel.

"Train Schedules So Much Waste Paper," is the way the newspapers were talking by the time Denver was reached, and indeed that splendid, great, clean, mountain city was crowded with belated Endeavorers. A host of them filled the First Baptist Church for a rally, with Treasurer Shaw to rouse their ready enthusiasm.

Probably never before has the Garden of the Gods held so much youthful enthusiasm. Everything on wheels was chartered for the delightful ride to Manitou, and many a farmer's big wagon was passed crammed with chairs. The Kissing Camels, the Lion and Seal, the Balanced Rock, the majestic Pillars of Hercules, — in and out among these marvels coiled and uncoiled a long procession of admiring young men and women, and many a prayer-meeting to come will be richer for that rich day's experience at the foot of grand old Pike's Peak.

The Royal Gorge! Well worth a journey across the continent is that impressive, silent witness to the power of the Creator. "No man

3

could put up this," murmured a buffet cook, as he knelt — an appropriate attitude — to gaze at those massive cliffs. The tumultuous river, between whose foaming, angry edge and the base of the frowning walls the cars found a narrow path, subdued its roar as if awed by the majesty of that vast chasm. All boisterousness was hushed, and only the waving of handkerchiefs as the abrupt curves brought the Endeavorers in sight of one another testified to their wonder and delight.

This was the beginning of a series of strange and stupendous sights that stretched out through the next twenty-four hours. The snow-fields along the summits of the Rockies, the snow-storm through which was passed the incomparable Grand Cañon, the paradise of Glenwood Springs, the awfulness of the desert,— nothing was familiar, everything was unique, in that strange day's travel.

Salt Lake City at last! The famous capital of Mormondom was swarming with Gentile youth. Every hotel room was crowded,— beds, cots, floor. Thousands used the Pullmans and Wagners for their hotels.

On account of the universal train delays, the open-air welcome at Saltair Beach was given up. The governor of Utah was there to welcome the delegates, but his guests were still largely on the way.

So it was on Sunday morning that the great Intermountain Christian Endeavor rally was really inaugurated. All the churches opened their pulpits to the distinguished visiting clergymen. The air was sparkling and cool. The glorious snow-crested Wahsatch Mountains glittered down on the city's broad streets that fluttered with banners of greeting, and with the badges of many thousand Endeavorers as they hastened — not to sight-seeing, though so many temptations allured, but to church.

Even before the regular church services, the prompt Juniors got in their Junior rally. It was held at the beautiful First Congregational Church, and that efficient Junior worker, Miss Anna F. Hulburd, presided over it. Mrs. Francis E. Clark told the wide-eyed boys and girls a host of interesting things about the Juniors she has seen in many lands in all parts of the globe; and that pioneer Junior worker, Mrs. Alice May Scudder, of Jersey City, followed with an exceedingly bright talk.

Of course the chief meeting of the Intermountain rally was that of Sunday afternoon, at the great Mormon Tabernacle. This remarkable building is the popular centre of the Mormon Church, as the vast stone temple near by is the ecclesiastical centre. Under its egg-shaped roof nine thousand persons can easily be seated, and every inch of standing-room also was occupied on this interesting occasion.

"Interesting indeed," said one, "as we sat and looked over the noble audience, the thousands of pure-minded young men and the happy, sweet faces of the girls; as we remembered the Christian homes from which they came, and contrasted them with the households of polygamy, all the evidences of wonderful Mormon industry were as nothing in our thought. Here were the representatives of a pure home in the midst of foul polygamy; the offspring of intelligence, in one of the greatest strongholds of superstition; the children of freedom gathered in the heart of a merciless despotism. Surely no one could look on that unexampled sight without lifting the prayer, O God, grant that as fully as, for this one afternoon, these blessed Endeavorers have possession of this edifice, so fully may purity, intelligence, and liberty come to reign in every Mormon home, and over this wonderful Mormon commonwealth; yes, and over our broad land!"

The great organ — one of the finest in the country, and a product of early Mormon skill — pealed out a noble introduction to the meeting. With the first words of the chairman, Mr. J. B. Caldwell, chairman of the Salt Lake City committee, the marvellous acoustic properties of the hall were made evident. Indeed, the lightest conversation could be distinctly heard from the rear of the room, 250 feet away. People *had* to be quiet, or they could hear nothing; and, being quiet, they could hear the speaker's slightest intonation.

Those speakers were Rev. B. F. Clay, president of the Salt Lake City Union, who voiced the welcome of Utah Endeavorers; Bishop Arnett, Dr. Pentecost, and Dr. Clark. Their theme was appropriate to the threefold significance that Dr. Clark discerned in the day, — the Sabbath, the Fourth of July, the first great Christian Endeavor gathering, on the backbone of the continent,— the theme of Christian patriotism.

Many references were made to the gracious queen who has just completed her sixty years of splendid sovereignty, and the hearty applause that followed every such reference showed the Canadian delegation that the "patriotism" in the afternoon's theme took thought of more than the United States.

Bishop Arnett spoke magnificently, and this distinguished African trustee of Christian Endeavor completely won the hearts of his vast audience. "I, my race, we, are the last children of the family of patriotism," said he. "We have not been long at the table, but we love our country just the same."

Dr. Pentecost urged, among other things, the *extension* of patriotism. He was grateful that the flag of our nation had been thrown over all this great Western land. His references to the possible annexation of Hawaii and Cuba were wise and eloquent, and at the same time free from the jingo spirit.

He related the story of the loyal Bostonian who, when some one told him how easily a foreign man-of-war could enter the harbor and blow our Modern Athens off the face of the earth, replied, "Never! Why, Boston is not a locality; Boston is a state of mind." "Our country," Dr. Pentecost went on to say, "is not to be found in its millions of square miles, in its rivers and its plains, its mountains and its valleys; but our country is a state of mind; it is a great incarnation of principles, of human rights, of human liberty."

Not only was the Chautauqua salute heartily given in honor of Dr.

and Mrs. Clark, but the assembly, in thought of the year of journeyings from which they have happily returned, arose and burst forth with the doxology. The president of the United Society drew some of the "lessons three thousand miles long" that are fairly to be deduced from this unparalleled trans-continental Christian Endeavor journey; he urged the Endeavorers to continue to uphold the four great bulwarks of national prosperity for which Christian Endeavor has come to stand,— civic righteousness, the Sabbath, the evangelical faith, the spiritual life ; he presented many an inspiring view from his recent travels among the Endeavorers of foreign lands.

The other participants in this historic meeting were Rev. James L. Hill, D.D., of Salem, Mass. ; Rev. Nehemiah Boynton, D.D., of Detroit ; and Rev. Silas Mead, LL.D., of Australia, who conducted the devotional exercises. The appropriate close was " America."

This was not by any means all of the stay in Utah and of the Intermountain Christian Endeavor rally. There were the denominationl rallies, in which the Christian Endeavorers of the Baptist, Presbyterian, Congregational, and Disciple churches, learned on this difficult home-mission field, and from the heroic workers themselves, much of the struggles and triumphs of these pioneers of the cross. Those impressions will remain. There were the Christian Endeavor meetings, in which the strong forces from all over the land flowed in upon and invigorated our brothers and sisters whose endeavors here are pressed down by so heavy odds. There were the evening services, a number of them held in the very mission churches built by the Endeavorers themselves. And then the next morning there were the visits to the strange Salt Lake ; to the tomb of Brigham Young and the various homes of that remarkable man ; to the varied institutions of the Mormon church,— their great co-operative store, their tithing-station, their publishing-house ; to the noble City Hall and State House. And finally there was the Ogden rally, with the ride to the magnificent cañon.

On the whole, as the unexampled procession of trains extricated itself from the confusion of the Salt Lake City stations, and wound up the valley to the Wahsatch Divide and out toward the Golden Gate, God was thanked for the privilege of sharing in the Intermountain Christian Endeavor Rally. It was a great occasion, an occasion crammed with significance and superb with hopeful omen. God bless the noble Christians in the uplands of our continent !

SIXTEENTH INTERNATIONAL CONVENTION
OF THE YOUNG PEOPLE'S SOCIETIES
OF CHRISTIAN ENDEAVOR.

THE GATHERING AT THE GOLDEN GATE.

THE long journey over, and Christian Endeavor's Sixteenth International Convention opened on time. To be sure, the toiling trains were still strung out between Ogden and San Francisco. An appealing telegram came,— "Illinois, eight hundred strong, asks you to postpone the opening of the Convention. Thirty-two trains behind us." But the Convention began as soon as the trains were set in motion, and lasted all the way.

How magnificent a close to the great journey was afforded by the welcome received at the hands of the reception committee! A truly Western greeting caught the delegates in its whirl. It sung and beamed and chattered all the way across the smiling bay, and at the city of the Golden Gate it took form in long lines of hurrahing young folks, their caps and handkerchiefs waving a welcome, their faces as well as their voices singing California's song, "Scatter Sunshine."

The brilliant streets of the Western metropolis at once caught the attention of all. At almost every hundred feet wires were stretched across the principal thoroughfares, and from these wires fluttered thousands of flags, while on each side large curved strips of purple and orange completed the arches. Moreover, half-way down Market Street was a splendid triumphal arch, glowing with Convention colors and bearing the significant motto that appeared throughout the city. "Maine, 1881 — California, 1897." Everywhere the purple and orange colors were displayed, in shields, hangings, draperies, banners, till the city seemed glowing with poppies. In the noble parks, also, the very flowers had grown together into Convention symbols.

Down at the ferry wharves was chaos confounded. Delegations swollen many times beyond the estimates of transportation managers, trains delayed many hours and then rolling in by scores at a time, trunks heaped in piles roof high, porters on the verge of insanity,— it was a situation requiring patience and good humor. The Endeavorers were equal to the situation. Nine hundred white-capped members of the reception committee sped on helpful errands. Delegates kept sweet, did without their fresher clothes till they could arrive, and looked the better for the travel-stained garments worn with such grace.

A word about a welcome that was extended far out on the prairies, — the San Francisco daily papers. These sent out magnificent preparatory numbers, gorgeous with colored illustrations, crowded with interesting matter.

The first glimpse of the Convention headquarters, the great Mechanics' Pavilion, filled all with an admiration that constantly deepened. The vast building was too large for an auditorium, so that an inner portion had to be partitioned off for ten thousand seats. This was furnished with a cloth cover, and was charmingly decorated within. Of course the color basis was the royal purple and gold; but there was an unusual and most charming use of delicate colors, of greenery, and of flowers. The seats in the rear half of the house were raised; the.e were many commodious galleries; the platforms were delights to the eye with their beautiful colors, and a practical joy with their convenience. It was a model convention hall.

Outside this inner hall two encircling tiers of rooms were arranged for all sorts of convention purposes. There were the brilliant newspaper quarters, where all the great San Francisco papers were taking multitudinous orders. There were the subcommittee headquarters, the press committee headquarters, where Mr. Littlefield kept alert hand on a thousand matters, the excursion bureau, the registration bureau the music committee, and the rest. There was the beautiful quiet restroom, softly carpeted, adorned with beautiful pictures, with palms and flowers and easy chairs, and tables to write on, and everything to rest the weary. In a bright corner was the floating society headquarters. where a most interesting exhibit was grouped around the splendid model of a ship. Opposite was a wonderful display made by the vigorous missionary-extension department of the California Union under the supervision of Miss Berry.

A most delightful hour was spent by many among the State booths. A large room nearby was handsomely decked in yellow, which covered wall and ceiling. Here the registration aids were as busy as bees, indexing the thousands of registration cards that came pouring in, so that any Endeavorers present might readily be discovered by inquiring friends. All were proud of the booths of the United Society and of THE GOLDEN RULE, under the efficient charge of Mr. Thomas Wainwright, "Uncle Tom," of Chicago. Never before have the missionary societies had such charming exhibits filled with curiosities, glimpses of foreign life, and mementos of all kinds.

But the gem of all the displays was California's. Entrance was beneath beautiful white arches, modelled after the style of the old missions. and delegates were bewildered by the beauty on either hand. Photographs and paintings of entrancing scenes, specimens of rich cereals, tropical fruits of all kinds, object-lessons, a myriad of them, as to California's fruitfulness and splendor, thronged every side.

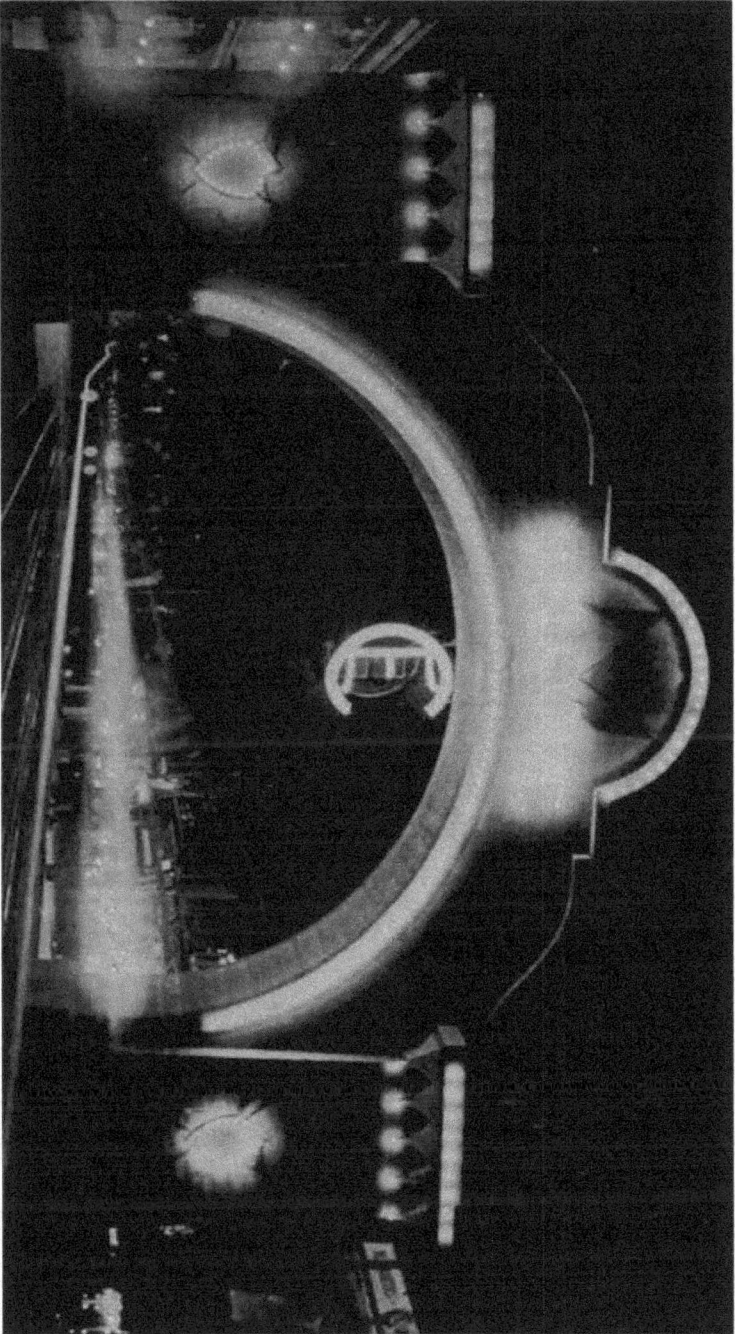

THE WELCOME ARCH ON MARKET STREET AT NIGHT.

IN SAN FRANCISCO.

Calvary Presbyterian Church.

THE Convention was not postponed, but the simultaneous meetings on Wednesday evening were held, according to the programme, in eleven different churches, though some of the speakers had not yet arrived, and their places had to be filled from the hundreds of able orators already on the ground. The interiors of the churches were brilliant with Convention poppies and stately with palms and other tropical plants. Large audiences crowded pews and aisles. The honored pastors of San Francisco, Oakland, and Alameda presided with dignity and cordiality.

No topic could be more suitable for the opening of a great religious convention than the one chosen for the opening twenty-two addresses, — "The Life Filled with the Spirit." Among the speakers were the two African bishops, the honored Arnett and Walters; those brothers named Tyler, big in heart and body; the eloquent Dr. Pentecost and Rev. Mr. Myers; those noble State Christian Endeavor presidents, Cochran and McKittrick; and those ministers of power, Dr. Davies, Dr. Boynton, Dr. G. R. W. Scott, and Rev. William Patterson. Dr. Clark also spoke, and Rev. Robert Johnston, of Canada, Dr. Powell, of Kentucky; besides Dr. Hill, Dr. Dickinson, Dr. Rhodes, and Rev. J. M. Lowden,— all trustees.

The pastor, Rev. John Hemphill, D.D., presided over the service with his accustomed felicity. His welcoming words were warm and hearty. The interior of the church was gracefully decorated with flowers and colors. After singing, "Blest Be The Tie That Binds," by the congregation, Rev. Robert Johnson of London, Ontario, was introduced to make the opening address.

Address by Rev. Robert Johnson, London, Ontario.

When Daniel Webster was asked by a friend on one occasion what was the greatest thought that had ever impressed his mind, the great man bent his heavy brows for a moment and then replied: "The greatest thought that has ever impressed me is the thought of my personal responsibility to Almighty God." The thought included in the word "responsibility" is very wide and far-reaching, but there is one aspect of it too often overlooked even by those who are by faith children of God; that aspect is the obligation of the redeemed soul to be all it can be for God. The good is oftentimes the enemy of the best, and as a sinner redeemed by Christ's blood it is not enough that I should be good for something; I am responsible to God to be the best that by God's grace it is possible for me to be. If in any department of my life I am failing to enjoy something of the Spirit's power that it is my privilege to enjoy, I am to that extent failing to live up to my responsibility. So it is that every child of God is bound to pray and to pray with desire, "Lord, give me thy best."

If one were to read the first fifteen chapters of Exodus, noting in particular the magnificent purposes and promises of God towards his people, and then should read the remainder of the book, noting as carefully the disappointments and distresses of the people as they wandered in their wilderness way, he could not fail to be struck with the incongruity between the purposes of God and their realization in history of the generation that came out of Egypt. "I am come down to deliver you and to bring you into a good land and a large, a land flowing with milk and honey," had been God's word to them, and yet as you read their disappointing story, you find them hemmed in on every side by foes, thirsty, hungry and heirs to a desert land whose sands are whitened by their bones as they die by plague, by pestilence, and in weariness of life. And as you read you say, "Something is wrong; the realization does not correspond with the avowed purpose."

So if one reads the promises of Christ to his Church in the Gospel, and fills his soul with the pictures of what he declared the Church should accomplish in the power of her ascended Lord, and then compares with that ideal the present position and history of the Christian Church, notes its powerlessness in the face of great evils, its restlessness in the uncertainties of thought and action of the age, the pitifulness of its conquests in comparison with the apparent magnificence of its strength, the reader is again compelled to say, "Here, too, something is wrong, the ideal and the actual are not in correspondence."

It is an awful thing to think that it is possible for a soul redeemed to frustrate the purpose of God. Feeble man cannot stretch out his hand and stay the king of day as he drives the flaming steeds up the vault of the eastern sky, but man can close his heart against the grace and strength of the Almighty, and can, with that will which constitutes at once his greatness and his grandeur, say "No" to his Creator and his King.

The rich sunshine of the oriental summer is streaming down, on Olivet's heights as the gathering band of pilgrims with Jesus in their midst make their way with hosannah shouts citywards. But in a moment their shouts are hushed, those by the side of him for whom they spread their garments have stopped; his eyes are filled with tears, his arms are outstretched towards the city which beneath them lies, temple-crowned, glistening in the sunlight— Listen! "If thou hadst known, even thou in this thy day, the things that pertain to thy peace." So methinks over many a soul that might have been so much that it has not been, that might have had so much of God that it has not had, that might have accomplished so much for God that it has not accomplished, does Christ mourn, saying "O Soul, how often would I, but thou would'st not!" My friends, God has more to give us than forgiveness of sins; we may win heaven; we may be saved, but we may miss much that makes that salvation precious. We may escape from Egypt, but fail of Canaan; we may be delivered from the bondage, but never enter into the rest.

I desire to-night to indicate first some of the characteristics of the life which it is the privilege of the child of God to enter and enjoy as opposed to the life with which so many of us are so unhappily satisfied. Paul, speaking of the experiences of Israel, says that "All these things happened unto them for our ensamples, and they are written for our admonition"; and as the picture is plainer even than the printed paragraph, and the actual more easily grasped than the theoretical, it is to the Canaan life of victory and rest as opposed to the wilderness wonderings that we shall look for our instruction.

First of all, then, it is a life of Possession as opposed to a life of Deprivation. The life of Israel in the wilderness was not a satisfying experience; true, the good hand of God was upon them. They had water from the rock and bread from heaven, but they missed the sensual enjoyments of the land in which they lived; they missed the many forms of activity and recreation and the interest in national affairs which even their slave life had made possible to them. In the wilderness ever moving, with no certainty of abode, their life seemed purposeless and unsatisfying. How different when their feet touched the Canaan side of Jordan's bank! True, there was struggle, but it was struggle for possession, and, soon established in the land and resting from war, they possessed their inheritance and longed no more for Egypt. The expulsive power of a new possession had done its work. They had a nation, a life, a land of their own which satisfied their longings, inspired their loyalty, and became the object of their love. More, it is a life of Victory as opposed to a life of Failure. Israel, a wandering people, the object of attack and plunder for roving Bedouin tribes, continually upon the defensive, ever on the watch, but never completely overcoming the foe, presents but a sorry spectacle compared with Israel in Canaan conquering at every step, subduing tribe after tribe, capturing stronghold after stronghold in their victorious march, until even Hebron, where dwelt the sons of Anak, fell before the old hero of a hundred fights, and the flag of Jehovah and of Joshua floated over the whole land; triumph marks every step; the strongholds of the enemy have become the citadels of the Lord's hosts, the vineyards of the foe refresh the wearied warriors, and at last the land rests from war.

One characteristic more. It is a life honoring to God as opposed to a life that is a byword to the world. It is, to state it mildly, to say that God got but little glory from the wilderness experiences of Israel. Their travels and trials were not of such a sort as to lead the nations around to believe in the goodness of the God to whom, in their songs of praise, Israel continued to abscribe all glory. But if the nations reviled Israel and Israel's God while they wandered a homeless people, their revilings were silenced from the day that the Jordan divided and the tribes set foot upon the land that was their own; then Israel became, indeed, what God had intended this people should be: "A people unto himself, for a name and for a praise and for a glory"; then, and only then, Israel fulfilled the end of its existence as a nation and became a witness to the grace, the goodness, and the glory of the God who had chosen it a nation peculiar to himself.

Time will not permit me to press the parallel as exemplified in our own lives, but let me ask you: Do you know this life of possession, of rest, of victory and of gladness? Of the blood of the Passover Lamb shed on Calvary and of shelter beneath it we know, of deliverance through it from sin's penalty we know, but do we know the resurrection experiences of Jordan and the triumph that succeeds? The inheritance is ours. Out here in the West, among the miners enduring a life of toil and uncertainty, a year or two ago there was living a young man who was heir to one of the finest estates in England. The inheritance was his, but he let it lie unclaimed. So do many Christians who possess in Christ unlimited supplies of grace, and who yet leave these treasures unclaimed. And this inheritance is for every child of God; there are no favorites in the kingdom of heaven; there is no spiritual aristocracy. Your vessel may not hold as much as another's, but you may have it filled. The great gold fields of our Canadian Northwest and Pacific province were until lately unappropriated; they were there for those who, fulfilling the conditions of settlement, would enter and claim the land.

We are not kept in doubt as to how this life of conquest and of power for God is to become the soul's possession. It was because of unbelief that Israel, under Moses, entered not in; it was by faith that, under Joshua, the tribes went up to possession. Believing that the land was theirs in God's promise, and that it would become theirs through God's might, they entered in, and this was the victory that overcame the world, even their faith. Not a little harm has been done, I believe, by emphasizing particular experiences through which certain souls have passed, and by setting these up as patterns by which the experience of every other soul must be framed if it is to lead to like results. This inheritance is mine in Christ; it is mine to possess it in the night of the Spirit. Whatever obtrudes itself and draws aside my soul to consider its own experience rather than to consider him in whom alone the inheritance is mine is a hindrance and not a help to my progress. God has many paths by which to lead his children; be it mine to surrender to his will, to follow where he leads.

For the spirit-filled life on man's side is simply a life of surrender; it is the handing over of the life to Christ without reservation. We cannot fill the vessel: it is ours to place it empty at the Master's feet. It is God's part to sanctify, it is man's part to surrender; it is his to use, it is ours to yield; ours to open, his to enter. It is not in our right to choose the extent or the form of service for which our King may use it; it is ours only to say, "Lord, this life is thine; over it none shall rule but thou alone." In the ruins where once the proud palaces of Bagdad reared their stately piles, the excavators and students of research find that in the walls of the royal palace every brick is stamped with the name of the king for whom it was built; thus the whole palace in its every part, from foundation stone to topmost parapet, bears testimony to its regal owner. Such is the surrendered life; every faculty of my soul, every power of my life, every avenue of my senses, every motion of my will is marked with the name of my King; and the brick that is stamped as Christ's he will not leave useless by the wayside, but in the power of the Divine Spirit he will use it in the upbuilding of his spiritual temple.

Into an old lady's cottage in the Highlands of Scotland came on one occasion a visitor who supposed herself unrecognized. She spoke kindly words to the lonely body, and read to her a portion of God's word, but when she rose to go the old lady took the stool on which her visitor had sat and said, "Your Majesty, no one shall more sit on this stool, unless you should yourself deign again to visit my cottage." It was set apart for the Queen. O soul! set your life apart for your Lord, and not once or twice will he come to your humble heart, but daily, hourly, aye continually. He will occupy the seat that you reserve for him.

Into the cathedral of a German town there came one day a visitor. He climbed to the organ-loft, and there of the old verger who was dusting the benches asked permission to play upon the organ. The old man shook his head. "No," said he, "no stranger's hand shall touch this organ." Again he urged his request, only to be again refused; still he persisted, for the fame of the organ was great, and at length his persistency won its reward, the verger opened the key-board and stood aside with suspicious look, bidding the man be brief. The stranger sat down and touched his fingers to the keys; the music stole forth; such music the old cathedral had never heard. It filled the nave and rippled and rolled up among the dusty carved arches and sunk in dying cadences to the crypt, and as it ceased and the stranger turned to rise he found the old verger on his knees at his side; and with outstretched hands, as though to bid him stay, and wondering look in his eyes, he whispered, "Master, who art thou?" And the visitor, smiling, said, "I am Mendelssohn." And the old man hid his face in his hands and tears trickled through his fingers as he said, "Stay, Master, stay, and forgive me that for a moment I refused to let thee honor my poor organ with thy wondrous power."

To-night to us there comes a greater musician, even an heavenly. He asks for the key of thine heart, child of God. Yield it to him and he will enter in, and from thy poor life he will bring music that will sweeten thy life and the life of the world, and will arise in glorifying strains into the ears of thy God in heaven.

After a hymn, Dr. Hemphill introduced Rev. B. B. Tyler, D.D., of New York City. It is regretted that Dr. Tyler's address was not taken by a stenographer.

"It is not enough," he said, "to be a Christian or to say that we are saved. There is something beyond to which we should aspire. We must be the very best Christians, and to do this we must be filled with the spirit of God. We are proud of this great organization, gathered from all parts of the country. We say that religion is not dying out; that it is successful; that we are strong, but we are looking in the wrong direction. It is not might or power we must seek, but the blessed spirit of God.

"The human body is the temple of the spirit," he continued. "Do we treat our bodies as the temple deserves? How many desecrate the temple and turn it into a tobacco box or a beer keg? How can men lead heaven-filled lives if their bodies are so degraded? The only way the body can be filled with the spirit of God is by an uncon ditional surrender to him. There are many people who profess religion, but they take it as a bitter pill. They prefer religion here to fire elsewhere,— a sort of fire insurance. But they are not filled with the spirit, and cannot be saved unless they surrender. To be truly saved one must be filled with the spirit of God, so that it may influence his every action. People who are in the church are not saved just because they pay pew rent and have been baptized. It is not enough to be a church-member : one must possess the heavenly spirit. Remember Paul's admonition to the apostles : " Be filled with the spirit."

The meeting closed with the singing of " God be with You."

First Congregational Church.

American and British flags partly hid the great organ of the First Congregational Church, while ·between them hung a Christian Endeavor emblem in California poppies. Purple and gold predominated, with plenteous palms and ferns. The pastor, Rev. G. C. Adams, D.D., presided. The singing was led by Musical Director Husband. Dr. Adams offered prayer. The first speaker introduced was Bishop Alexander Walters, D.D., of Jersey City, N. J.

Address of Bishop Walters.

The speaker announced as his subject, " Life and Light." He said : " For centuries there was a part of man that could not be understood — the soul All philosophers made lengthy and learned dissertations on it, and yet none of them touched the right chord. Nor was any real light shed on the subject until the coming of Christ. Christ is the author of all life, both natural and spiritual, and it was to him that we had to look for a solution of the enigma.

" Christ discovered to the world a new kingdom, a spiritual one. In order to enter it one must be born into it. Hence we read of being born into the kingdom of God. The result of his coming was the salvation of men, and it is for the salvation of men that the Endeavorers are banded together." Bishop Walters made a forceful application of his theme and concluded thus : " Let us go away from this convention with the thought that we have learned better than before how to engage in work for the Master."

Dr. Adams then introduced Rev. Nehemiah Boynton, D.D., of Detroit, Michigan. Dr. Boynton's address was vigorous and pointed.

Address by Rev. N. Boynton, D.D., Detroit.

He asked the young people to lay aside the idea that the spiritual life is a mystical one. " Christian life is actual, ample, active and aspiring."

Without manuscript it is impossible to give an adequate *résumé* of the address. Some of the points specially emphasized were these : The Christian life is a moving life, it is inspiring. Iniquity does not sing forth grand hymns. So pure an atmosphere of all that is good in man is found only in the fold of Christ. A Christian life cannot be satisfied with that which is common. We are always to be forging ahead for the things that are higher still, nearer the throne of the Almighty. This great convention in point of numbers will be fruitless if we do not learn more fully the lesson of Christ and the way in which to rescue the fallen.

The temptations of the young men of to-day are not the temptations of the lower planes of life. They are not the temptations of appetite, but of ambition. The young men of to-day put forth their best efforts in the direction of secularities, in the things that perish, and make their religion secondary. They devote their second-best energies to Christ and the Church.

First Baptist Church.

The decorations of the First Baptist Church were beautiful, elaborate, and original. The pulpit adornment was a magnificent and artistic piece of work. Above the pulpit and extending almost entirely across the front of the church was a great ornamental scroll traced in yellow poppies, marguerites, and green leaves against a background of purple gauze. The quotation, " Bring Forth the Royal Diadem and Crown Him Lord of All," was worked in eschscholtzias. The centerpiece of the scroll was a shield outlined in white against a yellow background, and bearing in purple letters the legend, " Jesus Reigns."

The church was filled when Rev. M. P. Boynton, the pastor, announced the opening hymn, " Onward, Christian Soldiers." The 98th Psalm was read responsively and Rev. Mr. Boynton offered prayer. After the song, " There is Sunshine in my Soul To-day," the chairman introduced as the first speaker upon the topic Rev. Joseph W. Cochran, of Madison, Wisconsin.

Address by Rev. Joseph W. Cochran, Madison, Wis.

Blessed be the men to whom God gave the arranging of this meeting. Our topic was born in a luminous hour. We are now in the robing room of this Convention. Put ye on the garments of praise and power, for the days that are to follow. What a blessing to realize that Christian Endeavor has gotten beyond the holiday idea of conventions! This is not an international picnic, but an international filling with the Spirit. Scenery, hospitality, decoration, music — all material excellencies — are the bright background of a simple scene transpiring here, — Jesus in our midst and we touching the hem of his garment.

Co-incident with the birth of Christian Endeavor is the dawning of the new day of the Holy Spirit's power. We cannot lose sight of this. It means something. It bespeaks intimacy between our society and the Spirit. It means that the church's realization that she has been living below the Spirit's fulness is to come through you. It means that Pentecost and Christian Endeavor shall be one and the same. It means that wherever your name and spirit go forth there shall Pentecost be known as a memorial of you.

The world of commerce is dependent on the unseen. It is not in the steel or the wood or the water. All the splendid locomotives that lifted us, ten thousand strong, over the mountains, all the engines in this wonderful city puffing away to give us drink, carrying us to and fro, lifting us through buildings, ferrying us across the bay, have not one ounce of power in themselves. It is all in the unseen force of steam. So an invisible life is behind this great movement, this engine of the Almighty, Christian Endeavor; so is every one who blesses this world born of the Spirit, filled with the Spirit. If the unseen should fail us, every motor in the world would rust where it stopped, or be dragged to the scrap heap. If the Unseen Spirit should fail us, these happy throngs in the brightly decked streets, the heavenly music bursts, the generous expenditure of means, all the marvellous machinery formed by the Committee of '97 to make this a memorable convention, would be tinsel and bombast, shoddy and sham.

The kingdom of God grows from within. It is life, not a machine; a growth, not a manufacture. A national political party was lately formed in Chicago to give the country better money. We were all soon to be rich. The birth of this party, full-armed, springing from the brain of one man into the arms of a national convention, was heralded over the world and we prepared ourselves for the worst. Its only members to-day are the president and secretary. Christian Endeavor was not begun in that way. It is great because it has had its solemn, silent moment, — because some one years ago walked apart with God. Just as in some moments of your life when without even the Bible in your hands you have felt the problems of destiny slowly working towards the surface, and you have asked, " What am I? Why am I here? Where am I going? How am I to attain?" And the answer came not from the distant heavenly battlements, not from reflected knowledge about God, but voice answered to voice in secret chambers of the soul, and the God-touch we rarely speak of pressed into all the channels of being, reformed motives, transformed ambition, clarified purpose. God and the soul in league, mind with mind, heart against heart, — God and the soul in league. Thus also came the silent moments to a great movement. They are here upon Christian Endeavor, and nothing must shake them off.

Beloved, we have always had a measure of the Holy Spirit. A higher note was struck at Washington '96—" Evangelism " our watchword, " Saved to Serve " our motto for the year. But have we had his fulness? Have we received the baptism? Born of water and the Spirit, yet perhaps only bottle Christians, dying, like Ishmael in the desert, for want of the well of water springing up within us into everlasting life. We may have drunk deep of the well of salvation, yet not been blessed with the fulness of which the Master speaks—" Out of his inward parts shall run rivers of living water."

I. *This fulness of the Spirit is to reorganize our denominationalism.*

If the church of God had always made this distinction between the Spirit for life and the Spirit for service and suffering, would we be so far away from the fulfilment of Christ's prayer " that we all may be one "? Can we believe that there is a fulness of the Spirit while there are one hundred and forty-three separate and distinct denominations in our land? With some it is a question of robes, and others of days, and others of color? Some splits are upon the matter of general policy, progressive or conservative. We are divided over psalm-singing, voting the national ticket, and who shall sit at the Lord's table, forms of worship, church polity, manner of administering the Sacrament—these are the little foxes that spoil the vines. Thus is rent the seamless robe of Christ. He has given us an illustration of the true unity in diversity. " I am the head, you are the branches." But the branches interlock in strife rather than fellowship. The battalions of the army have been set fighting one another. Denominationalism as it is to-day is a loophole through which millions of Christless souls have slipped into a sunless eternity. What then of the reunion of Christendom? The iridescent vision of a dream, the inflamed vagary of enthusiasts? Endeavorers, it is yours to prove it not so. That splendid new word of Endeavor coinage, " interdenominational," must be filled by you until tense with the Spirit's power.

II. *This fulness of the Spirit is to purify our methods of work.*

When we are ready to receive the fulness of the Spirit. what an array of mechanical methods will be swept away. In the time of the Spirit's flooding, how many fairs and suppers and clubs will go. Not all, but some. How many ingenious devices to make money and draw crowds and win popularity will be cast out. Not all, but some. The Spirit is an infallible detector between true and false social life. Revivals, too, will come—not forced, hothouse affairs, but bursting upon us like the bloom of springtime.

Why, the soul is fashioned after the similitude of a fountain, not a water-cooler. God meant that we should be full of his Spirit before we overflowed, that we should not give the dregs and drainings but the overflow of power. The disciples did not dare to leave Jerusalem until they had been filled. When the waters reach the very brim, then go forth. Strange, is it not, that the New Testament writers, though probably conversant with the laws of hydraulics as employed by the Romans, never used them as illustrations of the Spirit's power? Paul must have known the power of a " head " of water, but he never used it as a figure. That is what we are after to-day—the power, the power, the power of the Spirit. We want to tear away at the mountains of sin, as you in California once tore out the bowels of the earth with your hydraulic mining. But it is as disastrous in the spiritual as in the commercial world. We mistake when we look for the tearing, rushing power of the Spirit. Be not over-anxious for his power, but for his personality. The power will come of itself. We must open our arms to him. Christian Endeavor must be the full spring from which flow gentle rivers of influence, not an angry torrent, confined half-way down the mountain by a reservoir, to eat its way into the heart of the world's sin.

III. *This fulness of the Spirit is to dignify witness-bearing.*

The Spirit sends its sovereign blessing upon simple witness-bearing. This is the keynote of Acts, that Gospel according to the Holy Ghost. The Spirit was given for the purpose of witness-bearing, and its tragic meaning is expressed by the Greek word for witness, "martyr." The Spirit-filled life depends not upon the force of argument, for " Argument," says Bacon, " is like an arrow from the cross-bow; testimony like the arrow from the long-bow, the force of the latter depending upon the strength of the arm that draws it." Argument, then, does not feel the need of the Holy Spirit behind it, but testimony requires his strong arm. The world shall never be converted by arguments on the trinity of God, or the infallibility of the Bible, or the divinity of Christ. To be living, leaping witnesses! Gladly would we suffer the machinery of Christian Endeavor to grow rusty, if it could, provided there were an active, earnest, witnessing membership going out into the highways and hedges. Many of our societies are excuses for the lack of spiritual fervor. Too often we hear the grind and creak of wheels and pulleys, where there should be the fervent prayer and appeal to God for help, the cry of some sin-stricken soul for reconciliation.

IV. *This fulness of the Spirit is to glorify character building.*

Spirit-filled character is greater than all we can say of a noble soul. Cata-logue his bravery, classify his generosity, recite his sacrifices — and you have still left untold a glowing residue, an exhilarating atmosphere in which mean-ness withers like toadstools in the sun, or as a mouse dies in a chamber of oxygen. It was Spirit-filled character that cowed the cruel Ahab when Elijah fixed his eyes like arrows in that reeking heart. It was Spirit-filled character that silenced David before the uplifted finger of the prophet Nathan. It was Spirit-filled character that made Pilate quake before the Christ, and Agrippa loosen hold upon the Roman fasces while Paul stood before him. It was Spirit-filled character that lifted, in the history of the United States, an awk-ward country lawyer past the brilliant Douglas into the presidential chair, so soon to be baptized with tears and blood. It was Spirit-filled character that gives to-day Dwight L. Moody pre-eminence over many a silver-tongued pulpiteer.

Though Spirit-filled character rests in the splendid simplicity of witness-bearing, it is not insipid goodness. It does not make a man a pious bore. To be filled with Spirit is to enhance your individuality. You throb and tingle with life? There are bubbles in your blood? You are high-spirited? Well, Christ is looking for you. Christ did not intend a monotonous likeness in his followers. His life, so multiform, so universal, is not one which turns out wearisome rows and stupid platoons of stereotyped men and women. The church is not a Noah's ark of the toy shop. Shem like Ham, and Noah like his wife. Christ's test of Spirit-filled character is a brave individuality. He selected his disciples with this in view. Could you ever mistake John for Peter, or Thomas for James? The personalities stand out from the Gospel canvas. When we think of Christ's struggle against the tide of thought and action, his lonely protest against public sentiment, his divine carelessness of how men took him, how customary and forced appears much of our faith. Some one said, "Garfield, Grant, Lincoln, Gladstone, Queen Victoria, your grandfathers, were Christians." "Why, then, I will be one," you answered. What sort of Christianity is this?—a whitewash faith! Salvation by fashion! But, Endeavorers, if the cross of Christ means anything, it means that you must be a Christian whether or no there is another in the world. It means that you must be filled full of the Spirit whether any one else in the world is filled. What are you making of yourselves? An automaton for a heaven, a material machine for the spiritual energies of eternity? Do you give because some one else gave? Do you go to church, or belong to a society, or seek this new life of the Spirit, because others are doing so? Then you are living an external, shallow existence, upon whose horizon the sun of heroic character never rose. When Stephen of Colonna fell into the hands of his assailants, they asked him in derision, "Where is your fortress?" "Here," was the reply, placing his hand upon his heart. What, then, would be unseemly boldness in some is but the environment of Spirit-filled character in another. He robes himself in a great loneliness, he goes forth bending over fallen men, not to listen to appreciative murmurs, but with his ear close to the failing heart. How can it be that a life drifting with society, fearful of uttering one brave word that might mean loss of friends, shall some day, beyond, be strong and true? It cannot be. The natures that win victories for God run counter to the world's current. Spirit-filled character means obedience to Christ, whatever the world says of it; that these personalities of ours must be stripped for action, all the rich and clogging garments of selfishness cast aside, and selfhood, clean-limbed and clear-eyed, steps forth; that every talent, every capacity, be touched with the magnetic power of the Spirit.

The only true genius is Spirit-filled character. There are still Napoleons and Alexanders in the world, but their crown lies at the feet of their Lord. What famous linguists, soldiers, statesmen, capitalists, scientists, have poured their gifts into a heart of consecrated fire, until those gifts have fused and run into the channels of God's will? Thus are formed missionary lives; thus every life must face its mission. There must be a fixed point around which Spirit-filled purpose shall revolve. That point is this: "Whatever I do shall be for the glory of my Lord." How do we read that verse of St. Paul's to-day in the light of the world's higher criticism? Honestly and frankly, how do you read it? "I press towards the mark for the prize—" So far, so good. We can all say that. But here, perhaps, we part company with the apostle. "I press towards the mark for the prize of—a position in society; and I will miss my engagements with the Saviour to gain it." "I press—for political honors; and I will do as other politicians do to win them." "I press—for riches; and I will even foreclose a mortgage over a widow's head to gain it." "I press—for a scholar's career; and I will neglect my mission work to attain it." "I press—" says a preacher, "for a large church and heavy salary and the applause of thousands; and I will forget to preach the Gospel to reach it."

V. *This fulness of the Spirit will reveal the necessity for action.*

He who asks for the fulness of the Spirit must be willing to be used. Jeremiah, in his own figure, had closed up the fire of his soul and it was eating out his heart. "If I say I will not make mention of him, then there is, as it were, a burning fire shut up in my bones." This is a tremendous truth—the destructiveness of a restrained force. A man or a church can be destroyed by hoarded truth. Jeremiah had sinned against his soul's health and had the spiritual grippe—a burning fire shut up in his bones. Jesus had infused into humanity a life which lives only through activity, and which, when barred up within the soul, tears apart its very tissue. The Gospel is a treasure in earthen vessels which must be passed from one to the other, else its energies will rend the frail clay. In England a water pond connected with a dynamite factory becomes so impregnated with the deadly fluid that the pond must be exploded once a month. So the Christian Endeavor society which keeps the Spirit to itself becomes a menace. The darkest ages of the church's history were those in which she banked about the ministry of the Word the soil of pride and selfishness. And God withheld even the material glory of Christendom until she awakened to the call of the great commission. To-day the intellectual and scientific world has awakened to the newness of life, hand in hand with the missionary spirit of the age. With the release of God's flame has come the release of all the energies. The power of steam has been loosened, electricity set free. All the lines of relationship between East and West, North and South, were laid when man answered the question, "Who is my neighbor?" The Spirit is life, and you cannot chain life. I have seen a stone sidewalk broken in pieces by the silent push of a soft little toadstool. The root of a tender sapling once broke into the tomb of a German princess who by her will had taken every precaution for protection against the ravages of time. Amherst professors, several years ago, harnessed a squash to measure its lifting power. And such was the might of the mysterious principle we call, in our ignorance, life, that at first lifting sixty pounds, it lifted within a week five hundred pounds, in two weeks eleven hundred pounds, in three weeks seventeen hundred pounds, in four weeks twenty-one hundred pounds, until at length it lifted the incredible weight of five thousand pounds. This is a commonplace illustration of the resistless sweep of the Spirit. He must break forth into the world, and unless you are willing to channel him, he will rend the unwilling heart.

VI. *This fulness of the Spirit will show us our perils and opportunities.* As we look over our American heritage, what magnificent opportunity for the Spirit-filled life! When the Pilgrim Fathers sailed from Delft, 1620, their pastor said, " I am convinced that the Lord hath yet more truth for us, to break forth out of his holy word." We, the children of those times, given a new hemisphere, new stars to gaze upon, new mines of gold and silver, new tablets of God's writing. new mounts of liberty, new experiences in self-government, new problems of social regeneration, should have, withal, new revelations of his Spirit. Free as we are from the entanglements of tradition, we should be able to produce in our lives fresher, cleaner types — should be able to attain higher ideals of the kingdom — than anywhere in all the world.

For the very permanence of our American homes, we must have the filling of the Spirit. Isaiah saw Jerusalem grown heathenish and worldly, in a state of siege, and bitterly describes their miserable resources. They were stopping up the walls with materials of their own homes. He cries, " The houses have ye broken down to fortify the walls." What a picture of to-day! Home life is broken down to build up public life all about us — educational walls, political walls, industrial and commercial walls, society walls, ecclesiastical walls. In the Spirit-filled home the life lessons of the home are not resigned to the State, parenthood is not a mere physiological function. In the Spirit-filled home is found the altar of freedom, the fountain head of civic pride and loyalty. In the Spirit-filled home are found the best bricks for our political structure — home-made, not machine-made. " Here are our walls," we cry, as we point to the family kneeling at the home altar — every brick a Christian man or woman or child. Our crusade for Christian citizenship must reach back behind the actions of legislative bodies, back behind the ballot-box, back behind the textbooks and the schoolhouse flag, and find patriotism in the patriotic, Spirit-filled home. Our stupendous social problems can never be solved until our homes are purged and the living Spirit has free course. It is the home of Samuel that is the salvation of this land. Point me to the so-called Christian home that is prayerless, Bibleless, which cares little what the children are reading, where they are spending their evenings, who are their companions, and I will show you one of the worst menaces to society. The best Sabbath school and theological seminary in all this world is the Spirit-filled home. No man-made institution can make up for it.

VII. *This fulness of the Spirit is the key to the understanding of the Christ life.*

Society to-day asks for your soul. All life in the home, in the shop, in the office, in the factory, means, ultimately, the soul's crucifixion. The crosses of Calvary were all under the Spirit's law. Each life must suffer death as a savior or as a thief. Just two classes — saviors and thieves. Paul's was one — " I am crucified with Christ." The foolish rich man's was another — "Thou fool, this night thy soul shall be required of thee." The immortals are those who lose themselves in their own times, to be found in that to come. "Fame's eternal bederoll" is being revised in these days of the Spirit's open vision, erasing the Napoleons and writing the heroes of the battles of love. . . . John Howard will be there — he who became endungeoned for the prison classes of England. Wilberforce and Garrison will be there. John Brown, General Gordon, and Berkeley will all be there. Mary Ware, the fever heroine; Mary Stanley and Florence Nightingale, the angels of the Crimea, will be there. Such as these are the great, and the only great. Ah, the Spirit-filled life does not finger the fringe of consecration. The Spirit-filled life hears the angel that spake to Ulysses. In the fable, the spirit of the other world had returned to find bodies and work. One chose the body of a king and did his work; another the body of a poet and wrote for fame. At length Ulysses came and cried, "Why, all the fine bodies are taken! There is nothing left for me." And the answer came, "The best one is left for you, Ulysses." "What is it?" he asked. "The body of a common man; doing common work, for a common reward." The Spirit-filled Christian must get beyond the life-insurance feature of salvation. Not, "How little must I do to inherit eternal life?" but "How great a blessing may I be, since I am an inheritor?"

You are to live over again the incarnation, the crucifixion, the resurrection. The world is in the birth throes of an eternal incarnation. Whenever you accept the meaning of Calvary, there is another Bethlehem, and into the world a child Immanuel is born. The conversion of a soul is a new birth of Christ. If so, you shall meet the cross as surely as Christ met it. As he was made sin for us, Paul says, we are made sin to the world. Every Christ-born missionary is made sin to the sinners he turns. Cary was made sin for India, Livingstone for Africa. Then, too, the Christian life is an endless resurrection. Every rent in the social strata, every eruptive force, is but the push and stress of the Almighty Spirit, confined by the accumulated layers of ignorance, apathy, and sin, crowding its way upward through all

There stands Loyola, the brilliant Jesuit, on the banks of the Seine. Xavier, like an omnipresent spirit, has followed him thence, whispering, "What shall it profit a man if he gain the whole world and lose his own soul?" In the lecture-room the same question. In the chase, at meals, and at prayers, this same tragic question: "What shall it profit? What shall it profit?" In the hour of defeat the same refrain. Pleasure, fame, wealth, poverty, travels, success, failure — all were given tone and meaning by the question, "What shall it profit? What shall it profit?" At length the crust gives way; the flame bursts forth; the fiery hour has come; and Xavier leaves all to follow Christ. Born of that passion hour are these words, as he lands on savage shores, "Whatever form of torture or of death awaits me, I am ready to suffer it ten thousand times for the salvation of a single soul."

So through the luminous hours of this convention I trust may ring this question, for you who have not yet been willing to appropriate the Spirit's fulness as you appropriated the salvation of Jesus. It is yours to receive by faith. Accept it here and now — without the power, perhaps, without any rapt and glowing experience. "Receive ye the Holy Ghost for service." If not, "What shall it profit? What shall it profit?"

> " Therefore, O Lord, I will not fear or falter;
> Nay, but I ask it; nay, but I desire;
> Lay on my lips the embers of the altar,
> Seal with the sting and furnish with the fire.

Quick, in a moment, infinite, forever,
  Send an arousal better than I pray.
Give me grace upon the faint endeavor,
  Souls for my hire and Pentecost to-day."

After a selection by a quartet and another hymn, the presiding officer introduced Rev. Cortland Myers of Brooklyn, N. Y.

Address by Rev. Cortland Myers, Brooklyn, N. Y.

Earth's grandest possibility is in the subject of this hour. A life filled with the Spirit is a life passed upon mountain tops which pierce the clouds and touch the very threshold of heaven. This magnificent possibility is for all men, and, paradoxical as it may seem, it is for only one man. The condition precedes the blessing. The one man is he who fulfills the human part.

I. *It is possible for all men.*

The very greatness of the gift of the Holy Spirit has made many men believe that it was only for the few and not for any man anywhere. There have been no exceptions made in the Bible. "The promise is to you and to your children and to all that are afar off, even as many as the Lord our God shall call." "If ye being evil know how to give good gifts to your children, how much more shall your Heavenly Father give the Holy Spirit to them that ask Him." The same "Whosoever will" that stands above the gift of the Divine Son stands above the gift of the Divine Spirit. Almighty God has made no exceptions in his family. Neither ability nor position can stand in the way of this higher life. The weakest child in the lowliest place has often lived this Spirit-filled life and at last shook the world with its tremendous power. There may not have been much influence, but there was a Calvary earthquake of power. The Persian moralist had a beautiful fable. He took in his hand a piece of scented clay and said to it: "O, clay! where hast thou thy perfume?" And the clay said: " I was once a piece of common clay, but they laid me for a time in company with a common rose, and I drank in its fragrance and have now become scented clay." The humblest life in companionship with the Spirit of God becomes completely transformed and marvelously fragrant. The world pauses in its delightful presence and heaven rejoices to sing its praises.

Electric carbons are made in Nuremburg from gas-retort carbon and other waste products. These are powdered, compacted by hammering, pressed through cylinders, softened by steam, burned five or six days in crucibles. The resultant carbon rods fill the darkness with a blaze of light.

That is the divine method of lighting the world. He finds his material in factory and store and farm and office and kitchen and everywhere, and then hammers and presses and softens and burns and pours into them the mighty current of the Holy Spirit until the world's darkness is banished. This ideal life is not for any select few. It is not for preachers more than for citizens. It is not for missionaries more than a doctor or a lawyer or any other man in any other place. What a wonderful transformation would take place if men believed this was possible in every place where they live. A life filled with the Spirit is not incongruous with a life in factory or store or office or most care-stricken home on earth. It would not help you one iota to change your place- That is not according to God's programme. Believe in God's great gift for yourself just where you are, but possibly not just as you are.

II. *It is possible for only one man.*

The cup must be emptied at the well before it can be filled. The heart must be subjected to that same process. Tip it up and tip it over and drain out the last drop of the old poison. Hold it in the hand of surrender at the right angle, long enough to accomplish your purpose. Let the old self go, and shake the clinging drop off. You can only make room by the emptying process. Let the hand of God touch and control every part of your life.

Mendelssohn, the great composer, once visited Freiburg Cathedral and asked permission to play on the organ, but the custodian refused. At last, after much entreaty, he consented to let him touch it. but when Mendelssohn began to play the old man, who was also the organist, burst into tears and asked him for his name. When he heard who it was he wept afresh and said, "Only to think ! I had almost forbid Mendelssohn to touch my organ."

Recognize the Christ, and give him a chance at the keys of purpose and ambition and desire and thought and the entire manual. The whole heart must be surrendered to him, and hurled into the one sublime purpose.

They had a competition in plans for a monument for Walter Scott in Scotland, and a man who was a simple carpenter once, Mr. Kemp, won the prize, and the plans were accepted for that monument that stands now the tribute of Scotland's love to this matchless genius. Why did he succeed? As he passed along the road one day a dusty carpenter boy, a gentleman driving in his carriage saw he was tired and stopped his horse, and the great man said, "Get up and ride with me." So he became acquainted with Sir Walter Scott and learned to love and admire him. And it was one of the inspirations of his life that led him to become a master architect more than a carpenter. And when they threw the competition open to the world this man drew the matchless monument that now stands there incarnated in marble. Why? Because his heart was in it. Other men could not compete with him because he had put his soul into it.

That is the secret of any man's making the very image of Jesus. He is acquainted with him. He loves him. He has thrown his whole heart into the likeness. This changes the world for that soul. This is the expulsive power of a new affection. This answers all questions of dancing and card-playing and theatre-going and everything so common to Christian lives and so lowering. In the valleys when it might be an Alpine one. Even above all clouds. Tastes and preferences are lifted higher by something better. Many troublesome things may not be wicked, but oh, they are so useless! Whole lives are given up to this doing of an innocent little piece of uselessness. The question is not whether you are going to be punished for something, but whether you are keeping something better away from your heart and life. If your little useless innocency is an offence to you, thrust a knife into it now and kill it — that will be justifiable murder.

You remember when you were school lads, and the water seemed chilly. The first one ready went down to test it. He put in his toe; and oh! how slowly he got ready for the plunge. He said, "It is awfully cold." If you stand there, shivering on the bank, you put on your clothes again, and never go in at all.

Just make a complete surrender. Plunge right in and the joy will be unspeakable and full of glory. I remember an hour on my knees; it was the most sacred hour of my life. It was my life.

Some time ago there were 4,600.000 letters in the dead-letter postoffice at Washington,— letters that lost their way,— but not one prayer ever directed to the heart of God miscarried. Before the postal communication was so easy, and long ago, on a rock 100 feet high, on the coast of England, there was a barrel fastened to a post, and in great letters on the side of the rock, so it could be seen far out at sea, were the words "Post Office"; and when ships came by a boat put out to take and fetch letters. And so sacred were those deposits of affection in that barrel that no lock was ever put upon that barrel, although it contained messages for America, and Europe. and Asia. and Africa, and all the islands of the sea. Many a storm-tossed sailor, homesick, got message of kindness by that rock, and many a homestead heard good news from a boy long gone.

The waves of the old world almost roll over you, I know, but the prayer barrel is on "The Rock of Ages." Drop your message for the higher life in to-night.

First Presbyterian Church.

At the First Presbyterian Church the entrance decorations were prominently patriotic. In the background were draped the California colors, and over the central door was a banner bearing words of welcome to the Christian Endeavorers. Back of the pulpit a network had been stretched over royal purple bunting, and enmeshed in this were dainty sprays of California flowers.

Rev. E. H. Jenks, the assistant pastor, presided at the service. The great audience filled the church, and listened with wrapt attention to the words of wisdom and eloquence. The meeting opened with singing by the special choir under the direction of Professor Hughes. Mr. Jenks offered prayer and introduced Rev. E. L. Powell, D.D., of Louisville, Kentucky.

Address by Rev. E. L. Powell, D.D., Louisville.

The man who speaks for God and lives for God, whose message, spoken and lived, is righteousness, whose work is done under divine guidance and the constraining power of human need, and who gives himself to that work with a mighty passion that overrides all difficulties and dangers; the man who consecrates his powers of body, soul, and spirit to a holy cause with glad abandon and a noble disdain of tamer and less glorious living — surely such a man illustrates the meaning of "a life filled with the Spirit." Such a life is a felt force for righteousness. It is surcharged with the divine. It is a clearly marked life, for it bears the marks of divine ownership. Over its bare, bold brow we may read in other than printed letters, "Whose I am and whom I serve." Such a life is the divine product of that Holy Spirit which works in us both to will and to do God's good pleasure. The true prophet of God, whose character and mission have been preserved for us on those pages that never grow dim, embodies and illustrates in a most conspicuous way this life filled with the Spirit. In a brief study of the prophet doing the work of God so gloriously in his own age and generation that it has been preserved as an example for all future generations, "that we through patience and comfort of the Scriptures might have hope" — in this brief study of the prophet we shall feel the blessedness of a Spirit-filled life, even though we may not be able to describe it in the high and sacred speech it deserves.

Is it asked incredulously what have we of to-day to do with the prophet? What fellowship has nineteenth century life with the "olden, golden glory" of a day when the word of the Lord came unto men saying, "Whom shall I send and who will go for us?" Then let us answer boldly that the prophet, in certain essential elements of life and character, belongs to no particular age or race of men, but to every age and every nation. The realm of prophecy is limited only by fitness to enter and not by any arbitrary fixing of its metes and bounds. To use the imagery of another, we may not be able to shine with the brilliancy of Isaiah, the pole star of prophecy, or Jeremiah, the rainy Hyades of Scripture, or Ezekiel, the burning Sirius of Revelation, or even the minor prophets, the Pleiades of the Bible, but we may at least give forth the divine light that is in us—only a thread of light, it may be, but illuminative according to its intensity and persistence. To show that prophecy is not limited by sex, we have but to think of Deborah and Huldah; to show that it is not limited by condition we need only to remember that Moses was a herdsman, David a shepherd, and Isaiah a peasant's son; to show that it is not limited to any certain set of men, we may quote the language of an eminent theologian, who informs us "that no less than twenty-three prophets, besides those whose writings are preserved in the canon of the Old Testament, are mentioned by name, and that large numbers of nameless ones are brought forward at different points in Hebrew history." The field is open to all who are fitted to enter and occupy. The call to-day is for prophets in the house, whose words and life shall speak for God in the family circle; prophets in business who will say with a noted prince when invited to meanness, "The House of Savoy knows the path of defeat, but not of dishonor"; prophets in politics—"men who can stand before a demagogue and scorn his treacherous flatteries without winking; tall men, sun-crowned, who live above the fog in public duty and in private thinking"; prophets in literature "who refuse," as another has said, "to believe that that can be really beautiful which brings the blush of shame upon the brow of innocence or kindles the lurid glow of passion and unholy lust in the eyes of its youth and maidens"; prophets in art whose paintings and statues awaken within us an infinite longing for the true, beautiful, and good, and whose cleanness shall be a constant rebuke to all moral deformity; yea, prophets in the church of God who shall put the trumpet to their lips and shout once again: "Awake! awake! put on thy strength, O Zion! put on thy beautiful garments, O Jerusalem, the Holy City!" We need to cherish at this time the broad ambition of Moses: "Would God that all the Lord's people were prophets!"

There are few prophets, because there are few prepared. The Spirit-filled life is the necessary condition and prerequisite. With very great force it has been asked, " How then can we be prophets : we, the worldly; we, the sensual ; we, the idle and sluggish : we, the vulgar and conventional; we, who worship Mammon and love pleasure and delight so much in scandal and hatred and lies ? As we are we cannot be prophets ; but are the wings of six-winged seraphim — the twain with which they did fly — folded forever ? Is there no temple more ? Is heaven closed forever ? Burns there no fire on the altar ? Has the chariot of heaven ceased to descend to earth ? Are there no hot cords of fire to touch and purify the unclean lips ? Does the Lord say no longer from his throne above the cherubim, "Whom shall I send and who will go for us"? Our supreme need is a life filled with the Spirit. It is our poverty of soul, our worldliness, our cowardice, our materialistic conceptions, our lack of worthy ideals — it is such deficiencies in our spiritual life that incapacitate us to hear the divine word and to speak it out to the world. Not until the spirit of man has been quickened by the Spirit of God can he come to men in the "spirit and power of the prophets." Then shall he interpret for us the divine will ; then shall he make real to us the invisible ; then shall he stir the current of our sluggish life ; then shall he give to us worthy ideals and make them to shine with the brightness of beckoning stars ; then shall he speak, in word and deed, a message so clear, so brave, so strong, that the world shall own it as from God.

In the time that remains for this address, I want to speak of some of the characteristics of the prophet, or, if you please, some of the elements which enter into a life filled with the Spirit, and have you observe the imperative necessity of sharing them, if we shall do, even in a small degree, the work of a prophet in our generation.

1. The prophet must be an inspired man. Of the inspiration of the Bible prophet, a writer says — in summing up the Scriptural description — "the spirit of God 'comes' on him, 'rests' on him, fills him with power : inspires him or creates him 'a man of the Spirit,' making him to speak as he is 'moved.' that is literally borne along, as a ship is before the wind, by the resistless power of the Holy Ghost." It was a state of high mental excitement, "so that the people not unfrequently spoke of the prophet as mad." His powers were quickened, so that he became the orator, rousing the people as with a clarion blast. or the poet breaking forth in impassioned song, majestic as the myriad-voiced ocean. To what extent this inspiration of the Hebrew prophet has been shared by others I do not know, but one thing I do know, that only an inspired life can do the prophet's work in this or any generation. Is not the Spirit-filled life an inspired life? "The spirit of man is the candle of the Lord" and will remain cold and unresponsive until it has been kindled by the divine fire ; then it will flame and glow with power and helpfulness ; then it is inspired. What exhilaration and freedom in such a life! The ship, with anchor lifted and sails filled, treading the waves with the majesty of a king and bidding the winds obey its royal will, is only a faint representation of the sovereignty of inspired life. Life becomes worth living.

There are two things which have entered into the inspiration of all God's prophets. ancient and modern, two things which all prophets share with the greater lights of the Bible.

(*a*) The first is that the prophet must feel intensely that he is speaking and acting for God. That was the fundamental conception of Hebrew prophetism, and hence the frequent introduction of the phrase, "Thus saith the Lord." And so must feel every man who is standing for truth and righteousness. If he is not speaking for God, then, pray, in whose name is he speaking and whom does he represent? No man ever stood for any great moral issue; no man ever exalted the right or denounced the wrong; no man ever trod "in cheerful godliness the simple round of duty day by day" who was not representing God and speaking for God. It is this thought which sustains every true prophet and makes him strong in the hour of sorest trial. It is this, too, which makes him fearless in the denunciation of all wrong and serene in the confidence of ultimate victory.

(*b*) The second thing which must enter into the character of every true prophet — as a part of his inspiration — an element in every Spirit-filled life — is compulsion. "The lion hath roared: who will not fear? The Lord God hath spoken: who can but prophesy?" The prophet feels that he must speak. His message is as a fire in his bones until it gets delivered. As one thinks of the human need about him and the adaptation of the Gospel to that need; as he thinks of the solemn fact that his life must tell for either good or ill on the lives of those with whom he has to do; as he thinks of the worth of the smallest effort in helping the old world forward — that

> " To withhold the very meagrest dole
> Hands can bestow in part or whole
> And you may stint a starving soul."

As he hears the Macedonian cry, sad as the night wind's wail, coming from the slums, from the shops, from all the dark places of America and the still darker places of earth's heathen races, — a cry so loud and piercing that it sounds above the ocean's roar, — surely as one thinks and hears, he can but say with the divinest prophet of all, "I must work the works of Him that sent me while it is called to-day, for the night cometh, when no man can work."

2. The second characteristic of the prophet is goodness. This is the condition of his inspiration. "Holy men of God spake as they were moved." That he may fitly accept the call, the iniquity of the prophet needs to be taken away and his sin purged. He must be courageous, loyal to his convictions, open and receptive to the divine word, ready to do the thing commanded, — all these things enter into moral fitness. The goodness of the prophet is not "goodyism," or "amiable tamevers," or "insipid commonplace." On the contrary, it is virile and strong. It is not only good, but good for something. It walks with a firm step and has the "bare, bold brow," which is "better than the clasp of a coronet." The prophet of to-day, no less than the prophet of long ago, needs, as a prominent constituent of his goodness, moral courage. The life that is filled with the Spirit can but manifest this high quality of character — the courage, as Canon Farrar describes it, "which dares to confront an angry king, or, standing up before a raging mob, dares to say, 'You are wrong'; the courage which says, 'I will not follow the multitude to be lost'; the courage which sees nothing but feebleness in the plea, 'Every one else does it, so must I do it too'; the courage of the man who, when standing up against brute force for law and right says, 'No bullets and no threats shall cow me in the clear direction of my duty'; still more the courage which can face and shame down a wrong custom and the execrations of its votaries." This is the sort of goodness which the prophetic character requires. To live up to the truth as you see it — to stand for it in the face of opposition and death itself — this is to have the Spirit and to do the work of a prophet.

The call comes to you and to me — the divine call — "Whom shall I send and who will go for us?" O! that each of us may be so filled with the divine spirit that we shall give back the response gladly and joyously, "Here I am, send me." In accepting the call and doing the work, we shall know as we can never know otherwise, the blessedness and power of "a life filled with the Spirit."

EXTERIOR OF MECHANICS' PAVILION.

The next speaker was the Rev. G. F. Pentecost, D.D., of Yonkers, New York.

Address by Rev. G. F. Pentecost, D.D., Yonkers, N. Y.

It is a matter of regret that this strong and suggestive address cannot be published in full. He said in part: —

" I shall not speak to those who occupy the pinnacle of powerful influence, but to representatives of the common people. I shall speak to those who are distinguished in that obscure place to which God has assigned them.

" Christianity is a supernatural religion. It is not a religion of abstract creed or high philosophy, but a religion which has its whole being in something which came down from God. It has all its impulses from within and dominates rather than is dominated by its environment.

" The church to-day is waiting for the fruit of the Spirit — love, joy, peace, long-suffering, gentleness, meekness, truth, goodness, temperance and such things. When we bear such fruit the world will fall down and ground its arms before us.

" To be filled with the Spirit is to have unobstructed access to God. There is a vast difference between saying our prayers and praying. Independence comes from a Spirit-filled life. It is the life designed by the Master, which may be realized by all, and must be by those who are truly Christian. It has its beginning, middle, and end in God, its 'source. Its impulses are from within, and no other spirit could attract the vast throng of people to this coast. Such men and women are guides for themselves and others. They know truth and follow it, and as Endeavorers it is our duty to make more room for God's spirit ; then comes sanctification in its true sense, a baptism in the body of the Lord. The Christian Endeavor is the great God-given instrument to meet the emergencies of our age."

He spoke of the phenomenal gathering of 20,000 young people on the Pacific coast as something which no mere human attraction could have drawn. There must be something spiritual to bring all these people over such a wearisome journey to work together for Christ.

Plymouth Congregational Church.

The golden hue representing California predominated in the decorations at the Plymouth Congregational Church. Back of the pulpit was a large field of yellow, surmounted by evergreens. Upon this was an Endeavor emblem of eschscholtzias and the slogan of the society, " For Christ and the Church," worked in purple letters. Green plants and the Convention colors were effectively used in decoration.

The speakers of the evening were welcomed by Professor Lloyd, of the Pacific Theological Seminary, who is also acting pastor of the church. The first to address the audience was Rev. J. Z. Tyler, D.D., of Cleveland, Ohio, superintendent of Christian Endeavor for the

Church of the Disciples and a trustee of the United Society of Christian Endeavor.

Address by Rev. J. Z. Tyler, D.D., Cleveland, Ohio.

Dr. Tyler gave a Bible reading in which he helpfully considered three questions.

First.   Is it our privilege to be filled with the Spirit now ?

Second.   If so, upon what conditions ?

Third.   What are some of the normal results of a Spirit-filled life ?

In speaking of the first question he cited the prophecy of Joel in Acts, ii : 7, and the promise of Peter in Acts, ii : 39.

" There are indications," he said, " that not only are we to be filled with the Holy Spirit, but that it is to abide within believers, and they indicate that the life of the Holy Spirit is the richest and best of all the gifts of the Gospel.

" The conditions upon which the Holy Spirit is to come are clearly indicated.   Jesus said that the world cannot receive it.   St. Paul says that it is bestowed when we have believed.

" It is as impossible to catalogue the results of a Spirit-filled life as it is to catalogue the results of searching the Scripture.   We are taught that the Spirit resists our carnal nature ; that he sheds the love of God abroad in our hearts ; that he makes us to abound in hope ; that he fills us with joy, gives us liberty and helps our infirmities.

" The blessing of this Convention depends not upon its numbers, nor any spectacular display, not upon the eloquence of its addresses or upon its singing, but upon the presence and power of the Spirit of God within us."

The concluding speaker was Rev. William Patterson, of Toronto, Canada.

Address by Rev. William Patterson, Toronto, Canada.

He spoke of the necessity of a man's using his Bible with the Spirit of God, and the unspeakable joy of living a life filled with the Spirit.

" The Spirit gives power and joy.   He makes the endeavor of the Christian worker more effective.   The Spirit of God can be obtained by opening the heart in earnest prayer.   We are not to be annoyed by the petty things in this world, but are to try and rescue some of the millions that are going down.   The essentials in this rescue are, first, the Word of God, secondly, the Spirit of God."

A number of Christian Endeavor hymns were sung by the congregation, and a solo was rendered entitled " Hosanna."

Simpson Memorial M. E. Church.

Rev. W. S. Matthews, D.D., of San Francisco, presided over the large gathering that assembled in this church.   .The artistic interior of the edifice rendered profuse adornment unnecessary.   Sprigs of California poppies were prettily arranged about the pulpit.   A silk American flag was spread about the lectern and the Convention colors were draped about the alcoves on each side of the pulpit. The emblem of the Epworth League was used with the Christian Endeavor emblem in the decorations.

Rev. W. J. McKittrick, of Buffalo, New York, was the first one to speak upon the theme.

Address by Rev. W. J. McKittrick, Buffalo.

We regret that the manuscript of this address was misplaced. In his address he referred to the advance of Endeavor since its inception and of the sacredness of the labor, and also of the responsibility which is connected inseparably with it.

In part he said : " Our annual conventions are held for the sole purpose of instilling inspiration into those who are aiding our mighty cause. Whatever is done should be done well and with our whole souls. Our purpose is to endeavor to do all in our power for Christianity and to teach the blessed words of our Saviour, who died that we might live. Figuratively speaking, we should be always booted and spurred, that we may be ready when the trumpet sounds and not have to think of what might have been.

" The social mission of Christian workers should be to stand in dust and preach to dust-covered men, to lay aside all selfishness and take up the banner of loyalty to both man and God, for truly selfishness turns men into wild beasts, who refuse to be controlled by the teachings of the Gospel. It is impossible to legislate wickedness or crime out of the world or righteousness in, but the multiplication of good and God-fearing men may save the world, and this is what we are striving for.

" If the gospel of the Lord Jesus Christ cannot cleanse this earth, where is cleanliness to come from? If Christ is accepted, then we must accept his teachings, and this will be accomplished when the thought of denominational progress is laid aside and all our efforts exerted toward the sacred cause of Christian progress. Let us have on a banner ' Loyalty to Christ, and duty and courtesy to our fellow-man.' "

Rev. G. R. W. Scott, D.D., of Leominster. Mass., kindly supplied the place of Rev. Matt S. Hughes, D.D., of Minneapolis, who was on one of the delayed trains.

Address by G. R. W. Scott, D.D., Leominster, Mass.

Dr. Scott discussed the subject under the four thoughts that the Spirit-filled life must be, first, an illuminated life ; second, a consecrated life ; third, a life of unity ; fourth, a life of power.

The speaker forcibly developed these ideas, and laid especial emphasis upon the consecration of all the Endeavor forces to the ends of spiritual growth. " The advance of our cause," he said, " is being watched throughout our land, and the more strength and earnestness we may put in our movement will gradually, yet surely, increase our numbers. We will have true union when the spirit of our work fills our hearts. Heretofore, we have possibly had too little prayer and too much thought, but with reversal will come success and increased numbers. Let us preach, that the teachings of the Gospel may be sent broadcast throughout our land."

At the Central M. E. Church.

This church was taxed to its utmost to hold the throng of Endeavorers that sought admission. The interior of the building was beautifully decorated with the Convention colors. A Christian Endeavor emblem of yellow poppies also ornamented the organ. Long streamers of golden bunting was festooned beneath the gallery all around the auditorium. The front portion of the gallery was hidden by purple and yellow bunting, intertwined and caught up at regular intervals with gold stars and clusters of eschscholtzias. Over the choir gallery, in gold and crimson, was the motto : " For Christ and the church."

The presiding officer was the pastor of the church, Rev. E. R. Dille, D.D., a trustee of the United Society of Christian Endeavor. The opening hymn, "Bright Glory Land," was sung by the audience in an inspiring manner. "He Has Taken My Sins Away" and "Bright Glory Land" a second time followed, under the direction of J. J. Morris. Prayer was offered by Rev. C. McKelvy, D.D.

After " The Endeavorers' Marching Song" had been sung by the congregation, Dr. Dille introduced the speakers of the evening.

In introducing Rev. Charles A. Dickinson, D.D., of Berkeley Temple, Boston, Dr. Dille said that the great question of the time was how to reach the masses, and that this had been practically answered by the open church — the Berkeley Temple in Boston — of which Dr. Dickinson was pastor.

Address of Rev. Chas. A. Dickinson, D.D., Boston, Mass.

Passing over a Massachusetts road last fall, I was struck with the marvellous coloring of the autumn leaves. The woods were aflame with crimson banners, and the green and the gold vied with each other in their multitudinous shades. The hills looked as though a thousand Turners had been splashing the remnants from their easels over them, and in the maze and whirl of color one could almost imagine that he saw startling pictures. As I looked upon this gorgeous tapestry of the hills I remembered that only a few weeks ago these crimsons and golds and browns were all a livid green, and that a few weeks earlier they were a pale and tender hue, like that of buds just waking into life. How quickly the hues had come and gone ! How, in the ceaseless moving of the months, the same spirit of life working within had appeared now in this shade, and now in that, until at last it had burst out into this wild riot of color. Divers operations. but the same spirit. This is the law of divine action in nature and in the human soul. Whether we take humanity as a whole or in part, we find this law working itself out in infinite variety. Paul, in this twelfth chapter of first Corinthians, is illustrating this fact.

If you have really been touched and vitalized by the Divine Spirit, he says, this Spirit will be manifested in and through you in different ways, but it is the same Spirit, whether it appears in the flaming red of Peter's character, the mellow gold of John's, or the less pronounced colors of the characters of the other disciples.

The first thing to be noticed is that there is such a person as the Holy Ghost, and that he is none other than God himself working in man. Paul is very explicit on this point. "I give you to understand," he says, "that no man speaking by the Spirit of God calleth Jesus accursed." The Jews claimed to be of God when they were persecuting and crucifying Christ. This could not be. Like detects like. Spirit answers to spirit as face to face in water. God in the heart could not revile the Son of God on the cross. The Divine Spirit within can but recognize the Christ without. Many a man thinking himself a Christian, and assuming to criticise or condemn the professions of others, has been wofully mistaken as to his own faith.

"No man can say that Jesus is the Lord but by the Holy Ghost." The divinity and spiritual headship of Jesus Christ come to man as a special revelation from God himself. The pure in heart shall see God. The Holy Spirit in the heart convinces us of the divine character of Christ as no miracles or arguments can convince us. He flashes this divinity upon us as he did upon Peter when, amazed and humbled, that disciple exclaimed, "Thou art the Christ, the Son of the living God!" or as he did upon Thomas when, with hesitant finger upon the nail-prints, he exclaimed, "My Lord and my God!"

No person or church can monopolize the Holy Spirit. He comes to all who desire him. An earthly father is not more willing to give good gifts to his children than is God to give the Holy Spirit to them that ask him. The man or sect that presumes to an exclusive appropriation of the Spirit, and denies him to those who happen to hold a different opinion, or who differ from them in creed or practice, is doing just what Paul is rebuking the Corinthians for doing in this chapter from which our text is taken. There were certain persons in the Corinthian church who were very proud of their spiritual gifts, and had a great deal to say about them. For this reason Paul felt called upon to warn the church against being misled by these ambitious and vainglorious men. Do not, he says in substance, make the mistake of thinking that the Holy Ghost manifests himself only in showy ways, or in pretentious sanctities. He is the direct inspirer of varied ministrations, and is often most forceful in unpretentious service.

"To one is given, by the Spirit, the word of wisdom." Such an one is not able to talk much about his religion; he is a man of few words, but his words weigh much. Five minutes with him are worth an hour with some other men. His brain is made to distil truth, not to dilute it; and when the power of the Spirit is upon him, he is one of the most helpful counselors in Corinth.

"To another is given the word of knowledge." He is not born wise like the other man. He gets knowledge by hard work. His brain is a net which gathers fish from all seas, a repository of facts. He is not especially popular or practical. Like Gamaliel, he has no crowd at his feet: but serious people like Paul sit there, and when the power is upon him he stimulates men's intellects and strengthens their souls.

"To another, faith." Quiet, retiring, yet possessed of a strongly magnetic and inspiring personality, this man stands in the community as the daysman between multitudes of Little Faiths and the Lord. Men absorbed in worldliness lean upon him and believe in him, and all Corinth gets a glimpse of heaven through his upper window. God makes his faith a ladder upon which men climb up out of their sloughs of despond to ground where he gives them a ladder of their own.

"To another, the gift of healing." Some say that this was a temporary manifestation of the Spirit, which, like the gift of miracles, was to vanish with the early disciples. Others contend that it is as common in Boston to-day as it was in Corinth, and as much a privilege of the believer as wisdom, knowledge, and faith. Sure it is, the power of spirit over matter, the tendency of thought to quell certain physical disturbances and conquer pain, and the influence of prayer and a quiet trust in God over many bodily ills all belong to the acknowledged therapeutics of these modern times; and he who believes that it is the province of the Divine Spirit in man to make him not only holy, but whole, according to John's desire for Gaius, may be nearer right than some of us think. "Beloved, I wish above all things that thou mayest prosper and be in health, even as thy soul prospereth."

"To another, prophecy." The gift of vision. A John at Patmos, with the world's future swinging in dazzling cyclorama around him. The man and the woman of these latter days who are so full of the Divine Spirit that they see and foresee events something as Christ did; who stand out in the community and in the church as fearless denouncers of social and political corruption and mighty apostles of righteousness; who with eye ablaze with the light of the New Jerusalem, and ear resonant with millenial music, utter their oracles of rebuke or cheer, and with divine eagerness not unmixed with human impatience strive to bring on the day when the golden anticipations of the ages shall be fully realized, and the Christ shall be crowned Lord of all.

"To another, discerning of Spirits." A Peter who can look through and through a man, and detect the hypocrisy and imposition which are lurking in him, as in the case of Ananias and Sapphira. An Elisha who is able to see in the heart of the young Hazael a future of selfishness, murder, carnage, and devastation. The seer whom you will find in almost every band of disciples, whose spiritual insight is so keen that he can look into the souls and characters of men, detect their virtues and their vices, and lay them as bare as were the muscles of the flayed Marsyas.

"To another, divers kinds of tongues; and to another, the interpretation of tongues." The glottis gift, the power of the orator who sways men's minds and controls their wills. The power of the man who is master of men's thoughts and emotions, whose magnetic personality gives him free range through the hearts of men of every nation and kindred and tribe and tongue.

"All these worketh that one and the self-same spirit dividing to every man severally as he will." In other words, God can use every kind of talent; and when he takes full possession of a man he uses that man most efficiently along the line of his bent. He takes him just as he finds him, with the tendencies and powers which he first implanted within him, and develops him, just as he takes a bed of bulbs and tubers in the springtime, pours his sunshine and rain over them, and brings to their glory here a tulip and there a hyacinth, and later on, a dahlia, a lily, or a clematis, each beautiful in its time. This coming to full-blown tuliphood, or lilyhood, is the working of the same spirit of life. For a tulip bulb to say, "I, and I only, have in me this life power. We tulips have a monopoly of it. If you want to get it you must be like us, with a smooth, glossy exterior, and a straight, stiff stem, with one, and only one, blossom at the end. You hyacinths, with your gay, scented bells, and you dahlias, with your many tuberous roots aud multiplied branches reaching out in all directions, and blossoming high and low on all sides of yourselves, you make a great mistake in thinking that you have this life spirit,"—for a tulip to say this would be like what some good people are saying about other people who believe in Young Men's Christian Associations and Christian Endeavor Societies, and Institutional Churches. "You have too many roots and branches," they say. "You blossom out on too many sides of life to be a channel for the Spirit. You are too secular to be saintly. Come out from the world. Be separate from it. Seek the things that are above. Be singular, stiff, and blossom tulip-wise, and then we will grant that you have the gift of the Spirit."

The mere possession of the Spirit is not enough. Power is good for nothing until it is applied and becomes operative. The spirituality that shuts its eyes and sways to and fro and talks pessimistically and does little else but talk, may be of the genuine sort; but a more effective kind is that which our Saviour declared to be the one condition of discipleship—many-sided ministration in his name. "Inasmuch as ye did it unto the least of these." Here we have the application of the Spirit's power—not merely the possession of something, but the doing of something very practical and very secular because of that possession; the Spirit in us; Christ in us working out into tangible, helpful, every-day service.

This is the same truth that we have in our text and context—divers operations, varied manifestations. The Holy Ghost within us, impelling us to visit the sick, comfort the afflicted, welcome the stranger, care for the poor, is just as truly the Holy Ghost as he is when he helps us to pray and worship. He is just as real a presence in our lives when he helps us to control our tongues as when he helps us to use them. A silence which is full of the unpretentious deeds of love has far more spirituality in it, more of the Holy Ghost, than the most religious speech unaccompanied with the ministering hand. Prophesying and the gift of tongues are for the few. They are rare gifts; they are useful gifts. Blessed is he who by tongue or pen can move men to better lives. But the gift which our Lord speaks of when he talks about the man in prison, the stranger, the hungry, the naked, and the sick; the gifts of which he speaks in his Sermon on the Mount, and in his other discourses upon his new commandment — the gift of loving our enemies, letting our light shine, bearing good fruit, improving our talents, forgiving one another, suppressing revenge, and refraining from slander — these are the common gifts which all can have for the asking; which all, indeed, must have, or the inference will be that they have not the Spirit.

The practical lessons hang upon this twelfth of Corinthians as thick as the ripened fruit upon our New England apple-trees this year.

The true test of the Spirit's presence is the manifestation which he makes of himself. The man who claims to have a power and fails to use it will not be believed. Application, action, results, — these are the proofs of power. If you have spiritual power we shall all find it out. You may not make a show of it, but we shall discover it. You will find your place and fill it. The Holy Ghost does not need your position or your trade for his channel. He needs you. When he has possessed you, and filled you, and kindled the faculty by which he intends to make you felt in the world, he will set you to work wherever you are, to win the world to Christ. He will present the Saviour to men through you, by helping you to be Christlike. You may be a humble carpenter. That makes no difference. Apply your power. Show how the Holy Spirit can work through the carpenter. Be honest; be true. Saw your boards and drive your nails with a hand athrill with the power of the Holy Ghost. Let all the wheels of your inner life — love, hope, patience, forbearance, joy, peace, mercy — move ceaselessly on under the impulse of this power, so that their hum shall be as suggestive of energy as that of the dynamo. You and the Holy Ghost can make any calling a great one. If the Spirit divine appeared as the mighty Jehovah, the Creator of all things, when he first made the world, remember that he came in the lowly guise of a carpenter to remake it. The weak things has God chosen to confound the mighty, that no flesh should glory before him. No king by virtue of his kinghood can say, "I have done this great thing." God can do just as great and greater things through the king's servant. Joseph was greater than Pharaoh. Luther, the despised monk, was greater than the pope. The atlas-bearers of the world have made their muscle at obscure forges. The pauper with a righteous cause is often greater than a prince with a kingdom, "that no flesh may glory."

John Brown of Haddington was once visited by a young man of a very excitable temperament, and was told by him that he wanted to preach the gospel. The shrewd pastor saw that the young man's zeal was greater than his knowledge, and that his conceit was greater than either, and so he advised him to stay where he was. "But," said the young man, "I want to preach and glorify God." The old commentator replied, "My young friend, a man may glorify God making brooms. Stick to your trade, and glorify God by your life and conversation."

Then comes the thought that we are a part of "one stupendous whole." Your prophesying, and that other man's discerning, and that other's faith, are interlinked and mutually supporting members of one body. Your work and my work and our brother's work go together, as the hand, the arm, and the eye, and together we can strike a vigorous blow.

This is very comforting to discouraged workers and to those who have come to think that they have no great power spiritually. You stand in your place and toil on, wondering why, if you really have the power of the Spirit, you do not make more impression on the world and see more results. Men seem so busy and unresponsive, and to care so little for what you say. You put your heart into your work, and think you are doing it with Christ's approval, and yet the world does not seem to notice it. In fact, you have about concluded that the more unselfish your work is the more men will call you a fool or an enthusiast. You almost begin to doubt, and you say to yourself, "Does it pay, after all?" A finger plunged for an instant into the ocean and then withdrawn, a yellow leaf kissing the granite boulder and falling to decay, a raindrop brushing a rose petal and mingling with the earth, — each, you think, leaves about as much impression behind as you will leave when your life-work is done and the funeral tears are shed.

Failure seems to face you. Friends drop off one by one. You are getting old and the world is ever young; you are getting serious, and the world is gay. What is the use?

Mrs. Browning tries to comfort you a bit.

> " Though we fail indeed,
> You, I, a score of such weak workers, he
> Fails never. If He cannot work by us,
> He will work over us. Does he want a man,

> " The star winks there, so many souls are born
> Who shall work too. Let our own be calm.
> We should be ashamed to sit beneath those stars
> Impatient that we're nothing."

But to my mind it is *only* a bit of comfort that she gives you. Cold comfort, to think that God does not want a man or a woman to work with; that he could do without us just as well — cold as the starlight under which Mrs. Browning would have us sit in chilly, patient silence, meditating upon our nothingness. I find better comfort in our text and context: — "Members of one body," the less comely parts honored even more than the comely ones; something for each to do, and no thought of being left out alone, pining under the unsympathetic stars. God can work by us, and with him in us we cannot fail. Our work will last. It is as imperishable as the walls of heaven. It is a part of those walls. It may be but a bit of jasper, it may be but a tiny pearl, but somewhere in the colorings of the eternal city it will fill its place.

Yes, he fails never, and because we work with him we cannot fail. What we do becomes a part of his glory. Our toil and sacrifice and suffering are the medium of his power, the channel of his energy. Our tears make his rainbows. I saw a rainbow last week, magnificent, full-arched, and brilliant. There it lay off in the east, expanding from the dark bosom of the storm its seven-colored petals, a gorgeous blossom of the skies called into being by the westering sun. But how many raindrops it took to make that rainbow, falling, ever falling, in countless numbers! And how brief was the brilliance of each falling drop, and how many bows such a drop helped to make on its journey earthward, one for every angle of vision! How full was that dark cloud and that falling shower of rainbows, — rainbows which I could not see, which no one saw! And how these raindrops, after touching the earth for awhile, would in time get back again into the skies and help to make other rainbows, and so on throughout the ceaseless circle till the sun shall set forever. Your life, my brother, is a raindrop reflecting the Sun that never sets. It shines out upon this beholder and that; and when it gets below the angle of their vision they call it ended, and others take your place in the swift passage through the prismatic space. Even you do not see your own glory, and you get discouraged towards the end. But the end is only the beginning. Are they not all ministering spirits? Does not their work go on? Others take their earth places, and make rainbows for earthly eyes; but they, having fallen to the dust, have risen again a great cloud of witnesses, radiant ministers in the upper skies, reflecting still the Sun of righteousness, showing forth his glory, a part of the rainbow which encircles the throne of the eternal.

Dr. Dille then introduced Rev. M. Rhodes, D. D., of St. Louis, as

"The leading Endeavorer of Missouri." Dr. Rhodes took the place of Dr. Gilby C. Kelly, of Alabama, who was detained from being present at the Convention.

Address of Rev. M. Rhodes, D.D., St. Louis.

The speaker dwelt upon the necessity of putting sect into the background and doing real spiritual work for Christ's sake alone. He urged his hearers not to follow the banner of Luther or Wesley, but of Jesus Christ. Without the Spirit of God man is unable to accomplish anything. The Holy Spirit men must receive, through him pass from the realm of darkness unto that of light.

At the close of this winning address the choir sang, "Anywhere, My Saviour." A few moments of silent prayer followed, and then Dr. Dickinson made the closing prayer of consecration.

Trinity Presbyterian Church.

With a large choir and the leadership of O. M. Vesper the song service at this church proved attractive. Dr. A. M. Brush, of Alameda, acted as chairman of the meeting.

The first speaker introduced was Rev. John R. Davies, D. D., of New York City.

Address by Rev. J. R. Davies, D.D., New York.

TEXT: *Paul, a servant of Jesus Christ, called to be an apostle, separated unto the gospel of God.*— ROM. i. 1.

No department of literature is more generally useful than biography, because it is a reservoir into which flow many of the currents which have influenced our own lives; because it is a trysting-place where we hold fellowship with men and women of like passions, of like difficulties, of like victories, and, as we mark the ebb and flow of these experiences, we feel pouring into our souls the breath of a new life, and, inspired by such characters and by such conflicts, we say, I, also, can attempt this.

Our text is a biography, not bulky, but brilliant. You must look, not at the numbers of its words, but at their weight; not at the size of its chapters, but at their suggestiveness; not at the technique of its pictures, but at the timeliness of their teaching. Its keynote is found in the word "separate," and, as we study it, there will unfold before us, I pray, a life which, for purity of soul, grandeur of self-sacrifice, and lasting influence upon the world, is perhaps without a parallel among the sons of men. Our exposition of our text will be an attempt to answer the question, "Unto what was Paul separated?" First. as a believer unto the faith of the Gospel; second, as an apostle unto the work of the Gospel; third, as the servant of Jesus Christ unto the spirit of the Gospel.

First, as a believer, Paul was separated unto the faith of the Gospel.

Upon the threshold of this discussion we must define the phrase, "faith of the Gospel." The word "faith" here does not mean that act of the soul by which it centers all its hopes upon the finished work of Jesus Christ, but those doctrinal teachings of the New Testament which present to us with the profoundest philosophy, but also with the simplest style, God's plan of redemption. And by the word "gospel" we do not mean alone the sacred narratives which bear that name, but the teachings of those narratives expounded and expanded by the words and work of the Apostolic Church. And all through this faith of the Gospel there runs the expression of need which presents man as a prodigal, scorning the comforts of the Father's House, as the servant faithless to every trust, as the criminal bending under the growing weight of a broken law, as a temple defiled by all manner of impurities, and presenting at every angle those marks of decay and death with which for ages sin has separated man and God, and made necessary the reconciliation of the cross. And how clearly does the divinity of this faith of the Gospel shine in the presentation of this reconciliation, this remedy for the sins, the sorrows which pressed with such fearful power upon the souls of men. Various forces had been dedicated to the work of redemption; schools, systems, sanctuaries, had each launched their life-boats amid life's surf to save the human wreckage; teachers had taught, oracles had spoken, devotees had suffered, and priests upon myriads of altars had offered their sacrifices, but, as the lengthening shadows of the old dispensation foretold its coming night from the pillars of Hercules to the Euphrates, from the burning sands of Africa to the bleak uplands of Britannia, in all centers of life where men thought intensely and faced earnestly the problems of existence, there was a hungering for a revelation and for a redemption which would give an answer to life's questions and a deliverance from life's burdens. At last God answered these yearning voices in the person of his own Son, whose marvelous words, sinless character, sacrificial death, triumphant resurrection, brought to a decadent world that manifestation of divine life and love for which the wise men of three continents and many generations had longed and looked in vain.

But if Christ, the unspeakable gift of God, proves the divinity of the doctrine of the Gospel, that divinity is still further reinforced by its fruits in the lives of those who accept its message. To those who wanted to know the cause of the cure of the cripple at the Gate Beautiful, Peter replied: "And his name through faith in his name hath made this man strong whom ye see and know." And what was done through this name in Jerusalem by the same blessed instrumentality was repeated wherever the apostles went, so that both physically and spiritually the blind saw, the dumb spake, the lame walked, the dead lived, the prison doors opened, the captive rejoiced in freedom, and to the multitudes, poor not alone in abject poverty, but also in hoarded wealth, in boasted learning, in vaunted righteousness, was the Gospel preached; and thus was carried out that programme of Christianity which was prophesied centuries before by Isaiah, which was proclaimed by our Lord in the synagogue at Nazareth; and because this same programme has been followed with more or less of fidelity through all the intervening centuries we find such an unspeakable difference between the past in which the apostles labored and the gracious present in which we live.

To such a gospel with its sense of need, with its divine redeemer, with its blessed fruits of Christian character, to such a gospel was Paul separated, and though pressed with peculiar power by the sophistries of Grecian culture, by the subtleties of Jewish learning, by the brutal bigotry of those to whom he ministered, to betray his Lord and Master, Paul's loyalty to Christ was a river that, ever widening, ever deepening, flowed on without the ripple of a doubt, so that when at last he reached life's close, with great confidence he could say, "I have kept the faith." And all this to us is most instructive. The age in which we live is filled with subtle temptations, skepticism in the schools, paganism in the world, laxity in the church—these things are making vast assaults upon the believer's faith. Then the age in which we live is one which is filled with piteous needs. Multitudes are weary of the ashes of unbelief, multitudes are searching the foundations of faith, multitudes are dissatisfied with social conditions, multitudes inspired with generous humanitarian impulses are pouring their rain into the ocean and their sunbeams into the desert. All about us in home and foreign fields are the elements of a new order in chaotic confusion, which, if left to themselves, will produce a titanic tempest, but which, if wisely ministered to, will usher in the dawn of earth's fairest and noblest day. O my brother, upon whom the ends of time have come, called to the kingdom for a sovereignty almost divine, pray that as a believer you may be kept amid the temptations of the present, that you may be separated unto the faith of the Gospel so that you may do your part in giving God's remedy to a needy world and thus do much to save your country, your church, and yourself.

Second: Paul as an apostle was separated unto the work of the Gospel.

In the life of all of God's leaders a great crisis may be found. Such came to David when the prophet poured upon his head the annointing oil and set him apart to be Israel's king. Such came to Peter when Jesus of Nazareth looked upon his wondering face and said: "Follow me." Such came to Luther when amid the corruption of Papal Rome he learned the great truth, "The just shall live by faith"; and such a crisis came to Paul when upon the Damascus road the proud Jew, the bigoted Pharisee, the fierce persecutor received a call which changed his whole life and distinctly separated him to the accomplishment of the greatest enterprise ever attempted by any man since time began. That work appears to us in the explanatory words given to Ananias: "He is a chosen vessel to bear my name before the Gentiles and kings and children of Israel." And "What," a very common question asks, "is in a name?" That depends upon the one who bears it. John Smith of Virginia fame and John Smith the ne'er-do-well will illustrate my meaning; and when we think of that name which Paul was commissioned to bear, we see at once that person who is above every person, that Gospel which is above every gospel, and that Cross which lifts itself in superb triumph over every other scheme of redemption, as Mount Everest, the king of the Himalayas, lifts itself in lone and silent majesty above the other peaks which bow in worship at its feet; and this name Paul is to bear before the Gentiles and kings and children of Israel; and under the spell of these words we see this separated man going down to the sea in ships, hastening along the military roads of the Roman Empire, occupying the strategic centers of continents, proclaiming his message from the temple steps, upon the crest of Mars Hill, amid the mighty marbles of the Imperial City; and when in the hour of martyrdom the standard of the cross falls from the hands which had borne it from Damascus to the Gates of the West, it is grasped by others, among whom we see Polycarp, Tertullian, Patrick, Augustine, and the crowd of missionary witnesses who came after,—a glorious company of apostolic men and women into whose labors we have entered.

But we must not forget the one great condition which underlay the apostolic life and which made this separation possible, namely, a personal knowledge of Jesus Christ. This will explain the training of the twelve, as in high converse they walked with the Master through those mighty years, while, by parable and miracle, by speech and scene, natural and supernatural, he slowly revealed himself as Israel's Messiah and the World's Redeemer; and Paul was no stranger to such a privilege. He, too, saw the Lord; but what for others was vouchsafed through the space of years, for him was centered in one mighty vision, and amid the glories of that supreme hour were born convictions which burnt themselves into the soul of Paul, and which, like cables of steel, through all the surf and sacrifice of that heroic missionary life, anchored him as an apostle separated unto the work of that Gospel of which he was never ashamed; and no life can be separated unto this work upon any other principle. There must be a personal knowledge of Jesus Christ. The soul must have companied with the Master, heard his call, sat in the upper room, watched in Gethsemane, knelt at the cross, stood in the empty sepulchre, and made one of that little company who walked with him as far as Bethany, and who, with tear-stained but joy-lit faces, watched him passing heavenward. For this personal knowledge of the crucified, the risen Christ, I plead, and then a daily, a growing separation to the work which the Gospel represents will be a result most natural, because as all the machinery of the Corliss engine, in obedience to the impelling power of steam, moves with an ever-growing velocity, so all the machinery of the Christian life, in obedience to the impelling power of this personal experience of Jesus Christ, will move forward with deepening desire toward a life separated unto the work of the Gospel, as that work may come in pulpit or in pew, during the Sabbath or during the week, in places of conspicuous service or in quiet, obscure spheres where none but the Master knows.

Third: Paul, as a servant of Jesus Christ, was separated unto the spirit of the Gospel.

Upon the shield of the King of Bohemia in the battle of Poitiers was the motto, "I serve," and when the King of kings stood in the midst of the great conflict for the world's redemption, he said, "I have come not to be ministered unto, but to minister, and to give my life a ransom for many." This is the spirit in which he toiled, which he stamped upon the Gospel, and which he gave to all those whom he called to be apostles, and thus Paul speaks of himself as the servant, the slave of Jesus Christ.

Very marked was the progress of Christianity in the early centuries. Starting from the day of Pentecost, with marvelous rapidity, with superb strategy, it approached and entered the strongholds of the ancient faith; and to such an extent was this done that Tertullian, writing in the beginning of the third century, says: "We are a people of yesterday, and yet we have filled every place belonging to you,—cities, islands, castles, towns, assemblies, companies, palaces, senate, forum." And what was the secret of this success? Many answers have been given; for instance, that furnished by Gibbon, in which he speaks of the zeal, the doctrines, the miracles, the morals, the discipline of the Christian church as being responsible for its rapid conquest of the Roman world. But these things were simple effects of another cause — manifestations of a mightier power, and that power was found in a personal Christ, whose cross, crowned with thorns, garnished with blood, and eloquent with the mystery of a great sacrifice, stamped upon all his followers the same unselfish spirit, and before the overwhelming power of such a consecration Jewish synagogue and pagan shrine were compelled to say, "O Nazarene, thou hast conquered!"

The cry of a sorrowing, despairing, dying race rings as never before in the ears of the church. The appliances of modern civilization bring a world to our feet, its needs to our attention as never before. And what answer are we making to these appeals which come to us with such pathetic power. Look at our empty treasuries, our curtailed work, our crippled machinery, the vast possibilities of money, of brain, of soul, in all our churches which are untouched by the spirit of the cross. Do we not need to feel anew the power of Christ's sufferings, to have a diviner vision of him, who, though he was rich, yet for our sake became poor, and to experience a special visitation of the Holy Spirit, separating us as loyal followers of Jesus Christ to that spirit of self-denying service which permeates the Gospel. Do you shrink from this? Upon one occasion the boat in which Xerxes sat was in danger of sinking because it was too crowded. Some one said: "All those who are willing to make a sacrifice for the king leap overboard;" and the majority at once obeyed. And through every day, and in every department of activity, men are sacrificing themselves for the kings of this world. Can we do less for the Royal Priest. the Priestly King, who hath redeemed us, not with silver and gold as slaves are bought, but with his own precious blood, and made us to be kings and priests unto God? No, a thousand times no; and as we leave this scene of consecration let us bear as our motto a bullock standing between a plow and an altar, between toil and sacrifice, while underneath we write the words: "Ready for either." At Antioch the Holy Spirit said: "Separate me, Saul and Barnabas, for the work to which I have called them." In San Francisco, and at the beginning of this great Convention toward which the eyes of a world-wide church are turning, may the Holy Spirit now come with sanctifying power to separate us as believers to the faith of the Gospel, as apostles to the work of the Gospel, and as servants of Jesus Christ to the spirit of the Gospel!

Dr. Brush then introduced Bishop B. W. Arnett, D.D., of the African M. E. church.

Address of Bishop Arnett, Wilberforce, Ohio.

With his usual fervor and animation, Bishop Arnett spoke upon the objects and attainments of Christian Endeavor. "Spirit-filled Men" was his theme.

He described his trip across the continent — across the plains and over mountains. "Humanity," he said, "might be likened to the face of nature — all of us cannot be mountains. Some must tower above the others. Hence, a spirit of humility and obedience such as is shown in the life of Christ should be emulated. His life was filled with the spirit of obedience. It is not strange that God should have selected the seed of Abraham to carry out his great scheme of salvation to men. Abraham had faith in God, Sarah had faith in her husband, and Isaac trusted his father. Therefore it is not strange that this great Christian religion should have been established in such a house."

The speaker referred to these lofty Biblical characters as examples of Spirit-filled men.

"We are here," he said, "representing thirty-two denominations and the different sections of the country. Let us all pray that the spirit of the Master may be upon us. Let each denomination pray that the Lord may be with us as we strive to do our duty. What we need to-day is consecration and separation; become spiritual children of the living God; visit the widow and the orphan and relieve their wants. The children of God should be able to live in the world without being of it. The great work that the Endeavorers are doing is shown by their increased numbers in the last few years — 3,000,000 souls to-day."

In Oakland. The First Presbyterian Church.

Christian Endeavorers overflowed the First Presbyterian Church on the opening night of the great Convention. The session was a memorable one. Floral decorations and the California colors were everywhere in evidence. Rev. Robert F. Coyle, D. D., pastor of the church, presided. Rev. Alfred Kummer read the lesson, after which "Onward, Christian Soldiers" was sung by the assemblage.

Dr. Coyle and the leading members of his church who were present expressed themselves happy to have the Endeavorers gathered there. In the unavoidable absence of both Rev. Ford C. Otman and Dr. J. Wilbur Chapman, who were announced to speak, Dr. Coyle introduced as the first speaker a trustee of the United Society, Rev. J. M. Lowden, of Providence, R. I.

Mr. Lowden spoke briefly upon the general theme of the evening, "The Life Filled with the Spirit." He considered the topic one of peculiar timeliness on the eve of the great Convention. The watchword of Christian Endeavor is a high standard for Christ and victory over sin.

His words were earnest and suggestive, and at the close of his address were warmly applauded.

Fortunate the audience! After a prayer by the Rev. E. S. Chapman, Dr. Coyle introduced Rev. Francis E. Clark, D.D.

Dr. Clark was given an ovation as he arose to speak.

Address of Rev. Francis E. Clark, D.D.

Dr. Clark said in the course of his address : "I had not expected to take part in any service this evening because of the delay in arriving here in California. I am sure there are none who could speak more effectively concerning the spiritual life than my friend, Rev. J. M. Lowden. I esteem it a pleasure to look into the faces of Oakland people and be able to hold their attention for the good cause of our Christian Endeavorers.

"The organization of Christian Endeavorers has not come to California for the fishes and loaves of office. It is not here for what there is in it. This great army of earnest Christian young men did not give up their precious time and cross a continent for any such purpose. They came for fellowship and spiritual uplifting. That is the only topic, the topic, indeed the reigning idea of every hour of this Convention. Whether we talk of citizenship, of missions, of any subject connected with this vast work ; whether it be in evening prayer or in early morning consecration, it is the life filled with the Spirit of God.

"And glory be to God ! the success of these great conventions is due to that. There are fifty thousand little fires burning day and night. These are societies of Christian Endeavor. The conventions show the real work of the societies. A year ago I told the merchants of Boston, and I presume the same can be said of San Francisco and Oakland, that no secular attraction or combination of attractions — Patti, Irving, baseball, rowing regattas, intercollegiate football, or anything of the kind — could bring together such a gathering as a religous convention of this kind.

"Men want this, Christians are longing for it ; thousands thank God they have found this life-filling Spirit. The evidence is worldwide that this movement is universal. In India, Africa and Europe, the evidence is stronger and stronger. I attended the great Endeavor Convention in Liverpool a few weeks ago, and I found the people awakened. The power of God and the love of Jesus Christ is the thing for which you must seek. That is the purpose of this great Convention. That is how we shall get good out of the Convention, my dear friends."

In Alameda. The First Congregational Church.

All the Endeavor Societies of the city gathered in union meeting in the First Congregational Church. It was a noble rally. The walls of the church were decked with the signs of Christian Endeavor, and an immense national flag was draped gracefully across the platform.

Rev. W. W. Scudder, the pastor, presided. From an incident of a flag-raising which he once attended, he drew the thought that the Christian life should break before it should bend.

In the absence of Bishop Fallows and Rev. M. M. Binford, an everready United Society trustee supplied the address. This was the Rev. James L. Hill, D.D., so long associated with the movement.

Address by Rev. James L. Hill, D.D., Salem, Mass.

He spoke in part as follows : —

" Socrates," said the speaker, " when condemned to death, at Athens, was about to begin his oration on the immortality of the soul. He said, ' let us take each other's hands as we enter this deep, rapid river, and let us pray unto God for help.'

" Dr. Clark, the founder of our society, said he never entertained his audiences. He always appealed to the heroic in his listeners, and he once told me what surprised him most in all his travels was the undiscovered earnestness in young people. A spirit of consecration had developed in the little meeting which made his jokes surperfluous, for which he was always grateful. Rev. Edward Dorr Griffin, of Hartford, had found that his congregation was in a condition of spiritual drought while other churches were having revivals. He pondered long over this fact and came to the conclusion that a revival of religion must begin somewhere, or in some heart. It occurred to him that it might begin in his own heart, and he discarded his prepared sermon and started a new one, and his text was, ' My soul, wait thou upon God, for my expectation is in thee.' His tears wet the sacred page. His congregation saw that they had a new minister, and the spiritual drought in his church was succeeded by a mighty revival. In that one decisive moment there had been no time for a new language or ' acquired wisdom,' but there was time for the touch of the Spirit.

" I believe," continued Dr. Hill, " that there is a blessing which comes from the Holy Spirit upon the human spirit. Conversion establishes character. There are a great many churchgoers that lack one thing, the touch of the Holy Spirit."

The service closed with brief but helpful remarks by Rev. W. H. Scudder.

In all particulars these opening meetings in San Francisco and vicinity were a power in their inspiration and spiritual refreshment. Nothing could more appropriately introduce the great Convention of California, '97.

THURSDAY MORNING, JULY 8.

PRECEDED by the inspiriting services of the previous night and the nine early morning prayer-meetings, the Convention of 1897 opened in the great Mechanics' Pavilion, junction of Market, Hayes and Larkin streets, and in Woodward's Pavilion, Valencia Street between Thirteenth and Fourteenth streets.

In Mechanics' Pavilion.

Before the hour for the opening words the immense auditorium was filled. It is estimated that 10,000 persons were present at this first session. Song after song from the multitude carried the enthusiasm to the highest. Under the earnest direction of Mr. A. M. Benham, of Oakland, they sang "The Banner of the Cross" and "There's a Royal Banner." Then the Convention was opened by the president.

The day was most auspicious. There were no disappointments on the programme. The welcomes were heartfelt, the responses felicitous. When Dr. Clark arose to speak the opening word the multitude voiced their honor and love with cheers and the silent salute. Very fittingly did he ask the audience to read the one hundred and twenty-first Psalm. And so they rose and read in unison, "I will lift up mine eyes unto the hills from whence cometh my help. My help cometh from the Lord. . . He will not suffer thy foot to be moved. The Lord shall preserve thee. . . . The Lord shall preserve thy going out and thy coming in from this time forth."

Dr. Clark then introduced the presiding officer of the session, Rev. E. R. Dille, D.D., of San Francisco. He called upon the Rev. H. F. Shupe, of Dayton, Ohio, to conduct the devotional exercises. Together the audience read for the morning lesson from the fifth chapter of Matthew, and were led in prayer by Mr. Shupe.

President Clark announced as a business committee, Secretary Baer, M. M. Shand, of Washington, D. C., and C. N. Hunt, of Minnesota.

The "Welcome Song," rendered by the choir, was composed by J. W. Dutton. It was sung to the tune of "Onward, Christian Soldiers."

Welcome Song.

Welcome, Christian workers,
Welcome, noble band;
Welcome and thrice welcome
To this favored land.
Sunny California
Opens wide her doors,
Welcome, Christian workers,
Welcome to our shores.

CHORUS.

Welcome, Christian workers,
Welcome, noble band;
Welcome and thrice welcome
To this favored land.

INTERIOR OF MECHANICS' PAVILION AT THE OPENING SESSION. (PRESIDENT CLARK READING HIS ANNUAL ADDRESS.)

Workers from all nations,
  Joyous happy throng,
California greets you
  With sweet, swelling song.
Bright skies smile a welcome
  To the Golden Gate :
Ocean breezes waft you
  Welcome to our State. — CHORUS.

Brothers from the Eastland —
  Men by faith made free,
Welcome to the city
  By the sundown sea.
Fruitful plains and valleys
  Join the glad refrain,
While the vineclad hillsides
  Echo back the strain. — CHORUS.

Master, grant thy blessing,
  From thy throne above ;
Crown us with the virtues,
  Faith and Hope and Love.
Let us then, united,
  Join the sweet refrain,
And " May God be with you
  Till we meet again ! " — CHORUS.

Before introducing Rolla V. Watt to give the address of welcome, Dr. Dille said, " Your presence is an answer to four years of prayer. All California is paying homage to you. From Shasta, whose white clouds are bursting in your honor, to sunny San Diego, we greet you."

A myriad handkerchiefs saluted Mr. Watt as he arose to speak. Every one present appreciated the labor of love which showed itself in all the appointments and preparations of the Convention, and they were delighted to honor the chairman of the commitee who was responsible for them.

Welcome of the Committee of '97, by Rolla V. Watt.

Mr. Chairman and Fellow Endeavorers: —This morning our dreams are realized, our hopes are fulfilled, our prayers are answered ; for we witness the assembling of an International Christian Endeavor Convention for the first time on the shores of the mighty Pacific. God bless you ! We are glad you are here ; welcome, thrice welcome.

For a week past we have followed you with our prayers over valley and plain and mountain, from hamlet and village and city — from the rugged coast of Maine and the cowpaths of Boston, from Liberty Hall and the city on the Potomac, from Lookout Mountain and Missionary Ridge, from the plains of Abraham and the slopes of Mt. Royal, from the Crescent City in the South and the Windy City in the North, from the prairies and great plains of the Middle West, from the Rockies and the Selkirks, from the ranges of Texas and the forests of Washington, little streamers of humanity from a thousand hillsides, meeting at last in one great river, whose irresistible currents swept on and on through the land of Mormon and the sage-brush of Nevada to make glad the city by the Golden Gate.

It is my privilege this morning to welcome you to California on behalf of the Committee of '94 (New York), the Committee of '95 (Montreal), the Committee of '97 (Boston and Washington), and from this incident the old superstition is easily proven that "the third time charms."

I am also to welcome you on behalf of the Golden Gate and Alameda County Unions, your hosts, and on behalf of the California State Union, also your host in a broader sense, on behalf of all kindred organizations, which have united with us in one bond of fellowship in this, our labor of love.

We welcome you first and above all for the sake of our Master, whose banner of love is over all and whose servants you are. He has said if we lift him up he will draw all men unto himself; and just as we represent him in our thoughts, our words, our deeds, in our daily lives, so men will see him. He holds in his hands the solution of all our problems, social, political and spiritual. It is the part of Christian Endeavor to take these preferred gifts and offer them to mankind.

We welcome you therefore because you are seeking to present the Saviour of man to the world that the world may be made better.

We welcome you for your own sakes; your buoyant enthusiasm, your thoughtful earnestness, your calm determination, your intelligence, your integrity, your sincerity, your consecration to a great cause, command our admiration, beget our love, and make us your willing servants.

We welcome you because of the millions of young people devoted to good citizenship, temperance, and righteousness whom you represent.

We welcome you because we believe you will be among our people "living epistles known and read of all men," and that thereby the youth of our sundown country may be inspired to greater zeal in all right effort.

We welcome you because we believe your coming will direct the thoughts and attention of our young people to higher and holier things, and because many lives will be made better and more useful by what shall be uttered by those who will occupy this platform from day to day.

We welcome you because we see the development of reform in civil and political life through your patriotic and commendable good-citizenship movement. If this line of work is wisely and vigorously carried on, you will gradually but surely substitute leaders for "bosses," statesmen for politicians, and patriots for plunderers, — and may God hasten that day!

What shall we say of ourselves? We are Westerners of the true type. You see us as we are; not much sham or hypocrisy, not much "stealing of the livery of heaven to serve the devil in," for the devil's livery is quite popular enough.

There is no special premuim put on church membership, but if you are a churchman, you are expected to live it.

In some of our towns saloons must have clear glass fronts, and no screens; in others, saloons are not permitted all. But in most of the West saloons occupy the chief corners.

As in your Eastern cities, gambling is prohibited by law, but permitted without law. This vice seems to be increasing everywhere, and is one of the trinity of evils, "intemperance, gambling, and impurity," which Christian Endeavor must stamp out. In the West you will find as loyal, as consecrated, and as true Christians as anywhere on God's footstool. Bigotry is confined to a few narrow souls, but every man is accorded the right to worship God according to the dictates of his own conscience.

Philanthropy has marked the history of California, as is evident by numerous parks, monuments, museums, public institutions, and churches; for philanthropy on a large scale there are few parallels for Stanford University, the Lick Observatory, not to mention art institutes, hospitals, orphanages, and homes for all classes of unfortunates, and associations and training-schools for the young.

You will be particularly pleased to find on this Western coast one of the best equipped and costly Young Men's Christian Association buildings in America.

A trip through Chinatown will soon reveal to the dullest observer why the cry "The Chinese must go!" became almost universal; but you will also find that the Christian people were not deterred by popular prejudice from doing their duty. And while here you will doubtless visit the numerous Missions maintained by the various churches among the peoples from heathen countries. A score or more of the converts of these Missions to-day wear the white caps, with the purple band of our Reception Committee. Hundreds of Chinese girls have been wrested from the basest heathen slavery. There is no lack of opportunity here for missionary effort, and we are glad this is to be pre-eminently a Missionary convention.

We cannot offer you the historic settings of Boston Common, nor the beauties of a National Capital; we are too young for such things; but we are proud of our city, set on more hills than Rome boasted, and of our State with its varied and unequalled attractions. It is true we sometimes take measures of credit to ourselves for these features which have made California famous—such as geniality of climate, fertility of soil, richness of mines, beauty of scenery, advantageous commercial situation, and boast as though we had made them; but we do this only in our more enthusiastic moods; in calmer moments we realize with feelings of humility that all these blessings are an heritage directly from the bountiful hand of God.

While you are in our city I trust you will seek out the bright spots, rather than the dark ones; ascertain for yourselves what we are doing on the west coast along the lines you have chosen for your activities. Note the evidences of material, moral, and religious progress, and in so doing, remember that not fifty years ago on this little peninsula Yerba Buena was christened San Francisco; it was then scarcely a hamlet, and was not incorporated into a town until three years thereafter.

And now, in conclusion, let me remind you that at New York, and Montreal, and Boston, and Washington, we invited you to California; our invitation was broader than a city; and this morning, on our souvenir badges, on our flags, on our arch, on our banners, in flowers and shrubs in our parks, you will find inscribed the magic words which have induced you to leave your homes and to travel thousands of miles through the burning heat of the July sun —" California, '97."

To California, to San Francisco, to our homes and hearts, welcome, a thousand welcomes.

Dr. Dille next introduced, amid applause, the Rev. J. Hemphill, D.D., San Francisco, who gave the address of welcome on behalf of the Golden Gate pastors.

Pastors' Welcome, by Rev. J. Hemphill, D.D.

Several centuries ago a monk of Picardy, named Peter the Hermit, went up and down Europe preaching a fiery crusade against those who held the sepulchre wherein the Saviour of the world was laid, and he inspired the people wherever he went with his own wild, weird enthusiasm. All Europe flew to arms. The watchword, " Deus Vult," burst from ten thousand times ten thouand lips, and the armies of Christendom precipitated themselves upon the Holy Land with the awful war-cry, " God wills it," echoing from rank to rank.

Francis E. Clark—the Peter the Hermit of the nineteenth century—has for several years been going up and down our own land and other lands, preaching a far holier crusade, kindling the fires of Christian zeal and love on the altar of young hearts; and now, with a few battalions of his mighty army he has invaded California, and we have surrendered unconditionally to him and to them. Fellow soldiers in the Army of the Lord, we give you the military salute.

> " We are not divided, all one body we,
> One in hope and doctrine, one in charity."

What a mighty convocation of Christian Endeavorers do I see before me, coming from the East and from the West and from the North and from the South, like the great world-gathering in Jerusalem on the Day of Pentecost. I pray God that the results of this gathering may be the same. Assembled in one place with one accord, waiting upon God with earnestness and expectancy, I pray that Pentecostal power may descend upon you and us to fit us for larger and better service for Christ and the world in days to come.

Brothers and sisters in Christ, in the name of the pastors of the Golden West, in the name of our common heritage of faith, in the name of kindred ties which make us the heirs of all the ages, in the name of our common Lord and Saviour, we bid you welcome — thrice welcome — to our State, to our city, to our churches, to our homes, to our hearts. We bless you in the name of the Lord.

I have seen many great and notable gatherings in my time, but none of them affected me as this one does. This one inspires me — awes me. The spectacle I see before me reminds me of the old poetic images — the forest-crowned mountain, the field of corn swayed by the gentle winds, the crested waves of the ocean on a glad summer day, the sparkling stars on the midnight sky. What variety do I see before me! And what unity! We are many, yet one — one in Christ, one in aim, Christ for the world and the world for Christ; or, as Dr. Cuyler once put it, "Union in Christ for a world without Christ!"

Your society has had but a brief history, but most blessed. It has lifted hundred of thousands of young Christians off their "flowery beds of ease" and put them to work, and as a pastor I rejoice to bear this testimony before this Convention concerning the Endeavorers of my church: they have always been most helpful to me. I have never requested them to do anything that they have not done gladly, promptly, and efficiently. They have been eyes, and ears, and hands, and feet, and tongue for their pastor.

God bless this youngest-born of Christian societies! Live, live long, live vigorously; live to multiply in numbers, power, and influence, "forever blessing and forever blest." Its past has been rich in blessing, and our prayer is that its future may be richer far in blessing than its past, a time of clear-seeing, and of faith power, and of earnest work, and of much prayer, and of abundant outpourings of the Holy Ghost. May it rise equal to its opportunities, and exercise a resistless influence for good on all the world! May its roots strike downward as its branches spread outward!

May the expanding of its circumference arise from mighty motions at its center, and the living energies of divine love in the heart send impulsive growth along the whole radius of its life! True to its pledge, true to its past history, true to its God and Saviour, true to the eternal verities, may it go forward to new conquests and shake the pillars of unbelief in every land under the sun! In a word, may the members of this Convention receive such power from on high during these convention days as shall constrain them to say that the San Francisco Convention has been by far the best convention that has yet been held.

Some years ago I saw the stars through the telescope in the observatory on Mount Hamilton. Standing on the observatory on Mount Zion to-day, and looking through the telescope of faith, I see a grand future before the Society of Christian Endeavor. I see its horizon thick-sown with brilliant stars. We see only a few of them as yet. The lights of other stars are on the way. The darkness is not so dense as it was. The morning light is breaking, and you are helping its coming. To your ranks, then, and to your knees, gird you, brothers and sisters in Christ, for the blessed toil and speed its coming.

It has been a great pleasure to me, as I deem it a great honor to speak this word of welcome to you in the name of the pastors of the Golden West, and in the name of all who acknowledge Jesus as Lord. Once more we bid you thrice welcome. Once more we invoke such showers of blessings upon you that in the coming years the San Francisco Convention will be referred to as the Pentecostal Convention.

Dr. Dille said: "We are citizens, and because we are Endeavorers we are good citizens, and we honor the constituted authorities. Therefore, we will be glad to hear the Hon. William T. Jeter, who would welcome the Convention on behalf of the State and in the name of the Governor of the State, who is unavoidably absent."

Remembering the hearty Concurrent Assembly Resolution passed by the Legislature of the State of California, welcoming the Endeavor societies of the world, the audience gave to the State's representative a true Christiam Endeavor greeting.

California's Welcome, by the Hon. W. T. Jeter, Lieut.-Governor.

You seem to me to act as if you were already feeling quite at home, and to add anything further in way of welcome would be the merest form. To welcome means to receive with gladness, to make one feel at home; and after you have clambered over the backbone of our great State, then wheeled over her feet and thundered over her head at the North, you are now sitting, contented and happy, looking out over the Golden Gate, from which the ever-lasting doors have been lifted in order to reveal to you the glories of the Pacific, the possibilities of future extension work — it seems to me that under those conditions you are already sufficiently welcomed.

Furthermore, I cannot help but reflect upon the fact that Mr. Rolla V. Watt, who has been so active and who has extended to you such a cordial welcome already this morning — that when he, Dr. Dille, and others who are engaged in this great work of the Christian Endeavorers, bore to the city of Washington an invitation, followed it with legislative resolutions,—all of this must have convinced you that you would be welcome. And we are satisfied from the numbers that are now within this great city that you were so convinced, and come here feeling perfectly at home.

I regret extremely that Governor Budd was not able to be here this morning to say a word of welcome to you, because out of his big, generous heart welcomes bubble and flow copiously, naturally as the sparkling streams that come from the Sierra springs. But I must admit that on my part I must feel that a welcome is necessary really more than in form, in order to fully appreciate it; it must be an old-fashioned welcome that must come out of my nature, not bubbling out like the mountain spring, but it must be reached by the moss-covered bucket, and drawn up with some effort.

But I have become so accustomed to acting the part of a substitute in representing great and small men, too, that sometimes I think when the final call may come to some good man, he may not be entirely ready, and may ask that I take his place. And if he is a very good man, I am not certain that I would lose anything by the operation.

The most pathetic welcome that at this moment comes to my mind is that of the Prodigal Son. I think that most of you have perhaps heard of him. There were no reception committees in that case; no resolutions passed by the legislature, and under the great seal of State sent out to that wandering son when he was out having a good time with the boys. But the grief-stricken old father was on the lookout committee, and he looked afar off and saw this young man taking a walk upon an empty stomach. His affections went out to him, and without form he fell upon his neck and kissed him. The fatted calf was slain, and that young man received such a welcome as suits my notions of what a welcome ought to be.

I am not going to attempt, in representing the State of California, to personate this grief-stricken father on this occasion, but shall assume that your efficient Reception Committee have attended to this already. The fatted calf has been slain, the great California calf. You have perhaps already had an opportunity to taste of the meat, and we are going to slay on more and more, and keep on as long as you remain, and see that you get the choicest cuts.

I was somewhat impressed with the remark of one of the gentlemen who extended a welcome here, in referring to this youthful young man whom you recognize as "Father" Clark. The idea that he should be the founder and father of so great a family as this is beyond my comprehension. He was alluded to as entitled hereafter to be known as "Peter the Hermit of the West." It is also contrary to my notions that a hermit should have such a vast family as this, but

Father Clark has undoubtedly obtained a record in regard to building up a family that reaches to the uttermost ends of the earth, and has gathered into this fold, as I am informed, over three millions of people.

This organization has been able to grasp the idea of unity of purpose, and to appreciate what we used to have to write in the old-fashioned common school when we were learning to make marks: "In union there is strength." This is entirely in accord with my individual notions of these matters. I am glad to see that while denominational lines are not obliterated, that man's moral measure is not taken by the mode of baptism in which he believes; and that you meet together, work together, and act together as one people, with a common purpose, and without wasting your energies unnecessarily in discussing whether this way or that way of obtaining the same result is right. This organization works on broad lines, and this is the effective work that must and will tell.

You have come to California to hold this Convention, and I now predict that it will be known for years and years to come as the grandest convention that the Christian Endeavor has ever held.

If you had been two weeks sooner, you would have witnessed us in a little different mood for a few moments. You might have thought that we were having an earthquake, but we were not. It was simply the great State of California in convulsions of joy at the prospect of having this organization meet with us; and if, whilst you remain here, you should feel the trembling and quaking of the earth, be not alarmed: there is no danger. You are as safe as Elijah was in his cave when the awful wind passed by. It will simply be California and her way of shaking hands with you.

In extending a welcome to you on behalf of this State, I cannot resist also congratulating you that you are able to sit here at least for a brief time caressed by the chaste kiss of the California sun, while others less fortunate who have not taken this trip are subjected to the fierce heat, sunstrokes, and trouble on every hand; that you are not required to be back assisting the Government Surveying Corps in finding your state lines after one of those cyclones has passed by.

And now I am glad to know that you are all full of faith. I will ask you to use it as you pass about through this State. Unless you have more time than is probable, you will not be able to investigate and go into all the details of all the wonders that will be shown to you. I cannot take up your time telling you about all those things, and frankly, I don't think that I care to risk my reputation in telling you about the marvelous things that exist within the lines of California. Of course you will go somewhat about as you have time. I assume you will all go to the town where I live — that is, the city of Santa Cruz, surrounded by nature the most beautifully of any city in the universe. I say this without any regard for my reputation, because I know you will agree with me. And when you pass through the Big Trees, and are there shown, by the man who pilots people about, a tree sixty feet in circumference, that will take thirteen of your adult members' longest arms to surround, and you are told that it is three hundred feet high and that twenty-seven and one-half feet many years ago were blown from the top, please just accept the statement and don't go to asking where the piece is.

I greatly regret that my time will not permit me to remain through the deliberations of this Convention. I most cordially ask you all to remain as long as your business at home will permit; make yourselves entirely at home anywhere within this State. And when you are compelled to return home, arrange your worldly affairs as quickly as possible, and bring yourselves and your energies out here, where you can do better work.

We have broad valleys in the highest state of cultivation, broad acres that are now in virgin wildness,— and our people are in much the same condition. We have a large number of loyal-hearted, true, and active Christian people. We have a large number, the soil of whose hearts may be in virgin wildness, but it is ready to receive moral impressions, and it will not be long until you will have to look to your laurels in the East, if you expect to outvie us in the work of the Christian churches.

I thank you for the magnificent welcome you have accorded to me, and will now extend to you the welcome of the State of California, on behalf of the governor of the State.

Mrs. Martin Schults, soprano of the First Congregational Church of Oakland, accompanied on the piano by Samuel D. Mayer, sang "Praise the Lord, O My Soul." She was heartily applauded.

"We are going to be welcomed at Nashville, Tenn., in 1898," said Dr. Dille. "I want to taste the welcome of that State, and I hope it will not be so warm, but more hospitable, than some of the older of us met with in Tennessee in 1862. It is, therefore, fitting that we should be addressed by the Rev. Ira Landrith, of Tennessee, who will respond to the welcomes that have been extended.

Address in Response to the Welcomes, Rev. Ira Landrith, Nashville, Tenn.

Mine is an overwhelming embarrassment of riches. To me is committed the task tremendous of expressing the boundless gratitude of an almost numberless multitude, and all for a welcome as rich and beautiful as your glorious sunset land, and as deep and wide as the ocean which bathes your sound money shores with free silver spray. Who wouldn't be embarrassed by such riches? And to be compelled to spend all this fortune of fervent appreciation in fifteen minutes of time is just a little too much to expect of even this prodigal son. We are welcome — there can be no doubt about it, for hasn't Watt said so? and all Eastern Endeavorers have long since learned to look for a hatchet and heroic frankness whenever Watt has anything to say about a California cherry tree. Besides, hasn't the ministerial legislature of the Golden State enacted this welcome into a law of love and good cheer, and has not the governor of this Golden State authorized executive approval of this benign statute? On behalf of some thousands of young Americans who have taken Horace Greeley's sound advice, and on behalf of worthy representatives of most of the rest of the earth, I thank the Committee of '97, the Golden Gate pastors, the State of California, the rest of the delightful afternoon side of the Rockies, and a league or so of old ocean, for a welcome so evidently sincere, so gratifyingly substantial, and so admirably expressed as to helplessly paralyze all my Southern superlatives of appreciation, and to render weak and puny every gigantic adjective I had more recently appropriated for this occasion from the agents of wheat lands in Washington and the owners of fruit farms in Oregon and California.

No, no, I can't tell you how grateful we are for this welcome; but, in common with the host of my companions, I can show you, if you will watch the way we use your gift of hospitality through these days of duty and delight; and again I say unto you, Watch. He is the worthiest guest who leaves a blessing in the home where he is entertained, and in the name and for the sake of our Master we would be worthy guests. We have come across the continent, some of us across the sea, praying that God may use us in helping you as well as bless us through you. We have come to learn and teach "more, more about Jesus," and here, where the restless waves talk to us of eternity, and wealth, and productive soil, and mountains filled with treasure-trove tell of the riches of our Father's love, we expect a deepening of our own spiritual lives, a baptism of peace and power which we devoutly trust you may enjoy with us.

With this sure and steadfast foundation of consecrated and Spirit-filled life, we would be glad to exemplify in address and song and service all the holy purposes and fruits of Christian Endeavor. This is a practical age, men tell us; but there is nothing in all this practical age more intensely practical than Christian Endeavor, and nothing in Christian Endeavor more practical than our pledge. We believe in pledges. Safeguards they are, veritable guardian angels ofttimes; and yet objectors, driven to desperation for criticism, have complained at Endeavor because, forsooth, they do not believe in pledges. More than once have we heard even a man fresh from the altar of beneficent Pythianism or the open Bible of honored Free-Masonry, where vows most solemn have been taken, blandly declare, "I don't like your Christian Endeavor Society because I don't believe in pledges." There is nothing in our "covenant prayer-meeting pledge, the Magna Charta of Christian Endeavor," which most Christians did not in effect promise to do at the altar of church membership; and there is positively nothing in it that all Christians ought not to do. We shall have much to say also and somewhat to do about our cardinal consecration meetings. So long as we remember that Jesus found it necessary to go to the mountain-side to hold consecration and prayer services in the presence of his Father, so long will we deem it our holiest duty to consecrate and reconsecrate our lives to our Lord. If he had to pray, we must. We shall have frequent occasion to say that Christian Endeavor's committee work and methods signify merely that God's business is business, and that it ought to be done in a business-like way. If the average business man should attempt to conduct his affairs upon the haphazard, hit-or-miss, hat-collection plan — or want of plan — of some churches, he would be bankrupt, and that right early; and Christian Endeavor has undertaken, as necessary parts of the churches to which they belong, to put common sense and prayer-baptized method into the affairs of religion, "giving each active member some specific work 'for Christ and the Church.'" And, by the way, the true Christian Endeavorer puts in italics that little "the" in the Society's motto, — "for Christ and *THE* Church" to which the individual belongs, some well-meaning but none-too-well-informed people to the contrary notwithstanding. Christian Endeavor is fuller of proper denominationalism and freer from improper sectarianism than any on other earth. It believes in a paraphrased statement of an old truth,—none the less true for the revision,—" To thine own Church be true, and it must follow as the night the day, thou canst not then be false to any Church."

Thus believing, and with no unkind word or feeling for those who may not altogether agree with us, we find it quite easy and comforting to believe also that there are other godly people besides ourselves; hence the joy we have in interdenominational fellowship. Christian Endeavor believes that in interdenominational affairs communion is not only a bigger but a better word than union; and that if we are able to have glad interdenominational fellowship in heaven, we ought to be getting used to it on earth. Reading in our Bibles that we may know that we have passed from death unto life because we love the brethren, we cannot understand how we could find out that we were saved if we spent our time and our energies in interdenominational warfare. One of the late unhappy war's bravest and devoutest chieftains fell mortally wounded by the bullets of his own soldiery. That it was a terrible accident, friend and foe alike sadly declared. But upon many a religious battlefield have perished other Stonewall Jacksons, Christian leaders in all churches stricken down, not by the enemy, but by those who ought to be friends; and not by accident, but deliberately and for no better reason than that these heroes did not choose to wear the brass buttons molded by "our church." With a white flag, upon which is inscribed, "We be brethren," Christian Endeavor has rushed upon the field and declared that this fratricidal carnage must cease; and henceforth our churches will fire at Satan, and not at each other, all the ammunition they have or can get. Finally, Christian Endeavor, neglecting no other duty, will ennoble Christian citizenship until clean hands will cast no unclean votes for unworthy men and ignoble measures. As members of political parties, we will be loyal to our parties so long as they will be loyal to honor and truth. We will stand upon our political party platforms only so long as their planks will bear the weight of righteousness. But, like Paul, we were free-born, and we venture to believe that we have as many political rights and responsibilities as the party bosses who claim their monopoly of the rights and their independence of the responsibilities aforesaid. We will stand for political intelligence, integrity, independence, and industry; and we are rapidly reaching the conclusion that Democracy should stand for decency, Republicanism for respectability, and Populism for purity; or else we must obey the divine injunction by coming out from among them. In plainer English, after we have done our best, if we cannot clean our parties out, then we should resolutely undertake to clean them up.

These are some of the lessons which this school of methods, this Christian Endeavor Convention, will teach in San Francisco this year, and in my own ideal Southern city next year. And assuring you of the most prayerful wish for the largest success and usefulness of this Convention, you will pardon a parting word by way of invitation to Nashville, '98. Like our fellow Endeavorers of the West. we, the Endeavorers of Dixie, asked for an International Convention because we need it, and because we believe that this mightiest of modern religious movements needed just such a spiritual uplift and strengthening as it could get nowhere else on earth, California alone excepted, of course. "Come away down South in Dixie, to Nashville, '98."

Three times did Dr. Clark attempt the reading of his annual report, each time the cheers of the multitude prevented. Never before has President Clark received such a demonstration of affection as the one given at this Convention. When quiet reigned, he said : —

Annual Address by the Rev. Francis E. Clark, D.D.

A WORLD-ENCIRCLING MOVEMENT. — HOW SHALL IT FULFIL GOD'S DESIGN?

You can readily perceive why this year I have chosen for the subject of my annual message, the theme, A WORLD-ENCIRCLING Religious Movement; How Shall it Fulfil God's Design?

At the invitation of friends. and in obedience to the call of God, as I believe, I have, during the past year, been journeying in many lands, among people who speak many tongues. These journeys in behalf of Christian Endeavor have carried me more than 40,000 miles. to more than a score of peoples, who speak nearly as many languages. One factor I have found constant in all these lands : I have found Christian Endeavor principles everywhere the same.

The same pledge, the same consecration meeting, the same general lines of effort for the Master, called Committee Work : the utmost diversity in unessential details : the utmost similarity of purpose in essential principles.

Societies that are as widely separated in miles and manners as the Bengalis, who live in the swamps of the Ganges. and the Kaffirs on the uplands of Africa, from the Endeavorers of the Golden Gate and the Alameda, have subscribed to the same covenant pledge, and, better still, are keeping it.

I have attended conventions, since last I met you, in the Metropolitan Tabernacle of London, and in the Beels of Bengal; in St. Andrews Hall of Glasgow, and in the ancient capital of the Punjab; among our Irish Endeavorers in Belfast, and on the sunburnt plains of Southern India: in crowded Berlin, and on the lonely tablelands of the Transvaal; among the Alps of Switzerland, and on the vast veldt of the Orange Free State; in sea-girt Stockholm, and in the karoo of South Africa; in lordly Paris, and in quiet Wellington: in the Cape of Good Hope, made sacred to many of you by the life and labors of Andrew Murray and his associates: and everywhere, amid all these diversities of custom and costume, of manners and methods. of language and laws, I have found that the Christian Endeavor ideals are substantially the same.

Moreover. the peoples whom I have seen have been of diverse creeds and views of religious truth. All, to be sure, have acknowledged the supremacy of Jesus Christ as the very Son of God and the only Saviour of lost sinners; all have accepted the Bible as the Word of God, and the Holy Spirit as the sanctifier, comforter, and guide,— in such soil only can Christian Endeavor flourish.

But in minor particulars the creeds and forms of church government of these hospitable hosts of our Society differ as widely as their complexions. The shade of tan on a man's cheek does not make or unmake his manhood, the shade of his creed does not make or unmake his Christianity.

By Methodists and Baptists, by Presbyterians and Congregationalists, by

Friends and Disciples of Christ, by Episcopalians and Lutherans, by adherents of the State churches of Germany and Sweden and Holland and Scotland and England, as well as by representatives of every free church, have I been kindly received in the name of Christian Endeavor, and by every missionary society at work in India or Africa.

Why? Not by reason of any eloquent advocacy I could render Christian Endeavor, but because of the eloquent endorsement which a common and universal method of Christian service renders to its advocate.

Moreover, should you go much further afield than the months between two conventions have allowed me to travel, you would find the same thing true. You would hear Mr. Ling pleading for Christian citizenship in Foochow, and urging his fellow Chinese Endeavorers to drive the devils of civic unrighteousness into the Eastern sea, where they would be swallowed up like the Gadarene swine in the waters. You would hear Africander Endeavorers devoting themselves to world-wide missions. You would see Japanese Endeavorers seeking, as you seek, the life that is hid with Christ in God; and Malagassy Endeavorers looking up through their tears for a defeated and degraded nation to the God of nations; and Armenian Endeavorers groaning, as they think of their downtrodden and bleeding country, "How long, O Lord, how long!"

Could you have the invisible cap and cloak, you would see Christian Endeavor sailor lads on the briny billows fulfil their pledge under the eyes of jeering tars; and prisoner Endeavorers denying themselves their one weekly letter, that they might give to missions the two-cent postage stamp, the only possession they could turn into ready money. We would see faithful little Juniors as true to their vows as the hoary saint, and a multitude of obscure Endeavorers in every land, whose honest, conscientious service no man records, but whom God hath written in his Book of Life.

Only one denomination still seeks to prevent the increase of Christian Endeavor societies, and that has introduced Christian Endeavor principles, and, though we regret the absence of full fellowship, we are glad of the extension of the ideas for which we stand, — in that we rejoice, yea, and will rejoice.

Our Society, then, has these signs of a universal movement. It was born in obscurity and weakness. It has not owed its extension to human advocacy or ecclesiastical authority. It has spread to every land. It has been found adapted to every evangelical creed, and to every form of church government, and to every race and class and language and condition of people. It has failed only where the principles involved in our covenant pledge have been ignored, or where it has been crushed out by denominational authority.

This evident blessing of God, so vast, so unexpected, so undeserved, so far as human agencies go, should lead us to ask every year, with increasing humility and eagerness, what is God's world-wide design for the Society? What world mission has he for it to perform?

Our responsibility to fulfil God's purpose increases with our growth. The larger the movement, the more we conserve by our faithfulness, the more we wreck by our blindness or unfaithfulness to God's design. Let me then try to answer this vital question, How shall world-encircling Christian Endeavor fulfil God's design?

First. A world-wide movement must be true to its fundamental idea. For it is evidently to propagate that idea that God has established it. The fundamental purpose of Christian Endeavor is to raise the standard among young people of outspoken devotion and consecrated service.

This idea is embodied in our covenant pledge, and this idea makes our covenant *imperative* in a Christian Endeavor society.

This movement is not a conglomeration of every kind of young people's society; it is a movement for the spread of *definite ideas*, which God has owned and blest. *Its whole history shows the supreme honor which God bestows upon uncompromising, unabashed, out-and-out service.* O Endeavorers, be true ever to this basal thought of Christian Endeavor! for upon it, on every page of our history, God has set the seal of his approval.

Second. A world-encircling movement must necessarily be a UNIFYING *movement.* This part of its mission is too plain to argue. It has brought forty denominations together, so far as ecclesiastical authority has not interfered, and bound their young people in blessed bonds they have not before known; later, it has forged a link between forty nations that speak forty languages; more than all, it has woven new strands of Christian concord between the four great English-speaking sections of the world,—the United States, Great Britain, Canada, Australia. These bonds are made of many strands of common method and common name. The missionary colonies, too, of the English-speaking race, if I may so call them, are established in every clime, and a new connecting filament beween them all is found in Christian Endeavor.

Arbitration treaties may be amended, or accepted, or rejected. The world-wide Christian Endeavor movement is a new treaty of love and good-will between millions of those who speak the same language and who work by the same methods for the same Lord.

Every year some of our British brethren come to our American convention. In 1900 I hope that 10,000 of you will accept the invitation of British Endeavorers to London to ratify and seal the international treaty of Christian Endeavor.

Third. A world-encircling movement must be a PERVASIVE *force.* You have shown this sign of universal adaptability, Christian Endeavorers, by entering into prisons and asylums, lighthouses and life-saving stations, men-of-war and merchant vessels, soldiers' barracks and factory lofts, as well as into all the activities of church life. There is another place very near home where your power and principles are felt, and where they should be felt still more, and that is the weekly church prayer-meeting. I know of no way so good of making this suggestion practical as by forming senior societies, whose chief distinction shall be that, without increasing church machinery, they apply the Christian Endeavor covenant pledge to the weekly meeting of the church. Already these senior societies, which form the veteran and the permanent cohort of Christian Endeavor, have been formed; not only in America, but in Australia, India, Great Britain, and South Africa, and always with blessedly beneficial results.

Remember the lesson, so hard for some of us to learn, that we are all sixteen years older than we were sixteen years ago; that the responsibilities of the Young People's Society must some time be transferred to younger shoulders; and that our effort should be as we grow older to develop younger workers, and to apply our own energies directly to the church meeting and all church activities. Thus, in the Senior Society, we are no less part of the Christian Endeavor movement, but both the church and this movement of the church are infinitely strengthened. I hope to see the senior societies multiplied tenfold the coming year.

Fourth. A universal movement must be a sacrificial movement; in its very essence a missionary movement.

Let us make more determined *individual* effort this next year to obey our Lord's last command to evangelize the world. Go ye, — make it singular and personal, Go you, — Go you. Africa's, China's, India's unsaved millions plead; God commands: go you. It is no excuse to say that you live in America, and have family, business, social ties that imperatively keep you here. You may never leave your native shores, but the command comes to you none the less : Go, — go you. It is possible now, if you can give twenty-five dollars a year, and few of you who can attend a convention cannot give as much as this, to have your foreign representative on the mission field. Of course you will give as much to home missions to save your own country from the perils of civilized heathenism. This whole Convention with its long preliminary journey is a lesson in patriotism and home missions ; and home missions is another way of spelling patriotism.

A student in training, a catechist, a Bible woman, a pastor, a teacher, a village school, a mission church at home or abroad,—one or all of these is within the giving power of almost every Endeavorer to whom I speak. Have your representative at work while you sleep. Work twenty-four hours a day for God. Have your personal representative, above all, so that your heart and interest and love may be in the extension of the kingdom of God the world around; for where your treasure is, there will your heart be.

I know of no way so good for Endeavorers to make this thought a definite and tangible part of the new Endeavor year as by joining the Tenth Legion,— the legion of those who give at least a tenth of all God gives them, whether it be ten cents or ten million dollars, back to him for the spread of his kingdom.

Give this through your own churches and your own missionary boards; then will these appalling clouds of debt, which hang over so many of our boards, flee; and, better than all, if Endeavorers generally adopt this principle, they can never again return to darken the missionary horizon.

Fifth. A world-encircling movement must listen to God's voice, and continually obey it. It must not be led away by faddists or theorists or selfish axe-grinders; but it must always, if it would prosper, keep an open ear to God's voice, and will never rest satisfied with past achievements.

You have heard in other years, Christian Endeavorers, the voice of God, and you have aroused yourselves in your might to the interests of Christian citizenship. In every land your banner has been unfurled, bearing this motto, "Our Country for Christ." You have heard again God's call to a larger devotion to missions, and you have unfurled another banner with the grand device, "The World for Christ." The Endeavorers of California, our hospitable hosts, have done valiant work, as have many others, for the rescue of the Sabbath from the hands of the enemies. These banners we will always keep flying. No inch of ground once gained will we carelessly surrender to the enemy.

"My Country, 't is of Thee," shall be our song, under whatever flag we live.

> "Christ for the world we sing,
> The world to Christ we bring,"

shall be coupled with it. Indeed, we will press ever-advancing columns and take new redoubts. Sabbath-breaking, the saloon curse, the gambling-den, the brothel, shall receive no quarter at the hands of Christian Endeavorers. "Our Country for Christ," "The World for Christ." But is that all? Ah! there is another motto, which is more important still, "Myself for Christ." Are you disappointed, Endeavorers? Did you expect some new and startling message of aggressive warfare. Look closely, and perhaps you will find this well-worn phrase a greater advance step than we have ever taken.

Again and again we need to come back to this fundamental thought. The Christian Endeavor movement can only prosper as Christ is in its members and its members are in Christ. "As the branch cannot bear fruit . . . except it abide in the vine, no more can ye, except ye abide in Me," is as true of a movement as of an individual, and only through its living members can a movement abide in Christ.

This is a world movement, thank God! away from materialism, formalism, and a barren ecclesiasticism back to God himself. It is like the vast, vivifying current of the Gulf Stream, a mighty, resistless, continent-encircling torrent in the bosom of the ocean. It is called by many names, but everywhere the essence is the same. It is the "Spirit-filled life," the "life hid with Christ in God," the life emptied of self and surrendered to God. Everywhere and always it is life, life abundantly. Of this movement Christian Endeavor is a part, vitalized by it, and, on its part, contributing to it.

Endeavorers, let this be the motto, the purpose, the prayer of this our coming seventeenth year: to come within the blessed reach of this current, to abide in Christ, to surrender ourselves to him, to let him use us, to think less of our efforts and more of his fulness, to seek a larger infilling from above, deeper draughts of his life, more emptiness of self, more fulness of Christ.

Thus only will Christian Endeavor, and all for which it has come to stand,— Christian citizenship, Christian missions, and a thousand forms of benevolence, — receive ever fresh life and vigor.

That no one may accuse me of dealing in glittering generalities, let me be very practical and, if possible, suggestive. A life led with Christ in God does not come by chance. We must choose it, desire it, seek it. Let me, then, suggest two definite practical ways in which it may be promoted.

First. In seeking this closer walk with God, give more attention to *family religion.* A multitude of Christian Endeavorers have, within the past sixteen years, been set together in families. As the years come and go, other millions will enter these same relations. The Endeavorers of America can, within the next decade, distinctly raise the tone of the religious life of the families of the nation. Why not carry our Endeavor principles into the family? Promote family religion by making more of daily household worship, *and by having, at least once a week, family Christian Endeavor worship, in which every member, even to the lisping four-year-old, shall have some personal participation.* Let the children of Christian parents grow up as confessing, outspoken disciples of Christ in the family; making their choice of him very early, and never remembering the time when they did not love him.

Older brothers and sisters, as well as parents, can do much in introducing this, our fundamental principle of outspoken devotion to Christ, into the family.

Second. Remember the morning watch. Set apart, religiously and sacredly, at least fifteen minutes every morning to communion with God. More imperative than any business engagement, more sacred than any matter of family concern, more important than eating or sleeping, make this daily engagement with God. There look into the face of God. "Practise the presence of God" for at least fifteen minutes every morning, before the day's cares distract your mind, and you, like Moses, will be able to endure "as seeing him who is invisible."

"Remember the morning watch" was the last cry of the departing missionaries to their companions on the Liverpool pier, as the steamer which carried them to Asia cast off her hawser. "Remember the morning watch," I would repeat, as we cast hawsers from the old year of Christian Endeavor, and move forward into the future. Perhaps, within the ranks of Christian Endeavor we may form a band which we may call "The Brotherhood of the Morning Watch," or, "The Comrades of the Quiet Hour." Oh, if a million Endeavorers every day for a year to come would remember the quiet hour, the power of Christian Endeavor with God and man would be multiplied a hundred-fold!

THE WORLD FOR CHRIST.
THE NATION FOR CHRIST.
THE FAMILY FOR CHRIST.
MYSELF FOR CHRIST.

That fourfold Christian Endeavor cord cannot be broken.

"The world does not yet know what God can do through a fully consecrated man," America's greatest evangelist heard a passer-by on the street remark to another. And that remark influenced, and in a way transformed, his whole life.

The world does not yet know what God can do through a fully consecrated organization. O Endeavorers, hear that, and realize its vast import! It is for you to show what God can do through a movement dedicated unselfishly to him. We have the infinite might of the infinite God to use. We have Omnipotence to draw upon.

"Ask and ye shall receive."

Men lived for generations on the lid of the world's greatest diamond vault in South Africa, and never knew the priceless gems beneath their feet.

The gold-fields of the Rand have been ready for centuries to yield up the key of their untold treasure to the intelligent discoverer.

Electricity has been a mighty but dormant power in this world since Adam first walked in Paradise, but until Franklin flew his kite no man realized that there was a subtle, unseen power sufficient to turn every wheel, and drive every car, and light every city in the wide world. But so it was.

O Christian Endeavorers, there is a mine of undiscovered wealth on whose edge you are treading! There is a might inconceivable which you may have for the asking. It is the treasure of the Spirit's abiding presence; it is the might of God's power, which he offers to the humble and contrite heart. Will you take it? Will you use it for the coming of the Kingdom?

The seventeenth year of Christian Endeavor, whose white, unwritten page we, now turn with the opening day of this Convention, will show how you have answered this question.

The speaker was frequently interrupted by applause as the audience responded to the sentiments of the address. At its conclusion a perfect storm of cheers and kerchief-waving was accorded him. A song was rendered and the founder of the Christian Endeavor Union returned hastily to the rostrum.

"I have here," he said, waving over his head a short shoe-hammer, "a tool that once belonged to William Carey, and was used by him in cobbling shoes. This great and good man was known as "the consecrated cobbler." I had intended to call the Convention to order with this hammer It is not too late now. You are now formally in session," concluded Dr. Clark, rapping the table as he spoke.

Dr. Dille then proposed three raps in honor of the motto of the Endeavorers, the audience to wave their handkerchiefs as each blow fell: "The world for Christ, the nation for Christ, myself for Christ," said the presiding officer, and a maize of snowy white waved over the big building.

"I propose," said Dr. James L. Hill, of Salem, Mass., "three cheers for Rev. Francis E. Clark and Carey's hammer," and with hearty good-will the vast audience responded.

When Dr. Dille introduced the General Secretary, John Willis Baer, as a "composite figure of the Christian Endeavor workers," the Convention reciprocated the sentiment with a magnificent welcome to this tireless officer. After acknowledging his reception, Mr. Baer presented his annual survey of the world of Endeavor.

Annual Report of General Secretary Baer.

CHRISTIAN ENDEAVOR — A RIVER.

" There is a river, the streams whereof shall make glad the city of God." — Ps. xlvi. 4.
" And by the river upon the bank thereof, on this side and on that side, shall grow all trees for meat, whose leaf shall not fade, neither shall the fruit thereof be consumed; it shall bring forth new fruit according to his months, because their waters, they issued out of the sanctuary."
— EZEK. xlvii. 12.

And Christian Endeavor is such a river. Reverently the figure is borrowed from God's Word, to make plainer to you and to me what God really intends to do with this river which he caused to spring up in Portland, Me., sixteen years ago, and the overflow of which he has directed, until its waters now extend through the uttermost parts of the earth.

Careful observers of the onward sweep of this river of Christian Endeavor have noted that it has widened during the past year. Since last we met, this great current has been swelled by 5,000 new societies. Rejoice with exceeding joy, for the world-wide enrolment is now 50,747 local societies. What a swift and mighty flood! In 1881, one society and fifty-seven members. In 1897, 50,780 societies and a total membership of 3,000,000.

Of its large tributary State and Provincial streams in this country that have over one thousand local societies, Pennsylvania still leads, with 3,443; New York, 3,049; Ohio, 2,383; Illlnois has now passed to the fourth place, with 2,013; Ontario, 1,783; Indiana, 1,387; Iowa, 1,336; and Michigan, with 1,071, for the first time is entitled to a place in this class. These figures do not include the

Junior societies, with their boys and girls, the Intermediate societies, with their lads and lassies, the Senior and Mothers' societies, for the fathers and mothers and those who in years are no longer considered young.

Now we are reminded that Christian Endeavor has flowed into many and unlooked-for fields, for there are Christian Endeavor societies in colleges, in public institutions of various kinds, in prisons and schools of reform, in alms-houses, asylums, institutions for the blind, etc., on board ships, men-of-war, at navy yards, in life stations and among life-savers, among the boys in blue in United States army and navy, in large factories, among car-drivers and police-men, in the Travellers' Union, etc., to the total number of 231.

The Juniors now claim our attention, — the springs that feed this mighty river. The Keystone State, Pennsylvania, still leads with 1,397; New York, only a little behind with 1,288; Illinois, 993; Ohio, 970; California has made a mighty leap, and passed into fifth place, with 551; Indiana, 549; Iowa, 518; Massachusetts, 517, this ending the list of States with more than five hundred Junior societies enrolled. The Junior badge banner, given to the State that has made the largest gain in Junior societies during the year, was first pre-sented at Montreal to New York, and at the three annual Conventions since that time Pennsylvania has proudly carried it away; but this year our good "pig iron" friends must pass that banner over to the "buckeyes" of Ohio.

The other Junior badge banner, first given to the District of Columbia at Montreal for the greatest proportionate increase in number of Junior societies, and held successively by Delaware, Assiniboia, and Mexico, must now pass from Mexico to Spain. A Christian Endeaver banner to travel from Mexico to Spain! Strange history we are writing. O that it might be carried by the shortest route, by way of Cuba, and that to bleeding Cuba it might be an emblem of liberty, peace, and prosperity!

The Intermediate societies next claim attention. The first society was organized a few years ago by Rev. A. Z. Conrad, D.D., of Worcester, Mass. There are now 366 Intermediate societies enrolled. California leads the States with 51; Illinois has 44; Ohio, 32; Pennsylvania, 27. As busy pastors, espe-cially in large churches, are beginning to see the wisdom of banding the older boys and girls into separate societies, preparatory to graduation into the regular Young People's society, the growth of Intermediate societies the coming year is likely to be large. Make way for new applications of Christian Endeavor principles. Already the Mothers' societies number 70, Illinois having 30; Pennsylvania, 20; Kansas, 11; and the rest scattered here and there.

California, New Hampshire, and Pennsylvania each have three and Con-necticut two Senior societies. As far as we know Rev. H. N. Kinney, at the time a resident of Connecticut, and now of Syracuse, N. Y., was the first pastor to report a Senior society. In all twenty-seven churches have announced that they have organized their regular midweek prayer meeting into Senior socie-ties, by applying the Christian Endeavor idea.

England's Grand Old Man has well said : " Precept freezes, while example warms; precept addresses us, example lays hold of us; precept is a marble statue, example glows with life. There is at least one kind of exchange between nations which hostile tariffs can hardly check, the exchange of high personal example. " Our river is international and interracial, and bears upon its bosom this exchange of high personal example.

England has 3,925 societies; Australia, 2,124; Scotland, 433; Wales, 311; India, 250; Ireland, 169; Madagascar, 93; France, 68; Mexico, 100; Japan, 66; West Indies, 63; Turkey, 41; China, 53; Africa, 52; Germany, 32; and so on through a long list, with a total of 7,919 societies. In addition, all Canada has 3,390 societies.

The badge banner for the greatest proportionate increase in number of societies, which Oklahoma first secured at the Minneapolis Convention, which then was captured by Manitoba, New Mexico, West Virginia, Assiniboia, and which is now held by Scotland, will fall into the hands of the loyal Endeavorers on the Emerald Isle. The shamrock is ahead of the thistle this time. India, with her splendid advance, was very little behind Ireland. And the other banner, the one given for the largest absolute gain in total number of societies, is for the fourth consecutive year held by England. Indeed, this is the year of jubilee.

Ezekiel's description of his vision of the holy waters, from which I quoted in the beginning of this report, tells us, "by the river upon the bank thereof, on this side and on that side, shall grow all trees for meat, whose leaf shall not fade, neither shall the fruit thereof be consumed." Our attention is now attracted to the trees that line the banks of the river Christian Endeavor. In the United States, the Presbyterian trees are more numerous than any other, there being 5,531 Young People's societies and 2,934 Junior societies. The Congregationalists are next, with 4,156 Young People's and 2,407 Junior; the Disciples of Christ, third, numbering 3,208 Young People's societies and 1,322 Junior; Baptists, 2,640 Young People's societies and 1,080 Junior; Cumberland Presbyterian, 867 Young People's societies and 361 Junior; Methodist Protestants, 971 Young People's societies and 251 Junior; Lutherans, 869 Young People's and 324 Junior, and so on, until we have enumerated nearly forty different varieties.

In Canada, the Methodists lead, with 1,062 Young People's societies and 170 Junior; Presbyterians, 1,056 Young People's societies and 146 Junior; Baptists, 168 Young People's societies and 35 Junior.

In the United Kingdom, the Congregationalists, with 1,216, lead the Baptists by only six societies. Then the Presbyterians and Primitive Methodists follow. Under the Southern Cross, in Australasia, the Wesleyan Methodists are the most numerous.

Friends, will you please notice that all these trees on both sides of the river have very much in common, their roots interlacing, gaining vigorous life as they stretch their great limbs and sturdy trunks heavenward, each and every one pointing to the one Forester over all, none other than the King of kings and the Lord of lords? Look carefully and you will see that the fruit-laden trees are those whose roots are the closest to the deep water. And look again; don't you see that those same trees, the most prosperous and thrifty, in turn cast their protecting shade over the face of the river? Is my figure too dense? Well, in plain language, this is what I mean: that the denomination that wisely fosters and conserves its Christian Endeavor societies insures its own vitality and increases its own usefulness.

But better than any theory the following facts will prove my statement. A "missionary roll of honor" will be unrolled in one of our meetings next Monday. Upon it are the names of 10,468 Christian Endeavor societies that have given nearly $200,000 to missions *through their own denominational missionary boards.* And these same societies have given an equal amount for other benevolences. The largest gift to missions reported by any one society is the $1,437.01 of the Clarendon Street Baptist Society of Boston. The Calvary Presbyterian Society of Buffalo is second, with $1,016.85, and we must take off our hats to a Chinese society here in San Francisco, the one in the Chinese Congregational mission; it stands third, having given nearly $700 to its own denominational missionary board, and is supporting six missionaries in the field.

Thus the missionary roll of honor is emphasizing the seventh plank of the Christian Endeavor platform of principles, which is, "that all moneys gathered by the various societies of Christian Endeavor for the cause of missions be always sent to the missionary boards of the special denomination to which the particular society belongs.

"That Christian Endeavor officers and societies are affectionately reminded that appeals to them for money should come through their pastors and the officers of their churches; and when such appeals are addressed to the societies directly, they should be referred to the pastors and church officers for their approval before being acted on by the societies.

"Also, that the causes to which the societies give should be those approved by the denominations to which the societies belong. Thus the societies avoid recognition and support of independent and irresponsible movements."

THE OFFICERS AND TRUSTEES OF THE UNITED SOCIETY, THE "COMMITTEE OF '97," AND THE PRESIDENTS OF STATE, PROVINCIAL, AND TERRITORIAL UNIONS.

Yea, verily, "the fruit thereof shall be for meat, and the leaf thereof for medicine." Let us taste of the fruit gathered by some of our large city unions. Philadelphia, the City of Brotherly Love, at Washington last year gave up to Chicago the banner for the largest increase in the number of societies. This year Chicago may return the banner, for Philadelphia has accomplished more than any other city union in planting new societies, thus extending our blessed interdenominational fellowship. May we all, like Philadelphia, by loyal allegiance and energetic endeavor, reaffirm our increasing confidence in this interdenominational spiritual fellowship, through which we hope, not for organic unity but to fulfil our Lord's prayer " that they may all be one."

Our journeying down the river brings us to Cleveland, "the Forest City." We are immediately attracted by her abundance of all kinds of fruit. Indeed, we have not forgotten how Dr. Tyler and others from Cleveland proudly bore the citizenship banner at the head of the procession in Washington on the occasion of Christian Endeavor's memorable march from the steps of our National Capitol down Pennsylvania Avenue. In Cleveland, and everywhere, Christian Endeavor always stands for Christian citizenship.

" It is forever opposed to the saloon, the gambling-den, the brothel, and every like iniquity. It stands for temperance, for law, for order, for Sabbath-keeping, for a pure political atmosphere; in a word, for righteousness. And this it does, not by organizing a new political party, but by attempting, through the quick conscience of its individual members, to permeate and influence all parties and all communities."

Well, Cleveland, yours has been another year of splendid service. Toledo, Kalamazoo, Syracuse, Colorado Springs, Rochester, Chicago, and other cities, too, are entitled to honorable mention, but as a reward for the best reports sent in to the United Society, Cleveland will turn her banner over to Indianapolis.

During the past year, in view of the unprecedented peril of the Sabbath, especial activity has been put forth in organizing in societies Lord's Day committees, whose work should be to create a public sentiment which will be a menace to all forms of Sabbath desecration. It is not within the scope of this report to give a detailed report of this blessed fruitage. California has secured the Lord's Day banner which was offered at Washington by Dr. Crafts, of the Reform Bureau. Please do not think that California secures this banner because she is considered a model for Sabbath observance. I do not know that any of our States could be considered models in that respect; but it does mean that California Christian Endeavorers, under the leadership of their secretary, Mr. Francis W. Reid, have mapped out a campaign which promises a better day for the Pacific coast, and their aggressive methods should be a stimulus to every State in the Union.

In our meanderings along the river's course we have reached New York, the birthplace of the Tenth Legion. And what is the Tenth Legion? Simply an enrolment of Christians who promise to give God not less than one-tenth of their income. You remember that the glory of Cæsar's Tenth Legion lay in the unfaltering loyalty with which, in each emergency, they were ready to dare or suffer at his word. The United Society's Tenth Legion believes to-day is a time of crisis for Christ's army; the missionary advance has been checked at home and abroad. Our leader calls for larger self-sacrifice and braver service, and so we have emblazoned on our banner, not " Render unto Cæsar the things that are Cæsar's," but " *unto God the things that are God's.*" Will you enlist? It was the New York City Union that first conceived this plan of securing a revival of Christian beneficence, and it is the New York Union that transferred its plan to the United Society, with the hope it would rally thousands to its standard. Although the Tenth Legion is but three months old, it now numbers over 1,600 members.

With this spirit rife in New York it is not surprising that she again secures the banner for the largest number of members who give proportionately not less than one-tenth of their income to God. Return with your banner, New York, and long may it wave to inspire us to a closer walk with God, and may it, as it waves, also extend a principle which, when adopted more enthusiastically, will make a missionary board debt forever impossible!

Now let me bring our annual journey to a close. We have been a long way; your eye has caught many things worthy of mention that I have not noted. The waters of our river have turned many a wheel of industry, borne upon their surface many a burden, mention of which could be very worthily made; but let us now rest and be still. Come close to the banks. Is the river where you are clear — quite clear? Can you see God's face reflected there? It 's God's river, you know, not ours. Its bed is the church, the church of Christ. We won't forget that. The river in many places has deepened the last year. God be praised! Did the channel deepen in *your* vicinity? Listen! During the last eleven months 25,264 of the Juniors have joined the church. From the Young People's societies, 187,125; in all, 213,389. What a ransomed host! What a blessed testimony to God's grace and proof of fidelity to his church!

Once more I say that, if Christian Endeavor is the river, the church of Jesus Christ is its channel, its bed and banks. Dr. Henry Van Dyke has said: "The life of a river, like that of a human being, consists in the union of soul and body, the water and the banks. They belong together. They act and react upon each other. The stream moulds and makes the shore; hollowing out a bay here and building a point there. The shore guides and controls the stream; now detaining and now advancing it; now bending it in a hundred sinuous curves, and now speeding it straight as a wild bee on its homeward flight. The personality of a river is not to be found in its water, nor in its bed, nor in its shore. Either of these elements, by itself, would be nothing. Confine the fluid contents of the noblest stream in a walled channel of stone, and it ceases to be a stream. But take away the water from the most beautiful river-banks, and what is left? An ugly road with none to travel it; a long, ghastly sear on the bosom of the earth." And is it otherwise with Christian Endeavor? God speed the day when, in every community and in every land, the mutual relationship of the church and its subordinate life, the Christian Endeavor Society, shall be as truthfully set forth by mutual love and inseparable achievements as the relationship of the river and its banks is beautifully portrayed by the lines which I have quoted!

Verily, the river of Christian Endeavor is *one* of the streams that make glad the city of our God, for God himself is the fountain from which it must flow. May it be to this busy world "a pure river of water of life, clear as crystal, proceeding out of the throne of God and of the lamb"!

Mayor Phelan, of San Francisco, having entered the hall, was presented for a few words of welcome for the city. He said that a great compliment had been paid to San Francisco, and that she had opened wide her doors and thrown away the key.

Secretary Baer read amid great applause the following telegram and letter : —

Executive Mansion, Washington, June 24, 1897.

My Dear Sirs : — I beg leave to acknowledge receipt of your letter of 21st inst., which was promptly called to the attention of the President. Recognizing the scope and force of your great undertaking, the President is pleased to send you his congratulations on the approaching Convention in San Francisco, and asks me to express to you his sincere hope that it will be a completely successful reunion, productive of great good, both to its members and to the country.

Very sincerely yours,
J. Addison Porter,
Sec'y to the President.

To John Willis Baer.

Executive Mansion, Washington, July 7, 1897.

Secretary John W. Baer, San Francisco, Cal. : —

My best personal wishes for the success of the Convention.

William M'Kinley.

The chairman then introduced the Rev. C. A. Dickinson, D.D., of Boston, to present the "badge" banner to the country having the greatest proportionate increase in number of societies during the year. Scotland held it 1896–97.

Presentation Speech, Dr. C. A. Dickinson, Boston.

Mr. Chairman and Brethren : — I confess that I am in a strait betwixt two just now, for on one side of my family tree I am a Scotch Irishman, and so there is a sort of interracial warfare going on in my bosom. The Scotch part of me feels a little down in the mouth to-day. It seems to me that old Scotland has gone back somewhat on her usual record, for she is a thrifty country, as Ian Maclaren has said, and she not only knows how to get all she can, but she knows a good deal better how to keep what she has. On the other hand, the Irish part of me is feeling in high feather to-day. I am heartily glad that Ireland, although a little one among the nations, is ahead of us in the race, and I hope that she will keep ahead a good while. Although she has not been able to get home rule, she certainly has been developing the principles of Christian Government along the lines of Christian Endeavor very successfully.

I remember a story told of one of the Sons of Erin who came to this country and who was wonderfully impressed with the size of America. In writing to a brother by the name of Michael he said, " Brother Michael, shure America is a big counthry. ' T is an awful big counthry. You can lose owld Scotland in one of her big woods, and you could drown owld England in one of her fresh water ponds ; and as for poor owld Ireland, why, you could roll her through Ameriky from say to say and she would n't make a dint in the ground."

Now, if I should make an application of this story along the lines of Christian Endeavor, I should say that certainly there is no danger of Scotland taking to the woods along the line of religion ; and as for England, I do not think there is any danger in her getting drowned, if the report of Secretary Baer is true, for the Baptists are making a tremendous addition to their ranks there ; and as for old Ireland, she has been rolling over us all, and has made an impression which will last at least a year and we hope longer, and we are going to raise this banner in her honor to-day.

We are very fortunate in having with us another Scotch-Irishman on the Board of our Trustees, who is going over to Ireland next week, to whom we will entrust this banner. Dr. Patterson, I present to you this banner in the name of the Trustees of the Christian Endeavor Society and of this Convention. and we want you to take it safely to the Emerald Isle, give our hearty love to all the Christian Endeavorers there, and tell them we hope they may keep this banner at least three years and present it with their staff in London in 1900.

Response of Rev. Wm. Patterson.

I am very glad to have the privilege of receiving this banner for dear old Ireland. I think there is no country that Scotland would rather give the banner to than Ireland, for you know the first Scotland was in Ireland, and the first Scotchmen were Irishmen. That is an historical fact that I need not dilate upon now. You all know that Caledonia was originally a part of Ireland. And then again, you know a great many of the people in the North of Ireland are simply the Scotch purified. They have come over there two centuries ago, and by the long dwelling in the purity of the Irish air have become pure Irish. Then again, Scotland has stood by Ireland, and Ireland has always stood by Scotland.

Ireland is notorious for many things; but there is one thing we can say of her, and especially of Belfast, in which city I shall deliver this banner, and that is that in another year she will put upon the ocean the largest vessel afloat; and in 1900 she is going to have a vessel that will carry over 4,000 Endeavorers across to old London to the International Convention. Of course the Yankees are nowhere when it comes to Ireland, so far as beauty is concerned, or enterprise. So far as Christian Endeavor is concerned, she may not be going ahead so fast, but you know that though she has been somewhat long in starting, now that she has started she will move rapidly, as that is the way the Irish do. At one time she was the brightest star in the western horizon along the line of civilization, and I believe that through this agency of Christian Endeavor, welding together the different denominations, enthusing the young people of Ireland, the Golden Age will again return to her, and Ireland will be notorious, not for the "wee drap o' liquor," but for the Christian enthusiasm and Christian spirit of her people.

I shall be in Belfast on the 24th of this month, and I shall present this banner to the Christian Endeavor Society there with the best Christian wishes of this great Convention meeting now in San Francisco.

Rev. W. H. Vogler, of Indianapolis, Ind., was introduced to present the Junior " Badge " Banner for the greatest proportionate increase in number of societies the past year. Mexico has held it in the year just closed.

Presentation Speech, Rev. W. H. Vogler, Indianapolis.

Some years ago Dr. Meredith, of Brooklyn, New York, said that the church would soon abandon the method of sweeping converts into the church by spasmodic revivals, and instead would take her children from the cradle and keep and train them for the church. Christian Endeavor has begun to stand guard over the cradle, from Mexico all the way around the world; and in a generous rivalry to see who shall have the largest number of Junior societies enrolled each year, the victory has been won by Spain, and the banner will now go from Mexico to Spain. Who would have thought such a thing possible? I am very sorry the banner has been belated, but the United Society will transmit it to Spain, as there is no one here on the part of Spain to receive it. And while her Juniors are growing up, may the time speedily come when it will be possible for Spain to have all her colonies and never tyrannize over one as she has done over Cuba.

The Convention then adjourned.

Woodward's Pavilion.

The greater distance of this place of meeting from the centre of the city was the reason for the small attendance at the opening hour. But under the direction of Rev. H. B. Grose, of Boston, who presided, and the musical director, Professor J. J. Morris, of San Francisco, the interest was sustained and increased until before the adjournment it was estimated that four thousand people were present.

The " Welcome Song " was sung by the chorus. Mr. Grose called upon Rev. Soo Hoo Nam Art, of San Francisco, to conduct the devotional exercises. This leader appeared in regulation Chinese costume. The 121st psalm was read responsively, after which he offered prayer, beseeching a blessing upon the Convention. He implored strength and power for the Christian Endeavor Society. While his enunciation was clear, the strangeness of accent easily suggested the world-wide character of the movement.

" Onward, Christian Soldiers " was then sung. The devotional services were continued while delegates from the Mechanics' Pavilion found their seats. The singing was spirited.

With a few words of introduction Mr. Grose presented Mr. J. S. Webster, vice-chairman of the '97 committee.

Welcome of Committee of '97, J. S. Webster.

Not only on behalf of the Committee of '97 and of the societies composing Alameda County and the Golden Gate unions, but as the representative of the 55,000 Endeavorers in the State of California, am I privileged to extend to you the first words of welcome. " Cast thy bread upon the waters and it shall return after many days." California reversed this injunction, and her waters cast his bread on the land of Endeavor, and lo! after many days, the return has come in this grand Convention, the greatest assembly California has ever been privileged to welcome.

While we gather to-day in the Queen City of the Pacific, our beloved San Francisco, you have come here on the invitation extended to you in the name of California, and she extends a welcome as broad as her domain, as boundless as her products, and as warm as her own sunny skies.

We welcome you as the representatives of a great army of over three million youthful Endeavorers, mustered within the church from all parts of the globe, enlisted in a holy warfare for the uplifting of mankind and the redemption of the world to Jesus Christ.

We welcome you because our people will see in you what Christian Endeavor stands for to-day, loyalty to God, to the church, to the home, to the State, and to the nation,— a loyalty that will find expression in this Convention, gathered from the east, and from the north, and from the south, and from the west, and from the countries of the world, to sing the praises of him who is King of kings, the great Captain of our salvation, to listen to his leaders proclaiming his truth, to receive a new inspiration, to renew our vows unto him, and to give practical demonstration of our work.

We have been anxious for them to see in you the representatives of the greatest movement of this generation, an organization under no control but that of the individual church, yet bound together by the ties of Christian fellowship, and a controlling, dominating purpose to elevate and purify the lives of its members, and combine and concentrate their efforts in every good word and work until their numbers shall be as the sands of the sea, and the youth of every land shall be enrolled under its banner.

We welcome you to San Francisco because we believe there is a peculiar appropriateness in your assembling here this year. Two years ago you gathered in the historic city of Boston, a great army over 55,000 strong. Your hearts were profoundly stirred as you visited Plymouth Rock and Concord and Lexington and Bunker Hill and Faneuil Hall, and a new impulse was given you in your loyal and patriotic purpose to be better citizens and to do more to elevate the standard of local citizenship.

A year ago you assembled in the beautiful city of Washington, the Nation's capital, the seat of our Government, and by the great, white monument you reflected on the stirring events that marked the country's history from the days of Bunker Hill and Concord to the present, and you blessed God for the Union of all the States; and by the halls of legislation, as you sought to deepen the spiritual life, you prayed for a purer citizenship in every section of our vast country.

It was fitting that from there you should cross the continent and come to San Francisco, and learn, as only one can learn by travel, how vast our country is, and in your youth behold that immense section destined in the near future to wield a predominating influence in the legislation and life of the country, and by the natural force of emigration from the East, to be the home for the development of that type of sturdy, patriotic, liberty-loving, religious manhood sent out in early days to the West from the firesides of New England, New York, and Pennsylvania.

The record of Christian Endeavor work in many of the States, along the line of good citizenship, during the past few years, has been such as to be a marked incentive for others to follow, and the compilation and distribution of these records will prove a great stimulus to all well-directed efforts in this direction.

What more inspiring record could be presented than the heroic purpose, the gallant struggle, the hard fought battles, and the recent glorious victory of that faithful band of Buckeye Endeavorers in the city of Toledo?

We welcome you to San Francisco, and his Honor, Mayor Phelan, foremost in every effort in the cause of good government, will voice the city's welcome; but on the behalf of the Committee of '97, of each sub-committee, of the great chorus, and of the rank and file of the members of both unions, to all and to each of whom the great work of preparation has been a labor of love, I extend a royal California welcome to our homes, to our hearts, to our church houses, to our great pavilion, where we have sought to provide comfort and pleasure and hospitality. Above all, as a young, active, purely religious organization, we welcome you for the great work you have done and the good we expect you to do us.

This city and State need a great spiritual uplift, and your coming has been longed for, when the presence and power of Almighty God might be manifested to quicken and give new life and lasting zeal and enthusiasm to the members of all young people's societies and to all the members of our churches.

We need to get on a higher plane of spiritual living; we need to be more zealous and outspoken in the Master's service; we need a more thorough consecration to him, and we pray that God may use your presence to send us forth to this more consecrated and effectual work.

President Grose then introduced Rev. Dr. J. K. McLean, of Oakland, to voice the welcome of the Golden Gate pastors.

Address for the Pastors, Rev. J. K. McLean, D.D., Oakland.

Mr. Chairman and Christian Endeavorers:— I would like to utter some of the words that have been uttered by my predecessor in this order of welcome.

We began to hear of the Young People's Christian Endeavor as an organized form of activity, upon this coast, early in '82; we had optical vision of it in the autumn of the same year by seeing the first society officially planted in our San Francisco Bay. We have been anxious ever since to see more of this great body, for we have followed with beating hearts and bated breath the magnificent development of this movement, and its spread over the whole world. So, in 1895, we thoroughly wished for you out here; in 1896, we longed for you to come; in 1897, we fairly fasted and prayed for you, and we have got you at last.

We are glad to have you with us. I have been looking about for some measures of expression that would indicate to you my own personal gladness in this coming to our coast of this great international body, but without success. The nearest I can come to it is this: just seventy-two hours ago, almost to a minute, Mr. Chairman, about four hundred miles from here, I was landing a four-pound trout — four pounds and a quarter, to speak exactly. Those Endeavorers who are fishermen do not need to be told of the thrill I felt, but that is nothing to the thrill that I feel to-day in coming across the bay on the boat, and along the crowded thoroughfares, in realizing the presence of this great convocation. So I have laid aside my rod, bade a temporary farewell to my Indian comrade, left the glory of the woods and the magnificent splendor of Mt. Shasta, and I find myself a thousand-fold rewarded. The great mountain is sublime, but less sublime than this great assembly of earnest Christian men and women, gathered here to-day in the name of Endeavorers from all parts of the earth beside our Golden Gate.

Many most stirring events have transpired upon the sands here by San Francisco Bay, but I venture to say nothing of equal moral significance with that which is witnessed here in this assembly, taking place in these fair days of July. Therefore, with heart and soul I give you welcome, but my welcome is to be confined to the pastors of the Golden Gate. I will leave to his Excellency, the Mayor, the wider welcome from the city, and to the Governor, or his representative, at the other pavilion the yet broader welcome from the State.

I will only say in passing, that when you are looking upon this great State of ours, you are looking upon ultimate America, you are looking upon the field that is to obtain generations hence the highest results in American civilization for, my friends, Josiah Strong is here somewhere, or on the way, and those great vital forces which he describes so well in their tremendous accession of power as they move westward from the Atlantic coast into the great interior do not expend their energy in that short journey; they only get their second breath, they only take their second strength, and they pass on with more tremendous swing over our mountains. Let us remind you that the star of empire, which for generations has been unrestingly westward, when it arrives here has no further west to go, for, geographically and commercially, the west end is San Francisco, and a new East begins. So that the Bethlehem star which has guided you, resting here, rests in heaven over one of the high places of the world's future destiny. I am speaking in all seriousness when I say this, and out of that seriousness comes much of the significance of the welcome from the Golden Gate pastors to this assembly. For, in the first place, tremendous responsibilities are laid upon our unequal hands. We are with you, Christian Endeavorers, working for the time to come, but our work is distinctly foundation laying.

You will find in one of the papers of our city of a day or two ago a brief sketch of the religious history of California. Only forty-eight years ago last February, Protestant Christianity did not own a rood of ground, not a foot of lumber, not a bunch of shingles — not so much as a single nail. Whatever there was of it was wholly in the air, and fully one-third of this brief period passed before people seriously thought of planting those things which make for the highest in California. The East was home, and the highest hope or expectation that men had was the making of their pile, and by and by returning home to enjoy and spend it. So our constructive period is a very much shorter one than even the brief period of our occupation here. We are, therefore, only in the foundation period, but nevertheless laying foundations for great things that are to be.

But, my friends, it gives us new courage when we realize by the presence of such a gathering as this the mighty forces of prayer and sympathy and work and love that we have behind us, and it gives us greater assurance in those visions of the future when we comprehend — as we cannot, except by ocular demonstration — the incarnation of Christianity in our own and other lands; it gives us hopes of the recruits we are to receive by and by, those who are to be co-workers with us, and our successors in this work. Therefore, it gives us great gladness to see you here to-day. We ask of you to look upon our foundations; we ask of you to leave your sympathy, your prayers, your love, and your undying interest here.

In our great distance from the vast centres of Christian philanthropy, we realize sometimes our moral and philanthropic provincialism, and that the great heart-beats, in reaching these far extremities, have expended a great deal of their forces. We are glad, for once, to have the great heart of Christianity, so to speak, laid in our very hands. It brings us into a comprehension of the power of that Christianity, and we can understand better the feeling of the Apostle John, as he leaned upon the breast of Jesus, and we have a new interpretation of the omnipotence of faith and love and spiritual power. We are glad to be re-inforced, and we are glad to have you stand upon these western walls of the American continent, and we know that you will cast your thoughts across the great waters beyond, to meet the great work that is reaching out to Christian Endeavor. When you get out to our Cliff House, or when you stand at Cypress Point down at Monterey, and turn your eyes westward, I beg of you, dear friends, do not forget that there are more important objects than our seals and our pelicans, that there are things of more importance than all the interests of commerce, and that you are looking out upon the great highway of Christian missionary Endeavor, and that the hand of the Lord is pointing you across these vast seas into those newly awakening nations beyond us.

And once more, and lastly, we are very glad to have you here for another reason; I hope that when you go up and down our thoroughfares you will notice the names upon our signs, and see what a variety of nationality is represented here. I hope you will go off a little from our main thoroughfares, and not only go through Chinatown, but into other environs of the city, and see what a diversity of people we have. We are a Pentecostal population; we are from all parts of the world, and as there were presented at Jerusalem on Pentecostal Day fifteen or more nationalities and dialects, which Jerusalem represented, as related in the second chapter of Acts, so this is a Pentecostal place, and we have a Pentecostal constituency. And now, dear friends, our longing is that there might be a mighty sound from heaven coming down upon this place where we are sitting, and that the tongue of fire may descend and rest upon every head and face, so that when you go away, if go you must, there shall be left behind you a real Pentecostal blessing. There has been no place at which these conventions have been held, or can be held in future, better fitted to receive such a Pentecostal blessing, or that needs that Pentecostal blessing more than we need it to-day.

In the names of the pastors of the Golden Gate, therefore, we bid you welcome to our churches, our pulpits, our prayer-rooms, our city.

As the representative of the city which entertained the Convention, Mayor James D. Phelan was enthusiastically greeted, as he arose to welcome the delegates in behalf of San Francisco.

Address of Welcome to the City, by His Honor Mayor Phelan.

Mr. Chairman, Ladies and Gentlemen: — It might be appropriate for me to say that you are thrice welcome, since I am the third speaker detailed to welcome you.

But even as a San Franciscan and a Californian, accustomed to everything exaggerated in nature and art, I am surprised and gratified at the magnificent work which our local committee have done. They have provided everything for your comfort, and I wish to thank them for what they have done. They have provided everything, so far as I see within the range of my eyes.

San Francisco is very proud to-day to greet the Young People's Society of Christian Endeavor, because your fame has preceded you; your fame is known to us these many years, and the city is complimented by your coming. Across plain and over mountain, you have come to hold your annual Convention by the Golden Gate. At best, travel is a hardship, and we feel sincerely the compliment of your coming so far. In your philanthropic desire to spread the beneficent influence of your society over the entire country, you have wisely, at one bound, jumped from New England to the New El Dorado, have traversed the American continent, and many of you have seen, for the first time, the extent of our empire and the scope of your own work.

San Francisco, the metropolis of the Pacific States, welcomes you as fellow-citizens of the great Republic, welcomes you as co-workers in the common cause of doing good, and our people, eager to show you hospitality, eager to provide for your entertainment and pleasure, bid you welcome, cheerfully, enthusiastically, and freely, and trust that you will make yourselves at home, and not feel as strangers among us.

The worthy gentleman who has preceded me made several references to San Francisco. San Francisco is a unique place. Perhaps it is well for me to make a few references to things that concern us. Remote from the great centres of population, San Francisco, drawing upon the resources of mine, field, sky, and sea, has felt self-reliant and strong, and has carved out her own destiny with very little assistance from sources outside her immediate community. Here, life takes its color from her cosmopolitan population, because, as you have been told, the representatives of all nationalities are assembled here, and make of our city a little world of itself. So, in charity, I will say that it should not be judged by village standards. San Francisco is a metropolis, proud, and ambitious to excel. We welcome every ennobling influence which will serve to soften, while it does not mar, the rugged beauty of her character. The great breezes that sweep over the city from the ocean upon whose shores we stand make life in this city the most comfortable, enable man to work throughout the entire year, and thus multiply our resources, both individually and as a community, and give the advantage of a greater population, without its drawbacks. With a climate that is never extremely warm or cold, San Francisco presents a physical example of that moderation which belongs to the perfect life, for which your society so gallantly strives.

Ladies and gentlemen, let me say again that we welcome you. We trust that many of you will come and linger among us, not as sojourners, but as settlers; that you will come and share our possessions which the God of Nature has so bounteously bestowed. We are not unselfish in this. If we give, we know that we shall also receive. By making our population more homogeneous, and by bringing higher ideas of citizenship, the noble deeds and cheering words, and an Eastern population, such as yours, will serve to finish, as with the touch of the older States, the magnificent edifice which sprung from the untutored hands of the pioneer.

We say, Come and linger among us; be Californians; be a part of that great procession which is steadily moving westward, even as civilization, beginning in the remote East, has steadily moved westward, westward, westward, until, having arrived in California, not being able to go any farther, the natural tendency would be upward.

So, ladies and gentlemen, in concluding, permit me to say that San Francisco, such as it is, is hospitable. I think Californian hospitality is known throughout the East. We have done our mite; we have done our best; we have thrown open to you the Golden Gate of our hospitality; it is a gate that swings freely upon its hinges, and it is a gate which is open to all. But if we must have a preference to people who visit us, we will open our arms frankly, honestly, and heartily to the American people who have grown up in the substantial communities of the East. We want you, and we trust that you will be attracted here, as we know you will, not only by the fair face of California, which reflects the favor of nature and the happiness of our people, but also by your own desires, which we know is to help in preserving and promoting the permanent interests of our own common country and our common civilization.

The response of the delegates to this overflow of hospitality was voiced by the Rev. Silas Mead, LL.D., of Adelaide, Australia, president of the United Society of Australasia.

Response for the Delegates, Rev. Dr. Mead, Australia.

Mr. Chairman:— I count myself happy in being privileged to attend this Convention, and in speaking on behalf of the delegates here assembled this morning. I hardly know why I have been selected to speak to you on behalf of the delegates, except it be that I think I have come from a longer distance than any of you.

I and my fellow delegate, Miss Mead, have traveled only 17,000 miles. We have traveled 17,000 miles specifically to attend this Convention.

Our Australian Endeavorers believe in Christian Endeavor, and they believe in conventions, and because they believe in conventions they have sent us over here to convey to you their hearty, earnest Australian greeting.

You will be glad to know that Christian Endeavor has spread rapidly in our Australia; that I represent to-day some 60,000 Christian Endeavorers. Christian Endeavor seed was at an early date cast into our Australian soil, and it has sprung up and borne abundant fruit. We thank God for Christian Endeavor.

We were delighted to have Dr. Clark with us three or four years ago. We were so delighted with him that we tried every way we could to have him come again this year. But, in our self-denial, let me say, we thought he could do better work by going to South Africa than to revisit us in Australia and New Zealand.

I attended a convention (I only mention this to show you how Endeavor has spread in Australia) in Sydney on last September. I do not know the capacity of this pavilion, but the capacity of the hall in Sydney, where I presided, was an audience of 7,000, and admission was limited to Christian Endeavorers. We did not permit other people to come in, because we did not have room for them. I presided over that great audience for two nights in succession.

We thoroughly believe in these annual conventions, because they express to ourselves, to the churches everywhere, and to the world at large, our great and solid faith in the principles that underlie all this Endeavor movement.

Dr. Clark told us in Liverpool, at the British convention held there just before he came over to America, that the International Convention is to be held in London in 1900. I hope you will have a good Convention in 1898, and another in 1899, and then that you will all go to London in 1900. I do not see why you should not go there in chartered steamships of your own, to the tune of something like 15,000 or 20,000. Go to the London Convention, and you will find that London will give you a real London reception, earnest and hearty. I believe that the British Endeavorers will give you such an enthusiastic welcome as they have never yet given to any band of pilgrims that have visited these shores.

I want to say this: I have no doubt it was a very happy thought in naming the convention "International," but if I were on the committee, I am not sure but in due time I would propose an amendment,—that it should be called " Inter-Continental," Endeavorers. I was in India a year ago, and presided over a splendid rally in the city of Calcutta, but in India they are at the beginning of things. Dr. Clark will tell you at some period of this Convention of the splendid rally at which he was present in Eastern Bengal. I know Eastern Bengal quite well, and there is no reason why Endeavor should not spread wonderfully, splendidly, to the great honor and glory of Christ and of God and of his church, in India and in China, and in all the nations of Asia. We want Asia one of the great corners of Christian Endeavor, and also we want Africa as one of the great corners of Christian Endeavor, and I hail this gathering in San Francisco as a prelude and the harbinger of world-wide conventions, Inter-Continental conventions. Let us meet in London in 1900 — Australia next.

. My friend Dr. McLean said all that is beyond the Golden Gate is eastward, Oriental. I am an Oriental, you see. I have not the dress that I see in India, it is true, I have not the dress of our Celestial friends, either, but I suppose I am an Oriental. I am glad to be an Australian.

Mr. Mayor, you know that California and Australia have about the same climate — the best climate under the sun. California and Australia have entered into a co-operative union. I saw a great long train of trucks and no people in them as we came along, but there was *something* in them. What was it ? California fruit. We are co-operating with you, Mr. Mayor, in also undertaking to provide for the wants of the world in the way of fruit. The people want gold. California supplies gold, Australia supplies gold. You want silver. California supplies silver, and Australia supplies silver, and so, you see, we are a co-operative society.

But over and above that, we rejoice in co-operating together in the great and splendid movement of Christian Endeavor, and I am happy to be here to-day to bring you the thankful response of our delegates, and not only for those who are here with us, but I speak for the three millions of Endeavorers of these States, and sixty thousand in Australia, and for all the world. I thank the Mayor of the city, and the people of the city, for the glorious street welcome that you give to us. It is an object-lesson to pass through your streets, and to see everywhere the Christian Endeavor welcome. We thank you. We thank the Golden Gate pastors for their reception. We are sure they have been working hard, and we thank you Golden Gate pastors. We thank the Committee of '97. I think you have done splendidly. I heard what was done in Boston. When our representative from Australia, Mr. Closs, returned, he told us of that reception, but I think it was not exceeded by the reception that you have given here in your city. We all thank you very heartily.

The chairman then introduced General Secretary Baer to read the

report previously printed. As in Mechanics' Pavilion, Mr. Baer's appearance was the signal for demonstrative enthusiasm.

Mr. Grose read the telegram from President McKinley, which was **loudly** applauded, and, owing to the delay in commencing the session, **and the** consequent necessity for Mr. Baer to leave before he completed the reading of his report, the presiding officer concluded it for the secretary.

Presentation of Banner for Greatest Increase of Societies.

Rev. W. J. Darby, D.D., of Evansville, Ind., presented the banner for the greatest increase in the number of societies during the past twelve months. The banner was won by England. This country has held it for two years.

Dr. Darby expressed regret that there was no British delegate present to receive the trophy. He paid a high tribute to the Christian workers across the water, whose untiring efforts merited the Convention's testimonial prize. He referred in highly eulogistic terms to Queen Victoria, and said that this had truly been a jubilee year for England. He expressed a hope that the high Christian standard which Queen Victoria had set for her people would be maintained, and the growth of the Endeavor movement would continue as vigorously as it has been commenced.

The banner was accepted by Rev. Silas Mead, LL.D., for the English societies.

Presentation of Banner for Greatest Increase of Junior Societies.

As a surprise, the badge banner for Junior Endeavor work was merited by the State from which the speaker who was to make the presentation speech had come. Rev. J. Z. Tyler, D.D., of Cleveland, Ohio, accepted the situation drolly, and made a presentation speech that put his hearers in a merry mood.

"It seems never to have occurred to the committee," he said, "that Ohio had a chance of getting the banner, and it seems Pennsylvania has been so slow the banner has not yet arrived. So far as I know, there is no one else here from Ohio to receive it, so I have many parts to play. I have to present a banner which is not here to myself. I will take great pleasure in presenting this banner to Mr. Bomberger, the president of our union, who I had hoped would be here, metaphorically, to receive it. This banner means much to us. It means, either that we have more children than Pennsylvania, or that they are better children and join the Christian Endeavor. It means, too, that Ohio is in the lead in Christian work, and we are proud of it."

After singing, in the absence of Rev. E. W. Shurtleff, of Plymouth, Mass., who was to have read a poem at this time, the chairman introduced Dr. Clark to give his annual address. This was the climax to the enthusiasm. When President Clark finished the address, previously printed in this report, the Convention adjourned, after the benediction by Dr. Mead.

THURSDAY EVENING.

Woodward's Pavilion.

Not a single seat was unoccupied in this auditorium. Those who came late were compelled to attend some one of the overflow meetings. The fame of the speakers was world-wide. Their words would be helpful and inspiring.

The familiar hymns of Endeavor engaged the audience before the hour for opening. Under the direction of Dr. Clark the service was a memorable one. After Captain H. G. Smythe and Colonel J. H. Hallimond, of the Volunteers of America, had sung "Saved by Grace," Rev. C. A. Savage, of Orange, N. J., offered prayer.

President Clark urged all who were present to do their utmost to leave an impress of the Convention upon the city by their songs. He opened the session with a gavel presented by the Endeavorers from India.

Dr. Clark said : —

I hold in my hand this evening one of the belated gavels which has not been seen before in the Convention. It is too late to call you to order with it, but it is not too late to show you this gavel, or to let you hear its ring. This came from India. It was presented by the local union of Christian Endeavorers in one of the hill stations in northern India. They wished me to use it in calling this Convention to order. I wish to show it to you as a link binding India Christians to American Christians. It is made of three kinds of India woods, studded with rupees from the different native states, carved with curious hieroglyphics of the languages spoken in those states. It is from your fellow Christian Endeavorers, and they wished you to know, as you heard it ring, that their hearts beat in sympathy with yours, and that the ring of Christian Endeavor is just the same in India as it is in America.

Dr. Clark then introduced Rev. G. F. Pentecost, D. D., of Yonkers, N. Y. He was greeted with a warm welcome. His subject was " Christian Endeavor and Good Literature."

Address by Rev. Dr. Pentecost, Yonkers, N. Y.

Mr. President and Christian Brothers and Sisters : — It has been one of my misfortunes, if anything can be a misfortune in the line of divine service for God, to have been out of my own country almost coincident with the movement that is culminating for this year, at least on the Pacific Coast. This is the first Christian Endeavor Convention I have had the pleasure of attending. I should much rather have attended this Convention as a silent observer and as an eager learner, but one of the principles of Christian Endeavor is to do as you are bid, ask no questions, but simply render the best services in your power. I would much rather, certainly, that another had taken this subject, which is not entirely in my line, but I am here as a substitute. Just before leaving home I received a line from Secretary Baer, saying that I was desired to fill a vacancy that had unexpectedly been made. The topic is " Christian Endeavor and Good Literature. "

Paul tells us that man is a tripartite being, — spirit, soul, and body, — and each of these great parts of our personality needs careful feeding and conscientious nurture. For the body, God has provided the products of the earth and abundant exercise, which in one way, Paul says, profiteth little if the body only is attended to. For the spiritual nature, we have communion with God by the Holy Spirit. For the intellectual nature, we have the whole field of what we may call the literature of all time. We must, therefore, be careful that, as God has made provision for the spirit and for the soul and for the body, we give conscientious attention to the nurture of each part of our being; otherwise, we will go through the world, perhaps not visibly to man's eyes, but certainly as cripples or deformed in God's eyes. But the man who pays attention to his spiritual nature, to his psychical nature or consciousness, and his bodily nature, will be a symmetrical man.

Literature is so large a subject that it is difficult for me in a word or two, or in the short time that is given, to define it. But let me, for a brief, popular definition, say that literature is the record of man written in what we call history, biography, philosophy, science, travel, discovery, invention, and in the works of the human imagination, such as poetry and fiction. You can see, therefore, how large a field literature covers, and how much a man would have to do in a brief lifetime if he were to put himself in any kind of general fellowship with the vast field of literature.

But we divide literature into good and bad. And so we may, by a process of exclusion, get rid of a very large amount of matter that is generally classed as literature. Good literature is literature that has the spirit of life in it, and that has in itself a power, under the sanctifying influence of God's spirit, of nurturing life; a minister to the intelligent consciousness or the soul of man, literature may be a great aid to the Holy Spirit in building up the spiritual nature.

Now, I said that good literature is that which sanctifies. Literature, properly apprehended, may be the means of introducing us into a vastly wider fellowship than it is possible for any living man to have with his fellow beings. One of the words that is constantly heard in connection with the Christian Endeavor Association is fellowship. How delightful is the fellowship of this Christian Endeavor Association. During the nine days of rapid transit from Boston to the Pacific Coast I was shut up in one car with one set of men and women, and I never had nine days of more delightful companionship in my life. I would like to have all those who were my fellows on that trip constantly around me, within touch of my hand, within hearing of my speech, and would like to be always within hearing of their speech. That is fellowship.

By communication with these brethren, I have been nourished in spirit as well as in body. They have poured out in those days treasures of wisdom, treasures of fellowship, shown in the lives of their different individualities, until I began to comprehend, with some of these saints whom I had never known, what is the breadth, the depth, the height of the love of God that passeth all knowledge and understanding; because every man who knows God has a type of that love that no other man has, has it in his nature, and it is by fellowship that we who have so small capacity of comprehension can by that love and fellowship comprehend with the saints, or go into partnership with the saints and share with them all the wealth of the love of God.

Now, suppose that we could extend our fellowship beyond the boundaries of our church, beyond the boundaries of our city, beyond the boundaries of our country; suppose that we could put ourselves into personal fellowship with all the saints of England, of Germany, of France, of India, of Canada, of Australia, or of New Zealand; suppose we could keep in constant touch with the fellowship of the present world; — how vast and rich our fellowship would be! But suppose we could go beyond that, and we could get back into the last generation, or into the last century, or even into the sixteenth, the fourteenth, the tenth, and even the fifth century, back to the days of Paul and Peter, and the saints who were first called into the knowledge of Christ; suppose we go back even another century or two, back to Haggai, Malachi, Jeremiah, and Abraham, clear back to the days when God first had saints on the earth — what a wealth of fellowship we would have!

Well, literature is the record of man as expressed in history, as recorded on the pages of living biography, as poured out in the rich streams of human thinking and sanctifying speculation, and has found inspiration in the discoveries and the comments upon the wonders of God's works in nature, in the soaring of imagination sometimes touched by the spirit of God, and sometimes only the inspiration of mere human genius. Literature is that which brings us into living touch with all the ages, and gives us fellowship with all the best thought and the best birthright that the world has ever had. Who of us who have had some little of what we might call literary culture, and who sits down in his study and looks over the books on his shelves, and recognizes the name on the back of a book, telling what man has written it and what theme he has discussed, but feels himself every day thrilled and helped by the silent fellowship of good books ministering to him, even when he is not reading their pages, by memory of the things that are in them? That is one of the advantages of a literary fellowship. We have our living fellowships around us, but they are more or less limited by time and space; but the fellowship of the living dead,— that fellowship is bound and preserved to us in page and in volume, and is a fellowship that we have constantly at our hand.

This, of course, is a very crude outline or suggestion of what literature is. I have intimated that literature, or the fellowship of history in the various departments of human life, is to be found in books, just as fellowship is to be found in men. Now, I want, with the brief moments assigned to me, to make two or three practical observations which I trust may be helpful to my fellow Christian Endeavorers, and then very briefly chart out a little outline of the literature which comes within the easy possibility of the least privileged of the young men and the young women that make up the vast throng of the Christian Endeavor Association.

I would say, in the first place, that it is of the utmost importance, and it should be recognized as one of the serious responsibilities of every Christian Endeavorer, to put himself or herself into an immediate and practical, and, as far as possible, large fellowship with the best human thought that has been preserved on the pages of literature. We may, indeed, develop a good deal of enthusiasm in connection with our Christian Endeavor, but the human soul — and by the soul, I mean the consciousness, the intelligent consciousness, of man as distinct from his spiritual nature — the human soul is driven hither and thither by his environment in this world like a ship at sea without ballast, and it is only as we ballast our ship, it is only as we freight our intelligence with the fruit of good literature, that we are able to use the breezes that blow upon us, and to stand, sometimes, against the hurricane and storms of thought and the trend of human opinion, as Paul expresses it, beating upon us as " winds of doctrine." We want to ballast ourselves with the fellowship of the best thought that God has preserved to us in literature.

Now, when we discuss the question of literature at large, naturally we would say that the matter is far beyond the possibilities of the average young man and woman. Thanks be unto God, we live in a country that was established by men who had amongst their first convictions the supreme importance of what in these latter days we call education; we are an intelligent, educated people. That is the advantage which our good providence has enabled us to lay hold of literature. No young man and young woman who has had the advantages of common-school education — nay, I will go farther than that; no young man or young woman who has education enough to read the daily newspaper — but has it in his or her power to become possessed of the gist of the best literature of the world. Literature is the greatest human possession that we can have, and this is a fortune. It is a capital for life, and it lies within the easy reach of every conscientious young man and young woman, and our Christian Endeavor movement will be greatly strengthened, and it will be compacted and solidified, by the measure of its rich literary possession.

I know a young man who was converted when he was twenty, a young man who had paid little or no attention to education as a boy, who had rather resented it; but as soon as he gave himself to Jesus Christ, he was possessed with a great and profound conviction that he was unfurnished for the responsibilities of a Christian servant, and he went diligently to work. He called upon me and asked me to mark out for him a little course of reading. I gave him a little help, and within less than three years I have been amazed to find out what a mass of good reading that young man has. It was his first service to Jesus Christ, and he took this course in order that he might be a workman that need not be ashamed.

It is astonishing how much literature you can eat, digest, and assimilate by a little conscientious devotion to the service of literature every day. The amount of time that we waste upon unnecessary reading, the amount of time that we carelessly and thoughtlessly waste upon even vicious reading, — not ostensibly vicious reading, but actually vicious reading, — would enrich a half-dozen lines of the best literature that has streamed forth from the centuries down to us. I say that for your encouragement.

I will offer just one or two observations further than this: a very distinguished man has said of himself, "I early determined in the field of literature to know everything about something, and something about everything." I give you that to remember. It is impossible for us to be a master of history, of all biography and philosophy, of science, and of the works of imagination, but it is possible for us to select some literary theme — let it be history, biography, philosophy, science, art, or let it be what-not of the various departments of literature — and be the master of it, or at least the master of one great man in literature. I know a young man who says he has not time to read many books, but he has mastered Bacon's Philosophy, he has mastered Butler's Analogy, and he is a young giant. If an infidel, or a sceptic, or a scoffer meets that young man in discussion, he will find he has made a tremendous mistake if he thinks he can readily overcome him in argument, and he will meet them with the most irresistible logic, not only from what he has gathered from these two masters, but the reflex of the knowledge and culture which has been developed in his own mind.

I would say that the Christian Endeavorer is unworthy of his high calling as a servant of Jesus Christ who does not master some great and good book. If you cannot master two authors, be a master of one, and even then you have the key to a thousand others. One good book of one master mind thoroughly studied from cover to cover, not only in its letterpress, in its syntax, in its grammar, and in its argument, but also being saturated with the personality of the man who wrote it, and you may open a dozen books of the day and read them in ten minutes, and get every good thing that is in them.

Know "everything about something," and, as far as you may, "something about everything."

My next suggestion, in view of the subject that is assigned, is, that we must have the heroic courage to be ignorant of a great deal of literature. "Have you read this book? What do you think of so-and-so? What do you think of this and that?" Thank God, I know nothing about it. "Why, that is the book that is in vogue; that book everybody is talking about, and I do not like to say I have not read it for fear I shall be considered ignorant." Have the courage to be ignorant. Nine-tenths of all the books that pour from the prolific press of this century are not necessarily bad books, but they are unnecessary books. Nine-tenths of the books of the day are only a kind of shadow made of the chop-straw of the books of yesterday. They are the skimmed milk of preceding authors. Nine-tenths of the books of to-day will be waste paper to-morrow; they are unnecessary books.

I might name, if I were called upon, fifty books which any Endeavorer might become acquainted with and read, but I will cut it down to twenty-five books which I could name in the different departments of literature which, if this great Christian society would become more or less familiar with, would mark you for all the rest of your life as cultured men and women. It would put into your hand a cimeter that would enable you to fight your way through to the end, and not be ashamed of yourself in the world.

The president says I have five minutes more. I wish he had said it were fifty. One minute of that time I will take in making this remark: that as surely as a man or woman is known by the company they keep, so are they

known by the books that they read. Just as surely as your associations will act
upon your character, so surely do the books that you read mark, mold, and influence your character. Therefore, be careful. Give a little time and a little
thought to the selection of the books that you read.

I will venture with the other four minutes to indicate the field of literature,
and a few of the books. I have already said that the field comprehends history, biography, human thought, or philosophy, science, travel, discovery, invention, art, and works of imagination. This is the day in which all the critics
are saying to us that we have made a tremendous mistake in not dealing with
the Bible as literature, and a great many people are afraid, because somebody
has said, perhaps not because they desired to exalt or magnify God's Word, but
they have at least indirectly sought to undermine the traditional faith in God's
Word, and they have termed it literature, in order to get rid of what they describe as a superstitious reverence for the book, so that they could go at it as a
surgeon would dissect a body, hunting for the soul of it. But you cannot in
this way find the inspiration of God's Bible any more than you can find the
human soul by cutting up and dissecting the body. I should like to turn the
argument against them. I am like Nelson: I am deaf in both ears, as he was
blind in one of his eyes, so that he could not see the flag when he was ordered
to stop fighting. I want to take up the argument of the Bible as literature, and
turn it against the critics. Let us deal with the Bible as literature. It is the
summum bonum of all literature.

There never was such literature in all this world as is found in the Bible.
From Genesis to Revelation, where can you find such history? Where will
you find such biography as in those magnificent characters who have outlived
ten thousand of the princes and kings of the earth? A few people can tell us
something about the life of Plato or Socrates, or the thousand kings of
Greece and Rome, but millions will tell you something about Abraham, and
Isaac, and Jacob, and Moses, and Isaiah, the Judges of Israel, and the Prophets
of Israel, and of Peter, and James, and John, and Paul—these are the men
that have made the centuries that have come after them.

The Bible is the best history the world has ever had, because it was a history every line of which was guarded and superintended by the spirit of God.
If you want poetry, where will you find such poetry as is in the magnificent
writings of Job, Isaiah, or a dozen of the other prophets? There is no such
poetry in all this world as is found in the Bible. It has outlived the poets of
Greece and of Rome, and in the presence of ninety-nine one-hundredths of all
the twaddle that is published to-day in the form of poetry, it burns with the
blaze of an electric light, or the flash of the noonday sun, as compared to the
light of tallow dips.

The Bible in itself has power to give you culture. Do you want philosophy?
I will give you one word of philosophy,—the first word of the Bible, which is
also the last word of human philosophy and the science of the nineteenth century,— "In the beginning God." That is science. That is the last word of
science. Paul said two thousand years ago, "We look not upon the things
which are seen, but upon the things which are unseen, for the things which are
seen are temporal, and the things which are unseen are spiritual and eternal."
The last of the agnostic biologists is saying that the unseen is the eternal
substance of which all the creation is only the passing and temporary shadow.
The Bible had all the secrets of science and philosophy before modern or
Greek philosophy was born.

Read the Bible for culture. Look at the poor, ignorant man who was shut
up for twelve years in Bedford jail for preaching the gospel, and in the jail,
with only his English Bible and a Cruden's Concordance, he has left to the
world a classic in language, in imagination, in grammatical structure, such as
was never known in the world before.— John Bunyan's " Pilgrim's Progress." It
has been read by a million of intelligent souls where Plato's Philosophy has
been studied by ten students.

In Jesus Christ all the treasures of knowledge and wisdom are hid. I only
want to emphasize this study of the Bible, not simply as a religious book to

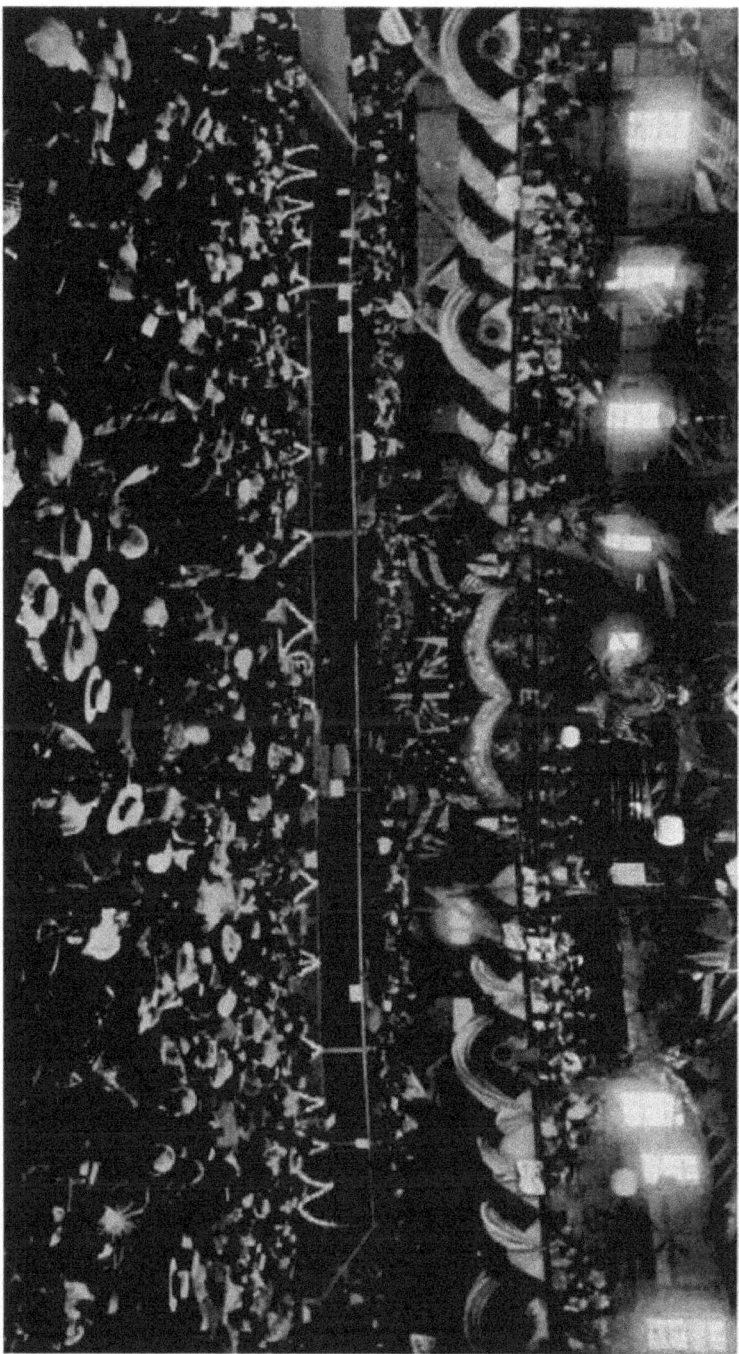

INTERIOR OF WOODWARD'S PAVILION.

help you in your prayer, to give you matter for your Sunday-school lesson, or a suggestion for a Sunday sermon, but as the key to all the literature of this world.

Do we want to study geology? behold, He is the rock of ages. Do we want to study astronomy? behold, He is the bright and morning star. Do we want to study botany? He is the lily of the valley, and the chiefest among ten thousand. Do we want to study biology? "I am the way, the truth, and the life." He is the secret of life. There is not a science in this world that is not suggested by that matchless, peerless Christ who is the living embodiment, the flower of art, and the inspiration of every page of that divine book. With the Bible in your hand, without knowing Greek or Hebrew, or any of the dead languages, you have the secret and the key of literature.

After singing, the banner awarded by Rev. W. F. Crafts, Ph.D., for the best work accomplished during the last year in defending the Lord's Day, was presented, on behalf of the donor, by Rev. Dr. B. B. Tyler, of New York.

Speech of Presentation, Rev. Dr. B. B. Tyler, New York.

It is unnecessary for me to speak words concerning this banner, or the meaning of it in this connection, after the utterance of the happily chosen words of our beloved president. But in the presentation of this banner to the secretary of the California Christian Endeavor Union, we call attention to the fact that the Christian Endeavorers of the great State of California have made the most heroic fight in behalf of the Lord's Day, and in that connection I am inclined to utter just a word concerning this great battle. It is fitting, it seems to me, that in this part of the country, where, if my information is at all accurate, there is an especial need of reform in this direction. The young people who have stepped to the front have done courageous service.

One of our ministers in New York City, not as well posted as he ought to have been concerning the Christian Endeavor movement, remarked: "It is about time the Christian Endeavor movement was doing something practical; we have had sentiment and gush and song long enough. Let them begin to do something that ought to be accomplished." The Christian Endeavorers were then doing needed things. More and more they are coming to the front, supporting our institutions, and rescuing imperilled customs that have been dear to us from the foundation of our Republic.

Know all men everywhere that the North American Republic is a Christian nation. Let us remember that it was religious enthusiasm as well as a desire of commercial gain that led to the discovery of this new world. The first act of Christopher Columbus when he set foot upon American soil was to reverently kneel; and erecting the cross, he took possession of the new world in the name of the Lord of hosts. The first settlers on our New England shore came to the new world because of their religion, and every State of the Commonwealth was founded by Christians. New York was founded by Christians; Pennsylvania was founded by Quaker Christians; Maryland was founded by Roman Catholic Christians; Virginia was founded by Episcopal Christians. The Carolinas were founded by the Huguenot Christians. Georgia was founded by Methodist Christians. Little Rhode Island was founded by the Baptists. Every commonwealth of this great country has had its foundation made by Christian men and women.

The corner-stone of what free state in the history of the world was ever laid by an agnostic? Only Christian men have led in this work. One of the peculiarities of this Christian Association is the observance of the Lord's Day. You may sneer if you will at the Puritan Sabbath, but that Puritan Sabbath and that Puritan faith made stalwart men, heroic women — made such men and women as have made this Republic possible.

The young people have done well to enter into this department of Sunday observance, and are working heroically.

It gives me pleasure to present this banner therefore to the secretary of the Christain Endeavor Union of the great State of California.

Response for California by Francis W. Reid.

On behalf of the Christian Endeavor Union of the State of California who have more organized day committees and who have done the noble work aggregating 5,353 credits inside of three months, I take great pleasure in accepting this banner from the Rev. Wilbur F. Crafts.

I wish to assure you that so long as this flag which appears upon the back of this banner exists, so long as its stars are bright and its stripes are safe, so long will we stand here in California in defence of a Christian country, in defence of the Lord's Day.

The last address was given by Rev. Josiah Strong, D.D., of New York City. Dr. Strong spoke upon "Christian Endeavor and Christian Citizenship."

Address by Rev. Josiah Strong, D.D., New York.

Blessed are the Christian Endeavorers, for theirs is the fellowship of the kingdom of heaven.

I know an elderly clergyman in New York who studied theology in New England. The question was once raised among his fellow students whether a Methodist could be saved, and they decided to submit it to a Congregational deacon, who was held in high esteem for his great learning and piety. They solemnly asked the question, "Is it possible, in your judgment, for a Methodist to be saved?" and he replied with equal solemnity, "No, not one!" I don't think that deacon has any spiritual descendants living to-day, but if there is one, I am sure he is not distinguished for his learning and piety, but for his ignorance and bigotry.

We Christians have been accused of "hating one another for the love of God," but this is true no longer. We have come near enough to recognize in each other's faces the likeness of Christ; and those in whom we see that likeness, whatever the name and whatever the color, we cannot choose but love.

But there is another step which the churches must take, if they are to accomplish their social mission, which includes Christian citizenship,— they must come near enough to grasp hands in Christian co-operation.

Let me show you, so far as I can in the few minutes allotted to me, the urgent and increasing need of good citizenship, which springs from the character and phenomenal growth of the modern city. Let New York illustrate the city's increasing rate of growth in recent times. Founded in 1614, it took New York 175 years to gain 33,000 inhabitants. During the next period of 50 years it gained 280,000; during the next 30 years it gained 620,000, and during the next 21 years, which period closed in 1890, it gained 859,000. The gain during the last short period was 26 times as large as during the first long period, and the rate of gain 208 times as great.

A hundred years ago the United States had only six cities; in 1880, 286; and in 1890, 443. A hundred years ago three per cent of our population was urban; now about 30 per cent.

Some have supposed that this tremendous movement of population from country to city was due to the exceptional conditions of a new civilization, but it is not peculiar to America. It is taking place in Europe, in Asia, and now in Africa; it is a world phenomenon. Others have imagined that it would prove temporary, that the flowing tide would soon ebb But such have not divined its causes. Permit me to touch them briefly. They are three. (1) The application of machinery to agriculture. A government commission reported in 1890 that four men with machinery could now do the work on the farm formerly done by fourteen. The ten are driven to the city. (2) The springing up of manufactures in the city to make these agricultural implements and a thousand other things, which of course draws workmen. (3) The railway, which makes it easy to transport population from country to city, and, what is more important, easy to transport food, thus making it possible to feed any number of people massed at any point.

Now, all these causes are permanent; the tendency which springs from them will, therefore, be permanent. If I could devote a half-hour to this point I think I could convince you that beyond a peradventure an ever-increasing proportion of the world's population must live in cities. We are to have not only a greater New York, but by the laws of our social life, we are destined to have a greater Boston, a greater Chicago, and a greater San Francisco.

Glance now at the significance of this effect. Because the city is composed of individuals, the city, like the individual, should have a harmonious physical, mental, and moral development. If the child's body grows and his mental development is arrested, he becomes an idiot. If mind and body grow, and the moral development is arrested, he becomes a criminal. Increasing power is rendered safe only when there is an increase of intelligence and of conscience to control and direct it. Precisely here do we see the supreme danger of modern, and especially of American, civilization.

There has been during this century a prodigious physical development; there has been no corresponding moral development.

If before Adam was driven from the garden he had eaten of the tree of life and had thus lived on to the present day; and if, like so many of his children, he had had the good sense to immigrate to America; and if he were eligible to membership in the Young People's Society of Christian Endeavor, — and when I look around on these gray heads and beards, I think he would be, — and if we could have called for his opinion, I am sure he would have told us that he had seen more material progress during this nineteenth century than during all the thousands of years he had lived before. Evidently there has been no such marvelous and unprecedented development of the conscience during this century.

The modern city is the best example, as it is the most striking product, of modern civilization; it exemplifies a disproportionate physical development.

The problems of a great city are vastly more complicated than those of a small one. The increasing growth of the city, therefore, demands for its successful government an increasing intelligence. But as a matter of fact, our great cities are generally under the control of the more ignorant portion of the population. The public health is sometimes committed to the tender mercies of saloon-keepers and low pot-house politicians. Some years ago health wardens of New York City testified before an investigating committee of the State that there were cases of "hyjinnicks" in their wards. Some of these guardians of the public health thought the people "had the hyjinnicks pretty bad," while others were of the opinion that the patients "got over" them quite easily.

I had it from the lips of Ex-Commissioner Roosevelt, a few weeks ago, that applicants for places on the police force of New York made the following exhibit of their intelligence when requested to name five New England States. One replied, "England, Oirland, Scotland, Whales, and Cork." They were asked to tell what they knew about Abraham Lincoln. Some twenty thought he was president of the Southern Confederacy. About forty thought he was a Union general. One thought he was a great general who won the battle of Bunker Hill. Some thought he was assassinated by Guitteau. One thought the assassin was Garfield, and one thought the bloody deed was done by Ballington Booth. That is the kind of men who actually get into office under the spoils system; that illustrates the degree of intelligence which until recently has ruled New York City for many years.

In Europe men of the highest rank and greatest learning deem it an honor to administer the affairs of their city; while we entrust authority to ignorant and corrupt men, who give us the worst municipal government in Christendom at four or five times the cost of good government in England.

Again, as cities grow larger, relations and obligations become more complicated; we need, therefore, a better developed social conscience. As we become more dependent on each other, we need to be more dependable; there ought to be a larger moral development. But instead, there is an increasing discrepancy between the physical and moral development of the city. So far as we know, the first murderer built the first city, and it would seem as if crime had ruled in the city ever since. In Philadelphia there are seven and a half times as much crime to the population, and in Pittsburg and Alleghany City nine times as much, as in the average rural country of Pennsylvania. The great moral forces or institutions of society are the home and the church; and these, instead of growing proportionately stronger with the growth of the city, grow relatively weaker. Our last census shows that of people living on farms about 66 per cent own their houses. In cities under 100,000 inhabitants 36 per cent own their houses; in cities of more than 100,000, only 23 per cent; and in New York, the largest of all, only about six per cent.

How about the church? In Boston fifty years ago there was one Protestant church for every 1,200 people; in 1890, only one to every 2,500. In Chicago sixty years ago there was one Protestant church to every 1,000 inhabitants; in 1890, only one to every 3,600. Our cities generally, which now contain about 30 per cent of our population, are only about half as well supplied with churches as they were fifty years ago, when they contained eight per cent of the population. Here is a marked tendency, and tendencies are prophetic.

Look, now, at the political aspect of the case. Our political structure is based on two foundation principles; viz., that of local self-government, and that of federation, which are alike necessary to the permanence of our institutions. Local self-government is necessary to the exercise of our liberties, and federation or union is necessary to their preservation. These two principles are like the two abutments of the Brooklyn Bridge; destroy either one, and you destroy the structure.

One of these two principles was endangered a generation ago, when we waged a great war, at unspeakable cost, to save the Union. But while patriotism was at the front defending one of these principles, the other was being quietly subverted at home. Men who never had a patriotic heart-throb in their lives sought the control of our cities, not for the public good but for private gain. Circumstances favored their designs. Many immigrants had acquired the rights of citizenship who knew nothing of its duties. Their votes could be bought and sold in blocks of many thousands. This constituted a paradise for the demagogue which enabled the political boss to perfect his machine and to compact his power, so that for years we have had in our larger cities not the government of the people by the people and for the people, but the government of the people by the boss and for the machine.

Of course, such government led to bottomless corruption, which has made our great cities a stench in the nostrils of the civilized world. Our friendly, but discriminating, English critic, Professor Bryce, says that the one conspicuous failure of American institutions is the government of our great cities, and every intelligent man knows this to be true. So true is it, that for years we have relied on the country vote to save us from the consequences to the State and nation of the city vote. So true is it, that our States do not dare to trust our cities with full self-government. The new constitution of New York State draws a line around the cities, limiting their liberties, and defining to what extent they shall be permitted to govern themselves. Thus is one of the two fundamental principles of our free institutions hanging in what Edmund Burke called "a dancing and hesitating balance."

We are now prepared to weigh the gravity of the fact that more than one-half our population will soon live in cities. If the rate of the movement of population from country to city between 1880 and 1890 continues till 1920, there will then be in the United States ten million more people in our cities than outside of them. They will then no longer accept limitations from the State, but take into their hands not only their own affairs, but also those of the State and of the nation.

What if the cities are *then* incapable of self-government? If their government is then, as now, "a conspicuous failure," what will become of our free institutions?

Wendell Phillips once said, "The time will yet come when our cities will strain our institutions as slavery never did." Is not that day drawing near? Most of our great cities have at some time been in the hands of a mob. In the summer of 1892, within a few days of each other, New York, Pennsylvania, and Tennessee ordered out their militia, and Idaho called on the United States government for troops to suppress labor riots. That is not self-government, but government by military force. There is peril when the Goddess of Liberty is compelled to lean on the point of a bayonet for support. Sooner or later it will pierce her hand.

The city, then, is the point of danger on which good citizenship must fix its attention. There is demanded for its safety a new patriotism, which is civil, rather than military, which springs to the defence, not of the Union, no longer imperiled, but of the other fundamental principle of local self-government, which is seriously endangered; not a patriotism which constructs fortifications and builds navies, so much as one which purifies politics, and substitutes statesmen for demagogues; not one which follows the drumbeat to battle, but one which goes to primaries; not one which "rallies round the flag," so much as one which rallies round the ballot-box; not one which charges into the deadly breach, but one which smashes the "machine;" not one which offers us itself to die for the country, but one which is willing to live for our country, which is as much more difficult as it is less glorious.

Now the practical question arises, What can we Endeavorers do about it? I have crossed the continent for the express purpose of raising and answering that question. This general subject of the social mission of the church, which of course includes good citizenship, the Evangelical Alliance has been making a study for several years. We have made observations, investigations, and experiments, and I believe we have reduced the problem to its simplest terms, and are prepared to offer the simplest practical solution. The problem of the social mission of the church is the problem of *education*. In her mission to the individual, which must ever remain fundamental, the church must go farther and aim at nothing less than regeneration; but her social problem is that of educating public opinion and the popular conscience. With us, the voice of the people is only less mighty than the voice of God. Every reform, whether political, social, or industrial, depends on the education of the people. Every reform, when new, divides the public into three classes, — its friends, its enemies, and those who are indifferent. The last class is the great class, and victory, remember, if won at all, must be won from the indifferent.

How, then, can we reach the indifferent with educating influence? Not by the pulpit, for they do not come within the reach of the pulpit. Our extended investigations show that less than one-half of the population profess to attend any church, Protestant or Catholic.

Nor can we reach the indifferent multitude by the popular meeting of the agitator. Suppose it is temperance reform, for instance, and we call a public meeting. It is those who are already interested that come, and the indifferent, because they are indifferent, stay away. We have reached precisely those we did n't need to reach, and have failed to reach those whom we did need to reach.

You say, "Let us write books and publish papers." Very well; but it is the interested who buy the books and papers, and the indifferent, because they are indifferent, do not buy. How shall we reach the indifferent with the truth? If the mountain will not come to Mahomet, evidently Mahomet must go to the mountain. If the indifferent will not come to us for the truth, evidently we must take the truth to them if they are to be educated.

Here is a vast work to be done, but there is in the church, providentially, a vast power, as yet mostly latent, which is entirely equal to it. I refer, of course, to the great organizations of young people, of which this is the greatest, and which altogether number some four million members in the United States pledged to Christian work and to needed popular reforms.

Our plan has been submitted to many of the leaders of those organizations, and in every instance has met with their hearty approval. Here is the plan. Let the pastors of every community organize a pastors' alliance, or union; call it what you please. If a ministers' association already exists, no further organization will be needed. Let them enlist as messengers as many of the young people as may be necessary. Let them divide the community into districts of from ten to twenty families in each, and assign to each a messenger. These messengers can with their bicycles easily reach remote and isolated farm-houses. Let the pastors, who know local conditions, decide what line of work should be taken up first. Suppose it is good citizenship; the Evangelical Alliance will furnish them on application specimen leaflets, prepared by the best brains in the country and at the smallest possible cost. These leaflets are not to be goody-goody stuff, better calculated to reach the waste basket than the conscience and the will, but something bright, attractive, true, valuable. We hope to get the Hon. Carl Schurz to prepare a good-citizenship series for our immigrant population; one on " The Meaning and Value of Naturalization ; " another on " The Rights of the Naturalized Citizen ; " another on " The Duties of the Naturalized Citizen ; " another on " The Fundamental Principles of American Institutions." Other series will be prepared, equally well adapted to American-born citizens, who need instruction but little less than the foreign-born. By means of the young people these leaflets can be systematically distributed to every family — one a month, or as often as may seem best.

Should only one in ten of the members of our several young people's organizations enter on this work, and should each messenger distribute only ten or a dozen leaflets each month, it would mean some 60,000,000 a year. It is entirely practicable to sow the length and breadth of the land with the seed of every needed reform, thus actually reaching and gradually educating the indifferent multitude, upon whom depends the future of every reform, political, social, and industrial.

But this is not all. The Christian conscience of the country, when educated, has no adequate means of expressing itself, and of moulding legislation. Every year there are bills introduced into our legislatures which outrage the Christian conscience of the State, but we have no means of defeating them. Suppose such an organization as I have outlined existed in every town of a State, and that there were a State committee of influential clergymen and laymen representing every co-operating denomination. If such a committee unanimously con - demned a given bill as immoral, they would undoubtedly represent the Christian conscience of the State. Let them prepare a petition calling for the defeat of the bill and send it down to the local organizations. Each messenger would circulate the petition in his or her district, and in three or four days hundreds of thousands of names could be sent to the legislature in protest against the passage of the bill. In many instances this would amount to the referendum, and be entirely decisive of the action of the legislature; and of course such a method would be as effective in the interest of a good bill as in opposition to a bad one. Thus by the method outlined we can educate the popular conscience, inform public opinion, and then bring them to bear upon the legislation of State and nation.

Here are possibilities entirely worthy of the Christian consecration, the splendid enthusiasm, and the mighty power of these great organizations.

Will you act on these suggestions?

Secretary Baer wrote us the other day that a good suggestion, like a crying baby in a concert-hall, ought to be *carried out*. You can help to carry out the suggestions made by speaking to your pastor concerning the matter, and asking him to write me at New York touching the subject.

I am not willing to close my address, leaving on your minds an impression of alarm and discouragement. There is no occasion for panic. There *is* occasion for alarm, if good citizens do not bestir themselves; but if we awake, our resources will prove fully equal to the emergency. A discouraged Christian is a sight for angels to marvel at. One discouraged who has access to divine resources! How is it possible for a Christian to lose courage and hope so long as he holds to his Christian faith ?

We have a divine warrant for believing that the city is to be redeemed. The Sacred Book, in its opening chapters, presents to us the beginning of the race in a garden; but John, in his vision of the consummation of all things, recorded in the closing chapters of the Word, represents the full salvation of the race, the perfection of civilization, the complete coming of the kingdom of God in the earth under the form of a glorious city, into which enters nothing that defileth or maketh a lie. We, as citizens of that kingdom, have a right to triumphant confidence, because we know that the kingdoms of this world are yet to become the kingdom of our Lord.

During the Battle of the Wilderness, a friend of mine, chaplain of a regiment of cavalry, became separated from his regiment by carrying wounded men to the rear. While hunting for it he came upon a tent somewhat separated from others. Its owner, in his shirt-sleeves and an officer's hat, was driving deeper his tent-stakes, which had been loosened by a high wind. The chaplain accosted him, " Colonel, can you tell me where such a regiment is ? " " Yes, you will find it in such a locality." " I understand," said the chaplain, " that General Grant's headquarters are near here; can you tell me where ? "

" They call me Grant," was the reply. " I beg your pardon, General," said the chaplain, giving the proper military salute. " That 's all right, chaplain. Do you hear those volleys of musketry ? " said the General. " It almost breaks my heart when I think what they are costing our boys. I could n't stand it, if I did n't know we're going to take Richmond." " Do you think we are going to take Richmond, General ? " " No, I don't *think* we 're going to take Richmond; I *know* we 're going to take Richmond." And that confidence was worth an army corps.

Citizens of the kingdom of God in the earth, touching the final issue of the conflict of ages between sin and righteousness, love and selfishness, we do not *think*, we *know ;* for we *know* who is the great Captain of our salvation, and we *know* that his is the power, and we *know* that when the kingdom has fully come his will be the everlasting glory.

After the address of Dr. Strong the Convention adjourned with the benediction.

Mechanics' Pavilion.

So great was the multitude that sought to enter Mechanics' Pavilion that three overflow meetings were successfully carried on.

Within the immense auditorium the theme was of the relation of the Societies of Endeavor to the Saloon and to Civic Righteousness. The atmosphere was charged with true Endeavor; the responsiveness of the audience was marked. Each speaker felt himself given a message of life in behalf of life.

The praise service began at 7.30, under the direction of E. D. Crandall, of Alameda. After the choir had rendered a beautiful anthem, the chairman, Rev. R. F. Coyle, D.D., of Oakland, introduced Rev. Ezra Tinker, D.D., of Wilmington, Del., to conduct the evening's devotions. Dr. Tinker read a chapter from Ephesians, offered a fervent prayer, closing with the Lord's Prayer, in which the vast company joined with one voice.

Secretary Baer made announcements concerning the overflow meetings, and at his request, Rev. W. H. G. Temple, of Seattle, invoked God's blessing upon the Wisconsin delegates who were injured near Chicago.

Dr. Coyle then introduced the first speaker, saying, " Dr. Russell is at the head of the Anti-Saloon League, and we may therefore expect to be enlightened by him in respect to his efforts as a Christian Endeavorer in that particular work."

Address by Rev. H. H. Russell, LL.D., Columbus.

The subject of Dr. Russell's address was "Christian Endeavor *versus* the Saloon."

I am glad to exchange greetings to-night with these picked regiments of the noblest temperance reform forces in the world. And while I try the vocal range of this far-stretching anti-saloon territory, and make sure that my voice, with the aid of your silent attention, is heard along these hills and valleys, and reaches the furthest temperance homesteader upon the distant gallery frontier, let us together, meanwhile, turn a page or two of Christian Endeavor history. The first scene is at Woodstock, Va., at the breaking-out of the Revolutionary War. The pastor of the village church, on a bright Sunday morning, after a thrilling appeal to his people on behalf of liberty, suddenly threw off his pulpit gown, and disclosed the full uniform of a Continental captain. The bugle sounded, and Pastor Muhlenberg led forth the men of his congregation, mustered them in as a company, and acting both as their captain and chaplain, he marched forth with them to a part in the battles of the Revolutionary War and a share in the final victory. This was Christian Endeavor *versus* sovereign oppression. Come back with me to Plymouth Church in Brooklyn. The conflict of the fifties had begun in Kansas. Mr. Beecher advocated the arming of the colonists, and a subscription was raised to supply every family starting westward with a Bible and a rifle. Plymouth pulpit was made an auction-block, and the slave girl was sold, but this time to freedom. At Sumpter's tocsin the first Long Island regiment was raised and equipped, for the war, by this church and congregation, with the pastor's eldest son a commissioned officer. Plymouth Church embodied and exemplified Christian Endeavor *versus* slavery. And the hour has come for the pastors of all our churches everywhere to lead forth their people to-day against a more baneful foe than that of 1776 or 1861; which slays more men every year than fell on both sides during the Revolution, and every five years than fell upon both sides during the awful carnage of the Rebellion. The first Declaration of Independence was written by Thomas Jefferson, against Sovereign Tyranny; the second by Abraham Lincoln, against Slavery, and the third will be written by Christian Endeavor, against the saloon. And as our English cousins, like Gladstone, now approve American Independence, and our Southern brethren, like Grady and Gordon, endorse the results of emancipation, so likewise all the world, including the liquor-dealers themselves, will, in the coming century, applaud the triumphs of Christian Endeavor *versus* the saloon.

The question to-night is by what method will more rapid headway be made in this reform than in the past. All Endeavorers agree the saloon is an arch-evil. All agree we must meet organization with organization. The saloon conspiracy must be overmatched with an anti-saloon combination. I shall, I am sure, have your quick assent that the churches — provided a proper method be proposed — are the most available and logical forces to federate for this conflict. It would be a profitable hour, if we had time, to consult upon this point the churches' chart and compass, the Bible. Take one citation of authority, — I John iii. 8. The apostle John was a conservative, but he knew the errand of the Gospel. " For this purpose the Son of God was manifested, that he might destroy the works of the devil." And there can therefore be no better King's business for the Church of Jesus Christ than to destroy this most desolating work of the devil, the drunkard-making, heart-breaking, home-blasting, soul-damning, hell-crowding saloon. The churches have all declared war — upon paper. No great power in history has ever uttered more equivocal ultimatums against another great power than the church *versus* the saloon. Take the Presbyterian Church, for example. This church is usually thought to be conservative. Here is a sentence from its General Assembly: " The pronounced and stupendous need of the hour to meet this enemy is an aroused church, consecrated to the extermination of the traffic." That sounds belligerent, but what is needed now is a cessation of the paper-wad bombardment, and the beginning

of the real warfare for active extermination. Christian anathema must be succeeded by Christian Endeavor *versus* the saloon.

I have no patience, however, with wholesale strictures and attacks upon
the church. We have been waiting, as Christians, for the proposal of a tangible method, and our brethren of the churches in some localities have at last
found such a method. They have named this timely and effective federation
of the churches and temperance organizations " The Anti-Saloon League."
During the past four years this league has been endorsed by every church
organization in Ohio; likewise by the State Christian Endeavor Union and
every other young people's society. In other States it is meeting with similar
approval. Several national religious bodies, including the General Conference
of the Methodist Episcopal Church, and the United Presbyterian General
Assembly, and many others, have voted to co-operate with this league in its
lines of work. It is therefore quite proper to enter upon a brief exposition of
this method here.

This organization was begun only after long deliberation and much prayer,
and the exercise of extreme caution in planning the lines of constituency and
method involved. As a matter of constituency it is agreed everywhere that
the league must be omnipartisan. A league of the churches which would present its cause from the pulpits, and carry on its work in the church buildings,
and become one of the regular benevolences of each congregation, must elimi-
nate all political partisanship from its organization. It must not directly further nor oppose the interests of any particular political party; otherwise we
should have a greater confusion of tongues than we have had in the past. So
we enroll together Republicans, Democrats, Populists, Prohibitionists, Nation-
alists, Socialists, and Mugwumps of every kind and variety; and last year in
the heat of the Presidential campaign, you would have been pleased to have
seen, as I frequently did, men who had been debating hotly the question of
gold or silver, sitting together in a friendly way planning for the extermination
of local saloons. As a matter of constituency, also, the league is thoroughly
interdenominational. There was an early coherence of members of the Protestant faiths, and a friendly hand was held out to our Catholic brethren, and in
December, 1894, Bishop John A. Watterson, of the Columbus Diocese, addressed our great Convention. He made a most eloquent plea for a federation
of all the opponents of the un-American saloon. Rev. Dr. Levi Gilbert, of the
Methodist Church, clasped hands with Bishop Watterson, and pledged Protestant fellowship with the Catholics in this fight against the saloon; and he said
he " hailed the coming day, whose dawning was now discerned, when Catholi-
cism and Protestantism, marching together under one banner, shall sweep
irresistibly forward, clearing the way for justice, for righteousness, and for
temperance!" The young people of all denominations are actively enlisted in
our anti-saloon conflict. In our last legislative campaign they opened a joint
headquarters at the Capitol and maintained a force of clerks, and did valiant
service in co-operation with the league superintendent.

With this explanation of the constituency of the league I come to speak of
the methods of work. These may be summed up under four departments.
The first department, and the most important for many years to come, is the
"Agitation Department." Through the agency of systematic and aggressive agitation by tongue and pen and printing-press we seek the most rapid improvement
of the general public sentiment which it is possible to attain. Wendell Phillips,
the greatest agitator of our anti-slavery reform, laid great stress upon this educational agency. He frequently said, " Agitation is the marshalling of the
conscience of the nation to enact and enforce its laws." and in his historic
address upon " Public Opinion" he said, " If you will take a fact, and place
it upon two legs, and send it from Maine to Georgia, you are just as certain to
change the government as if you exploded gunpowder beneath the Capitol."
One of the facts now thoroughly established by the experience of the past generation in this reform is that the success of either restrictive or prohibitive
legislation depends upon local public sentiment upon the question. This is true
of any police regulation. For example, I was once visiting a brother minister at

Plattsburg, Mo., and while driving with him upon the outskirts of the city, we saw some men and boys fishing with a seine. I said, " Is not that against the law of the State?" He answered, "Yes, I believe it is; but then, that is the way we all fish around here! Nobody cares for the law." That is local public sentiment upon a question of prohibition. The fish and game law was a dead letter there; and the same principle applies to the saloon question. About two weeks later I was at Ottawa, Kan., a city of about 10,000 inhabitants, where they have not had a saloon for twenty years. In 1890, you remember, the "original-package" decision was announced by the United States Supreme Court, which, until the amendment of the law by Congress, allowed the sale of liquor in pasteboard boxes in prohibition territory; and a liquor-dealer came down from Kansas City to Ottawa to start an original-package saloon. They rang the largest bell in town, and summoned the citizens, and I saw a thousand people come together with clenched hands and eyes flashing fire. They said, " He shall never sell liquors in this town, law or no law!" It was a case of determined public sentiment. They appointed a committee of a hundred business men, with a circuit judge as chairman, and they waited upon the intruder and served notice upon him that he could not sell liquor in that city. He thanked them for their hospitality and warned them that he should mind his own business and he expected them to do likewise. But he found an unlooked-for obstacle and was compelled to move on. He tried to rent a vacant room, but he could not rent one. Such was the pressure of public sentiment that no man could rent his property for a saloon and hold the respect of the community. And may God speed the day when that shall be true everywhere! And it will be, in the course of time. And that day, as it comes in locality after locality, will be ushered in as it was at Ottawa, Kansas, by the persistent and united agitation of the question. It will come as it has at Cambridge, Massachusetts, where there are eighty-five thousand people and no saloons, and the " no-license " vote was the largest last fall ever registered in that city. It will come as it has in seven other Massachusetts cities with over thirty thousand population, where anti-saloon avalanches have swept the drunkard factories away. The Anti-Saloon League is a public-opinion-building society. By the public Union Anti-Saloon Meeting regularly held, by the circulation of literature, by the organization of educational work in the public schools, in the pulpits, the young people's societies, and the Sunday-schools, we persistently press the agitation and keep the awful fact warm upon the hearts and consciences of the people, until a stern and determined public demand has been created and fostered to the pitch where the people of the community will not tolerate in their midst a crime-breeding, disease-engendering, poverty-producing saloon. And you can readily see that the best agency for most rapidly developing this kind of sentiment is the federation of the local churches. Christian Endeavor *versus* the Saloon!

The second department of the Anti-Saloon League is the " Enforcement Department." In this department we seek the enforcement of all existing laws and restrictive regulations. The saloon-keeper is a chronic and ubiquitous law-breaker. In 1894, investigation was made in thirty cities and towns in Ohio, and of the five thousand persons found present in the saloons visited, the majority were boys under age, in violation of law. We insist that this and other restrictions shall be enforced. We do not lose sight of the proposition that the best way to shut a saloon on Sunday is to close it seven days in the week, and the best way to prevent sales to boys is to lock the door, but while we are raising public sentiment to the prohibitive point, as a means of making progress toward that goal we demand rigid enforcement of all legal restrictions. The league believes in the wedge principle. Put in the thin edge and hammer diligently upon it. If we cannot get the whole loaf, or the whole baking, we will take a slice, or a crust, or a crumb, and we will nourish the cause on half rations, while we fight on for a full meal. Do you ask, " How are the laws enforced?" Not by the " Law and Order League" methods. We do not hire lawyers and detectives, and prosecute the cases in courts, as a league. On the other hand, we secure the facts and then insist that the officers of the law, who have been elected, sworn in, and are paid for their services, shall prosecute the law-breakers. If they fail to respond to the demands of the people, then we rally to the primaries and the polls at the next election, and nominate and elect some honest officials, who will enforce the laws.

Before speaking definitely of the political methods of the league, I will name the third department of the work, which is the "Legislative Department." This means the careful and systematic effort to hold all present ordinances and statutes and the securing of better enactments. In both the enforcement of present laws and the securing of better legislation, political action is indispensable. How does the league accomplish this? Here is a question of interest to young women as well as men. For whatever we may personally think or prefer upon the question of woman suffrage, it seems quite certain that the twentieth-century women will be endowed with all the rights and responsibilities of citizenship. In political action, the Anti-Saloon League, as has been said, leaves every member free as to his party relations, but it does demand that every member shall perform his citizenship functions in that party with which he affiliates. And this, when carried out, works a great revolution. The fountainhead of government in this country is the party primary, and the kind of men who prevail there settle the kind of policy of the public officials. The methods of the league may be illustrated by our recent legislative work in Ohio. Thirty-six members of the House voted for our county local option bill in 1894. The Legislature soon after adjourn.d. I submit it was the duty of the league, without regard to party, to stand by the men who stood by the right, and I am glad to testify that not one of the thirty-six men was allowed to be defeated by the liquor-dealers. Not only so, but we made a Christian endeavor to defeat the men who voted against us, and over twenty of them were defeated, either at primaries or polls. For example: One would-be statesman who thought his political bread was buttered by the saloon-keepers and voted against us went home from the Legislature and ran for Congress. But he was defeated by the church people. He sought a circuit judgeship with like result. He then ran for the next State Senate; and if there was any office where we did not need him it was in the State Senate, and by very careful organization and hard work he was defeated again. A few days before this last convention he made a remark to a political associate, which was repeated to me, and which I will ask permission to quote here to-night. It may sound a little harsh, for the language of the machine politician is not always elegant; but there is so much truth in it, after all, that it will bear repeating. Our machine statesman had grown apprehensive after two defeats, and he exclaimed, "If the Church vote is thoroughly organized, it will knock hell out of things!"

You have, perhaps, heard of the two Irishmen, just over, who walked up Fifth Avenue past one of those grand New York cathedrals, and one said to the other: "Sure, faith, and this bates the divil!" "Why, yes," said Pat; "sure, faith, and that's the intintion!" If the church work is ordained for anything, it is to knock that very kind of ingredient out of things, and when our presumptuous, truckling, machine politician was defeated, it was a speedy fulfilment of his prediction. This kind of retributive political justice is needed everywhere. Fresh illustrations arise continually. Take the recent cases of the two apostate governors of Missouri and Iowa. Governor Stephens of Missouri recently appointed a beer-brewer to the office of police commissioner of St. Louis, I suppose upon the old theory, "Set a thief to catch a thief." The Governor has been a prominent member of the Methodist Church. The church militant everywhere will rejoice that Governor Stephens's church associates did not hesitate to condemn him and his action. The *Methodist Christian Advocate*, of St. Louis, used this style of Anglo-Saxon: "The devil, backed by a thousand bartenders, and a thousand bartenders backed by a brewer, and a brewer backed by a Methodist governor, are a spectacle on which devils, men, and angels are gazing in amazement and wonder." Governor Drake, of Iowa, a prominent member of the Christian denomination, soon after out-Heroded in official depravity the recreant governor of Missouri, when he signed the bill which legalized the return of breweries and distilleries to that State. Here, again, the associates of Governor Drake in his religious denomination, in common with all church people, have unsparingly denounced the deep damnation of his official shame. In the *Christian Standard*, the national organ of his church, in a scathing indictment of his perfidy, in which a demand was made for his expulsion from his offices of trust in the church, the editor said : "When Governor F. M. Drake attached his name to the bill legalizing distilleries and breweries in the State of Iowa, he sinned against God, against the church, against patriotism, and against civilization. He gave his countenance to a business which brutalizes men, robs women and children of their natural protectors and supporters, encourages prostitution, corrupts politics, and is a cause of four-fifths of the crime which disgraces our land." The Anti-Saloon League is formed for the purpose of administering political retribution for such high crimes and misdemeanors against the home, the church, and the State. It is the highest duty of the Democratic church voters of Missouri and of the Republican church voters of Iowa to see that Governor Stephens and Governor Drake are never again allowed to so compromise and dishonor the Church of Christ; and the manifest way of prevention is to defeat their nomination and election to any official position to which they may aspire. With this end in view everywhere, the Anti-Saloon League organizes within the dominant parties, whatever they may be, and holds its pre-primaries, and gets out the vote to the primaries, and defeats bad men, and nominates and elects good ones to all the offices possible. And when defeated we adopt the tactics of the saloon men and come up smiling at the next election, with a predominant vote after our own kind.

As a matter of course, the carrying-on of such systematic and aggressive lines of work in organization, agitation, law enforcement and enactment, requires generous financial support, and this is provided for in the fourth department of our work, the " Financial Department." . This home-mission work is made one of the regular benevolences of all our churches. We raised in Ohio in 1894 eight thousand dollars, in 1895 twenty-four thousand, and in 1896 over thirty thousand dollars for a year's work in one State. The Michigan League will raise the first year over ten thousand dollars. This provides for the employment of reputable, scholarly, college-bred men to carry on the work. This missionary enterprise will not run itself. That was an intelligent Yankee who said he " had never seen anything run itself exceptin' something that was running down hill! " Of the fourteen field men engaged in Ohio last year nine were ministers, called from the pastorate to this church temperance work. Twenty-two persons were employed to give their whole time in the headquarters' offices and the field.

The results thus far of this church combination and activity are most encouraging. The Liquor League has given every evidence of apprehension and alarm. Public sentiment has been quickened to a point never before known. It is more unpopular to drink alcohol and more disgraceful to keep a saloon than ever before. It follows that the laws upon the question are better enforced than they have ever been. The last two Legislatures have been induced to pass four laws in the interest of temperance. On the other hand, although the liquor-dealers have introduced eleven bills, not a single one has been enacted into law. As to the reduction of the number of saloons, a surprising record has been made. Before our league began business the saloons increased in number from 1888 to 1893 at the rate of 468 a year, upon the average, or over twenty-three hundred in the aggregate. In the past four years, since the beginning of our work, the increase of saloons has been stopped, and the number actually reduced to the extent of more than twenty-six hundred rum-shops in the State. Allowing a frontage of twenty-five feet to each saloon, over thirteen miles solid frontage has thus been closed by this alliance of Christian Endeavor *versus* the saloon. Further organization is now being made elsewhere through the American Anti-Saloon League. Already sixteen States have leagues auxiliary to the American League. Permit me to urge you to take part earnestly in this permanent campaign in your locality, as you have opportunity. And if no opportunity presents itself, seek out the opportunity.

I can think of no better way, in closing, to stir you to earnest activity in the field of reform than to tell you very briefly why I am in earnest, and why I think you should be. I have no testimony to give of personal rescue from this habit, but I know what it means to look upon the face of a near and dear friend who lost his life in the darkness and the storm of a winter's night, frozen to death on the way home from a saloon. Then for fifteen years I encouraged and helped my dear brother to make the fight against an inherited love for liquor, that most imperious demon of appetite which rules the human body, ever lashing its victim on toward self-destruction, and all those anxious years I was asking, "Why must these man-traps stand along the streets to tempt in the erring feet of my brother again?" But my brother was no dearer than thousands of brothers and husbands and sons wrecked to-night upon these Christian shores. Then, as a pastor, I saw the horrors of the saloon in tragedy succeeding tragedy. Glance at one or two scenes and you will be ready to go out with me to battle. An aged mother met me at the door in the Armour flats. She could not speak for some moments, but silently led me in to look upon the face of her boy. Not twenty-one yet. A fair face, from which rum had not yet had time to daub out the nobility his mother had stamped upon it. Brokenly she told me how he had come from New York State to Chicago to a good position. "He was going to make a home for me, in my old age," she said; but he was stabbed in a saloon brawl on a Sunday afternoon, and yesterday he had died in the hospital. He was the only son of his mother, and she was a widow. One more scene. A wife dead this time. The neighbors have brought the flowers and tidied the home, for she was a noble woman. Her husband used to be kind, but the saloon transformed and embruted him. He beat his wife fiendishly, as she lay in bed, because she could not rise to minister to his wants—a new-born babe by her side. The doctor came and found her feverish, and wrote a hasty prescription. "Get this medicine quickly!" "I have no money," said the man. "Here is money," said the doctor; "you must hurry and bring it!" He turned into the nearest saloon and drank to stupor with the money. The doctor said the poor woman lost her life for lack of the medicine. And on the day of the funeral there were gathered the seven weeping children, and where was the husband? He lay dead drunk upon the floor in the back room of the house. And I made my vow to fight this archdemon to the uttermost. Will you not vow likewise? I beg you one and all to gather close about me to-night and let us covenant together, as did the brave clans of old. Let us revive that oath, with a change of a word or two, which William Lloyd Garrison wrote and printed in the first copy of his "Liberator." And let us take it and make it to-night our solemn and mutual declaration, and then let us forward together upon the united, persistent, and, please God, victorious conflict of Christian Endeavor against the saloon: —

> " I swear, while life-blood warms my throbbing veins,
>   Still to oppose and thwart, with heart and hand,
> Rum's desolating sway, till grog-shop chains
>   Are burst, and Freedom rules the rescued land,
> Trampling oppression and his iron rod:
> Such is the vow I take, so help me God!"

After this address Miss Josephine Patterson and Robert Husband sang " Saved by Grace."

The banner for the best progress during the year in promoting Christian citizenship was fittingly presented at this time, Rev. Howard B. Grose of *The Watchman*, Boston, making the address. The banner had previously been held by the Cleveland City Union.

Speech of Presentation for Christian Citizenship, by Rev. H. B. Grose, Boston.

Mr. Chairman : — Since Mr. Lumbar, who was to have presented the banner, has altogether lost his voice, I, who soon shall lose the rest of mine, have been called upon to take his place. I do it with exceeding great pleasure.

The best Christian is the best citizen. Christian citizenship is one of the latest developments of Christian Endeavor. Christian Endeavor has led from one discovery to another. First, the young people discovered themselves; that was one of the greatest discoveries of this nineteenth century, which is remarkable for discovery. And second, the Church discovered the young people. Then, of course, since the young people found themselves, they found out that they had duties and responsibilities. And so it has come to pass that a great many other people have found out that Christian Endeavor is here. The railroad men have found it out; they are trying to get the rest of it here. The hotel men have found it out, and the waiters at our hotels have found it out, though we have not always found them out. But, better than that, the saloon law-breakers have found it out, and the Sunday desecraters have found it out and are finding it out, and have found out that Christian Endeavor is here and that it is here for business.

Now, there is one thing that is not here, and that is the banner. It came very near happening that I was to present a banner that was not here to a representative that was not here, but the representative fortunately is here, and, metaphorically at least, will receive the banner. The banner is in a trunk, and the trunk is where most of your trunks are, and if you know where that is, I wish you would tell me.

Now, I am especially glad to present this banner to-night to Indianapolis, the city of Indiana that takes it from Cleveland-by-the-Lake, in Ohio, that takes ·it because of the practical work that has been done; and if any one doubts the practical character of the Christian citizenship of Christian Endeavor, just listen while I tell you in a word what the Indianapolis Union has done. In the first place, it took up the question of Sunday baseball. Baseball in Indianapolis on Sunday was a new proposition, and the Christian Endeavorers said it should not be. And although all the influence that could be brought to bear was brought to bear by those who had fitted up a park for this kind of amusement, the movement was defeated by the Indianapolis Union. They moved upon the sheriff until he felt compelled to arrest the players or stop the game, and they gave up in disgust. Then these Sunday desecraters went into the Legislature in the winter, and, backed up by the influence of the most influential newspaper in the State of Indiana, sought to carry through a bill permitting ball to be played on Sunday. The Christian Endeavorers went to work and obtained 17,000 signatures in opposition, and these signatures carried a weight with them that defeated the bill.

They say they can't do anything! They did do it. Then they went to the primaries. They gave notice to their members in the various societies of the day when the primaries were to be held, and laid upon them the obligations of their Christian citizenship. Then they took up the question of obscene literature, and if you only knew some of the shocking details of the spread of obscene literature in this land of ours, and the work it is doing, you would see that it is high time that somebody took up this matter. They practically took up one of their newsdealers who was selling this kind of literature, and he does n't sell it any more.

Then they took up the saloon campaign, and they made their investigations wisely and well, and found where a saloon-keeper had been selling liquor on Sunday, and they made it such expensive business for him that by the time he had paid $500 in fines and lawyers' fees, he decided to quit the Sunday selling. Then they took up the question of screens, and they have made them come to time on that.

This Indianapolis Union has proceeded practically in the line of Christian citizenship.

But in regard to this banner which I now hand to Mr. Buchanan, of the Indianapolis Union — well, we will see that he gets it.

Response for the Indianapolis City Union, by Mr. Buchanan.

We have met the enemy, and they are ours. By the "enemy," I do not mean the Good-Citizenship Committee of our sister city, Cleveland. I mean that we have a common foe, and the enemy that we have to down is Sunday baseball, Sunday saloons, Sunday theatres, a lax Mayor, and a wide-open town.

Now, I want to warn the citizens of Cleveland, Cincinnati, St. Louis, Louisville, and all the cities that surround us, that our gamblers have left town. There is a very fast train between Indianapolis and Cleveland, called the "Knickerbocker." We have an idea that they have gone over there, and that is what has swamped Cleveland. If they should visit Cincinnati, you would know them. They are a slick-looking set; they are slick citizens, but we were a little too much for them.

Now, we have restricted the saloon business, and that is one great object for which we have striven, and you may take encouragement from what we have done, because we have driven them out, and they will probably be with you to-morrow or the next day. But you will have to give them a warm reception, and they will leave you — and that is what we want them to do.

Dr. Coyle introduced as the second speaker upon the program, Rev. Cortland Myers, of Brooklyn, N. Y. Mr. Myers's subject was "Christian Endeavor and Civic Righteousness." It was vigorous and patriotic.

Address by Rev. Cortland Myers, Brooklyn, N. Y.

The best Christian in America should be the best American. The best American should be the man who believes in the citizen, and in the citizen's country, and in the citizen's country for Christ. The strength of the Republic depends on the individual. The citizen king must hold his own sceptre and swing it from that throne which rests upon the eternal granite of right. This hour calls for strongest emphasis to be given to the responsibilities and the rights of American citizens. The machine may drive men out of factories, but it shall never drive them out of our politics. That is death to the principles of your government. If one man grasps ten thousand sceptres in his hand and swings them above slaves from whom he seized them, he ought to be sent to the penitentiary instead of the United States Senate. It is a dark day in this land when machines take the place of men. They ought to be smashed with a thunderbolt from Sinai or an earthquake from Calvary. Every citizen must be king, or Republican institutions have lost their prosperity and perpetuity. The patriot bears his own responsibility and bears it all the time. Patriotism is not only the willingness to fight and die for one's country. It is also the willingness to live for the country. The husband may fight ruffians who attack the wife at his side, but that is only an accidental part of his relation to her. He loves her to live for her. A man can be just as patriotic at the ballot-box as upon the battlefield. He who runs away from his duty at the polls ought to be branded as a traitor. He should be imprisoned on Decoration Day and Fourth of July. It ought to be a criminal offence on his part to sing "My Country, 'tis of Thee." The individual citizen holds the future of America in his grasp. May he never relinquish his grip for politician, or policy, or party. Principle should be ever the ruling force.

"God, give us men; a time like this demands
Strong minds, great hearts, true faith, and ready hands.
Men whom the lust of office does not kill;
Men whom the spoils of office cannot buy;
Men who possess opinions and a will;
Men who have honor, men who will not lie;
Men who can stand before a demagogue
And scorn his treacherous flatteries without winking;
Tall men, sun-crowned, who live above the fog
In public duty and in private thinking.
For while the rabble, with their thumb-worn creeds,
Their loud profession, and their little deeds,
Mingle in selfish strife — lo!
Freedom weeps, Wrong rules the land, and waiting Justice sleeps."

That splendid Jew, Nehemiah, in his sublime patriotism said, "I will not hearken to Sauballat," "The Boss," or Geshen, "The Ward Politician." But so do not I because of the fear of God. American walls will be rebuilt and made immovable and glorious before all earth only when that same stone-and-mortar spirit is used. That conquered all enemies of your ancestors. The profound belief in the citizen won their hard battles. Pilgrims and Puritans came for that and fought for that. That was the conviction behind the sword and the pen. It was the hand of citizen kings which moved across that immortal document, the Declaration of Independence. The same hands rested upon muskets at Lexington and Bunker Hill. Every boy in blue realized the meaning of citizenship and was pushed by his personal responsibility into the thunders of a Wilderness and Gettysburg and Lookout Mountain. Married to this responsibility of the citizen is his rights. Something is demanded of him, but he demands something in return. I am convinced that our method of increasing the recognition of obligation is by the recognition of rights. If the American is assured that the Stars and Stripes will protect him wherever he stands upon this planet, his loyalty to that flag will be assured. If he can be starved and imprisoned and killed in Cuba or any other place the strength of citizenship is weakened at home. He ought to be protected by every gunboat in the navy and every rifle in the land. In heaven's name give him his rights if you would give him his duty. England sent an army across a sandy desert and seven hundred miles inland, at an expense of twenty-five millions of dollars, to take one English citizen out of an Abyssinian dungeon. Do you wonder at British loyalty in the heart and life of an Englishman? It is born in the spirit of his country. The son is born of such a mother. If that is true in England, it ought to be a thousand times more true in the land where every citizen is a king. Believe in the citizen; it is a part of your Christianity as well as your patriotism. Righteousness in politics begins here. The best American believes also in the citizens' country. For him this is the best nation in the world. If any other is better, life is too short for him to stay here an hour; he ought to live in the best land. God speed him to the other side of the sea! An Irish-American ought to live in Ireland. A German-American ought to live in Germany. Cursed be the lips which speak of the "Irish vote," or the "German vote," or "Italian vote," and the "Chimpanzee vote." This land of liberty, of public schools, of ballot-box, of government of the people and for the people and by the people, has only one name. It stands alone under heaven's light, and by citizen kings will be kept spotless.

If the Statue of Liberty in New York harbor could speak, it would continually utter one word for all the oppressed of Europe to hear: "Welcome! welcome! welcome!" There is room for all who come to be loyal to our institutions, but there is not one square inch of room for any other man, woman, or child. America shall forever be first to the dwellers of our country. At a great dinner on the other side of the Atlantic sat Benjamin Franklin between an Englishman and a Frenchman. Some one proposed that they each give a toast to their own country. The Englishman arose and said with all possible assurance of greatness, "Here is to England, the sun in the sky, around which the world revolves." The Frenchman next responded, and said, "Here is to France, the moon in the sky, which moves the tides of the world." Then our own Franklin shook himself like a lion, and true to himself and his beloved country, said, "Here is to George Washington, the Joshua of America, who commanded the sun and the moon to stand still and they stood still." That is the patriotic material out of which every American should be fashioned. Believe in the principles of this great republic as the best for yourself and for all men. Believe that they come from Christ and this land of their home shall be given to him. America for the Christ, and that may mean the world for him. This is the centre now of the greatest movements in the kingdom of God, and the power emanating from this western world is destined to increase as the years move on. Any Christian whose eyes are open to see the relation of this land to the world will be a most loyal citizen, and will work hand in hand with every movement toward political righteousness, which means also

PRESIDENT CLARK ADDRESSING AN IMPROMPTU GOSPEL MEETING AT RAILROAD STATION EN ROUTE TO CONVENTION

A SAMPLE OF THE WAY MANY OF THE MERCHANTS DECORATED THEIR BUILDINGS.

the establishment of the kingdom of God. The Ten Commandments and the Golden Rule and the Sermon on the Mount are not out of American politics, and they never shall be, but rather increase their force everywhere. The Christian has a large political duty, just for the sake of Christianity. It is a part of his business as much as the worship on Sunday is a part of his Christian service. In the casting of a ballot, or any other patriotic act, there may be the highest worship. If there is to be righteousness in politics, it is our duty to bring it to pass. That is a part of the great commission and every other command of Jesus Christ, " Go ye into politics and preach the Gospel." Drive out the demagogue with the Decalogue. Give Christ his throne on our soil. He made it. He redeemed it. He cares for it. It shall be his. From Atlantic to Pacific, from Gulf to Lake, it shall be forever his. The Christian citizen carries in his heart this motto: " AMERICA FOR CHRIST."

After the benediction by Rev. Dr. Laverty, of Los Angeles, the Convention adjourned.

Overflow Meetings Outside Mechanics' Pavilion.

Several thousand people who were unable to gain admittance either to the Mechanics' Pavilion or to the overflow meeting in Odd Fellows' Hall were addressed in front of the main entrance of the Mechanics' Pavilion by Rev. J. C. Ohrum, one of the prominent members of the Seattle delegation. It was a large and enthusiastic audience, and the meeting continued until 9.30 o'clock. A number of the chorus in the Mechanics' Pavilion were assigned to duty at this overflow meeting, and entertained the gathering with a number of Endeavor hymns.

Odd Fellows' Hall.

Odd Fellows' Hall was utilized for the first time last night to accommodate the overflow from the big meetings in the pavilions. It was filled with Endeavorers and their friends, who listened to well-known speakers, who took for their theme, " The World for Christ." Rev. Warren P. Landers, of Middletown, Mass., was chairman. The stage was decorated effectively with the Endeavor colors, which were also draped from the balconies and in the vestibule.

Rev. C. A. Dickinson, D.D., of Boston, spoke of his long acquaintance with Dr. Clark and the early history of the movement. He contrasted in an effective way the present position of a boy in the church and that which he himself occupied when he desired to become a Christian.

Bishop B. W. Arnett, D.D., of Ohio, followed. He said in part: " As Christian Endeavorers, we are interested in everything which is for the promotion of the cause of Christ throughout the world. Our society lays great stress upon the interdependence of man. God has nowhere in his great empire an independent man or an independent angel. All form a part of a mysterious whole, from the smallest atom that dances in the sunbeam to the tallest archangel that flames in the presence of the Almighty.

"You and I are children of a common parent, responsible each to the other for the welfare of the common family. Help'ng each other

— that is Christian Endeavor. This spirit is the great unifier of the church.

The last speaker was Rev. H. H. Russell, LL.D., of Columbus, Ohio. Dr. Russell easily held his audience while he explained the practical workings and necessity for the Anti-Saloon League.

The singing was spirited and the whole effect of the meeting uplifting.

FRIDAY MORNING, JULY 9.

Mechanics' Pavilion.

THE third session of the Convention opened with a large attendance. Enthusiasm was at all times present. At 9.30 the praise service began, under the leadership of Mr. Robert Husband, of San Francisco. The presiding officer was Mr. H. J. McCoy, general secretary of the Young Men's Christian Association of San Francisco.

In opening the session, Mr. McCoy referred to his first coming to San Francisco, sixteen years before, and said : —

" Since that time, the young Christian workers of this great city have been instrumental in erecting the handsomest building of its kind in the West. It is a mistake to think there are no Christian young men in San Francisco. The city is full of them, and more are coming into the fold each day." The morning's devotional exercises were conducted by Rev. W. K. Spencer, of Adrian, Michigan. He read Psalm 122, and offered prayer.

Under " Aggressive Work," the first speaker introduced was Mr. George W. Coleman, of *The Golden Rule*, Boston, who spoke upon " The Intermediate Society of Christian Endeavor."

Address of Mr. George W. Coleman, Boston, Mass.

Did you ever look at the patent marks on a Bell telephone, or a Pullman car, or any other like marvelous creation of these modern days? Well, you found recorded there a series of patents, with various dates. Every great invention has its subsidiary improvements. The Intermediate Society is not a new invention, but simply an improvement added to the Christian Endeavor movement, the greatest invention of the age in the realm of applied spiritual dynamics. Dr. Clark deserves a place by the side of Sancho Panza's hero who invented sleep, for neither of them were so selfish as to patent their invention.

The Intermediate Society is simply a device for stopping a leak and thus saving a great waste of force. There is a mighty waste in all the affairs of every-day life. From the coal to the steam, and from the steam to the power applied, more than half of the initial energy is lost. Think of all the running streams that drive no wheels. Think of the mighty rise and fall of the tide twice every day, a matchless display of unused force. There is leakage and waste on all sides. The problem is everywhere to reduce this leakage and waste to a minimum. There is need of the same watchfulness in conserving the forces of the church.

From the earliest days since little children were first welcomed into the church, it has been an ever-growing problem how to so lead their lives that their footsteps might never be turned from the paths of peace and righteousness. Thank God, Christian Endeavor has come to solve that problem, and now the Intermediate Society can be applied to stop the last great leak.

Everywhere the cry has gone up, How shall we keep our young men in the Sunday-school and the church? A very bright New England pastor thus tersely expressed what every lover of the church has many times had pressed home upon his heart and mind, as he contemplated the picture of any given church. " The danger line in the church," said this pastor, " is where the bald head touches the beardless chin." Here is where there has been and still is a tremendous leakage in the forces of the church. By the grace of God, and through a proper understanding of his revealed Word, we have opened wide the doors of the church to the little ones, and have established spiritual nurseries for their nurture and care; but what shall be done with those who have ceased to be children but are not yet men and women, the girls and boys between fourteen and eighteen?

There is nothing peculiarly distinctive about the Intermediate Society, except in the age limits. If you will read the model constitution of an Intermediate Society, published at Christian Endeavor Headquarters, you will find it practically the same as the regular Y. P. S. C. E., except that, if desired, a superintendent may be appointed by the pastor or the church, who shall have general charge of the work of the society. The pledge is essentially the same; the consecration meeting and committee work are identical.

I think it was Rev. A. Z. Conrad, of Worcester, who first discovered the value of an Intermediate Society. Dr. Dickinson, of the Board of Trustees of the United Society, has long had a flourishing society in his church, and both of these pastors, with many others, are earnest advocates of the idea.

The need of an Intermediate Society makes itself most strongly felt in a large church, where there are 200 or more young people. There, it is plainly manifest that young people between fourteen and eighteen are out of place in the Junior Society, and yet not mature enough to take their place with advantage to themselves in the regular Y. P. S. C. E., where the ages run from twenty to thirty and older.

The Intermediate Society affords just the opportunity for the continuous and natural development of these young Christians. They are not held back in their development by the presence of a lot of little children, and they do not suffer the natural embarrassment and repression incident to contact with a large company of older people.

It would be quite as reasonable to jump a boy or girl from the Primary to the High School as it would in many churches to plunge a Junior Endeavorer into membership in the regular C. E.

But there is another very emphatic reason why the Intermediate Society should be established, fostered, and maintained. I have previously in my talk spoken only of the immense advantage to the church in saving to itself the lives of these young people who might otherwise drift into indifference and inactivity. But there is another side to it. Suppose these young people were simply lost to the church for four or five years, and then by some miracle of grace returned to the active church life to pick up the threads that had been laid down years before. What think you would be the difference between that set of children, with their four or five years of coldness and inactivity, and another set who knew no interruption in their service for Christ, but who had steadily followed the Master, growing in grace and wisdom from day to day from earliest infancy to ripe manhood and womanhood?

The world has long understood the power of cumulative force as manifested in the continually accelerating speed of a falling body. To-day business men appreciate the cumulative force of constantly repeated advertisements. And now we are beginning to apply this same cumulative force to the Christian life by that tremendous power called "habit," so long associated with the devil and his imps. Now we know our destiny is not our fate, but is to be worked out on this line. As Thackeray expresses it, " Sow a thought and you'll reap an act; sow an act and you'll reap a habit; sow a habit and you'll reap a character; sow a character and you'll reap a destiny." This is the cumulative power which Christian Endeavor has brought to the church.

The child in his progress from the Junior Society to the Intermediate, and from that to the regular C. E., finally reaches the point where, with all the power of a tremendously accumulated force, he is ready for membership and active services in the Senior Society, which is the church itself.

Can we afford to slacken or omit the training of the Christian life at any period? If we do, the church will lose many of the young men and women who would have been its strongest supporters, and these same young people, though Christians nominally, will have missed the effect of that wonderfully accumulative power in their training, and will ever after be the weaker for it. Let the Intermediate Society come in and stop this waste and save these young people from an early grave in the backsliding cemetery.

Look at the process of education that is requisite to-day to turn out the best-trained and best-equipped minds,— kindergarten, primary, grammar, high, college, and professional schools. There is no missing link in that chain. Shall we do less for the training of the Christian life of our young people, who to-day are but children learning the way of life, but who to-morrow are the bone and sinew of the great nation, through whom we hope to win the world for Christ?

" Christian Endeavor Extension in Country Districts," was the subject upon which Rev. Joseph W. Cochran, of Madison, Wisconsin, spoke.

Address by Rev. J. W. Cochran, Madison, Wisconsin.

Mr. Chairman and Fellow Endeavorers:— I presume Mr. Baer asked me to talk upon this theme for a few minutes because he wanted a brawny farmer to represent Endeavor extension in country districts.

It was a few years ago, in Los Angeles, in a Christian Endeavor meeting, that while the meeting was quietly progressing, a man who had become notorious as an interrupter of Sunday services arose and cried out vociferously, " I don't believe in Christian Endeavor; I don't believe in endeavorin' at all. I believe in a 'git there society.' We all felt shocked at the time, but enclosed in that crazy setting was there not a gem of truest wisdom? A "get there " society — endeavoring to accomplish. Getting somewhere. Beginning at Jerusalem but not staying there. That is the kind of a society we want for Endeavor extension in country districts.

Perhaps some of you will see a picture in this of some of your own district conventions. The secretary reads a list of silent partners. One-third to one-half the society is not represented. Then follows an earnest discussion as to how can we interest them? Some one suggests that a great many of the societies have already disbanded. This reflects upon the corresponding secretary, and she is very sorry. Then some one suggests that there are a number of isolated unions in the country districts that are only waiting to hear the summons, "Child, disband." And so fervent speeches are made upon the necessity of doing something. In desperation a Lookout Committee is appointed. It meets for perhaps ten minutes and then disbands for the year. The chairman of the committee writes a few letters to the discouraged, urging them to cheer up, and to be sure and send in their money. The members of the committee are waiting for the chairman to do something. He tries to do all the work, which of course is impossible, and so the year rolls by without any practical results being accomplished, and this is followed by the same procedure in the next twelve months.

O beloved Endeavorers, this is disastrous — as much so in the spiritual as in the commercial world. It is spiritually penny-wise and pound-foolish to do this.

If we have not enough enthusiasm, if it is not long enough and strong enough to go out into the Macedonian byways, how shall God open up the way for larger missionary enterprise? The life blood of this nation is purified in the country. Farms are the lungs of the nation, and if the lung-power be weak, the whole body politic is weak.

When we realize that Christian Endeavor is one of the world movements of the age, and if so it must be found in all its freshness and strength in the vital portions of our national life, does it not behoove us to take care of the country districts and not put them off with the impromptu programs carried out by inefficient speakers? We should give them the best that we have, the truest hearts, the brainiest heads ; the best that the most energetic and cultured society in Boston can furnish is not too good for the poorest country district in the far West.

We are, I am afraid, sinning against the verdict of history by refusing to abide by the significant events in our nation's life, if we do not serve our country districts. The bravest and noblest souls that ever threw themselves into the thick of God's battles were those that came up from the country,—the little towns and villages, the farms. Some spirits are there given time to sink knee-deep in nature, to worship in the groves, — God's first temples,— to enter into the mysteries of up-springing life all about them — these are the spirits that can tell the rarest lessons to us who have been long in cities pent.

When God found time ripe in our day to set a fire blazing in the hearts of the youth, that might run around this wide world as the prairie-fire runs before the gale, he did not roll together the logs of the great city churches to make the fire, but he used the kindling that he found in one little rocky portion of the nation; and with the little twigs of Williston, he truly set the forests of Endeavor blazing.

And so we are to go home from this Convention and pay more attention to the twigs, and the stems, and the branches. We have been heaping high the fires of the altar for this great pillar of fire in this Convention. But we must not forget that there are those little twigs and branches waiting to be kindled as we have been kindled. And so we are to go to our district unions and prepare for them the best programs, the best speakers, sing the most rejoicing songs, and make those district unions chips off national and State conventions.

One thing that I feel is important is that we should look out for strategic points in the country, not wait for the district and State officers to organize. The machinery there is slow. The individual societies should go out into the field and work for the Master. Oh, how some of these societies have grown noted in our history, in Massachusetts, in Illinois, at Fort Atkinson, in New York, and in Wisconsin — these are the mother societies of whole scores of Endeavor chickens. The powerful Endeavor society that does not pay attention to the weaker society will soon have its own life snuffed out. I warrant you that the powerful society that does not have an interest in the smaller society dies down, down, down until the next missionary meeting. But the society that is enthused and alive with the missionary spirit, that is the society that has the best missionary meetings, because its interest is being constantly increased by what it does for the country districts.

Our United Society is ready to co-operate in this matter and to make each powerful society a mother of other societies by giving us free literature, giving us every opportunity of spreading the knowledge and principles of Christian Endeavor to those who know them not.

Bus-loads of Christian Endeavorers ought to go out into the neglected portions, hold their picnics and lawn conferences on Saturday afternoons, then leave their best leaders there for the Sunday meetings. Then there should be after that the training of leaders, leaders, leaders, the great need of this age.

Beloved Christian Endeavorers, the master weakness of our movement, it seems to me, is that after organizing these societies we leave them to linger and languish alone.

It reminds me of a tale that a fellow townsman of mine told me the other day. He located it in Wisconsin. He was telling about a tombstone he saw out in a Wisconsin cemetery. Perhaps he was straining his conscience, but he said he saw it. The engraver had been given instructions by the bereaved husband to put four certain lines on the stone. Perhaps the workman was in a brown study during the first three lines and a half, for when he came towards the end of the fourth line, he found that the stone had run out; there was no more room. The last line was to read, "Let her rest in peace." He simply put in the initials of the last three words, and it read, "Let her r. i. p." So it seems to me that is the motto that is graven on the tombstone of a defunct society to-day. But while we have endeavored to have them "rest in peace," we have really let them "r. i. p."

Some of the societies wax fat in idleness; some of the societies find their very life in this great movement of country extensions; some of the societies do not know what they are organized for. As I go through our State I am sometimes reminded of the Chinaman that was hacking away at a log of wood in China. A missionary came up to him and said, "What are you making?

What are you doing?" "Oh, don't know; maybe idol, maybe bedstead." We should know what we are living for, what our mission is.

Said an old salt to an old man who was drifting on a log on the outgoing tide, "How did you come to fall in?" The old gentleman replied, "I didn't come to fall in; I came to fish." We should know what we came for. We didn't come to fall into a rut of conventionality, or a pit of idleness. We came to fish for men's souls.

Now this is for State officers: Keep in touch with Sabbath-school missionaries by all means. Teach them the vital relationship between Sabbath school and Christian Endeavor Union. Furnish them with literature, and thus, without the expenditure of a single cent, you will have organizers in your district. Well and good.

And again, put on as your superintendent of evangelistic endeavor the most spiritual man in your State. Send him out every year with a corps of trained workers. An illustration of that to-day is Superintendent Buswell's campaign within the foreign districts of Milwaukee and vicinity, to which city we expect to welcome you in 1901.

In closing I would say, with the realization of the necessity, the cry in our ears of these neglected districts, and our hearts going out to those isolated ones, What is God's mission for us? What shall we do? Shall there not be some crystallization of this thought? And as I think of it, I see, perhaps in prophetic vision, after all the three hundred and sixty-five days of extension in country districts, one special day that we shall go out into the highways and byways, after canvassing all the needs of our neighborhood, and yonder one society would be strengthened in methods; yonder another strengthened in spiritual life; another told about missionary extension, and there yonder a society holding its meeting for the first time. Oh, what a blessed day that would be! What a glorious experience for many of you who have never tried it! What magnificent reports for "*The Golden Rule*" there would be.

I wonder whether we shall ever have an "Extension Day," in which we shall all leave our city unions and go out into the highways and byways? Let us pray, then, for the coming of "Extension Day."

But all these methods are futile and worse than nothing unless we have the Spirit's fulness—not by might nor by power, nor by method nor by mechanical devices, but by God's spirit; for Christian Endeavor is a life, not a machine; it is a growth, not a manufacture. Just, perhaps, as it has been with the Bible in your hands, you have felt the problems of life and destiny working slowly to the surface, and these questions have been answered: "Where am I? Where am I going?" So Christian Endeavor is great, not from some answer from some distant heavenly battlements, but because we have had our solemn, silent moments with God. Because away back sixteen years ago some one walked apart with God like Enoch — but, thank heaven, he has not been taken away from us yet.

So let us go on, with the spirit and with these methods, to claim the country districts "for Christ and the Church."

It was a pleasant surprise to the audience when Fong Sing, by special request, rendered "Christ Died for All." His voice, a deep, rich baritone, reached every nook and corner of the big building, and so delighted were the listeners that the great Chinese Christian worker was compelled to repeat the song. Rev. Gee Gam, another Celestial of more than ordinary repute, was formally introduced to the audience by Secretary Baer. The latter said that Mr. Gam would speak at the evening session, and that he had merely brought him forward at that time in order that the people might better know the man who had done so much for the cause of Christ. The famous Chinese, clad in the costume of his country, bowed twice to the great throng and then walked with dignified mien to his seat on the platform.

The second division in the thought of the morning was "The Essentials of a Model Christian Endeavor Society." The first address was very appropriately upon "The Pledge." This was forcefully presented by Rev. E. L. Powell, D.D., of Louisville, Ky.

Address by Rev. E. L. Powell, D.D., Louisville.

If the proof of the pudding is in the eating, then the worth of the pledge is established beyond peradventure. It has been tried and not found wanting. One was lamenting the materialistic tendency of the times to a painter, who replied, "The more materialistic science becomes, the more angels I shall paint." The best answer to all criticisms of the pledge is the pledge at work. If a man insists that the pledge is a failure, you can only give him the gospel invitation: "Come and see;" better still, "Come and try."

In the meantime, let there be no trifling with the pledge. It has surely passed its tentative period. It can now stand with the serene independence that comes from successful experience. Better, in this instance, at least, let "well enough" alone, since "well enough" meets all the requirements of a successful and useful society. Those who have tried to improve the pledge or adapt it to a lower spiritual condition than the pledge contemplates, have invariably met with failure. We must hold fast to the pledge in its integrity, for it is essential to the life of any Christian Endeavor Society. "In the lower division of the brain is the medulla, a cord about an inch in length, which connects the spine with the brain, and which is the most vital part of the whole system, for it is the centre which presides over the respiratory organs." Injury to this part means the stopping of respiration — and consequently immediate death. The pledge is the medulla of Christian Endeavor. When it is impaired, the breathing of the society ceases. It does not even go to sleep. It dies.

One is amazed at the wisdom displayed in the preparation of this pledge. It says just enough, and in just the right way. It avoids all controversial matters, and emphasizes only the essentials of Christian life; it has to do with practical Christianity, and avoids all speculation. It offers a basis for interdenominational fellowship, while insisting on denominational loyalty. It contemplates congregational co-operation, and yet makes paramount the duty of the local society to the local church; it is a binding pledge, but not made binding by human authority, the individual being answerable only to the Lord Jesus Christ; it proclaims freedom of conscience and life, but freedom within the limitations of love and loyalty; it lays down a few particular Christian duties, and then in the broad statement, "Whatever he would like to have me do," takes within its compass all of life; its details save it from infiniteness, and its principles are expansive enough for unlimited growth. It is like that magical and elastic tent which could be compressed within the limits of a walnut, and expand until it covered the king's army. To my mind, it is a model of wise and effective expression. I do not say it is perfect, but adequate to all the requirements of successful Christian Endeavor.

Christ is the centre and circumference of the pledge.

First, "I promise him." The pledge is not made to any man or society, and, therefore, no human court can hold you responsible for its breach or require its observance. It is a promise made to Christ, and to him you must give account. Before him, you stand or fall. Christ and your own soul are parties to this transaction. If you can offer an excuse for imperfectly keeping the pledge, that you are willing to give to him, the society has no jurisdiction in the matter. Your own conscience, in the solemn light of your promise to Christ, must approve or condemn. There can be no inquisitorial or impertinent interference in this covenant between the individual and Christ. The constraining thought is that you are pledged to Christ, and if that does not keep you loyal, no penalties can. Every promise is sacred, but a promise made to him whose promises are "Yea" and "Amen" should be kept with an unfaltering allegiance. In the presence of men and angels, with a mighty cloud of unseen witnesses looking upon us, this promise is made. To write it in blood could not make it more sacred.

Second, you are to keep this pledge in his strength. "Trusting in the the Lord Jesus Christ for strength." The strength which comes from Jesus is life. He strengthens from within and not from without. It is the difference between the tree standing erect, because of the life that courses through its trunk, and the tottering wall supported by means of external pressure. The one is strong in the strength of an unseen power; the other is kept from collapse only so long as it is buttressed. It is the difference between the law and the gospel, the one seeking allegiance through command and penalty, the other through the impartation of life, renewing the heart, and strengthening the will. Jesus offers unto us life, and it is in the strength of this life we are made able to keep the pledge. If we rely on the strength of our resolution, or the force of habit, or even on the solemn obligation of a promise, we shall fail. We are trying to support the wall with external props and stays. The sick man may resolve to walk, and may make his way for a little distance with crutches, but he can never run without weariness, or walk without fainting, until life tingles in every vein and artery of a sound body. Let the life of Jesus Christ flow into you until you shall be able to say, "I can do all things through him who strengthens me."

> "'Tis life whereof our nerves are scant ;
> More life, and fuller, then, we want."

And keeping the pledge thus in the strength of life — the strength which comes from Christ — we have liberty. The pledge is not kept under a sense of restraint, but because it is the inclination of spiritual life thus to express itself. It is the principle taught by the very familiar story of Ulysses and Orpheus in passing the Isle of the Sirens. Not by means of resolutions or regulations shall we be enabled to keep the pledge. But let us once be filled with the life of Christ, — let us hear its throbbing music beating in our souls, — and the "thongs" will not be necessary. The higher music has set us free from the necessity of external restraint. Be filled with the life of Christ, and do as you please; for you can but please to do the things he would like to have you do.

Third, you are to seek his approval in the keeping of the pledge: "Whatever he would like to have me do." It is one thing to do a duty because commanded; it is quite another thing to do it with the view of winning the approval of one whom you love. In the one case there may be only the recognition of statutory enactment; in the other case, there is the recompense of a person whose favor you earnestly desire. The one is the obedience of the slave who fears penalty; the other is the obedience of a loving son, who is seeking a smile. "What would Jesus like to have me do?" is the question of one who feels the sentiment,

> " Nor is there aught more fair
> Than is the smile upon his face."

It is told of a Frenchman who fought in the Napoleonic wars, that on every battle-field, when tempted to play the coward, or to shirk duty, he whispered the magical word, " Francais," and then pressed on to victory. "What would my country like to have me do ? " was his inspiration. So when you are tempted to neglect any duty mentioned in the pledge, when you feel like giving up and going back whisper " Jesus," that sweetest name on mortal tongue, and lo! you shall be strong again. " What would Jesus like to have me do ? " is a question the very asking of which will give us new courage when we are disheartened, and new strength when we are weak.

And it is the doing of what he would like to have us do that will save us from all trouble as to the things he would not like to have us do. Said a passenger to a pilot 'of thirty years, " You must know every rock and bar and shoal on the whole coast." " No, I don't, by a long ways," said the pilot, "but I know where the deep water is." What Jesus would like to have us do is sail in the deep-water channel. Keep in the deep water, and the rocks and bars and shoals — the things we should not do — will never vex us. We shall sail right onward in the current of duty and safety.

Finally, the pledge is a stereotyped reminder of our Christian obligations. It is true that the pledge requires nothing more than is involved in our primary acceptance of Christ, but that surely is no objection to the pledge. Can it be hurtful to make explicit that which is implicitly declared by us in our original acceptance of Christ? Can it be harmful to crystallize that which our confession of Christ holds in solution? Is it dangerous to stereotype a conceded duty that thus the duty may be made plainer and more emphatic? The pledge is simply putting in black and white certain known Christian obligations — the making of them visible, that we may constantly be reminded of them. It sustains to our Christian vows the relation which the wedding-ring does to our marriage vows. One may be married without the wedding-ring, but the ring simply emphasizes the vows of love and is an ever-present reminder of those vows. So the pledge is a constant reminder of the soul's vows to Christ. It speaks to us from the walls of our churches; it confronts us on our prayer-meeting cards; it looks upon us from the pages of our Christian Endeavor journals. It says to us in language we may read, in our native tongue, in simple words that a child may understand, " This is what your acceptance of Christ means; this, in brief, is your original obligation put before you in definite form. Read, and remember, and act."

What a gloriously successful Christian life the keeping of this pledge would make ! The world then will take knowledge of us truly that we have been with Jesus.

After a selection by the Knickerbocker Quartet, the chairman introduced Rev. W. H. G. Temple, of Seattle, Washington. Mr. Temple's address was bright and pointed upon " Committee Work."

Address by Rev. W. H. G. Temple, Seattle, Washington.

If there is one thing that the Christian Endeavor Society has insisted upon all through these sixteen blessed years of its existence, it has been that Christianity is not a sentiment, but a service. While it has always been ready to look upon the beauty of what a man may be, it has demanded that he must measure the height of his being by the loyalty of his doing. There are some people who fancy that they can sing themselves away in Zion to everlasting bliss. I am afraid when they wake up, they may find it everlasting blister.

James the Just believed that, for he said that a dreamy faith that did not find anything to do was only waiting for a coffin and an undertaker. " Faith without works is dead," said James. Jesus himself emphasizes the fact when he said, " Not every man that saith unto me Lord, Lord, shall enter into the kingdom of heaven, but he that doeth the will of my father which is in heaven."

So when we come to talk about Christian Endeavor, we talk about something that has not only a heart to feel and a mind to plan, but hands and feet to execute a blessed service that shall put an additional crown upon the brow of the Master, for whose sake the work is done, and shall lift up some poor erring or lethargic spirit until there shall come new inspiration into his life, and he, like the worker, shall also find his duty

Christian Endeavor, then, is something so practical that it places before every single one some specific act. Hence the great committee work that has been given to these young societies to do.

What do I mean when I say Christianity is not a sentiment? I mean this. Let me show you how it is with us. We find ourselves all overburdened with sin. We look up into the face of God and expect to confront inexorable justice, but we find instead the sweetest smile that ever broke on a human soul in the face of that pardoning Father, and at once we turn from the darkness of conviction of sin into the light of reconciliation and communion. We are away up there, bathing in the light of God, and we are prone to think that that is religion. By and by Jesus, who was the most practical Master that ever set servants to work, comes to us and says, "Come, my child, here is a duty to perform. Go to work in the kingdom." And we look at the duty. Perhaps it is not one of those loud-mouthed duties that goes proclaiming the character and singing of the man who performs it. It may be a simple act of benevolence, an act of faith; something that does not invite us, something that will sting our pride, something that will take two or three or ten stories off our conceit. We look at it and we say, Is that Christianity? Then there comes to us a new vision, and we go at the simple duty and we throw all the intensity of our soul and all the ingenuity of our brain and all the skill of our hands into this little task, and we accomplish it. Then Jesus says, "Come up with me into the Mount of Transfiguration and see me through the eyes of service, in all the glory of my kingly being." Then we get our first real view of Christ. And if, like Peter, we want to stay there in that spiritual contact all the time, we have a glow upon our faces that will not afterwards be noticed by the world. But if, like Moses, standing in the presence of God and getting his spiritual marching-orders, we go down the mountain-sides into the common walks of life to lead three million people through a desert into the promised land, our faces will glow so that everybody will know that we have been in communion with our Father.

What do I mean by a sentiment? A brook is a sentiment that finds its source somewhere among the brushy heights of the mountains, and comes tumbling and pirouetting and cascading down the mountain-sides, scattering its spray on the leafy banks, and then runs over its pebbled path into the level country until it becomes a river, and flows through the fertile valley until it finally comes to the sea. But turn that brook into a mill race, and let it go to work grinding corn and pushing ahead the industries of life, and your sentiment has become a service.

Sunshine, as it breaks over the hilltops and dances on the sea, is only a sentiment. But sunshine that warms up the roots of plants and makes them blossom more beautifully — that goes into the camera of a photographer and imprints the pictures of nature on the plates — is a service.

A thought may be as high as the clouds, as deep as the mountain gorge, as emblazoned as a California sunset; but if it has not harnessed itself to something, it is only a sentiment. But let it drop off the nibs of some transient pen, let it speak from the lips of a man on fire with some new reform, and your thought has become a service.

Oh, then, Christian Endeavor stands and begs that you look upon Christianity not as a thing of the mind, but as a thing of life; not as a theological creed, but as thorough service; not as faith in science, but as activity; not as a formulation, but as a following after Christ.

The great question has been, What shall we do with our boys and girls — especially the boys? I belong to that sex. I remember that once I was a boy. I have sympathy with every wide-awake, mischievous, tantalizing, lazy, shirking-off, irreproachable, irrepressible, irresistible, indefatigable kind of a boy. A girl always does just as she ought to do. When she is mad she pouts. When she is glad she smiles or sings. When she is in love she looks silly. But a boy, he laughs the hardest when it hurts the most. He breaks down and cries in almost agony in the ecstasy of joy. He will dilly-dally by the way when he knows that promptitude will nearly save a life that morning. He will go five miles to hunt up an excuse to stay at home. He will bribe his more worthy brother to do the thing his mother asked him to do, and then go to her and borrow the money to pay the bill. Oh, is there a contradiction under the sun like a boy?

Now, the most independent being on the face of the world is a growing boy. The most independent kind of a growing boy is an American growing boy. The most independent kind of an American growing boy is a Congregational American growing boy. (I belong to that denomination.) And the most independent kind of a Congregational American growing boy is *my* boy. I found it out years ago. I had to cope with his independence for years afterwards. And yet that boy found his chief joy in a Christian Endeavor prayer-meeting, and doing work on a Christian Endeavor committee.

If you want to save your boys from the devil in the world, set them to work. If you want to save your boys from the devil in the church, set them to work. Give them such an exalted view of their Master, of whom my brother has spoken so touchingly.

Have we any better illustration of what can be done in the way of committee work than in the Committee of '97 of this city? We came in by the Southern Pacific Railway to your State. We arrived at Bonicia, on the other side of the arm of the bay, and we found an advance guard of committeemen. When we came across to Port Costa, there was a whole bevy of them, and they gave us a California welcome as well as they could manage so big a thing. The ladies pinned button-hole bouquets on all the gentlemen. We received our instructions as to what to do when we got to the Oakland Ferry. There a detailed lot of young people came over with us and showed us what cars to take. One very attractive young lady even sat down alongside your humble servant in the street-car, and engaged his wearied mind in bright conversation until we arrived at the Baldwin Hotel, and then proceeded through the door just before him, so that he might not by mistake find his way into the theatre just below. Why, what this committee has not thought of is n't worth getting inside of a man's brain.

If my brother, Ira Landrith, of Nashville, Tennessee, who has been running a sort of tilt with me up in the Tacoma Convention, can only employ his big head and those associated with him half as successfully as this committee has, he will cover himself with glory. But that 's not Ira, not a bit of it! He intends to double it, just as sure as you are born.

Now, unless we can go into this committee work with a complete spirit of service, our work will become merely perfunctory; and after a young man becomes perfunctory, he generally becomes defunctory.

Once when I was sitting in my South Boston home trying to get through the second meal of the day, there was a fellow outside grinding away on one of those hurdygurdies. Why, if you young ladies who spend many hours practising runs, fearing to lose a note, could play those runs as skilfully as that man ground them out on the hurdygurdy, you would be wild with delight. And though we had " The Beautiful Blue Danube," the " Thousand and One Nights," and others of those splendid waltzes of Strauss,— I am speaking now from a musical standpoint, not from a religious one,— the whole thing was so mechanical from beginning to end that no girl would flatter herself if she put as little soul into her music. But let some person with the thought of music in his soul, find it growing and expanding until he has got to get rid of it through his finger-tips or burst, touch an instrument, and you will find that that spirit will by and by make a Verdi, a Rossini, a Schubert, or a Paderewski.

You can go into any store where pictures are sold and buy a glorious chromo for ten cents, with a splendid sunset on it, and a big tree over in the corner, and a purling brook running through it, with its perspective in mathematical correctness. But after you look at it you see it is only a chromo at best; it is only the product of machinery. But let some person with a thought of beauty in his soul develop that thought until he must seize the brush and put that beauty on the canvas, and then you will have a Turner with his glory on the sea of the sunset sky; and then you will have a Raphael portraying the face of the Christ. You must have the spirit in your soul before you can accomplish with your finger-tips. I suppose the phonograph is mechanically sufficient for any orator to use. But tell me, is oratory only distinct enunciation, only correct grammar, a mathematical figure? Unless there be a soul in the man to respond, there is no fire or life in the speech.

This spirit of service, then, must precede all else, or the work will be so mechanical that it will end by being entirely perfunctory. Above all in the committee work must stand the Prayer meeting Committee. The Prayer-meeting Committee stands for the soul of the society. There before God the society gets the power by which afterwards it will execute with glorious success. Oh, then, young people, no matter what prayer-meeting you may be in, whether it is that which is successful spiritually or socially, believe that all you may do must be done first of all as unto your God; then it will be best done for humanity.

Are you on the Lookout Committee? for we must always bring this thought back to the local society, to the local church. That is where the primary of all this movement is. We go back to the local society and say, "Are you on the Lookout Committee?" If you are, see to it that your desire is to bring into the society such as will be an ornament on the brow of your Christ, — not those half committed to the pledge, — so that when they come into the society, they will know the solemn responsibility of the vow they have taken.

If you are on the Social Committee, see that you are just as spiritual in your work there as on the Prayer-meeting Committee, or on the Lookout Committee. By the way, please remember that it is not always the meeting that goes the most glibly that shall leave the best impression. There was a young man in Seattle who belonged to a certain society. Said he the other night, " We had the grandest meeting to-night we ever had in the experience of our society. There was not a single second left vacant. Two or three people were on their feet continually." I said, "How is that?" "Oh," said he, "there was an old fellow in the meeting and we were told he was coming, and knew that if we gave him a chance to open his mouth he would never get through. So the young people headed him off." And that was the spirituality of the meeting.

If you are on the Social Committee, oh, do please give them a good social! Have an entertainment that the world won't laugh at. If there is any person or institution that ought to have the best thing there is on earth, it is the Christian and the church. Don't let the devil get the best music. Don't let the devil's people have the most interesting time. And when you have refreshments, have them of good quality, and enough to go around — don't let them be short, like our programs. The proverbial Christian Endeavor oyster stew, with the solitary oyster, an island in the middle of a great sea of juice, is not the kind for Christian Endeavorers to give.

I believe that to be honest is the biggest part of being spiritual.

If you are on the Good-Citizenship Committee, see to it that the young people have continuously put before them the duty of their citizenship, and the opportunity that every young person should have for being just and true to his country; but see to it that they get something to read on those subjects that will inform their minds, so that when they begin their duties in that line they will have some knowledge. See to it that all the people on the Missionary Committee will be served with about a ton of Allcock's porous plasters. You know what they are for — to draw the money out of the skinflints. Be sure to get the belladonna kind; they will soothe the patient while he is undergoing the process. No matter what you do, do everything as unto the Lord — whether you are in the Senior Society, or in that society that stands at the danger-point we have been told of this morning, where the bald head meets the beardless chin.

Let me turn quickly away from this that has been more or less jocular, and hold up to you the one great model. If you would be a Christian Endeavorer in very truth and deed, pattern after the One who came to this earth; One who was so beautiful that I do not believe any limner has been able to catch his features; and although all the great artists have given us sketches of what Jesus was, I believe we shall only see him in his glory when we see the King in his beauty. It was not the beauty, however, of Jesus that served the Lord. I remember One who came and spoke as never man spoke when he opened his lips; even the common people heard it gladly. So sweet was his message, so authoritative was his style, that he was at once contrasted with the Scribes and Pharisees that taught, but were never powerful in their teaching. And yet it was not oratory that brought Jesus to the world's heart. I see One standing among the crowds as they stood on the slope of Mount Hermon, and heard him utter that magnificent sermon. I see him walking all up and down the streets of Palestine, and wherever there was a distressed one or a downtrodden one, one with such a longing in his heart that nothing of earth could ever satisfy it, that Jesus, by the magnetism of his character, became all in all to his soul. Yet it was not magnetism that made Jesus powerful. He came to serve the world, to serve it with shining face and with parted lips in speech; he came to save it with his hands, all spiked and dripping with blood, and his feet, as they walked up that bloody hill of Calvary with a cross upon his shoulders that weighed him down, and upon which he poured out his life, saving the world with his life, saving the world in his death more gloriously still — serving the world to-day as he stands before the great white throne, presenting his hands and his feet, and by the meritorious, substitutional, vicarious sacrifice of his life and death, demands of justice that every sinner who believes in him shall enter the gates of eternal life, and every poor, faltering Christian shall be sent again on his way rejoicing toward the throne.

Follow him. He is your model. He is the one whom only you dare follow. Let this mind be in you that was also in Christ Jesus your Lord, who, though he was in the form of God, thought it not robbery to be equal with God. He made himself of no reputation; took upon him the form of a servant and the likeness of man, and being found in the fashion of a man, humbled himself and became obedient even unto the death of Christ. Therefore, God hath highly exalted him and given him a name which is above every name; that is the name of Jesus; every knee should bow, and things on earth, and the things in the heavens, and the things under the earth, and every tongue should confess that Jesus Christ is Lord, to the glory of God, the Father.

The Chinese quartette then sang, and Chairman McCoy presented Rev. Robert Johnston, of London, Ontario. His subject was the central one to the Endeavor prayer-meeting, "The Consecration Meeting." It was a suggestive address:

Address by Rev. Robert Johnston, London, Ontario.

It is heart power, rather than head power, that moves this world. Whitfield's mighty and magnetic influence did not lie in his thrilling oratory, nor in his marvelous voice, so much as it lay in his power of sympathy and love. It was because the great preacher's own soul wept for the souls of men that he made thousands around him weep under his piercing gospel utterances.

Henry Martyn, lying on the sands of India weeping over the lost millions of that land, was a greater power than when with his mighty intellect he led his English classes in the university. It is the power of heart, rather than power of head, that leads the great movements of the world.

Victor Hugo, the greatest novelist of the age, has told us the story of Jean Valjean, who, after suffering prison torture, cruelty, and everything that the law, in its cruelty, could inflict, finally escaping, found every door in the world shut against him, until even the door of the dog kennel was closed to him for a night's lodging. Then it was that he met a heart, a true heart, the soul of one man throbbing with sympathy for his lost fellow-creatures. And when the eyes of that good bishop looked into the heart of that poor convict, Jean Valjean, he was redeemed.

As it is in the individual, so it is in the society. The consecration meeting is called the heart of Christian Endeavor. To all that the first speaker in this part of this program said concerning the pledge, I say a hearty amen. To all that the second speaker said on committee work, I say likewise. But, as the body may still be a body, lacking the power of the backbone,— not a complete body, not a perfect body, but lacking the power of limb and the organs of speech and sight, still, behind all that, there may be a soul which will give the body a mighty influence in the world. We cannot do without the pledge, which is the backbone of the society, from which all of the structure is built up. We cannot do without the committees, which are the limbs and the organs of the society, that carry it into all the different departments of its aggressive work. But better can we do without these than we can do without the heart, which is the very centre and soul of all success. Without that, all pledges and all committees' work will be utter failure.

We are asking on all hands, — 10,000 Endeavorers are here to-day and coming to this Convention, who ask,—" Why is it we have not done greater work in the past year?" "Why is it we have not won the young men of our cities and of our land?" "Why is it that the Christian Endeavor Union, with its grand organizations and its splendid multitude of earnest hearts, has not taken fuller possession of the land for Christ?"

We are looking in wrong quarters for the answers to these questions. I volunteer to any that while we talk of poor equipments, poor methods, too many of us would fail to look at the spot where failure must begin, and where in nine cases out of ten the cause for failure rests — the heart of the society, the consecration meeting. If the consecration meeting is true, if the hearts are there, in sincerity and in earnestness made over to the disposal of Christ the King, then whatever our equipment, our numbers, our methods, success will be ours.

I wish to speak now simply of two things: first, its meaning; second, its mechanics. What is the meaning of the consecration meeting? Sixty years ago, a week or two past, our gracious Queen, a girl of eighteen, left her home and took her way to Westminster Abbey, whence so many sovereigns had preceded her, to be crowned. She was met by the multitudes, and presented to them as their rightful and legal sovereign. And as the Archbishop of Canterbury placed the crown on the girl's head, every peer and peeress doffed their coronets in token that the Queen had come; and then they advanced one by one, and spoke their words of allegiance: "I do become your liege man of life and limb and of earthly worship and faith, and truth I bear to you against all manner of foe, so to live and die." It was a handing-over of their possessions; a handing-over of themselves; a handing over of their loyalty to her whom they called their Queen.

So it seems to me the consecration meeting is the gathering where the hearts who know Christ Jesus come together, openly and publicly, to lay themselves at the disposal of their Lord.

Some of you are mothers, fathers, and in your home one day you will hear a little one say to another, "You must not touch that." "Why can't I touch that?" "It is father's; hands off. It doesn't belong to you; it is father's." Consecration is writing upon your heart and upon your life, " Christ's; hands off, the world, I am Christ's." What party do you belong to, Endeavorer? I want to see the party that I belong to. I want to see the party that can put hands on me, and that can use me. Do you belong to a church, and are you a thing that can be used by any power in the world? No; I am Christ's. His name is upon me. Life and limb and liberty and all that I am and have, Christ, are thine, to be used by thee. That is the meaning of the consecration meeting.

But, you say, Is not that done once for all? When consecration, as a real, genuine act, is completed, is it not finished? Is it not true that there is nothing more to do? Hamilcar led his boy Hannibal, when but eleven years of age, to the altar at Carthage, and there before the altar and shrine he made him swear eternal enmity to Rome, and Hannibal did it. But he did not do it once for all. Every sun that rose on the burned and bleeding cities of his land made him renew that vow to give his life for the destruction of Rome. And day by day, and year by year, as he saw more of what was to be done for the liberation of his land, as he learned more of the awful power of the greedy and gloating Rome, he repeated that vow, and reconsecrated himself to his life's work.

So, Christian Endeavorer, as you go forth, it may be that at your conversion you have given yourself wholly over to Christ; that you have said, "I am thine." But you get out into the world and find evils and temptations yet to be conquered. You find many things of which you were ignorant, and the Christian life is not a complete thing anywhere between the cross and the crown; but it is a growing and extending thing, and so, month by month, we come together, having learned more of ourselves, more of our brothers, more of the byways of this wicked world in which we live, and we give ourselves again to be Christ's, and his only, in every avenue of life; and wherever he is, his providence will reach us. Monthly, just as the key-note is struck on which the music is to be sung, just as the leader of the orchestra strikes the note and all the instruments take it up and carry it along, so the consecration meeting strikes the key-note of our lives, and we take it up and carry it on and on.

Now, what are the mechanics? It is impossible to try to tell you how and along what mechanical line a Christian Endeavor consecration meeting should be conducted. Just as different as are our places of abode, just as different as are our societies, so different must the methods be which we may use in our meetings. There are two principles which I believe there must be in every true consecration meeting First of all, we must magnify the pledge. I have known Christian Endeavorers to repeat that pledge, "Trusting in the Lord Jesus Christ for strength, I promise him to do whatsoever he would have me do," and I have known them to go away and live a life of seclusion. I have known Christian Endeavorers to come to their meeting and repeat that pledge, and then, with their ball-dresses on, and the gentlemen with their dancing-pumps, go away to the ballroom and dance until morning. And both of these thought they were real Christian Endeavorers.

Now, what I think that means is this: we must magnify that pledge; and not merely trusting him, *promise* to do, but *do*. It seems to me that the pledge is in our minds like a blurred picture on the screen, improperly focused. There it is; but what it is you do not know. One says one thing and one another. You must get the light focused on the screen. How are we to do that? Behind the pledge you must let the light of the life of Jesus Christ shine upon it. Let the light of the man, the ideal citizen, the ideal son, the ideal friend, the ideal Christian — let his light shine on the pledge, and in that light interpret it.

O leaders of consecrated meetings, hold up high the ideal of Christian life, and let it never settle one iota below the perfect life of Christ; that is the pattern for all.

The other thought is this: magnify the Spirit and give prominence to the remembrance of Jesus Christ. Oh the power of remembrance! The secret, the keyword, of consecration is in remembrance. The mightiest consecration meeting this world knows is in all our churches when, in obedience to the command of our Risen Lord, we gather around the communion-table, and there, in the token of his body and blood, we remember him, remember what he has done for us.

It was in a little village of Germany that Count Zinzendorf, a gay Lothario, saw that wonderful painting that sets forth the suffering of Jesus Christ; and underneath it he read, "All this I didst for thee. What hast thou done for me?" It was the sight of that that led him to the remembrance of Jesus Christ, and he said, "Thou hast done that for me. I give myself to thee."

And so, leaders of consecration meetings, do not make prominent your own view, do not look too much into your own life, but hold up the life of the blessed Christ, and as men and women look at that life, their souls may be brought to remember what he has done for them, and they in response will give themselves to him. "This do in remembrance of me."

As every monthly consecration meeting comes around, let us remember Christ, and, remembering him, let us give ourselves to his service.

It was only two weeks ago that we lit our bonfires around the world, from Vancouver's highest point to Florida; across the broad Atlantic, on every masthead that flung the Union Jack, we lit our triumph of joy; across the British Isles; across Europe, and on to Himalayan peaks and Hongkong; even across the Pacific, that washes your beautiful shores, we lit our fires in joy and gladness that a Queen who has sweetened girlhood, dignified wifehood, and glorified womanhood reigns over us. But listen! When the fires of consecration light up every Christian Endeavor meeting all around this great world, and from Alaska's snowy peaks down to Mexico's burning plains, all through South America and over every continent — when the fires of consecration and devotion and of whole-hearted surrender of ourselves to the living

CALIFORNIA'S MISSIONARY EXTENSION HEADQUARTERS IN THE MECHANICS' PAVILION.

ALAMEDA COUNTY'S SECTION OF CALIFORNIA'S HEADQUARTERS IN MECHANICS' PAVILION.

love of Christ are lit in every Christian Endeavor prayer-meeting, then shall we take up the shout of loyalty to Jesus Christ; and he upon whose head we shall place the crown, and under whose feet we shall lay out as a stepping-way both the cross of the Union Jack and the stars and stripes of your own brave flag — then Christ shall come and we shall crown him our only King.

"Oh that with yonder glorious throng "— aye, better than that —oh that here and now; oh that in these closing days of the nineteen century, by reason of the giving-over of ourselves to Christ; oh that here we might join the glorious throng and crown him, in this glad and beautiful world, here and now, ere we die, Lord, Lord of all.

After the benediction, by Bishop Arnett, the Convention adjourned until the evening session.

Woodward's Pavilion.

The vital questions that affect Christian work, more especially the departments of Christian Endeavor, were under consideration at the morning session in Woodward's Pavilion on Friday. Under the direction of Rev. Dr. Philputt, of Philadelphia, the "Open Parliament" was spirited and full of interest.

The choir, ushers, and the president, Rev. Dr. Clark, were promptly on hand. R. Powell Evans, of San Francisco, directed the musical features. Rev. E. J. Lyall, of Mellbrook, N. Y., led the responsive service from Ephesians vi. 11. A moment of silent prayer followed, including, at Dr. Clark's suggestion, supplications for the bereaved ones who sorrowed through the accidents *en route*, and then Rev. Samuel Dunham, of Binghamton, N. Y., voiced the desires of all before the throne of grace. "Loyalty to the Church " was the central theme of the session. The first address was upon "The Senior Society of Christian Endeavor," by Rev. Barton W. Perry, of San Leandro, Cal.

Address by Rev. Barton W. Perry, Ph.D., San Leandro, Cal.

For two or three years I have felt, with other Christian Endeavor workers, the need of something especially adapted to the older members. The Endeavor Society was designed to promote work among, and to build up the spiritual life of, the young people. The eldest of those who entered into Christian Endeavor work some twelve or fifteen years ago are somewhat like the Irish minister, when asked his age, who answered, "I can distinctly remember when I was younger." Many of these older members are inclined to become statesmen — I do not like to say politicians. They have conquered everything in sight at home — filled all the offices — and are now out to capture county and State positions. I do not say that this is wrong, but simply wish to point out a better work, a more excellent way. This excellent way is more love for our own church. Though we may speak with the tongues of men and angels at county and State conventions, and have not love for our own church, we have become as sounding brass or a tinkling cymbal. Christian Endeavor was organized for Christ and the church, and our own local church is the first and best place to honor the name of Christ.

I believe in unions and conventions; but the fountain source of all Christian Endeavor work is the local society in the local church. To increase the volume of this perennial fountain is the object of the Senior Society. Each new year we close up the history of the past, and turn over a new leaf. When a member of a Christian Endeavor Society arrives at the years of discretion — say about thirty, but the nature of the problem forbids exact days and dates —

then it is advisable to turn over a new leaf, and take up work in the Senior Department.

The first step to take is to consult with the pastor and church officers. While holding to the general plan of Christian Endeavor, which has been so successful these many years, there will be variety in the senior organization in order to conserve local interests. It is the design of the Senior Society to be vitally connected with the mid-week prayer-meeting. In large churches the organization will be simple — not much more than committees to increase the attendance and spontaneity of the regular prayer-meeting led by the pastor. In the average church the organization may be complete,—officers and committees, connection with County Union, regular Christian Endeavor topics, and with different leaders. The pastor, in his remarks, can introduce a new subject, if necessary.

This, in brief, is the plan. What will it do?

It has been said that each new society reduces the real work of the church, as a church. It is likened to an onion — peel off a layer here, and peel off a layer there, and keep on peeling until nothing is left. This is not true. Healthy societies make a healthy church. It is possible that the Senior Society may not work as beautifully as it may appear to do in print. Human nature is the same the world over. There are many who have mothered and fathered the Young People's Society for years who will object to going into the Senior Society. Will not such a one set his common-sense philosophy over against the instinct of the eagle when she pushes her eaglets out of the nest? The young people need exercise, and, like Jacob, to wrestle alone with God. Others are not willing to work in either society, and will take the change as an opportune time to withdraw. Wise workers will endeavor to show these how the blessing has been lost. A little boy was on his way home from church with his mother. The mother criticised the minister and his sermon. But the little fellow said, " Ma, you can't expect much for the cent you put in the box." If we put nothing into the Senior Society, we will get nothing out. The Endeavor work will die, as will any other live thing, if it is not fed. The nourishment is from the Holy Spirit pushing us out into good, honest, Christian work. This work is exemplified by the lives of Caleb and Joshua. We see them returning from that God-given work, searching in the promised land. They alone of the twelve were ready to go up and possess the land— in the face of the giants, of the walled cities, and many other difficulties. They failed, humanly speaking. But in the sight of God their work was a great success. They turned back with the rest of the children of Israel, and wandered in the wilderness forty years. At last these two, and only these, of all those who were seniors when they turned back, ever entered the promised land. Our duty is to follow the Lord. We may not see the success, as men count success, but if we are true to our God we will receive the " Well done, thou good and faithful servant."

Christian Endeavor is a force in the world, an engine. This force has been working as a Young People's Society for some time. A few years ago the Junior power was added. Now I am pleading for the Senior engine. In coming over the mountains your train took on two, sometimes three, engines. The Young People's Society has indeed been an engine hitched to the church. It has moved the church up into better work for our Master, not only in this land, but in all lands. This work was first taken up by those between the ages of fifteen and thirty. But the church must be pushed through and over the highest mountain of wickedness in this world. Then the Junior engine came in, puffing, whistling, and singing, and the church moved to a higher level. But there is another high peak to climb. We desire to see the average church-member lay aside all business cares and avocations on the night of the mid-week prayer-meeting, and to find a working-place in that meeting. The Senior Society is the new engine to furnish this power. I would hitch the Senior Society on behind to push, and hold the young people as the principal Endeavor Society of the church.

The mountains back of San Francisco Bay temper and change the course of the wind. The Senior Society will be a great factor to transform church members into mid-week prayer-meeting, mountain-top Christians. Each member of the Senior Society feels responsible for the meeting. Each is prepared with a definite topic for the study, and, like a prepared or moistened sponge that will quickly absorb water, will be in condition to absorb all the good things of the prayer-meeting. The Senior Society will help us to stand four-square to every wind that blows. Instead of being turned away from Christ by Sabbath desecration, beer saloons, and infidelity, we will turn these evils and drive them — foreign monsters that they are — out of this free American land.

Rev. Jacob W. Kapp, D.D., Richmond, Indiana, followed with an interesting address upon " Christian Endeavor and the Sunday Evening Service."

Address by Rev. J. W. Kapp, D.D., Richmond, Ind.

It may truly be said in many churches, with reference to the evening service, " To be or not to be, that is the question." Many pastors have seriously studied this subject with tears and prayers. I believe that if the young people will help the pastors to answer their prayers, it may be said, " As a prince thou hast power with God, and hast prevailed." In very desperation some pastors have said, " The young people's meeting is to blame for the lack of attendance at the evening service ; they attend their own meeting, but neglect the second service." If that can be truly said of any Christian Endeavor Society, it is the endeavor left out on Sabbath evening.

I recently heard of a pastor who abandoned his young people's meeting in the evening, hoping thereby to have a larger attendance at the second service. That was a denominational society, by the way. We are not going to cure the difficulty by putting aside the means to solve the problem, by disorganizing our forces. We, need, rather, to gather them together and work the more earnestly because of the difficulties before us.

Without question, in many of the churches of our land the evening service is a very difficult one to maintain ; indeed, here and there it has been abandoned entirely for lack of an audience. In many cases members of the church attend only the morning service. Old people and young married people think that one service a day is sufficient. And then there is a large number of non-church people who, for one cause or another, do not attend the morning service, but will attend the evening service. And it seems to me that because the evening service is especially adapted for the people who are not members of the church, it opens a great field for us as Christian Endeavorers to do missionary work. Whatever the cause may be, — and it is not my business to discuss that matter to-day, — it is undoubtedly true that there are a very great many people in all our communities and cities who have no idea of what is said or done in a church which is within easy reach of their home. They hear the invitation of the church bell Sabbath after Sabbath, but give no heed to it. And there comes to be more or less of a division between a certain class of people in every community and the church. This is a condition that every one of us laments, and a condition against which we must fight, and seek to bring the church constantly in contact with the people, that there may, not be a division or a separation. There never was a sterner piece of democracy than Christianity. It is not like the Pagan religion ; it withdraws from nothing, except it be from insincerity and from hypocrisy. We want to be in touch with the people. And because there is a large number of people who do not attend the service of the church at any other time than that of the evening service, it may be made especially adapted for that class of people, and it thereby opens a great missionary field for the Christian Endeavorers to go out and get people and bring them into that service.

A pastor of one of the prominent churches of Chicago says that if it were not for his Christian Endeavor Society he could not have an evening service at all. I am sure that many of the pastors could testify, if not every one of us, that because of the Christian Endeavor Society our evening audiences are very much larger than they would be without the society, and that many of us could not maintain the evening service at all if it were not for the Christian Endeavor Society.

If we are going to solve the problem, it is necessary that we should remember that it is a difficult one, and that there are some things we must understand. There is prejudice to remove, false notions about the church that have come into the minds of some people; we must put aside Sabbath desecration; we must work for the better preservation of the Sabbath, and incidentally this will be a great work in aid of the evening service. I am glad to learn that the California Endeavorers have done such good work in this direction. May you go on in your good work with continued success.

We need also to get rid of some false notions. We need to put aside the idea that the pastor alone is responsible for the success of the evening service. We must stop putting upon his shoulders the great burden of making a success of that service. In some churches the strength and popularity of the pastor is so great that the easy-going and self-indulgent Christian prays that God may bless the pastor in the second service, and enjoys himself quietly at home, relying upon the pastor's popularity to bring out the people, and so concerns himself but little about the evening meeting.

Very little success has been made in that line; but where there has been a pastor who was attractive and eloquent, if you study even such cases a little more closely, you will doubtless find out that these pastors have a consecrated band of workers who are ever active in going out and trying to reach the non-churchgoers, and persuade them to come in and hear the gospel. There are pastors who are able to fill every pew in the church, but the simple fact remains that God did not make enough of that kind of men to go around. I think it is an evidence of the wisdom of God that he did not do it. We need to stop seeking for men to fill our pulpits who draw the people because of their eloquence simply. The church needs to seek for men to fill the pulpits who are filled with the Holy Ghost, and those who are resolved to go to work and do their duty and bring the non-churchgoing to the second service. When we have done that, we shall have done much to solve the question. The truth of the matter is, we are very much more in need of people who can talk religion every day of the week than we are in need of men who can preach religion from the platform.

We must also get rid of any coldness and indifference to strangers. If Mr. Coldness and Mr. Indifference are standing in your church door, bid them to go home, and give them a long and final farewell. See that they are ejected, and put your Social Committee in their place, with warm hearts, and with hands that are able to give the hearty grasp to the stranger. The truth is that the Social Committee at our evening service has almost as important a part in the service as the pastor himself. If there be a hearty grasp of the hand, and a cordial welcome, it is a key that unlocks the heart, and thus enables the Word of God to find an entrance and bring forth fruit to the honor and glory of Jesus Christ.

See to it that in the pew no longer the chief places be occupied by Coldness and Indifference, but let the Christian Endeavorers be scattered throughout the audience, with a book ready and a smile ready for the stranger, so that every one who shall come to our churches shall have to say when they go home, "Well, there is one thing certain: I was made welcome at the house of God."

Considering all the difficulties that we have to face, it seems to me that the Christian Endeavor Society should say, with reference to the evening service, "We will put an end to the sickliness and the insufficiency of our evening service. We will, *we will*, WE WILL make it a success!" Be determined that it shall be a success. Very much is gained by a determination of that kind. When we have studied the problem over carefully, let us then not only vote for a resolution, but carry that resolution into effect. If we fail again and again, and if we have tried one method and another, and did not succeed, let us not say that it is no use to keep on trying. What we fail to do to-day let us try to accomplish next week, and let us keep to work week after week, and month after month, until success crowns our efforts. Do not depend upon announcements made here and there in a haphazard way, but by organized effort resolve that success shall come.

We need to enter more and more into personal work, and come in contact with men. We must go after them. The difficulty is not so much with the work inside the four walls of the church as it is with the work outside of the church. We do very well, so far as the inside of the work is concerned, but we do not do so well when we leave our church doors to go about our ordinary business.

Let us remember, as Christian Endeavorers, that Jesus Christ said, "Go ye into all the world and preach the gospel to every creature." Some think they are doing very well when they contribute or set apart a little money for foreign missionary work, to send a substitute into a foreign field. Do not send a substitute in the person of your pastor to those about you. Christ said, "Go *ye*." He sent each of us to preach the gospel to every creature in the world in which we live. You have no right to say that when Jesus Christ gave that commission he used the word only in extent of territory; he meant the world in which *you* move, the society in which you live; your own business circle, your own sphere. That is the world in which you move, and where you are to preach the gospel.

A lady said to me a short time ago, in talking upon this subject, "Well, it is very much easier to give money for the foreign missionary cause than to go out and invite people to come to the services." Certainly it is. We can do that very much easier than to go to the homes of your own neighborhood and urge them to come to the service, that they may hear the gospel. In fact, it is very often that Christians know very much about the condition of the heathen in Africa, or in Japan, or here or there, but they do not know anything about the condition of their unconverted neighbor. They know about the success of this and that mission in the foreign lands, how many have been converted, what success has been made, and the various lines of work that are being carried on, but cannot tell how many people were at the evening service, because they were not there themselves, and did not take the trouble to inquire. We are glad of the wonderful interest that is being shown in missionary work. These things we ought to do, but not to leave the others undone. We need home work right in our own community, as well as work in foreign fields. We need to work heart to heart, carrying the gospel from one individual to the other; and in this way we shall get the non-churchgoing people into our evening service, and we will not get them in any other way. We like to be, sometimes, like the cook who prepares the food down-stairs, and then sends it up on the dumb waiter to the dining-room. We like to send the gospel by an invitation through the mail; or possibly we will say to the pastor, "Now on our street there is a family we know that does not attend church, and it is possible that you might get them to come if you would go and talk to them." We like to make a dumb waiter out of our pastor. Christ does not say, Go ye and hang up a sign in the hotel, or in some prominent place in you city. He says, "Go yourself, and carry the gospel." Go out and bring your neighbors and friends with you into the service, and thus, it may be, you will bring them to Jesus Christ.

There is nothing that has the power of personal touch. The people of old, as they went out of Jerusalem, preached the word from house to house, individual to individual; and if we do the same we shall be able to solve the question of attendance upon the evening service, and the evening service will be a mighty power and means to lead many to Jesus Christ, and the glory of God will be accomplished, and the kingdom of Christ carried forward.

After singing, Rev. E. W. Thompson, Patterson, N. J., spoke upon "Christian Endeavor and the Mid-week Prayer Meeting."

Address by Rev. E. W. Thompson, Patterson, N. J.

CHRISTIAN ENDEAVOR AND THE MID-WEEK PRAYER-MEETING.

Christian Endeavor is no longer an experiment. Its existence has been justified. Man realizes this effect and believes in it. God blesses it. Christian Endeavor has a divine enterprise which enables it to carry out its principles. It is not the church, but a force within the church, and the most ambitious of us had no desire that it shall be anything else; "For Christ and the Church" is its motto. Forwards and backwards it is Christian Endeavor, — C. E., Christian Endeavor; E. C., Everything in the Church. For Christ and everything in the church. Let it realize the meaning of this in the fullest extent, and anything or any one belonging to the church, from the Sunday-school to the prayer-meeting, from the choir-loft to the pew, from the pulpit to the organ, from the janitor to the preacher, from the usher to the chorister, from the squeaking weather-vane on the top of the spire to the coal-bin in the cellar, will realize that it, or he, or they, have in the Christian Endeavor Society a firm helper and friend.

I am reminded that I must be short, even though I am six feet long. "Dominie," said a suffering elder one day, "I wish you would preach shorter sermons." "Shorter sermons?" was the reply, "why I am commanded to give the people the sincere milk of the Word." "That's all right," said the elder; "but these are the days of condensed milk."

Part of what I shall say about Christian Endeavor and the midweek prayer meeting will be founded on theory — not very deep theory, because I am not much of a philosopher —and part on experience — not a very long experience, because I am not very old. But I have certain theories about Christian Endeavor, and the Christian Endeavor societies with which I have to deal have never failed to do all that was expected of them.

THE RELATION OF THE CHRISTIAN TO THE MID-WEEK PRAYER-MEETING.

Some Christians dread this meeting. They manifest their dread as much in their presence there, and even more, than they would by absence. They are not always blameworthy. Many a successful pastor dreads this meeting. Mr. Beecher once said that as a boy he hated to have his hair combed, but he recognized the necessity of the operation and passed the ordeal, and that as a minister, he had come to dread the prayer-meeting in the same way.

The service is a service of privilege much more than of duty. Think of natural sympathy and fellow-feeling; of the many interests we have in common with our fellow-men; of the hundreds whose desires are the exact counterpart of ours; of the many demands which we make upon others, in religious just as in professional or business life, and we will see that the prayer-meeting finds its theory in the unity of the human race, the equality of the human nature, and the commandments and promises of one God and Father of all, who would have his followers who are agreed touching anything come to him in the unity of faith, and commune with him with one heart and voice. Add to this the influence of the prayer-meeting in counteracting the secular spirit of the age, and we will see that this mid-week hour of communion is a natural and logical and spiritual necessity in the lives of those whose chief end is to glorify God and enjoy him forever. The prayer-meeting has properly been called the thermometer of the church, for it affords the only real opportunity for the pastor and people to view the whole range of Christian sentiment in the church. As Christians we must exchange views in the recalling of Christian experience, exchange praises in the singing which makes melody unto the Lord in our hearts. We must be givers as well as receivers. As Christman Evans says, "We ought every one of us to be temples of God's praise, and not graves of God's benefits."

THROUGH THE PRAYER-MEETING THE CHRISTIAN HELPS THE CAUSE OF
CHRIST AND THE CHURCH.

Here, more than in any service of the church,

> "Our echoes roll from soul to soul,
> And grow forever and forever."

Christian makes the character and spirituality of the church. Only as the
Christ-life is made manifest in the individual, can it be made manifest in the
church. Those who have confessed Christ and are pledged to him must have
a deep sense of their responsibility for the growth of grace in themselves and
in their fellow-men. The Christian who does not make use of every means that
God has blessed to the salvation and help of man is greatly lacking in his work
for Christ. The prayer-meeting is such a means of grace, and every Christian
who is not present, and present with a word of encouragement or help, or petition for God's blessing to rest upon this assembly of the saints, is losing many
of the privileges of communion and service; unless, of course, he is hindered
by some reason which he can conscientiously give to his Lord and Master. "Inasmuch as ye did not this for one of the least of these brethren, ye did it not for
me."

THE CHRISTIAN ENDEAVORER SHOULD THEREFORE SUSTAIN THE MID-
WEEK PRAYER-MEETING.

I. *The pledge requires it.*
The prayer-meeting is a part of the work of the church, and is included in
the promise to support the regular services of the church. No one with the
true spirit of Christian Endeavor in his heart would ever dream of saying that
the word "attend" means only that we occupy a seat in the room while the service is being conducted. It means our worshipping presence, and our helping
presence, in the spiritual prayer service of the church of Jesus Christ. "Attend" should always be used in the sense in which St. Paul uses it in the seventh chapter of First Corinthians: "This I speak for your profit; not that I
may cast a snare upon you, but for that which is comely, that ye may attend
upon the Lord without distraction."

II. *Christian training looks to this end.*
The work of the society is not only to develop our hearts Godward, and
promote our growth in grace, but also to lead us to confess Christ in word and
deed. All committee work in the Christian Endeavor Society is organized
with this end in view. It is not arranged so that none need be offended by having
their names forgotten when prominent positions in Christian Endeavor work
are to be filled, but it is to train all in service for some line of Christian work.
The requirements of the pledge are only rules for training in Christian work.
The Christian Endeavor Society is not a mere training-school, but it is a place
where we are trained for the work of Christ's Church. The time is coming —
and when it does come, I am sure there will be no more dead prayer-meetings —
when the years of training in the C. E. Society will reap an abundant harvest,
when those who have kept the pledge diligently in their society work will be
found ready to say a word in the church prayer-meeting that will give others a
new idea and incentive to serve the Lord Jesus Christ. All the Church in the
Society and all the Society in the Church is my ideal of Christian Endeavor,
and I pray God the time may soon come when that ideal will be realized. I
will have no trouble in finding Sunday-school teachers, or helpers in the mid-
week prayer-meeting. The principle that is behind the wisdom of Solomon,
when he says, "Train up a child in the way he should go, and when he is old
he will not depart from it," will find its best illustration in the short, terse expressions of Christian experience, and the brief and humble prayers of earnest
petition, which will be heard in the mid-week prayer-meeting of the future,
when every member of the church has had years of training in Christian Endeavor work.

In conclusion let me say, I have in my own church in Paterson, N. J., a
Christian Endeavor society which has done for me everything I have asked of

you to-day. Any place can do anything that Paterson can do. We have furnished the Vice-President of the United States and the Governor of New Jersey, and you can any of you do that. I told my society a few weeks ago many of the things I have told you to-day. The result has been that they are proving a great help to me and the whole congregation in the mid-week prayer-meeting. Take your Bible and read the twelfth chapter of Acts and learn from the account given of the mid-week and midnight meeting held in the house of Mary. You will find that many were assembled there even at a time when it was dangerous to attend a prayer-meeting. You will find that it was faith that brought them there and led them to pray for the release of Peter from the prison, and you will find that it was a damsel who discovered for the petitioners that their prayers had been answered. Cannot all Christian Endeavorers gather in such a meeting and pray for the race of men imprisoned by sin and evil habits? Will it not be that God will permit the young men and maidens to announce to the prayer-meeting that many chains have fallen and many imprisoned ones been rescued? "What's brave, what's noble, let's do it."

The two "Open Parliaments" were then consolidated into one and Dr. Philputt took charge. He prefaced his conduct of this part of the meeting with a brief address upon the same subject presented by Rev. Mr. Thompson.

Open Parliament, Conducted by Dr. Philputt, Philadelphia.

It is a coincidence of divine providence this morning that this building is not full. We wanted an object-lesson of what we wanted to do, and we have it. Now here is a morning service and here is a preacher with a half-full house. I envy young preachers who have small buildings. Now, the problem this morning is how to combine the mid-week service and the evening prayer-meeting. Let us start with this proposition. Who will be the first to speak?

A MEMBER: Let the young people keep that part of the pledge that says, "We will attend all regular meetings of the church."

A MEMBER: One way is to get the Christian Endeavorers and the members of the church to begin at home before they come to the evening service by praying that the Holy Ghost shall be present with them. When we can start that way, all of our plans will follow easily, naturally, from the heart loyal to Jesus, and because we are led by the Spirit; and in all my experience I have never yet known anything so attractive as going to the house of God in the power and presence of the Holy Ghost.

A MEMBER: I make a point of shaking hands with every person who comes into our church, and making them feel very much at home before they go out.

ANOTHER MEMBER: I make it a point that a member of the Christian Endeavor Society who can attend only one service should talk about the meeting, like any other business affair, to all he may meet; and I try to show the people I would rather be there than anywhere else.

A MEMBER FROM TENNESSEE: My way is this: Be just as cordial, and show just as good fellowship, during the week to those you wish to attract, as during the evening service.

JOHN T. STANLEY (New York City): In my opinion, the best way to fill up the prayer-meeting is this: For every one who professes to be a Christian to do his duty and be there himself, and there will be no vacant seats in the church.

A MEMBER FROM HOUSTON, TEXAS: We not only help our pastor to fill the pews, but we help him to fill the pulpit. In the summer-time we combine our two services, and the Christian Endeavorers hold the first part of the service, and the pastor winds up with a fifteen-minute talk. In the winter-time, we are so in love with our pastor, and so in love with Jesus Christ, we think we can't afford to let the services go down, so we rally round both and hold up their hands, and look to our pastor and help him in the evening service. That is the way we work up these things.

D. R. WELDON (Humboldt County): My plan on Sunday evening is for the Endeavorers to pick out the strangers who are there, and shake hands.

A MEMBER FROM TEXAS: The most successful plan we have tried is to make the meeting so interesting that they can't stay away.

MR. PHILPUTT: How do you do that? That is the gist of the whole matter.

A MEMBER FROM MICHIGAN: The evening service should be a continuation of the Christian Endeavor service. The Christian Endeavorers should pray before the evening service, and then come to it.

S. S. LEWIS (Pond Creek, Cherokee Strip, Indian Territory): Let us give our young men who come to the Christian Endeavor meetings as hearty a welcome as they get in all other places by us. Let us be to them as friendly when we meet them through the week as their companions are in the world.

J. W. WEBB (Fresno, Cal.): Let us keep in touch with the masses. Let us show our sympathy in a practical way. Let us attend such other gatherings as are lawful, and show a public spirit; and then say to those we meet there, "You can help us in return by coming to our meetings."

A MEMBER FROM LOS ANGELES: I would like to suggest that you make more of singing and music on Sunday evening, and not depend exclusively on the quartette choirs, but bring all the young people in.

A MEMBER FROM NEBRASKA: A good, live, Lookout Committee is a great help. Not that the Lookout Committee shall do all the work, but be wide awake to influence those without. Some particular persons have more influence than others with those without. Send them to them, and they are more likely to get them. Send out those who have influence.

LADY FROM SAN DIEGO: We have a special committee of six young men and six young women. It is the duty of these young men and these young women to look out for strangers; and then, when they come in, our Social Committee does not let them get out of the door until they have had an invitation to attend every meeting.

MR. PHILPUTT: You would have a recruiting committee of six young ladies and six young gentleman, but how do you keep all these committees in line and at work for more than two or three weeks?

A MEMBER FROM PENNSYLVANIA: I would give everybody a hearty welcome. One hundred members of the Christian Endeavor should be all on the lookout for the church service. Have two meetings, one following the other, and make it the plain, simple gospel.

ANOTHER MEMBER: My opinion is that preachers lack terminal facilities. If they would keep their sermons inside of thirty minutes, they would turn away people from the church.

A LADY MEMBER: I would say, "Remember the Sabbath Day to keep it holy." The sewing-girls that work until 12 o'clock Saturday night, and the young men clerks who have to work until 10 and 12 o'clock, do not care to come to church. They go elsewhere for amusement. If that were remedied, we would have our churches full.

A MEMBER: My experience has been that young men or young ladies will go where they get what they want. Every nature has a demand which must be supplied, maybe for good or evil; but I think all human beings have desire for good when presented aright. I should begin by greeting those who come with a warm hand-shake and a warm welcome, and being just as cordial to those who during the week may have been laboring with soiled clothes and dirty hands. I think the Reception Committee of the whole society should make it their business to speak to the people who come to the church. I don't believe any young man or woman will resent a hearty hand-shake.

A MEMBER: A great problem before the Christian Endeavor Society is to decide upon a proper night of the week on which to hold our prayer-meetings. In Western New York we always hold our prayer-meetings on Tuesday evening; it hurt the prayer-meeting but helped the Sunday night meeting. It is proverbial on this coast to hold the meetings on Sunday evening. This is one of the things that has injured the Sunday evening services on this coast.

ANOTHER MEMBER: The true point has not been touched here. To-night there will be five thousand open saloons in San Francisco, and five thousand young men will go there, and those young men will influence five thousand young ladies who will not attend the Christian Endeavor meetings. I say, blot out the saloons. Keep those things away from the people, and every seat in this place, or any other place, will be filled.

ANOTHER MEMBER: We have always had our meeting on Friday night. We found that Sunday was overcrowded with services. I have not it in my heart to ask any one, after attending morning services, Y. M. C. A. services, and Y. W. C. A. services, to come to a Christian Endeavor meeting on Sunday night. It is too much for any one to do.

ANOTHER MEMBER: Just one sentence more. We have had a great many good suggestions. I was once coming through a pine forest up in Maine, and lost my way. I asked a woman, whom I saw standing before a cabin door, how to get to a certain lake. She said, "Take this road for about two miles, and then you will find three or four paths leading in different directions. Take the one that seems to you most likely."

MR. PHILPUTT: Before we go on with the next exercise, let me give you a few statistics. The impression may have been given that the Endeavorers are not faithful to the mid-week and Sunday evening services. We have taken great pains to collect statistics on that point. A little while ago thousands of postal-cards were sent out to the churches of all denominations in all parts of the country, and the result proved that fifty-seven per cent of the Christian Endeavorers attend the mid-week prayer-meeting, and that eighty-three per cent of the active members attend the Sunday evening services; and of all the church, young and old, only twenty-seven per cent attend the mid-week services, and only forty-four per cent attended the Sunday evening service; so you see that, although we have not reached the pinnacle we hope to get to, in the main, the Christian Endeavorers are faithful to these services.

At the request of President Clark, "Tell the Glad Story Again" was sung. The chairman then introduced Rev. E. W. Shurtleff, of Plymouth, who read the Convention Poem. The poem was upon the program for Thursday, but its reading was postponed, owing to the non-arrival of the author. Mr. Shurtleff read his excellent contribution with much power. Its sentiment and beauty made it one of the features of the session.

Convention Poem.

THE ARMY OF DAYBREAK.

BY REV. ERNEST WARBURTON SHURTLEFF.

" Ye are the light of the world."

I.

WHERE morning stars in Oriental lustre
  Like camp-fires flickered in the darkness cold,
I saw the Army of the Daybreak muster.
  With swords of fire and javelins of gold:
They came with great awakening flame, outstreaming
  Their silvern pennons from the purple night:
They hurled their golden spears in volleys gleaming
  Across the zenith like a storm of light;
But joy was blazoned on their misty banners,
  And forest songsters rang their bugle-calls,
And Nature led them with the wind's hosannas
  In martial music through her mountain halls.
O snow-clad summits towering proud and regal!
  O white cascades that rich with rainbow spring!
O roaring pines! O freedom-loving eagle
  That soarest through the light with tireless wing!
O Nature's self! What grand transfigurations!
  What revelations hath this hour unfurled!

How like the light of Christ upon the nations
  When Charity illuminates the world,
When through the heights and depths of mortal night
  Love's mastering voice commands, "Let there be light"!

I saw from Faith's high mount another morning,
  It broke in Portland, by the sounding sea;
And on the spire of Williston its dawning
  First shone prophetic of the day to be.
It was as if that hour Jehovah's finger,
  As in Judæa, had pointed from the height,
And left its print, a star of dawn, to linger
  Where Shiloh's day should bring its holy light;
For lo! Messias, beauteous and mild,
Again had come to Bethlehem, a child.

Around that chosen shrine the morning breaking —
  A smile of love amid a world of sin —
With deepening tides grew brighter, till, awaking
  The sons of earth, it brought the new day in;
And, just as in its earliest hour the morn
  Crests here and there some single mountain's spire
That, rising highest toward the day new-born,
  May first receive its kiss of glowing fire,
So did the splendor of this coming day
  From spire to spire bestow the light it brought,
And flashed from Williston, by Portland's bay,
  Far to the Old North Church, of Newburyport; [1]
Then on the Christian Church, of Scituate,
  In fair Rhode Island's rose-embowered plain;
Then, speeding like full day through heaven's gate,
  Increased till all the earth was its domain.
That vision was the grand prefiguration
  Of that new era born of love and truth,
Earth freed from night by dawn's emancipation,
  Immanuel's morning in the hearts of youth.

Beneath the dome of azure skies o'erarching
  I saw, like myriad sunbeams blent in one,
A second Army of the Daybreak marching
  Upon earth's darkness like the rising sun.
White-vestured in the glory of Messiah,
  Baptized with morning's chrism of light they came;
Methought I saw the chariots of fire
  That kindled Dothan's heights with holy flame.
Sin's darkness fled; Grief's mournful Miserere
  Was turned to joy by Marah's bitter spring;
And, like the mountain eagle from his eyrie,
  Hope soared before them on triumphant wing.

Methought that these were they of whom Isaiah
  In words ecstatic spake in centuries old,—
"Arise and shine, O Zion, for the fire
  Of Elohim hath lit earth's altars cold."
Their columns bloomed with banners, and, wherever
  The eye of man did for their mission search,
The love-emblazoned ensign of Endeavor
  Its theme displayed — "*For Christ and for the Church.*"
And then came other multitudes as royal,
  Hosts meeting hosts with flags of peace on high,—
The Epworth League, the Unions tried and loyal,
  The Legions pledged for Christ to live and die.

Yet not alone in majesty of numbers
  And stateliness of outward might they came;
That gentler power by which day breaks the slumbers
  Of night was manifested in their flame.
As morning's smile so gracious, yet courageous,
  Invades with light the forest's deepest gloom,
Till, 'mid the solemn, pathless aisles umbrageous,
  The violet answers with its modest bloom,
So through the shades of sin and doubt and terror
  Came down the tides of this celestial morn,
Till in the forest shades of mortal error
  The answering flower of human faith was born;

[1] The second local Christian Endeavor society was organized in the North Church, Newburyport, Mass., October 18, 1881.

[2] The third local Christian Endeavor society was organized in the Christian Church, Scituate, R. I.

For, like Abou Ben Adhem's shining angel,
  Who wrote in book of gold with starry pen,
This daybreak brought to earth the sweet evangel:
  They best love God who love their fellow-men.

So was the Army of the Daybreak founded,
  The faiths of youth in federation bright,
And like a bugle-note the roll-call sounded,
  And marched they forth in their armorial light.
Nor can the voice of gratitude be dumb
  To speak of him whose spirit, like the lark,
First sang of that sweet day that was to come,
  That prophet of youth's morning, Francis Clark!
To him be heaven's honor, man's renown,
  And love divine in human garlands given;
And long may earth add lustre to that crown
  E'er angels seek another prince for heaven.
And other names there are whose echo thrills
  The ear of Love with Memory's gratitude;
Shall Faith forget how on her morning hills
  All worthy of her praise her captains stood?
Nay, nay; wait not until life's song is sung,
  And death hath silenced tongues whose words were dear,
Till Love's low bell, with measured curfews rung,
  Bids Memory drop her offering with a tear;
Wait not till then to speak the gracious word,
  And pay the noble tribute doubly won;
But tell the living how your hearts are stirred,
  And pay your praise 'neath life's meridian sun.
So speak we, that, amid this moment's span,
  Our leaders' names may be with light enshrined;
God cannot work without the hand of man,
  And they for us his purpose have divined.

II.

In panoramic light again reviewing
  The Army of the Daybreak as it passed,
I saw how heaven was more and more enduring
  Their dawning lives God's light on earth to cast.
I saw their crowded tents in many a city,
  A white encampment 'mid the surging throngs;
Above the city's din, in heavenly pity,
  I heard the benediction of their songs;
I saw the multitudes that paused in wonder,
  The tribes of every tongue, the sad, the lost;
And thousands felt the Spirit's power as under
  The cloven tongues of fire at Pentecost.
I saw the conquering dawn, with beams unfading,
  From Washington gleam to the Golden Gate;
The Army of the Daybreak was invading
  The continent with light, from State to State.
Their beauteous feet were radiant on the mountains;
  Their Rose of Sharon lit the desert plain;
Their shining squadrons swept the ocean's fountains,
  While nations clasped their hands across the main.
Then came a change upon the vision; grander
  Their cause became, and mightier their word;
They stood in zeal like Him, that great Commander,
  Who cleansed the temple's shrines with Truth's swift sword.
They turned their search-light on Administration,
  Where false Ambition, robed in power of state,
Raised high its brow in self-aggrandization,
  And bade republics on its mandate wait.
Take heed, O ye that stand in civic power
  Where senate halls to pompous dictum sound;
The gift of office is a sacred flower
  Whose seed our fathers sowed in holy ground;
Ye shall not wear on false and lustful bosom
  The bloom that felt the pulse of Sumner start;
Ye shall not grasp with greedful hand the blossom
  That lay in death on Lincoln's bleeding heart!
They who would bear the honors of the nation
  Shall honor by their lives the nation's cause;
For there is rising now a generation
  That views by Sinai's flash its country's laws.
Republican or Democrat or Tory,
  'T is men we seek, not demagogue and clan,
Not outward pomp of grandeur's tinselled glory;

For character's the stature of the man.
Law unenforced is chaos, black, abhorrent;
 But, when the courts of day revere its might,
Then, like Niagara's awe-impelling torrent,
 It thrones itself in overwhelming light;
And like the storms of music, grand, incessant,
 That great Niagara thunders in its psalms,
It voices God, and zones with rainbow crescent
 Its earthly majesty with heavenly calms.
Then give us men, men like Savonarola.
 To wake Law's organ, though it shake a throne;
To honor God as sovereign Controller,
 Whose earthly courts are governed by his own.
Then give us Lincolns, Gladstones, Sumners, royal
 In honor's birthright and their country's pride,
Great souls who first to manhood's self are loyal,
 Who fear their God and know no fear beside.
Such men shall teach a despot that high heaven
 Shall smite at last the scepter from that hand
That from Armenia's sacred shrines hath driven
 A martyred faith in carnage from the land;
That, though from Athens for Constantinople
 The Grecian armaments may march in vain,
Yet over Russia, flaming like an opal,
 The lightning eye of God knows no disdain,
And he who reigns in majesty supernal,
 The omnipresent and all-seeing God,
Shall ask before his judgment-seat eternal,
 Why Russia shed like Cain a brother's blood;

That like Mont Blanc with snows eternal drifted,
 It peaks a shrine where earth and heaven commune,
By day a temple to the sun uplifted,
 By night a cloister for the stars and moon,—
In silver mists its roseate brow now veiling,
 Now hurling down its avalanches grand,
Yet ever pouring forth its streams unfailing
 To Italy and France and Switzerland,—
So God, though seeming lost 'mid heavenly wonders,
 Where starry angels smile their praise in awe,
Yet sends his rills of peace to earth, and thunders
 His judgments down in avalanche of law;
Not blind like Nature in her moods sublime,
But weighing justice in the scales of time.

Thus from the mount I still beheld the vision,
 And witnessed Youth in armor for the right;
What wonder that with radiance elysian
 I saw that host a synonym for light.
That army of redemption from man's sorrow
 Of which so long the poets' harps have rung,
That broader day, that unhorizoned morrow
 Sprung from the shriven spirits of the young?
Oh, lovely was the vision beyond telling;
 Prophetic though in part its stirring view,
Yet to its fair fulfilment time is swelling,
 And history already claims it true.

III.

But mark, ye soldiers of the dawn's redemption,
 "Love" is the watchword, "Love," the countersign;
They who serve God from love have no exemption,
 For God is love, and love is power divine.
And charity alone, most sweet of graces,
 Can bring that heavenly dawn to light the earth,
And they who bear its sunrise on their faces
 Must in their spirits give its dayspring birth,
And know that love, though gentle in its diction,
 Is like the sunlight, warmth as well as light,
And able to expel, by its eviction,
 Man's hatred from its wintry fortress white.

I stood once on the mountain's snow-clad towers,
 And like a pilgrim waited for the dawn;
The night's dark lake was lilied with star-flowers,
 And there the crescent floated like a swan.
Then burst the roseate rills from morning's fountains,
 And glistened through the east with deepening glow;

The stars grew pale, the moon sank 'neath the mountains,
  And dawn flashed on the ice-bound world below.
That glowing light unlocked the marble palace
  Where winter kept the spirits of the flowers,
And lo ! the wild rose oped its lovely chalice
  When scarce the frosts had left its lonely bowers.

The warbling birds returned ; the ice-bound river
  Leaped glad and free, its chilly heart grown warm ;
The dews, like sparks, did on the grasses quiver ;
  The rainbow spanned with peace the passing storm ;
The fair earth raised again each lovelier feature,
  From sea and shore ; from meadow, vale, and wood ;
And all sweet nature, like a gladdened creature,
  Grew beautiful with spring's beatitude ;
And all because the light had come, and given
  A gracious warmth that had in silence won,
Earth's frosty lips, so sadly raised toward heaven,
  Caressed to smiles with kisses of the sun.
O, ever thus, when heaven's light is blended
  With love's pure warmth to melt man's wintry scorn,
The icy thraldom of the heart is ended,
  And summer is in mortal spirits born.
Then shine, ye Christ-beams of the dawn's endeavor,
  All luminous with love for human right.
Then gird your loins, O youth, and shine forever,
  Till all this darkened world is filled with light.
Down with Oppression, Bribery, and Treason,
  By Sinai's law, by Shiloh's cross and crown !
But ever let Love plead for Truth a reason,
  And Light, in mercy, strike Night's kingdoms down.

So shall ye bring indeed that holy dawning
  That finds the hills with dews of joy impearled ;
March on ! Shine on ! and, brightening like the morning,
  Expand God's halo, love, around the world.

Ye have the pledge, the soldier's bond of duty ;
  It links the grace of heaven with human needs ;
It touches all the way with faith's own beauty ;
  It garlands in one crown the Christian creeds.
O, call it not a covenant of iron,
  That seal that binds the noble and the right ;
Nay, but the holy marriage vow of Zion,
  The bridal of the soul with heaven's light.

Go then, and. like the daybreak on the ocean
  Whose roaring waves, tempestuous and grand,
Beneath that glory cease their wild commotion,
  And turn to kiss with peace the wave-washed land,
Shine on the sea where human fates are drifting,
  Till storm of tongues and social strife shall cease ;
And in your light the Christ, with hand uplifted,
  Shall walk the waves and say to tempests, "Peace ! "
March on ! Shine on ! Your light shall be your glory.
  Tread ye the path the Christ before you trod ;
And ye shall hear at last in heaven the story,—
  The Army of the Daybreak marched with God.

At this point the chairman read a telegram of congratulation from President Charles Cuthbert Hall, of Union Theological Seminary, New York, as follows : —

" The Union Theological Seminary sends greetings to your Convention."

It was received with hearty applause and itself supplied the connecting link between the previous papers and discussion and the address immediately given.

" The Claims of the Ministry upon Young Men" was the topic upon which Rev. B. B. Tyler, D.D., of New York, was introduced to speak.

Address of Rev. B. B. Tyler, D.D., New York.

I desire, first, to appoint a committee, and I beg you to accept the appointment, if you should be named as a member of that committee. I desire to appoint the men and the women who are here present a committee to report to young men, pious young men, as far as possible, the things that I shall say this morning.

I would that I could speak to this room, packed with young men, concerning the ministry of the claims of Jesus Christ, the claims of the ministry, on the young men. I would be delighted to present this to them personally, but I cannot; they are absent. Indirectly, I would reach them through you. Hence, the appointment of this committee.

The claims of the ministry on young men, of course, mean the claims of the gospel ministry on young men. I begin what I have to say with this remark, having studied the matter: Do not enter the ministry if you can help it. If you can be satisfied with farming, with practising law. or medicine; if you can be satisfied as a mechanic, as a banker, a railway president, a merchant prince; if you can be satisfied with holding office in the municipality, in the State, in the Republic; if you can be satisfied before God in any of these lines, pursue these vocations; do not, I tell you, seek a place in the gospel ministry. Do not become a minister simply as a profession; do not enter this calling as you would enter a calling merely to make a living, and to have a respectable and honored place in the world. Enter the ministry because God lays the work upon you in such wise that you cannot resist the call; but facing life with its duties and responsibilities, consider whether or not the call comes to you. I urge you to consider the claims of the ministry as you are standing upon the threshold of your career. "Can I preach the gospel of Jesus Christ? Have I the natural requirements? Have I, by God's grace, the ability to proclaim the unsearchable riches of Jesus Christ? Ought I not to do it? Is there not a place for me, and is there not a demand for my service along this line?"

This, then, is my first point,— standing on the threshold, thinking seriously of life, with its responsibilities and calls to duty, "Ought I to enter the gospel ministry?"

When this conviction fastens itself upon you, enter that work, not counting the cost. Start out on this career, burning the bridges behind you, and say with Paul, "This one thing I do." We were reminded yesterday by our beloved president that William Carey said, "Preaching the gospel of Jesus Christ is my business. I mend shoes to pay expenses." That is the spirit. Henry D. Palmer, of Illinois, used to say, "I preach when I can; I work when I must." He was a pioneer in that great State. He wrought with his hands and preached the gospel of Jesus Christ. In that spirit men ought to enter this holy service.

I desire to remind you, in the next place, that the gospel ministry is not the only place of service, nor is it the only place of holy service. Paul blotted out, I think, that line between the sacred and the secular when he said, "Whatsoever you do in word or deed, do all in the name of the Lord Jesus, giving thanks to God and the Father by him." The man who studies and practises the healing art is a servant of Jesus Christ just as much as the minister of the gospel, if he undertakes this work and carries it forward in the spirit in which the Master would have all of us render service. It is a mistake to suppose that the only place in which sacred service can be rendered is in the gospel ministry. You may render a more valuable service in a business life than by preaching formally from the pulpit to the people. I have known men whose lives were richer in blessing to the world, who were business men, than they would have been had they entered the gospel ministry. This, then, is not the only service. You may serve God in the school-room, in the counting-room, at the carpenter's bench, in the shoe-shop, in the merchant's stall. anywhere, everywhere, if you are inspired by love and desire to do something that the world needs.

My third point is that the gospel ministry is the highest and the holiest service that can possibly be rendered. When Jesus was leaving the earth, and when he would have his message of redeeming love proclaimed to the whole creation, he did not summon the angels to render the service. He could have done so; they were subject to his order. When his enemies were putting him to death, he said, "Know ye not that I could call upon my Father, and he would send more than twelve legions of angels?" Jesus could have commissioned angels, but he did not. He did not call upon the angels of the upper world, but, coming down to us, whom he loved, and for whom he gave his life, he said, Men, women, go, ye who are my disciples, go! I call you into partnership with myself. Go! As my Father hath sent me, so I send you. Go, go preach the gospel. Go upon my authority, and make disciples of all the nations; go to earth's remotest bounds."

You talk to me about an honored place as a preacher of the gospel of Jesus Christ. If I am true to my vocation, I outrank the highest office-holders of the world, for I am an ambassador of the King of kings and Lord of lords. May I refer you to my own experience? The greater part of my life is behind me. Thank God, I have not crossed the "dead line" yet. But when a man has preached thirty-six years, the best part of his life is behind him. If I were looking into the faces of ten thousand young men this morning, and I knew that I was making my last address, I would say, if I had to live my life over again, I would preach and do nothing else; if I had a hundred lives to give, I would give them to this holy service. As a preacher of the gospel of Jesus Christ, I have never engaged in business — no, not for an hour; I have never made investments. Upon looking back over this stretch of years, I am glad that in boyhood I gave my heart to Christ and my life to his service. I believe my mother ordained me before birth. My earliest recollection was of that sweet, sainted mother talking to me about preaching the gospel of Jesus Christ. I cannot remember when the thought was never in my mind that the highest service, and only service that I must render, should be along this line. When my father, who for fifty-three years was a pioneer preacher, heard me speak first, the old man stood up, and while the tears rolled down his furrowed cheek, he said, "Neighbors and friends, I would rather see my boy stand where he stands to-day, I would rather hear him say what I have heard him say, than to see him ruling the Senate of the United States." Such a father, such a mother, consecrated me to this holy service.

The world needs you, young men. If you can preach the gospel of Jesus Christ, you are needed. We talk about the crowded professions. A young man would enter the law, but the profession is crowded. Daniel Webster said, "There is room at the top." There is room for you, if you will consecrate your life to this service unselfishly, and tell the old, old story of a heart that has been baptized in divine love. Your own country needs you.

> " My country, 't is of thee,
> Sweet land of liberty,
> Of thee I sing." — of thee I speak.

Dr. Stone greatly impressed me last night when he called attention to the fact that our progress along moral and spiritual lines has not kept pace with our material progress. Sad, sad fact! We are the richest people on the face of the globe to-day — rich in the aggregate, and rich *per capita*. We are rapidly accumulating wealth, notwithstanding our murmurings and complainings! Oh, what strides we have made, and what strides we are making, and are destined still to make, unless we make of our country a moral and spiritual wreck! This country of ours needs a moral elevation, needs a spiritual uplift. There is need in this land of ours for consecrated men to go out and preach the gospel of Jesus Christ. Young man, if you want to stand in a place where there is a demand for your service, and where there is the most room for the largest exercise of your highest intellectual and moral powers, enter the gospel ministry.

Finally, turning from the young men, I turn to you, Christian men and women. Pray ye the Lord of the harvest that he will send laborers into the

One of the "Outdoor" Meetings on Van Ness Avenue. (Stand No. 3. Secretary Baer Making the Closing Prayer.)

field. Are you praying? Is your heart so fixed on this that you are willing to give your own sons to the service? When you are praying that laborers shall be sent into the field, are you praying that your son may be inspired to undertake this work? Let us pray that young men may see the field ripe for the harvest, and may hear the call of God to enter in.

. My heart is full of this. I would like to talk longer. I would be delighted to talk, as I said in the beginning, to ten thousand young men. But tell them, *tell them*, TELL THEM, as you meet them, that I stood in your presence, and with tears in my heart and on my face, I besought young men upon their knees to decide their course of life, and to listen if God does not call them. Tell them that if I had a hundred lives to live, I never would be a lawyer, nor a doctor, nor a farmer; I would never strive for the presidency of the United States; but I would strike for the highest honor that can come to man,—I would strive to be a worthy, earnest, humble, consecrated preacher of the gospel of Jesus Christ.

After singing the doxology, the audience was dismissed with the benediction by Bishop Alexander Walters, D.D., of the African M. E. Zion Church.

First United Presbyterian Church.

A MOTHERS' CHRISTIAN ENDEAVOR SOCIETY MEETING.

One of the most important meetings of the Convention was the Mothers' Meeting in the First United Presbyterian Church. Mrs. Francis E. Clark presided, and the meeting was a grand success.

The church was filled. and many disappointed ones were turned away. The decorations were of eschscholtzias, arranged in Christian Endeavor monograms, pansies, sent by Juniors, satin banners of the Junior societies, and a floral flag, which ornamented the front of the reading-desk.

Three speakers were absent, Miss Frances LeBaron, of Chicago, who was to have presented the report of the Mothers' Society; Miss Jennie T. Masson, of Indianapolis, who would have told "What Mothers Can Do To Help the Junior Superintendents;" and Mrs. Alice May Scudder, of Jersey City, N. J., who was assigned to conduct the "Question-Box." But Mrs. Clark readily supplied these vacancies, and there was no break in the program.

Words of greeting were brought by Mrs. E. G. Wright, of San Francisco, and Mrs. E. Y. Garrette, of Alameda, Cal. The devotions were conducted by Dr. Kin Eca da Silva, a sweet-faced Japanese lady.

Mrs. Clark then explained the purpose of the gathering,— to bring the Junior superintendents and mothers together with mutually helpful suggestions. Her introductions were felicitous, as always. The addresses and reports were inclusive and bright. We regret that we cannot supply them all in full.

Miss Myrtle Simpson, of San Francisco, presented the report of the Junior Society of Christian Endeavor. She said in part:—

"California comes fifth in the list of States, with 551 Junior Societies. It seems to me," she continued, "that the Junior work is the true centre of Christian Endeavor. We have all the committees the Seniors have, and they are not committees in name only. Within the last eleven months 2,511 Juniors have been brought into the church. That is what the mothers appreciate."

The report of the Intermediate Society of Christian Endeavor was given by Mrs. James L. Hill, of Salem, Mass.

Mrs. Hill said in part, " I once heard a Junior recite a poem upon the ' Trials of the Middle Boy.' When he would ask to accompany his older brothers and sisters upon some excursion he was told that he was too young, and at another time he was too old to cry because he could not go with his mother, although she took the babies with her. There are a great many ' middle boys ' and girls who are glad to enter the Intermediate Society, and there are now enrolled 366 of these societies. California leads, with 51.

" The first society was formed a few years ago by Rev. A. Z. Conrad, D.D., of Worcester, Mass. It is easy to see that their chief mission is in large churches where there are many boys and girls. Their place is analogous to the grammar grade, between the primary and high school. If there are but a few Juniors in a church, by all means let them grow together until they come into the Y. P. S. C. E., but do not say there is no place anywhere for a graded system, for in large churches it has been found necessary to have the Intermediate C. E. S. This gives the multitude of boys and girls opportunity for confession and participation, the natural expression of Christian experience."

After singing, the presiding officer introduced Mrs. H. N. Lathrop, of Boston, to speak upon " The Relation of the Mothers' Endeavor Society to the Junior and Intermediate Societies."

She said that sending a child to the Junior Society, to Sunday-school, to Bands of Mercy and to Loyal Legions, did not relieve the mother of her responsibility, because the impression on the child's heart, so carefully made by the Junior superintendent, might be dissipated in a moment by an indifferent mother, or deepened immeasurably by a Christian mother, who was with the child all the time, instead of an hour a week.

The next speaker was the wife of the Canadian trustee, Mrs. William Patterson, of Toronto, Ont. Her paper was on the theme " What Junior Superintendents Can Do To Help the Mothers "

Paper by Mrs. William Patterson, Toronto, Ont.

The Junior Christian Endeavor Society, like the Sabbath-school, was never intended to be a substitute for the home as far as the training of the children is concerned ; neither was the Junior superintendent designed to take the place of the parents in teaching the children. Nevertheless, the Junior superintendent can greatly assist them in their work. It is essential that the Junior superintendents should realize the importance of the work in which they are engaged.

The great majority of the men and women who shall be holding important positions twenty-five years from now are at present in our Junior Christian Endeavor Societies, or should be. If they are not converted and influenced for good when young, the probability is they may never be. It is easier to bend the tree when it is young than when it is old, or to mold the clay when it is soft than when it has become hard. How much better it is for a boy or a girl to be saved at the age of twelve than at fifty, for the probability is they will have so many more years in which they can work for the Master; and who can tell the number of souls they may be instrumental in saving during that time? The Junior superintendents can help the parents by teaching their children while young their duty with reference to the temperance cause and the importance of becoming good citizens. They can teach them the value of votes and prepare them for the time when they shall become voters by impressing upon their minds the value of purity of thought, word, and action. Show them the privilege and responsibility of casting votes for right or for wrong. Educate them to look forward to the time when their vote will be cast and their influence wielded against many of the now existing evils. The Junior superintendents can, with more grace and effectiveness, instil into the minds of the children the duty and privilege of honoring and loving their parents. This they can do by taking concrete examples from the Scriptures, and by contrasting the results of obedience and disobedience. Take Jonathan, for instance, and show how he loved and shielded his father, notwithstanding that he was very unamicable. We cannot but look back and admire Jonathan for his fidelity and love to Saul.

We see the results of evil which flow from dishonor and disrespect of parents in the case of Ham, who showed his lack of proper respect and love for his parents by exposing his father, and as a consequence his descendants suffered and were enslaved. There is another beautiful story, teaching children to honor their parents, in the case of Joseph. The superintendent can show how Joseph had risen in the estimation of the king, so that he held the highest position he could possibly hold under the king, and how he loved his father, who was only a humble shepherd, and he was not ashamed to present him to the king. We cannot help appreciating Joseph's kind treatment of his father. In this and other ways Junior superintendents can assist the parents by teaching the Juniors not only love and honor for the parents, but also willing obedience. Frequently we find parents who hesitate to speak to their own children about their salvation. This should not be the case. There must be something awfully wrong if it is. If there are any parents here to-day who have this feeling of hesitation in regard to this matter, let us ask God to show us what is the cause of it, and to give us grace to overcome it. May God remove this obstacle, whatever it may be.

In our Junior Endeavor Societies we find children whose parents are not Christians, and who apparently are not under any control. The Junior superintendent will try to win these little ones to Christ, and will teach them to pray for the conversion of their parents. In many instances parents have been led, through the prayers and Christ-like lives of their little ones, to seek that salvation which has made such a marvelous change in the lives of their children. Their deportment in the home and elsewhere will be improved. Parents should know with whom their children associate; but it sometimes occurs that they do not, and they sometimes associate with others whose companionship is very injurious. The Junior superintendent may hear of this before the mother, and by kindly talking the matter over with their mother she may induce the children to give up these associations, which can only be hurtful. The more that the Junior superintendents and the mothers co-operate the more help they can give to one another. A Junior superintendent requires the sympathy, help, advice, prayers, and hearty friendship and co-operation of the parents in order to be successful in the work. Together they may be enabled to check evil habits which may be forming, such as use of bad language, bad reading matter, untruthfulness, selfishness, and bad temper. And together they can help on the little ones to holier and higher aspirations. A superintendent can help a mother by letting her know when her little son or daughter has prayed in the meeting that God would enable them through his grace to overcome some particular fault, such as bad temper or selfishness, etc. Would not the mother gladly assist the little one in every way she could? How much good is often left undone for the lack of a word of commendation when it is deserved! Give it when you can, parents; it encourages your little ones to try to do better.

Don't forget, then, superintendents, to acquaint the mothers with facts concerning their children, for are they not the ones who are most anxious to commend their children for good they have done, and to encourage and to help them when they are trying to overcome temptations? It sometimes happens that a child's heart is touched at a meeting, and the superintendent sees that the child has longing to live nearer to Christ. Then don't neglect to write a little note to the mother, so that she may know how best to help her child. Call on the parents and tell them of the work, and it will prove a mutual help. Invite one of the parents occasionally to visit your meeting. It will repay you. I have three little children, members of the Junior Society, and I was helped when the superintendent spoke to me in words of commendation of my little daughter's paper, which she had written for the Christian Endeavor meeting. On Sunday nights when I stay at home with my children, we have an Endeavor meeting, in which all take part. I was greatly impressed with the suggestion Dr. Clark gave in his address yesterday morning, when he suggested that a family Christian Endeavor meeting be held weekly in the home, in which every member should take part. Good results must surely follow this suggestion of Dr. Clark's.

Mrs. Clark said: "I have the pleasure of being a Junior superintendent, and one of the pleasantest features of my winter in Berlin was the letters I received from my Juniors. I have also the pleasure of being the mother of two very lively small boys, both Juniors. I have an advantage that you do not all enjoy, and the Junior superintendent and mother often consult. I urge you all to consult each other. Mothers should give more time to preparing the children for their Junior meetings, to the daily prayer, and to the spiritual life of the children."

Then Mrs. Clark asked all the ladies to remove their hats, so that no one might be deprived of a sight of the Chinese children who were about to sing. It was the Christian Endeavor Society from the Occidental School, organized on January 2, 1896, by Miss Mendora Berry. There were fourteen members, and the seven-year-old secretary read the report. The children sang "Jesus Loves Me," and other hymns, in English. A boy of four recited a patriotic piece which ended, "I wave my flag and say hurrah for the United States!" Ah Lou recited "Gentle Jesus, Meek and Mild," and one of the older girls sang a hymn in Chinese. The singing and showing of work done by these transplanted and motherless Juniors was the event of the day.

Miss Elizabeth W. Richardson, of Salem, Mass., read a paper on "How Can the Mothers' Society Help the Day School?"

Paper by Miss Elizabeth W. Richardson, Salem, Mass.

A good Jewish Rabbi once remarked that the Lord could not be everywhere, so he made mothers. Had he lived to-day he might have added that the mothers' most interested co-laborers are teachers. They have the same noble aims. Every Christian teacher realizes that her calling and election is not of man but of God.

The salvation of the world is born anew in every child. The relation between the mothers and the teachers is so important that every opportunity should be improved to make the tie closer. This is one of the purposes of the Mothers' Society. Nothing would so encourage the teacher as to feel that standing shoulder to shoulder with her in this society. She needs co-operation in impressing upon the children the importance of truthfulness, punctuality, fidelity, and natural helpfulness.

Opportunities to help the day school are inexhaustible. Interest should be taken in ventilation, lighting, pictures, and libraries. These are needed everywhere, especially in the poorer districts. It needs but a hint to the mothers to show what may be done for children less fortunate. The teacher sees the child from quite a different view than the mother. She can discover other beauties and defects in character, and they should reason together. An open conference could be planned by the society with great profit.

" Mothers and the Band of Mercy " was the subject of an address by Miss Elizabeth W. Olney, Providence, R. I.

Miss Olney made a forcible and stirring appeal to the mothers upon this topic. She asked for maternal help in checking the early destructive tendencies of children. She voiced a plea against docking horses, cropping dogs' ears, and the wholesale destruction of birds for the sake of pulmage for millinery.

Rev. J. Z. Tyler, D. D., of Cleveland, Ohio, spoke for " The Sunday Morning Church Service and the Boys and Girls."

He asked for a better attendance of children at the morning church service, because they are not forming the church-going habit, and that their absence meant fewer conversions and a decline in Sabbath observance. He lamented the transformation of Sunday from a holy day into a holiday, laying the blame in part on the voluminous and elaborately illustrated Sunday paper, on the character of the morning sermon, and on the decline in family worship. He urged the mothers to remedy the evil by setting a good example.

The last address of the morning was by Rev. C. A. Dickinson, D.D., of Boston, on " The Pastor and the Mothers' Society."

His words were full of practical suggestion. He thought it desirable for the pastor to meet the mothers once a week. He told of the talks on food and hygiene which he had with the poor mothers in Boston. In his church the older Christian Endeavorers take care of the little babies in an adjoining room while the mothers attend divine service. The helpful session closed with the question-box and a short service of prayer.

FRIDAY EVENING.

Mechanics' Pavilion.

It seemed as though everybody sought to anticipate the great rush for seats at the evening session in Mechanics' Pavilion. To come two hours before the time of commencement appeared to be a necessity. An hour after the doors opened every available spot was occupied by an enthusiastic Endeavorer. At 7 o'clock the great doors were closed ; the thousands must go elsewhere. And they did, and overflowed into the halls of the vicinity.

The director of music, Mr. J. M. Robinson, of Oakland, did not wait for the gavel. The multitude followed his lead in an hour of song. By special request Director Robinson sang " Homeland " with such sweetness and effect that the last verse was repeated in response to the loud encore.

The devotions of the evening were conducted by the Rev. Sydney Gulick, of Osaka, Japan. After reading from Eph. vi. 10–16, he offered an earnest prayer. The choir rendered an anthem.

When his welcome had quieted, Dr. Clark, who presided throughout the evening, said, "Friends, we are already ahead of time, but I want to say just a word or two. The place is crowded, filled in fact to overflowing, and no others will be permitted to enter. Now, there is just one thing I wish to say: please do not go out unless it is a case of life and death. It is not Christian Endeavor-like to do so.

"We are going to have a great feast to-night. There are representatives present from all over the world, and they will tell us of the Christian Endeavorers in far and strange lands."

The first speaker introduced was Rev. K. Inazawa, Japan.

Address by Rev. K. Inazawa, Japan.

Fellow-Citizens: — It is a heavenly boon to mankind, this religion of humanity. Since Christianity taught the world the common fatherhood of God and the common brotherhood of man, what tremendous changes have taken place amid the family of man, amid humanity! The world now rises and enjoys the prizes of Christian fellowship. Now God has become common to all, and true religion universal. The clasped hands of Christianity and civilization are joined in the interests of humanity. It was a good omen of the epoch to have the hand of the old world joined-with that of the new. Since then, as the power of civilization has progressed, the dominion of our Supreme Master has advanced. For instance, turn your eyes to the far East. About a half-century ago, you Americans scarcely dreamed or imagined of Japan, beyond the Pacific Ocean. She was a secluded portion of the far East, who had never come in contact with the enlighten d world for ages. Columbus fell in love with her fair name through Marco Polo, but he failed to find her, and gained an immense new world. Time went on, and providentially she has been brought out upon the world's stage, and has been brought into fellowship with all the nations. Consequently, she awoke from her sound slumber of centuries, and soon was clad in the newly cut garments of modern civilization. To-day she sits as a bright and effulgent star in the western horizon, and Christianity is slowly yet steadily gaining ground in the Sunrise Empire. Indeed, the sun of righteousness brightly cometh forth as a bridegroom out of a chamber. This is the gift of modern civilization and international contact. It has been of the highest advantage to our nation for our people to come into international affiliation. Truly isolation is bad. Communication has opened hospitality and is going forth to push out the star of Asia into the open firmament; and true Christian sympathy can warm the spirit of Christian fellowship.

Dr. Clark, in introducing Tamil Evangelist David, said: "A few weeks ago, when I was in India, everywhere I went I saw that the spirit of God had been in that place, working very largely through the instrumentality of a certain evangelist whom God had raised up and greatly blessed in his work among the churches. This evangelist, I am delighted to tell you, we have with us to-night, the Tamil Evangelist David, as he is familiarly known. I will not attempt to pronounce his whole name. Perhaps he will give it to you. I am delighted that he is here, and you will be most glad to hear him. Our representative from India, Tamil Evangelist David."

Address by Tamil Evangelist David, India.

It gives me great pleasure to stand here and testify in the name of Jesus Christ. I have got only five minutes, so you know I do not want to waste my time. When I was beginning to talk, my conversational preaching did last twelve hours; but since I have been here I have learned something, — we ought to be punctual and prompt when it is needed. Please excuse me, but I want to tell you just a few words concerning India; and if I am going to give the whole account of India it will take at least twenty-five years. I will give you a little account of India Christian Endeavor, short and sweet and to the point — just to take two minutes. Well, I began my ministry nineteen years ago in Ceylon, but the Lord wonderfully opened the door just eight years ago. He anointed me with the power of the Holy Ghost, and sent me to preach the gospel in India — not only in India, but England, Scotland, Ireland, Australia, Sydney, and all through the place the Lord took me to preach the wonderful gospel of Christ. When I went throughout India I had to visit lots of churches; and glory be to God, hundreds and thousands of people came out, and in consequence of it they asked me what to do with them. I say, start a Christian Endeavor. Now I asked them bring the young ones together and bind them up with the blood, word, and spirit, — the word and the blood of Christ, and the spirit of Christ. If Christian Endeavor people have been brought together and bound by these three bands the work will go on. So accordingly in Bombay, Calcutta, Poona, and other places. — oh, many places, — Christian Endeavor bands have been started. Glory be to God, they are going ahead. But when I went to Maggella, that was the time I met the instructor (pointing to Mr. Clark). There we had a little conversation; it came to my heart I wanted to speak to him on the subject. I said I was going to America, so I would be very glad to see him there, and he gladly asked me just to pass through San Francisco and give a few words here. According to his invitation, the Lord brought me here. The Lord just here is going to give you the real message, just two or three minutes. When I went around this way in different lands I found one thing that was lacking. The Lord God put it into my heart to press home one idea: that is, Christians all are alive, but they had no life more abundant. Just two years ago, when I dwelt upon this all-important subject, the life more abundant, the Lord raised many many thousands of souls among Christians. Within three months of our work there ten thousand people were converted; and out of those ten thousand, thirty-six evangelists without any money, voluntary workers, started to go anywhere and everywhere for the Lord. There I found one secret out of this: life more abundant is absolutely necessary for Christian Endeavor people. So let me spend another two or three minutes upon that word.

Dear friends, if you want to be a success for Christian Endeavor, let me just tell you a few words concerning the life more abundant. Christian Endeavorers, you ought not to live for yourselves. You are saved that you may live for Christ. Christ did not save you that you may have eternal life alone, but saved you that you may become a real savior for the world. Through you, thousands of souls may be converted. And if you want to get such spirit in you, abundant life, it means fruitful life. The abundant life means victorious life. The abundant life means satisfied life. The abundant life means strong life. The abundant life means praising life. That is what you will get out of the Lord Jesus Christ. As he says in John x. 10, "I have come to this world that they may have life, and have it more abundantly." How can you get this abundant life? Here it is: ask the disciples of old. Christ told them. "Go preach the gospel." He said, — Mark xvi., — he told his disciples. "Go into all the world and preach the gospel;" and Acts, first chapter. fourth verse, not to go, — to "tarry." One side he said, "Go;" another side he said not to go, "Tarry." First, you must understand "Go." Second, you must understand not to go, "Tarry." Third, you should understand "Receive." Fourth, you must understand "Preach." Four points: go, tarry, receive, preach; go, tarry, receive, preach. Go, the command that is given to all Christian Endeavor people. You are responsible. You are to be a soul-winner. Snatch those out of the horrible pit and miry clay. Bring souls ; go. But if you want to know where is the power, tarry, tarry, tarry at the feet of Christ. Get this power, the power of the Spirit. When the power of the Spirit comes, he shall sanctify, fill you with himself. Here is the power of the Spirit, was given to the disciples in the upper room. Peter and Thomas and all were filled with the Holy Ghost, and then they opened their mouths. They were not to open their mouths before ; but when they got the power of the Spirit, they just stood in the street, opened their mouths, and preached the gospel, and three thousand were converted. Before Pentecost they were not able to convert souls because they had no power. They went and preached the gospel. That was just like a locomotive engine without steam, or a clock without a spring. So many people try to win souls. You can't unless you have the life more abundant, and that is the power of this Spirit. O Christian Endeavorers, teachers, pastors, clergy, all soul-winners, I tell you one thing here, it is Jesus Christ : get the life more abundant.

Rev. Jee Gam, in his Chinese garb, read an interesting paper.

Paper Read by Rev. Jee Gam, China.

Our Fellowship.

Old China was an isolated nation having no fellowship with other nations, and desiring none. Her conceit of superiority was very great. She called her people Celestial, but all outsiders barbarians. She built a great wall and sealed up her ports to keep these foreign devils out, for she wanted no intercourse with them. And this is the spirit of the old China to-day.

New China recognizes her long-continued mistake. She has opened her ports to foreign intercourse. She is reaching out to nations she once despised, and learning from them. Old China kills missionaries; new China calls for them and offers to support them. She has invited aid from Christian nations in her colleges and other schools. Professorships of English, French, German, and Russian have been established. Many leading men, without waiting for the government, have opened schools where the English language is taught. Three of our California converts have been employed as teachers in this school. The directors of the Sui Ying College in Ci Ning said to our preacher, whose chapel is located close by, "If your superintendent will furnish us a professor of English, we will believe in Jesus every seventh day," i. e., every Sabbath this professor is granted the privilege to teach or preach Christianity to these students. You may be sure that our brother Lew Chong, who has been called to this professorship, has seized this grand opportunity. He has not only been holding services on the Sabbath day, but has evening Bible readings also. The students of all the government schools at Tientsin on Sabbath days have been granted permission to attend Christian churches.

How were all these remarkable concessions brought about? Christianity is the mainspring of this new movement. It will keep on working until China is thoroughly Christianized, for, until then, she could never have perfect fellowship.

Christianized Chinese in California will do what they can toward accomplishing this end. They have grasped the Christian Endeavor idea; welcomed the opportunities for fellowship which it provides. The Golden Gate Union and other Christian Endeavor unions throughout California have not only taught the precept which says, "God is no respecter of persons," but have practised the same — practised it to the Chinese, as well as to any other nationality, and, of course, this adds much fellowship, which we all appreciate.

The first Chinese Christian Endeavor society organized in America was at our mission in Santa Cruz, California, in 1891. The second one was by the Congregational Chinese in this city, on July 24, 1892. Now there are about twenty-five societies in California, embracing a membership of over a thousand.

We will carry this fellowship to China. Indeed, it is there already, and large Christian Endeavor conventions have been held during the past three years at Shanghai. These societies number 119, and embrace a membership of 4,321.

This will help to harmonize the Chinese in China. When this is done, the fellowship of the East and that of the West will unite the hemispheres, and make real and visible the oneness of our human race in Christ.

Now, dear Endeavorers, in behalf of the Chinese Christian Endeavor societies of California and those of China, I ask your co-operation in hastening the work of fellowship. I trust hundreds, yea, even thousands, of you will go to China as missionaries, for she is the greatest mission field in the world. Her call is, " Come over into China and help us."

Dr. Clark introduced as England's representative, Miss Harriet Green. As was true of the reception of each foreign delegate, Miss Green was warmly welcomed.

Address by Miss Harriet Green, England.

I have only five minutes, dear friends. I hope you will not think that I am not loyal because I am here to-day. Dr. Clark has said that because of the Jubilee, nearly all the loyal Christian Endeavorers would not leave to come to this Convention. But I can assure you that the Mother Country is looking on her children who have so far outstripped her in energy and in numbers in this Christian Endeavor work with admiration, and I rather think with envy. The mother is always slower than the children, is she not? It certainly is so with England. While the Englishman is thinking what he will do, the American has already done it.

Coming from the Mother Country, dear Endeavorers, I want to ask you to let me say a few very serious words to you. We have heard just now of the need of the Spirit, the fulness of the Spirit, in our work. I belong to a part of the Christian Church which rose up years ago in England when the work of the Spirit was almost, if not entirely, ignored in the churches. Praise God, it is not so to-day. But, beloved, let us think for a moment how it is that we are met here in this city of San Francisco to worship God and promote the interests of the church. It is because a man of God walked so close to God, and so listened to the Spirit, that when the Spirit said to him in his work, " Thou shalt not go further that way," he stopped and waited. And there came a voice from Macedonia, a cry, " Come over and help us." And he went there in obedience to the Spirit of God, and the blessed gospel has spread all over Europe to-day, and over the world, and we are here to praise God for the gift of the Blessed Spirit.

Beloved, I fear sometimes in these days of conventions, in these days of blessed fellowship one with another, that we may ignore or almost forget the blessed work of the Spirit of God. Can the Lord Jesus Christ find still a quiet place in thy heart and my heart, where he can speak the message which we have to take to that neighbor going down the broad road to destruction? Can he find a still place in our hearts to hear that word that we have heard already, bidding us go, go, go, into all the world?

Last year a friend of mine was back at home in England from China on a holiday, and she told me this. An old woman in China had become a Christian. My friend wanted her to join her own church, the Baptist. But she said with tears streaming from her eyes, " No; I shall never be able to join the Christian church." " Why not ?" She was unwilling to tell, but at last she said, " You know the Lord's last words, ' Go ye into all the world.' My dear, I cannot do it." Her feet had been bound and she could not go around easily. She said, " I have been into that village over there; I crawled into that village; but I cannot go everywhere, and so I can never be a member of the Christian church, for I cannot keep that command of his." Of course it was explained to her that the Master did not expect her to do what she could not do. But, beloved Endeavorers, what a lesson for you and for me. The same Master says to us, " Go ye into all the world and preach the gospel to every creature " China is lying in darkness; Africa is lying in darkness; in India millions are going down to the grave without the Christ that has made your life and my life what it is. Let us not be satisfied with our glorious conventions, with our fellowship one with another, but let us listen to the voice that says, Go. Let us not be selfish in our holiest things, but ask God what we can do, you and I, to take his message, the message of a glorious Saviour, to a dying world.

To show that this country is interested in some other features of Alaska besides her gold and seals, President Clark introduced one of her Christian workers.

Address by Dr. B. K. Wilbur, Alaska.

Mr. President and Beloved Fellow-Endeavorers: — A country of vast icebergs and a country of tangled forests; a country of rich gold-fields and a country of barren rocks; a country of wild natives and a country of wilder white men; a country of untrodden forests and a country of water-courses, thronged every year with thousands of tourists, greets you in the name of Christian Endeavor to-night. Of the United States, yet hardly in the United States, one thousand miles from our nearest neighbor, Alaska thanks God for Christian Endeavor; thanks God for that bond of fellowship which we consider to-night, that bond which binds you and me in Christ, that bond which, traveling from island to island, across from ocean to ocean, from mountain peak to mountain peak, binds you to us in Alaska in one great bond of love in Christ.

Alaska is a neglected country. Look at these letters around the hall. What are those letters on the shields? State after State, side by side, bound each to the other, inspiring each other, supporting each other. Away up there in the corner is Alaska. Beyond that is another shield without any name. That is for Cuba next year.

We hear everything of the United States *and* Alaska. We hear in the papers, in correspondence everywhere, of United States *and* Alaska. It seems to me very much as if Alaska was tied to the United States as the tin can is tied to the tail of the unwilling dog. But a strong, helping hand has come to Alaska, and back of the hand is a great Christian heart. And to-day many of our missionaries, and the only hospital in all that 580,000 square miles, is supported by Christian Endeavor.

Dear friends, beloved friends, forget not Alaska. Peter and James and John, as they stood on the mount and saw our Lord in all his glory, said, "It is good for us to be here. Let us build tabernacles and here abide." And so you and I have felt, as we have dwelt in the presence of our God in these meetings, that we would like to abide here and build tabernacles. But the Master said, "Arise, there is a work to do down at the foot of the mountain. There is a demoniacal boy to be healed." And so you and I must arise and go forth. But we shall go, better men and better women, even though some of the inspiration is lost; yet we will bear the impress of these meetings. And as we go, oh, forget not Alaska. She is neglected. She is poor. You have helped her much — oh, help her more.

And now, how can you help us? Alaska is a country almost unknown to many of you. Christian Endeavor has landed there. Two years ago, when our Boards were so distressed by debt — our little society at Sitka has only seven members, and none of us rich, yet we raised $300 to save three scholars from that school from going back to ignorance and darkness. One of our workers receives $500 a year, her only support, and yet she gave one-fifth of that to save a girl from the life of sin and shame.

Oh, forget not Alaska, and as you go hence with all your love and power, use that love and influence in helping Alaska more thoroughly, for she is your very own. And now as you go away, God grant that it shall be with Alaska on your hearts, and that trusting in the Lord Jesus Christ for strength, by his mighty power working in you and through you, you shall take and hold Alaska for Christ and the Church.

Rev. J. S. Conning was next introduced to the audience as a delegate from Canada, and the Chautauqua salute was given twice before he could begin his address. Rev. Mr. Conning spoke fluently and rapidly, and was interrupted repeatedly by applause. At the close of his talk the choir began the opening lines of "God Save the Queen," which was taken up by the entire audience. One verse of this was sung, and then the first verse of "My Country, 'T is of Thee," and both were rendered in excellent style and in perfect unison.

Address by Rev. J. S. Conning, Canada.

I greet you to-night in the name of 200,000 Canadian Christian Endeavorers. In no country in the world has Christian Endeavor been more cordially welcomed than in the fair dominion to which I belong. It is found in every province and in every denomination. You will find its banners and its badges in every city and town, from the sea pastures and the coal-fields of Nova Scotia to the golden sands of Columbia, and from the great river of St. Lawrence to the ends of the earth.

We Canadians are proud of our country, the land of the maple and the beaver; the land that lies in the North, that has ever been the home of industry. We are proud of our Queen, God bless her! — that Queen who for these sixty years has ruled her vast empire in the fear of the Lord, whose virtues have transmitted the sacred principles of loyalty into a personal affection. We are proud of our flag. You will see it up there — look upon it, the grand old flag; the flag with the double cross, that, like the Stars and Stripes beside it, has ever stood as the symbol of liberty and of civilization. We are proud, also, of our Christian Endeavor, for several reasons. Some of you may not know that Christian Endeavor had its origin in Canada. The United States may claim the honor of being the birthplace of the first society, but Canada claims the greater honor of being the birthplace of the beloved founder of this movement. If the United States can point to Williston Church, we can point to Cherry Cottage. And we would rather have the cottage, the cottage in which was the cradle where lay the boy who became Dr. Francis E. Clark, the leader of this great movement. If you want to find Christian Endeavor at its best, come to Canada.

Everything that Canada produces is, like its Manitoba wheat, number one, hard to beat. Canada has the largest society of Christian Endeavor in the world, and you will find there that Anglicans, Methodists, Presbyterians, Baptists, Congregationalists, and all denominations are bound together by the ties of Christian Endeavor, and the young people go forward under the one standard, "For Christ and the Church." We are not only proud of Christian Endeavor in Canada, but we are proud of the future that lies before it. We realize that there is a great future before this movement in our country, and we hope to see the day when all our Provinces will be bound together by this blessed tie of Christian fellowship, when our young people will be won for Jesus Christ, when all denominations will be bonded together by the ties of Christian sympathy, and when Christian citizenship will be exalted in our fair land, from ocean to ocean, from the Great Lakes to the North Pole — that our country shall become Emmanuel's land. And what I wish for our own country, I wish for your country, the country of the United States, the land that I love next to my own.

May this blessed work go on until Canada and the United States, and these lands that have been represented to-night upon this platform, may all be one for Jesus Christ; until God's angels in the heavens will arise and cry, "Hallelujah, for the Lord God Omnipotent reigns, and the kingdoms of this world have become the kingdoms of the Lord, and of Jesus Christ."

Mr. L. A. Dickey, a young lawyer from Hawaii, an ex-president of the Christian Endeavor union of the Hawaiian Islands, was next introduced.

Address by Mr. Lyle A. Dickey, Hawaii.

I have the most hearty good will for Cuba, but I hope I stand here for that " No-Name " shield there. Representatives here from countries encircling the globe make us think to-night of the missionary spirit, of the world-wide spiritual love that encircles the world. The first missionary field of the United States was the Hawaiian Islands. The first missionary Gulick was a missionary to the Hawaiian Islands. You all know that first of all the Christian Endeavor movement started in the United States, and had its first foreign society in the Hawaiian Islands. But the Hawaiian Islands are small, though there are several of them. The English-speaking population is massed in a few churches, and for many years Christian Endeavor societies did not increase in Hawaii. In the last few years, though, the young people of the Hawaiian Islands have been getting a little more of that fellowship displayed in the missionary spirit of their ancestors, and in the last year, for the first time, the Christian Endeavor pledge has been translated into the Hawaiian language.

Our country is small. We are more cosmopolitan in our conventions than the United States. At our convention a month ago the Hawaiian language was used almost as much as the English language. In our convention next year we expect to hear the Japanese, the Portuguese, and perhaps the Chinese language. But an announcement that will be of more interest, perhaps, than any other from the Hawaiian Islands, is that a Christian Endeavor society has been started among the lepers of Monokai. There has come with the delegation from the Hawaiian Islands the first president of the first native Hawaiian society, Mr. D. L. Naone, the minister of the church of Hau Wai Hau. I will not speak to you longer, but will introduce to you Mr. D. L. Naone, and he will give you a Hawaiian song.

Mr. Naone was greeted with applause. In reply he said : —

Brothers and Sisters : — Before I give my Hawaiian song, I will speak to you a few words. The Sunday before I left my country and my Hawaiian congregation, that congregation, and my Hawaiian Sunday-school, and my Hawaiian Christian Endeavor society, gave their love to you. And so I announce, in my own language, Aloha Oe Oko.

Mr. Naone then sang a hymn in his native tongue. A very hearty response was accorded by the audience.

Dr. Clark then introduced Australia's representative, the Rev. Dr. Mead.

Address by Rev. Silas Mead, LL.D., Australia.

I am very glad, Endeavorers, that Australia greets you to-night in the person of the one now addressing you. Mr. Close, our delegate to the Boston Convention, was not very successful in one idea that he had. He hurried home to Australia in order, by means of the phonograph, to give us a part of the speech of Dr. Clark that was delivered in Boston. Somehow, by reason of the delay in the post-office, the phonograph did n't come. But I have come really and truly, and I am not a phonograph, but I speak to you with the loving voice representing the earnest love and the earnest sympathy of all our Australian Endeavorers.

It is very proper indeed that we have as our subject to-night " Fellowship." I think there is an old saying that an ounce of fact is worth a ton of theory. But instead of theories upon this subject, Christian Endeavor puts it into fact. Here is a great fact to-night, and we have hearty, earnest, deep Christian Endeavor sympathy in all this great audience, and in all the audiences gathered in San Francisco to-night at the various Christian Endeavor meetings. I have not heard a word since I reached San Francisco but that has been in perfect accord with all our earnest sympathies for the cause of Christian Endeavor. Not only is this meeting, and the other meetings, evidence of our fellowship, but will you allow me just for a moment to make two or three references in order to confirm this thought? You all know about the idea of the world's chain of prayer. I think as time goes on, more and more will join in that great circle of prayer, so that in due time millions and millions and millions all around the globe will unite in the fellowship of prayer.

There is another bond of fellowship,—our president to-night; the president of the Christian Endeavor Union first, and I hope the one who will be president for many years. We in Australia feel that Dr. Clark is as much our president as yours. I know that the India's Endeavorers feel that Dr. Clark is their president also. I was at the Liverpool Convention the other week, and I am quite sure the Liverpool Endeavorers felt just as truly and earnestly that Dr. Clark is their president as you feel that he is yours.

And so we have in Dr. Clark a wonderful, living bond of fellowship. More people know Dr. Clark in India than perhaps anybody else in America, even including your President.

I was going to tell you about *The Golden Rule* being a bond of union, and some other things, but my time has expired. I am very glad to-night, however, to express on behalf of our Australian Endeavorers their earnest congratulations and rejoicings in our fellowship, — a fellowship that is not only for this country, but for all countries; a fellowship in Christ; a fellowship in the service of Christ; a fellowship in the church of Christ.

Dr. Clark regretted the absence of Mr. Robert Somerville, who was to have spoken for Scotland. But as he presented Mr. Somerville's sister, the audience accorded her a flaky-white Chautauqua salute. Miss Somerville acknowledged the compliment with a graceful bow.

President Clark suggested as a pleasant and appropriate conclusion to the fellowship greetings and the international symposium, that the national air be sung, and the Convention might supply the words of either " America " or " God Save the Queen." The multitude suited the action to the thought, and the effect was such that if English and American statesmen should do the same in their respective halls of legislature, it would abolish all necessity for a board of international arbitration.

Secretary Baer came forward and announced " just as one would break an egg," that is, " gently," " Dr. Conwell is not here." The audience felt the disappointment, but, like all C. E.'s, rallied. When President Clark introduced a substitute in the person who is behind " Nashville '98," Rev. Ira Landrith, he was heartily applauded and closely followed in his address.

Address by Rev. Ira Landrith, Nashville.

There is a homely story which in spite of its great age has done me valued service on more than one occasion. I remember to have used it when people said, " You can't get the Convention in Nashville in 1898; and if you did get it, you wouldn't know what to do with it, and you couldn't entertain it." We answer that sort of people now by telling them that only last week Nashville entertained from 50,000 to 75,000 strangers every day, and it can do it again. But to the story. It is said that on one occasion a man who had a favorite dog was out hunting, and when he came back he told this story of his cur. " When out in the woods," said he, " a bear got after my dog, and the dog ran, and the dog ran, and the bear ran after him, and the dog ran, and the dog ran right up a tree." But the man who heard it said, "I beg your pardon, but a dog can't climb a tree." And then he said, "*But that one had to.*" My point is this: I knew I could n't fill the place of Dr. Russell H. Conwell, and I said I could n't fill the place of Dr. Russell H. Conwell, but a Baer got after me and *I had to.* Now, will you please not press that figure any further? There is a dog at the other end of it. Some years ago, I think it was at Montreal, the president of the United Society of Christian Endeavor proposed three systematic endeavors. They were systematic and proportionate,—giving to missions, Christian citizenship, or good citizenship, and interdenominational fellowship. I have heard an eminent Southern Methodist minister say, as he expressed his own regret that his own church had seen fit to withdraw from Christian Endeavor, "Our mistake was that we did not stop to remember that great reforms must be accomplished by great multitudes, and that Christian Endeavor, with the co-operation of Methodists and others, would soon have been a power, as by and by it must be without us, which will be so tremendous as to be irresistible." I believe that this Christian Endeavor movement is three practical endeavors, three great necessary reforms, which could not have been accomplished without these immense multitudes. Why is it that the splendid press of this splendid city, and of the whole wide world for that matter, is giving even more attention to this movement and to this Convention than it ever did give even to that little incident which occurred in the Fitzsimmons commonwealth of Corbett? Because we are here, and here in such tremendous numbers — and let me as an individual Endeavorer, and I believe I speak for three millions of others, express gratitude and appreciation to the secular press for what it is doing. And after all, Christian people, have n't you about reached the conclusion that it is about time we were to quit abusing the press and go to using it more?

I believe that these three great practical endeavors were divinely suggested, just as I believe that when our president stood here yesterday and suggested home religion as the next endeavor of Christian Endeavor, God's spirit was in him and in the suggestion. Interpret that pledge of ours, "and to pray by my own fireside," and Christian Endeavor will in the next year accomplish more than it has in the last sixteen. God bless the suggestion, and let us take it down from here fifty thousand strong to fifty thousand firesides throughout the world.

Systematic giving was that first endeavor. We do not stop to dwell upon it. We remarked that giving is the most natural thing in the world; that every other creature of God gives abundantly, and that man, the last, best work of our Master, is the only creature in the world who holds all God gave him. We believe that giving should be systematic and regular. Do you know what the nickel habit is? Got it in your church? It is dreadful in mine. The nickel habit is this: a man starts down here by suggestion of the pastor to raise a missionary collection. Up this aisle and down that goes the collection-basket. But back yonder sits a man who ought to give $5, $10, $15, who sees that everybody else is giving, and he must, not because he ought to for the Lord. He has no desire to aid the work of the mission, but he wants to do and take the credit for doing what other people are doing, and he reaches into his pocket, fingers there among the coin, finally finds a nickel, grasps it very hard and long, drops it into the basket with a half-dollar clutch, and then goes on singing "How I love the Lord!" That is the nickel habit. It is catching. If it is possible, keep it out of your community. We believe, and I am sure he believed who suggested this practical endeavor, that the nickel habit ought to be cured, and cured by systematic giving.

And I believe he wanted to cure another thing. I don't know. I have not consulted him and do not undertake to speak for him; but I believe he wanted to cure that abnormal, almost monstrous effort we are making to serve the Lord with a large amount of ice-cream. Or, to put it otherwise, to give entertainments for revenue only. I believe that Christian Endeavor, as such, in its genius, is opposed to such a hap-hazard, legalized mendicancy as these methods suggest. I don't believe I have the right — I don't believe, as a Christian, I ought to go begging for the Lord when I would feel disgraced to go begging for myself. If I would not give a parlor entertainment to raise money for my wife and children, I have no right to do the same to raise money for my King of kings, and then sing, "I am the child of the King." Giving is worship, or it is nothing. It is worship or it is blasphemy; and it is high time we were learning that if we loved the Lord we would give to him, and if we loved him more than we do ourselves, we would give to him at least a tenth of what he has given to us.

That other practical endeavor was Christian citizenship. I remember that when Paul, that great ideal Christian citizen of the ages, was approached on one occasion by one of his enemies, and the suggestion was made that you had better be a little particular, we purchased our freedom at a great price, Paul looked his insulters in the face, and said, "I was free born." And as an American citizen and a Christian American citizen, and even a Christian minister in America, let me say that though I have the right to button this clerical coat to my chin, I still was free born, and I don't believe, and Christian Endeavor doesn't believe, that the red of nose and black of heart professional politician who exists in the land has any particular monopoly on statesmanship or political duties. The movement stands for political integrity, — first of the voter who regards the ballot-box as sacred as the ark of the covenant, so that he who would touch it with unholy hands must suffer the same social death — be careful that you understand me — as he suffered who touched the ark of our God, and died physically. Let us elevate the ballot-box until people will not smile, but hiss, when the suggestion is made that an American citizen is ever for sale.

There is another thing which Christian citizenship must do, and that is to elevate the office until cleanliness will care for position. You have heard the story a thousand times — perhaps it will bear repeating for a thousand and one — of how a father did not know what to do with his boy. The fellow didn't seem to have any special inclination any way, and so he said to his wife, the old man did: "We will put John here in this room and shut him up, and I will put a dollar in there, and an apple, and a Bible. If he takes the dollar, I will make a banker of him; if he takes the apple, I will make a farmer of him; and if he takes the Bible, I guess we will have to make a preacher out of him." That is the way parents feel about it, God forgive them! Then, by and by, he brought his old lady back, and they pushed open the door gently and peered in, and there stood the boy, like a young American always, with the apple in his mouth, and the dollar in his pocket, and the Bible under his arm; and the old man said, "Maria, the boy is a hog; we will make a politician of him." Now, what made you laugh? Honestly, what made you laugh? And wasn't that laugh eloquent with the suggestion that we have allowed political position in this country to sink so low that I came pretty near telling the truth about it in many cases? And if that be true, isn't it high time that Christian Endeavor, and Christian citizenship generally, were working to elevate political position until such a story as that would be accounted too far from the truth to arouse anything but either disgust or resentment? God help us to improve social conditions at least to that extent. Let us have political intelligence, and independence.

I believe Christian Endeavor ought to stand for good laws and the enforcement of them. I believe that Christian Endeavor was back of the movement which in my own State passed a law a few days ago, by unanimous vote of the legislature, that if an American dude wanted to commit suicide he would have to choose some other route than the cigarette. To Chicago we owe some good things, because, after all, some good things can come out of Nazareth. To Chicago we owe this new definition of a dude: "He is the unimportant appendage to the damp end of a cigarette."

Passing now for these closing moments to the special theme of the evening, interdenominational fellowship as promoted by Christian Endeavor, let me say, first of all, that it does promote interdenominational fellowship, and I need go no farther than this audience to prove it. Present evidences are sufficient. In that last platform of Christian Endeavor before the one proclaimed here, and I hope there will be no special change, and I believe there is none, the fourth plank is: " Our interdenominational and international fellowship, based upon our denominational and national loyalty." I believe that no true American, no true citizen of the United States, is any less loyal because with all our hearts we joined in singing " God Save the Queen," that blessed international fellowship. Nor do I believe that, as Christian Endeavorers, we who have stood and peered out of the window of the Cliff House with opera-glasses will ever again feel like shedding any good American and English blood because of a few ugly old seals. What does this new fellowship of the denomination stand for? What does it mean after all, except that as we get closer to Christ we are getting closer to each other? We have been praying, " God bring us closer together;" and finally we quit that, and in the name of Jesus Christ, Christian Endeavor has merely been praying for fifteen years, " God bring us closer to Jesus," and we found to our utter amazement that when we got to Christ we were denominationally very close to each other. It means merely that we have come to know each other better. Some reference has been made to that particular " Canadian from the Emerald Isle "— I remember those of you who were at Cleveland— those of you who in spite of Debs succeeded in reaching Cleveland— that this same William Patterson — those who know him well are irreverent enough to call him Billy Patterson — said: " The worst fear I ever had in my life was from a plain sheep, a plain sheep. My father had brought me home and turned me loose in the back yard and I never had seen a sheep at all at all, and was a little boy, and I ran out into my father's back yard, and the sheep came bleating at me and it scared me within an inch of my life. I had never seen a sheep; but when I came to know him right well, I loved the sheep better than any other animal in my father's barnyard." And so here, as we have come to know each other, we have found that the other denominations were not so desperate and dangerous as all the while we had thought they were.

The Christian Endeavor motto of my own denomination is: " In work denominational, in spirit and fellowship interdenominational." And I believe it is a good motto. We are clinging to those things that seem to us vital, and then we are magnifying those things upon which we can agree. It was a heathen, the founder of a great heathen religion, who said to his own followers, — in some way it seems that we might learn this lesson from the heathen,— " Magnify your own creed, but do not, do not slander the creed of other people."

This movement does not mean that we are rapidly, through Endeavor, approaching denominational union. I believe that organic union is never as good a term as co-operation and communion, anyway. I believe — and so I believe the leaders of Christian Endeavor believe — that it is not quite practicable; and whether it is or not, it was never the mission, and is not the purpose or intent, of Christian Endeavor to secure or seek denominational organic union. It will be hard to do. All men are queer, except, as the Quaker said, " Except me and thee; and thee is a little queer;" and it will be some time before we change conditions. Some of the efforts for organic union have been very interesting. You heard the story of the old gentleman and his wife who did not quite agree about the kind of sheets they slept on, and the old man was telling about it. He said, " My wife wanted linen and I wanted cotton, and we compromised on cotton." If we could just have organic union on a Cumberland Presbyterian basis, I am for it. If you will just compromise on my own denominational platform, we will unite right away; and that is the way every other denomination on the face of the earth feels about it. Well, I doubt if it is necessary. Somehow the Lord didn't seem to paint the sky always the same color. Somehow he didn't give all the flowers the same hue. Some way he put variety in this earth, and I believe there is beauty in variety; and after all, it is sometimes better for the success of a cause that we have various portions of an army; and if it shall continue in the church of Jesus Christ as it does in the world that we shall have soldiers on hand, and some who come by water, who cares so long as the work is done and done right well and early?

You know what stravaging is? That is the conduct of the Methodist who

A Corner in the State Headquarters, Showing Tennessee's Booth.

would just as soon be a Presbyterian as anything else, who would always go to hear the best preacher in town without reference to what church he belonged to, and who would particularly attend any prayer-meeting except his own. That is stravaging, and it applies to all churches. It is the conduct of the young man who said he wanted to be employed, and the man asked him what church he belonged to, and he said: " I am a Presbyterian, sir, but I can change if that does n't suit you." Most of us have had our periods of singing an old song in a new way, but thank God it is over now, —

> " I love thy kingdom, Lord, the house of thine abode,
> But other churches I despise, for they are on the downward road."

After Mr. Landrith's address, the audience sang " Blest Be the Tie that Binds." The Mizpah benediction brought this very profitable and inspiring session to a close.

Woodward's Pavilion.

The capacity of the pavilion was taxed to its utmost. There were special musical features to heighten the character of the program, and the happy presiding of Rev. C. A. Dickinson, D.D., of Boston, carried the session upon a top wave. All present felt the power of the addresses, and the responsiveness of the audience was noticeable.

Musical Director Vesper, of Oakland, led the singing. The opening words were of the national anthem, which swung everybody into line. Rev. A. J. Turkle, of Omaha, Nebraska, conducted the devotional exercises.

Before introducing the first speaker Dr. Dickinson said : " This Convention will go down to history as the greatest and grandest of our Christian Endeavor gatherings. The world and our country marvel at the fact that more than twenty-five thousand people have traveled from all parts of the earth to the Golden Gate for a Christian purpose, for a purely religious meeting "

Rev. M. S. Hughes, D.D., pastor of the Wesley M. E. Church, Minneapolis, Minn., delivered an address upon the " Promotion of Denominational Loyalty by Christian Endeavor."

Address by Rev. Matt S. Hughes, D.D., Minneapolis.

My subject is, " The Promotion of Denominational Loyalty by Christian Endeavor." To those who have made a study of the principles underlying this mighty movement of our times, my task will seem a violation of that article of our creed which declares against works of supererogation. As citizens we must move within the limits of the Constitution of the United States; as Endeavorers we must build for the future upon those basic principles which have furnished the foundation of past successes. To stir up " pure minds by way of remembrance " is as essential as to illuminate with new truth. So the wisdom of the assignment of this topic to a place on the program is apparent in every particular except in the choice of the speaker.

Charles Dickens, in " Bleak House," gave us his characteristic creation, the immortal and typical Mrs. Jellaby. Mrs. Jellaby was a woman with a mission ; but her mission, unlike charity, did not begin at home. Her eyes are described as having been telescopic. They had a curious habit of looking afar off, " as if they could see nothing nearer than Africa." Mrs. Jellaby devoted her talents to the business of benevolent societies, but chiefly to the grand project of a great Christian, coffee-growing colony at Borioboola-Gha, on the left bank of the Niger.

She had a sublime disregard of all home duties, and an astonishing unconsciousness of her responsibility as a wife and mother. So Mrs. Jellaby spent her time writing circulars and appeals connected with her African work. She herself was an amiable slattern, and she was assisted by her ink-stained and unwholesome looking daughter, Caddy. The home was dirty and disordered, and the Jellaby children, with tangled hair and torn clothes, decorated with dirt and bruises, existed in a semi-barbarous condition. But all domestic affairs were as dust in Mrs. Jellaby's estimation when compared with the proposed settlement on the banks of the Niger. To be sure, the portrait of Mrs. Jellaby has the exaggeration of a caricature, but it is none the less profitable on that account as a warning against what Dickens called "Telescopic Philanthropy."

We all have home interests and responsibilities. It goes without saying that each Endeavorer has a church home. "The man without a country" is no more an anomaly than the Christian without a church. The wandering Christian is as pathetic a figure as that weird, legendary personage, "the wandering Jew." We are all Endeavorers, but we are also Congregationalists, Presbyterians, Baptists, Methodists, or representatives of some other one of thirty denominations. What is the relation of Christian Endeavor to the denominations? That relation should be clearly defined. I venture to say that this program has no subject more vital to the integrity and perpetuity of the movement.

In its relation to denominations, Christian Endeavor adheres to two fundamental principles : the first is loyalty to the denomination, the second, fraternity between the denominations. These principles give the individual Endeavorer a centre and a circumference. The centre is the church particular, the circumference is the church universal. These principles provide for fidelity and fellowship — fidelity to the denomination, fellowship with all other denominations. These principles foster conviction and co-operation — conviction concerning the doctrines, polity, and methods of the denomination ; co-operation in the common work of bringing the world to the feet of the Master, which is the supreme object of all denominations. These principles represent the centripetal and centrifugal forces of the Endeavor movement. The centripetal force of loyalty holds the Endeavorer in his true relation to the body of which he is a member ; the centrifugal force of fraternity binds him in loving ties to all these who follow Christ. In the balanced action of two apparently antagonistic forces is found the secret of the harmony and security of the heavenly bodies ; so in the proportionate influence of the two principles of loyalty and fraternity will be found the pledge of the permanent power and progress of this great Endeavor movement.

I am here to emphasize the distinctive principle of denominational loyalty. It is always a difficult matter to maintain two seemingly antagonistic principles in equilibrium. The law of proportion is one most difficult to obey. Hence, the wisdom of having these two fundamental principles emphasized by two speakers at the same meeting. The dangers of failure in this respect are two. First, the over-emphasis of loyalty to denomination will inevitably result in exclusiveness, narrowness, and sectarianism. On the other hand, fraternity, to the exclusion of loyalty, will result in Jellabyism, that neglects the simplest home duties, and expends its energies in barren sentimentalism. Hence, this subject will be up-to-date and vital in the conventions of the latter part of the twentieth century.

Denominational loyalty is connected with the object of Christian Endeavor. The original society of Williston had for its end the training of young converts in the duties of church membership. It was born of a pastor's desire to make his young people loyal and efficient members of the Church of God. This he sought to do by the promotion of a vital Christian experience, and by education in methods of usefulness. The double purpose of developing Christians and producing workers is expressed in the name, Christian Endeavor. This was and is a movement of the church, by the church, and for the church.

Denominational loyalty is written in the motto. Emblazoned on the banners of Endeavor are the words, "For Christ and the Church." The church, for the individual, is primarily that church whose records bear the name, whose hand of fellowship was extended in personal welcome, and whose altar witnessed the registration of vows. The Endeavorer who possesses the spirit of the motto is not a disciple of Mrs. Jellaby, disregardful of home duties, and devoid of domestic sympathies.

Denominational loyalty is indicated in its sphere. The local society is found in some church — not simply attached to some church in barnacle fashion, but it is a vital part of the church. The church is its home and the basis of its operations. Its work is church work; the duties of its members are the duties of church membership. Not that the society is to be in close confinement in the church. Its influence is to reach beyond the church, but it is to be no more separated from the church in its outreaching activities than is sunshine to be divorced from the sun or the perfume from the rose. The Endeavor society is the young life of the church expressing itself in vital piety and consecrated enterprise.

Denominational loyalty is necessitated by its economy. If not to your denomination, then to what will you offer your allegiance? What is your alternative? The United Society absolutely refuses to assume any control or authority over any local society. It is organized simply as a bureau of information, and its only work beyond that is arranging for these international conventions. And these conventions are held not for purposes of legislation, but solely for fellowship. They are simply a feature of Endeavor fraternity. The United Society does not even make a financial claim on the local society in levying a tax. The United Society specifically and emphatically directs that each local chapter must manage its own affairs in harmony with its denominational polity. Thus the United Society consistently adheres to the fundamental principles of denominational loyalty, and repudiates as false to the spirit of the movement any schism between the local chapter and the church.

Denominational loyalty is inculcated by its leaders. The leaders of the movement — those who are best qualified and authorized to speak on the subject — declare that the local society owes allegiance only, and altogether, to the church of which it is a part. Any vexed question arising in the society is to be submitted to the final decision of the regularly constituted church authorities, and that decision is final. The list of officers nominated by the society is to be subject to revision or veto by the church. Reports of the activities of the society are to be regularly submitted to the official board of the church. In brief, in every possible way the local society is to put itself under the control of the church. Such is the official opinion on the subject, as you will find by consulting any officer of the United Society, from President Clark down.

Thus it will be seen that Christian Endeavor, judged by its principles, is entitled to be known as a society for the promotion of denominational loyalty. It stands in each denomination for loyalty to doctrine, for loyalty to polity, for loyalty to usage, for loyalty to authority. It insists upon the Presbyterian being a true-blue Presbyterian; upon the Congregationalist being an all-round Congregationalist; upon the Baptist being an up-and-down Baptist; and upon the Methodist being a Methodist, first, last, and all the time. If you wish to become a first-class Endeavorer you must begin by asking what is required by loyalty to the denomination to which you belong. Loyalty to the denomination and to Endeavor principles must be one and inseparable.

Let me also emphasize, in closing, the fact that upon strict adherence to this principle of denominational loyalty hangs the principle of interdenominational fraternity. You must have the national before you secure the international; you must have the collegiate before you can have the intercollegiate; so we must have the denominational before we can have the interdenominational. To attempt anything else is to do violence to what may be termed the instinct of self-preservation to be found in every organized body. A society for the overthrow of institutions founded upon convictions is an organized impertinence. It is not too much to say that Christian Endeavor will maintain its magnificent influence as an interdenominational factor only by strenuous observance of the principle of denominational loyalty.

In all our relations to each other as followers of Christ I know of no better guide than the comprehensive directions contained in the famous words of an old church father: " In essentials, unity ; in non-essentials, liberty ; in all things, charity."

The ever-welcomed " Saved by Grace," was then sung in duet by Mr. Robert Husband and Miss Josephine Patterson. Recalled by the audience, they responded with " The Banner of the Cross."

The next address was a complement to the first, upon " How Christian Endeavor Promotes World-wide Fellowship." The speaker was the Rev. J. C. R. Ewing, D.D., of Lahore, India.

Address by Rev. J. C. R. Ewing, D.D., Lahore, India.

It is my joy to-night to bring to you the greetings of two hundred and fifty societies of Christian Endeavor in that great country of India. During the decade ending 1861 the increase in the number of native Christians in that country was 22 per cent; from '61 to '71, 41 per cent; from '71 to 81, 58 per cent, and from '81 to '91, 82 per cent. This represents in a vague way the increase in the number of our Christian brethren and sisters in that land across the sea. The promotion of international fellowship through the agency of the Christian Endeavor Society is a theme which can best be grasped, I believe, by us all if we aim to understand that some of our brothers and sisters on the other side of the world have entered with us into this great organization, and that they are rejoicing with us in the same blessed service. It was our privilege during the past winter to have a visit from the Rev. Dr. Clark, the president of this society, and as we looked into his face, and in our feeble way aimed to give him a welcome and some imitation of those great welcomes which these conventions give him, we felt that, after all, we were but a part of this great army which has risen up in this world to win this country and the whole world for Jesus Christ. The brethren and the sisters of far-off India look out across the great sea toward us to-day. They are not unaware of the fact that there is here in this city of the West this great gathering of Christians, and they say to themselves, and they say to their neighbors, We are but a part of that great army.

Let us for a moment turn our thoughts to that from which they came, and rejoice with them in the distinction which they have gained in being members of such an army as this. There are two hundred and sixty-seven millions of people in that country. Think of England and France and Germany and Russia and Turkey proper, and these great United States, and take the population of all, weld them into one great heterogeneous mass, and you have only a population equal to the population of that country of which I speak, and which has as yet but two hundred and fifty organizations of Christian Endeavor. It has sometimes been said of recent years that there are five million native Christians in the world,— the black and the brown a' d the red,— but this is not all. Besides these, if you will only allow your imagination to work through that which you know, and will hold upon the thought that many of them, through great tribulations, have entered into the Kingdom, you will understand something of the Christian church in those far-away countries of the world. They did not pass away as in the vision of Mirzah, for there is no vision of Mirzah. They did not pass into the Buddhist hell; but we saw them pass out across the dark river of Death, and enter the very paradise of God, and we heard them sing the songs of Moses and the Lamb. You have brothers and sisters in that country who through great tribulation and without the vision of Stephen to cheer them on, have suffered martyrdom, and some of them, because of their faith, are suffering a practical daily martyrdom now.

Some years ago it was my privilege to baptize a young Brahmin lad. On the Sabbath morning he was baptized, and in the evening his father came with an uncle and took him away to his house. He came back after a week had passed by, and I noticed a marked retrogression. He came again and again, and our hearts were saddened as we saw that, instead of an increase of faith and hope and love, there was a deadness, a blindness, and a darkness.

We sent a Christian brother to find the cause of this to a village about fourteen miles away. He came back and told us this strange story. I wish you to take it as a significance of what it means to be a Christian and an Endeavorer in far-away India. His mother had administered surreptitiously opiates, and had applied to him a temptation awful in its debasing character. She succeeded in winning him away from righteousness, and was glad of it. The last I saw of the lad was five years ago. He was then a drivelling idiot, drawn away from the path of God. You know how you feel to stand up in a Christian congregation at home and say, "I believe in the Lord Jesus Christ as my Saviour," and how your mother and father fell on their knees and thanked God that he had given you grace to say that. It is there so different, and there are multitudes to-day that have what Joseph Cook calls a solar light in their faces — the light which you and I saw in those noble leaders of this society yesterday — the light which comes from personal experience with Christian effort.

The society to which I belong, in the City of Lahore, away up in the northern part of India, is a working society, and is, I believe, a type of the other societies of that country. They are looking for your prayers, that God may give them strength to carry forward their good work. A week before I left that land, one Sabbath afternoon, one of those Endeavorers accompanied me to the Bazaar to preach in the city. We took our stand on the street-corner, and soon drew a great gathering around us. At the beginning of the exercises, in order to draw a greater crowd, we sang a hymn. That hymn was this:

> "Jesus Christ is mine.
> For my sins and my salvation,
> Jesus came from heaven above.
> I have taken him as my own.
> His it is to guide and lead,
> Mine it is to follow whithersoever
> He shall tell me to go."

We saw about us a great gathering of Hindoos, Mohammedans, and Parsees. There were all classes. There was the poor outcast, who makes his living as a scavenger of the people; a high-caste man with a countenance very much like the face of a respectable cow; there were others having no interest in the affair except to gain popularity for themselves. A man soon came up through the crowd, slick and oily and impertinent — with an impertinence imprinted upon his face superior to any which I have ever seen upon the face of anybody. He took his place in front of the preacher, and began in this wise (the preacher had at that time proceeded through the beginning of his discourse to the point where he desired to be very emphatic). Presently he interrupted the speaker and said: "I hope that your great majesty is entirely well. I hope your great majesty will allow your slave, for a very short time, to interrupt this proceeding." The "great majesty" continued to preach for a little time. The man, unwilling to be put down, again interrupted, saying: "The question I wish to ask is this. I have heard that you are one of the wisest men in all the world, and, having heard this, I know I will get a correct answer. Do you believe the Bible?"

"Yes, I do."

"Do you believe the Old Testament?"

"Yes."

"Do you believe those books called Leviticus, and Numbers, and Deuteronomy?"

"Yes, I do."

"Then, I want to know why you Christians eat pork?"

I shall leave this for the Christian Endeavorers to answer.

You will understand that this is merely a typical question. There are many other exceedingly frivolous questions asked of those who labor in these far-away lands; such as, "How is it possible for God and man to be so united as to be a savior of men?" "Explain to me the Trinity, and how the Godhead has suffered upon the cross." These questions call forth all the clear thinking of the clearest-headed missionaries to answer. There are some of you who are thinking about being missionaries, and may God help you to be such. I believe nearly all of you are anxious to be missionaries, and to be amongst those who will be sent forth into the dark places of the earth to preach the unsearchable riches of Christ. But it is not true that any sort of a thing in the shape of a man will do for a missionary. If there is any place in the world where I believe the very best that the Church of Christ has ought to be expended, it is in such countries as India, China, and Japan, for there are no people in the world more ready to see and to recognize in an instant inefficiency and incapacity in the individual who has been sent out by the Christian church. The Hindoos of India are a people possessed of a most fascinating philosophy, which exercises the mind while it distorts the faculties. It is possessed of a great many crazy things, but, with all its craziness, there is, after all, underlying it, a keenness of thought and an earnestness of purpose that appeal to us as Christians in the hope that we may go forth, with the help of the Lord, and win those people for the Lord Jesus Christ.

I sometimes think that Christian Endeavorers, and other Christians, do not realize that all the world is not heathen, in the same sense as we in childhood were taught. The people of India — the Christian Endeavorers of India — are not naked people. There are many of them capable of standing side by side with us, in our homes and in our social life. There are lawyers, and doctors, and people of other professions among them. The leader of the Christian Endeavor Society of Punjaub Colony is a professor in a university. He is a man who stands away above his fellows among the Hindoos and Mohammedans, and among a great many others, in his desire to serve his Master. The people of that country from which our brothers and sisters have come cannot be fully understood by us to-night. But there is one statement which I desire to emphasize. There are those who have addressed audiences in this land, and made statements concerning the Hindoo religion, which, if they were true, would be most beauteous; but I stand as a representative of the Christian Endeavor societies adhering to the principles of your religion, and I say there is nothing in the Hindoo religion to answer any one of these tests. There are 250,000,000 of Hindoos, four-fifths of whom are bowing down in adoration of an obscene object. One of the priests of Punjaub, ten years ago, was accustomed to sit upon a table, and to be looked upon by all as a holy man. Women and little girls came from their homes, went to a well near by, and drew water, which they took to this holy man and asked him to wash his holy feet. Then these poor women and children drank the water to the last drop. Can you understand, dear friends, what this means to us — those who have seen this man, and seen the people do those things which I have described? Yet he has now come forth as a preacher of the religion of Jesus Christ.

O brethren, what is it that Jesus Christ told us to do? "Go ye into all the world, and preach the gospel to every creature." That is what we ought to do, that is what we must do, if we as a society, as a church, are to live in the world, or if we have any right to live in the world. We must do what our Master told us to do; but I am sometimes afraid of the result of our not doing what we have been told to do. May it not be in the experience of us that that may take place which took place off in the deserts and jungles of Africa, where the African priest, having heard a missionary stand up and tell about one who came nineteen hundred years ago to save mankind, rose to his feet, and raising his hand to heaven, defied the missionary. "You tell me that eighteen hundred years ago the great God sent down from heaven his own son that all men might live, and you people in England and America have known about it for nineteen hundred years, and have never told us? I will tell you what I will do. I will go away, and when the Great Day comes, we will take our stand right before the great God, and we will say to you who stand before him too, 'O God, thou Infinite God, do justice between us.'"

O brethren and sisters, there is before the Church of Jesus Christ in that country of which I speak a necessity which fills my heart as I think of it to-night, and as I see your eager faces here, and realize what it would mean to those brethren if they could but look in your faces.

I have in my pocket to-night a foreign post-card which reached me yesterday morning here in San Francisco. Upon that card, which was written by a native brother, a young man, in the English language, are these words about his father, who was a member, when I left Lahore, of our Christian Endeavor Society: " Last Tuesday my dear father died, and his last words were, Tell Dr. Ewing that I say that at this last hour underneath are the everlasting arms.' " Does not that bring us very near together? Do we not realize as we hear that, that after all the same arms that have been underneath and about you and me in our childhood, in our manhood, throughout all our life, amidst its cares and trials, — those same arms are underneath our brother away off in dark Hindoostan, sustaining and helping him? Is not that a world-wide fellowship? Is not that something which ought to help us to realize that we are one in Jesus Christ?

A student in the senior class in Lahore was a Hindoo a year ago. After his baptism, his wife and friends refused longer to have anything to do with him. These relatives came to Lahore one day and desired to see the son and brother. He said, " I dare not go to a Hindoo house; they will poison me. Won't you go with me? " I went with him down to the city to the house of a friend of his and of ours, and as we were about to enter the room where his mother and his sister and his wife were, he said to me. " Sir, I want you to sit just here by the door, because I shall be tried, and I am very weak. Sit here and pray all the time. The fact of knowing you to be there will help me much." I sat there for three-quarters of an hour, and I wish you could have heard the cries from within, the pleadings from within, as that bright, dear boy stood against those who were nearest and dearest to him. But when he came out his face glowed; there was a glow upon his face, a glow which came from a victory over himself and over all his natural longing, a victory for Jesus Christ. The first of all the band who, during last winter, when Mr. Mott was in Lahore, offered themselves as missionaries was this young man, who rose in his place and said, " I must be a missionary." When asked, " Why? " he said, " I cannot be anything else but a missionary for Jesus Christ. He has done so much for me, I must do all I can for him." But that does not mean for him money and wealth. He knows that there are hundreds of rupees waiting for him if he will enter the government service, and that in doing so he will be honored by his own people.

" Go ye into all the world and preach the gospel to every creature." After Mr. Judson had been in Burmah for a long time, his friends wrote to him again and again asking about the prospects, and the answer came back. " Bright as the promises of God." A year passed by, and again they wrote to him as to the prospects, and again the answer came back, " As bright as the promises of God." So we want to feel to-day, in regard to the conversion of the world to Jesus Christ, that the prospects are " as bright as the promises of God." Shall we not here to-day, fellow Christian Endeavorers, lift our hearts in prayer to God that those, our brethren and sisters, across the sea in India and in Africa may be brought to the Lord Jesus Christ, and that we may be baptized with the Spirit of God, which it is our right to be baptized with. Are you and I going to be satisfied longer to live at this poor dying rate, always doubting, always fearing, or are we going to lay hold upon the promises which the Son of God himself gave when he told his disciples to go forth? We need to be filled with the Spirit of God just as Peter was filled, just as Paul was filled, before we have any right to claim it over across the sea. Fellow-Endeavorers, let us claim the gift of the Holy Ghost. Our dear brother, leaving behind him all material wealth, went forth carrying nothing but what he needed for each day's living. He went to one of the missions in Punjab, and there was a day of Pentecost as the result of his influence. Eleven men and women rose in the congregation and said " We shall leave all for Christ." One of our American sisters, with these eleven brethren from that country, is going forth with them, without charge to any man, preaching the gospel of Christ; and that Christian American sister is going barefooted on her way from village to village, preaching the unsearchable riches of Christ.

They are stretching out their hands to us from across the sea to-day, and they are asking us for more men and more women, and, above all, for more prayer, that the Spirit of God may come upon them and upon us, and that we and they may be so filled with his power that we shall be fitted for his service, and we shall look to the day when we shall say with them, " Hallelujah, for the Lord omnipotent reigneth. Hallelujah, for the kingdoms of this world have become the kingdoms of our Lord and of his Christ."

The address of Dr. Ewing was attentively heard and heartily applauded.

The banner to be presented to the local city Christian Endeavor Union reporting the best work accomplished in promoting fellowship last year, by organizing the largest number of new societies, was won by Philadelphia. Though the banner was not actually present, Canon J. B. Richardson, of London, Ontario, made a bright little speech as he passed it over — metaphorically — to the Quaker City Union.

Speech of Presentation, by Rev. Canon J. B. Richardson, London, Ont.

Mr. Chairman : — As a Canadian, it always affords me a great deal of pleasure to be mixed up with United States affairs. It is because those affairs have always been to myself so exceedingly happy and so profitable.

I feel that a very great honor has been conferred upon me by the Board of Trustees in making me the humble medium of presenting to the local union of the city of Philadelphia a banner for having inaugurated the largest number of societies within the area of the union.

I regard it as a double honor; first, because I become the humble medium of bringing a great deal of pleasure to a most distinguished and honored local union ; and secondly, because in a still humbler way I become an arbitrator between two very important cities of this great Republic.

In response to a telegram received by Secretary Baer a few days ago, it appears that the city of Philadelphia is entitled to this honor by all odds.

This day week I had the pleasure of visiting Chicago, for the first time in my life. I had heard a great deal of the wickedness, and immorality, and sin of that place, but I was told, during my visit there, that Chicago was becoming very much changed in this respect — very much improved. Who knows but that the influence of our fellow Christian Endeavorers in that great city has been the instrument, under God, of conferring the blessings in which Chicago now seems to rejoice. I do not know how it is, Mr. Chairman, with other local unions, but I am very sorry to say that with our local unions of Canada, and with many others with which I am familiar, they are the most useless department of Christian Endeavor work that I know of. They seem to have little or nothing to do, can scarcely gain a quorum at their monthly meetings, and their whole energy seems to be expended in making arrangements for the reports of the general conventions. But in Chicago last year, and in Philadelphia this year, they have been most important factors, and I hope that the representatives of the local unions here to-night will take warning and take encouragement, and in the future exercise the true power which belongs to them, of extending Christian Endeavor within their own limits.

I am not surprised that the glorious " City of Brotherly Love " and Christian fellowship and Christian affection receives the banner this year. I have very much pleasure in bestowing it upon the representative of Philadelphia who is here this evening.

I may just say that the banner is really here in spirit, though in material it is somewhere else. I promise you that you shall see it, before the Convention closes, in all its magnificence and beauty.

The response, on behalf of the Philadelphia Union, was made by its president, Mr. T. J. Grant Shields.

Response of President Shields, Philadelphia Union.

My Dear Friends: — I was officially informed to-day, at the hotel at which I am stopping, that the slow State of Pennsylvania had again received the banner. I can assure you that it was a surprise to me. I left Philadelphia on the 28th day of June, and when I left one of my advisory board said to me, "Brother Shields, do you think Philadelphia will again get the banner?" I said, "By no means. Chicago has the banner, and she will evidently keep it." So you can imagine my surprise to-day at being informed that we should have it. But, my friends, it is but the return of the prodigal son, coming home to where he belonged.

During the past year the local union of Philadelphia has concentrated all its efforts, after losing the banner last year at Washington, to strengthening our weak societies. This we have done in a magnificent manner. The Lookout Committee was not instructed to put all its force into the forming of new societies that we might gain the banner, but that committee desired to strengthen our societies, which we have done.

If the local unions represented here claim that they are not a success, there is a secret which you have not as yet found, because at our executive meetings at our Philadelphia unions we very seldom have less than one thousand present. At our northeast branch, one evening when I spoke there, there were 1,300 present, and all were treated to ice-cream free. At our west Philadelphia branch the doors are always crowded. At our Germantown branch the doors are crowded. At our northwest branch they have most glorious meetings, which are crowded with men from the mills and girls from the factories — all Christian Endeavorers.

Therefore to-night I come to you, thanking Chicago for handing over this banner, for which, I might say, we did not really work. To the representatives of other local unions I would give encouragement. Go forth in this Christian faith, having before you, as we did, this one thing: as Paul, we planted; as Apollos, we watered; but God has given us the increase.

I hope to receive the banner before I go to Philadelphia, so that I can take it with me.

After the presentation of the banner the Convention adjourned with the doxology. Dr. Hughes pronounced the benediction.

Overflow Blessings.

The Convention had compassion upon the multitude. Many hundreds were indeed like sheep without a shepherd. And they were fed. Available halls in the centre of the city, churches, and the open air — all heard the gospel song and the word of life.

Before Mechanics' Pavilion.

Disregarding the incessant passing of cable-cars, hundreds stood for two hours in front of the main entrance to Mechanics' Pavilion, and held an inspiring service. Treasurer Shaw, of the United Society of Christian Endeavor, presided and spoke. The hymns of Endeavor were sung. Others, including Rev. William Patterson, of Toronto, and Rev. Alan Hudson, of Brockton, Mass., addressed the gathering.

Calvary Presbyterian Church.

Dr. J. Hemphill presided, and introduced Rev. Ralph Brokaw, of Springfield, Mass., a trustee of the United Society of Christian Endeavor, as the first speaker. Bishop Samuel Fallows, of the Reformed

Episcopal Church, followed. The last speaker was Rev. W. H. Vogler, of Indianapolis.

Odd Fellows' Hall.

Postal-Inspector Irwin, with his stereopticon and a collection of views belonging to Rev. J. Lester Wells, of Jersey City, illustrated a lecture given by Rev. L. R. Dyott at Odd Fellows' Hall last night. The hall was crowded to its utmost capacity, and hundreds were turned away to other overflow meetings. The subject of the lecture was, "Christian Endeavor Among the Life-Savers," and was to have been delivered by Mr. Wells, who is deeply interested in the work at the East; but owing to serious illness, a substitute had to be supplied in the person of Mr. Dyott. Dangerous coasts, collisions at sea, storms upon the coast, ill-fated ships, throwing out life-lines, saving passengers, and heroic deeds by the life-savers were portrayed upon the screen and described by the lecturer.

Central Methodist Church.

A large audience gathered in this church and held an enthusiastic overflow meeting. All of the speakers but one were trustees of the United Society. Those who spoke were Rev. H. B. Grose, of Boston; Rev. James L. Hill, D.D., of Salem, Mass.; Dr. U. F. Swengel, of Baltimore; Bishop Walters, of New York; and the Rev. Alan Hudson, of Brockton, Mass. Rev. E. R. Dille, D.D., pastor, presided.

SATURDAY MORNING, JULY 10.

Mechanics' Pavilion.

TWO features entered into the great success of this session : the varied and practical character of the program, and the genius of the presiding officer. The pavilion was full. Every moment was taken in address or discussion, and it was altogether among the first meetings of the Convention. The chairman was Rev. James L. Hill, D.D., of Salem, Mass. Dr. Hill was most happy in his pithy introductions and in his direction of the symposia.

Mr. W. C. Stadfeldt, of San Francisco, had charge of the musical parts of the program, and the singing was spirited. The opening hymn was " Onward, Christian Soldiers." Other songs followed, and then Rev. Dwight C. Hanna, of Springfield, Ill., conducted the devotional exercises with Psalm and prayer.

Dr. Hill introduced as the first speaker Mr. Giles Kellogg, of San Diego, Cal., last year president of the State union. Mr. Kellogg spoke upon " The Floating Society of Christian Endeavor."

Address by Mr. Giles Kellogg, San Diego, Cal.

THE FLOATING SOCIETIES OF CHRISTIAN ENDEAVOR.

Dear Christian Friends : — During the past few days our hearts have been raised to a high plane of aspiration, that the Word of the King might reach those parts which he intended that it should reach. " To the uttermost parts of the earth " is the command, and nothing less will satisfy the King.

How is it that this Word shall get to the uttermost parts of the earth ? Oh that we might have the volunteers who would take the Word to the uttermost parts when the money is provided; and oh that we might have the coffers full of the money when the volunteers are ready !

Is there any middle ground, dear friends, which we may take and whereby we may hasten the coming of the kingdom ? Do you realize that one nation alone of this world of ours, England, has 500,000 men of the merchant ships alone passing hither and yon over this globe ? Is it a possibility that these men shall carry the gospel of the Lord Jesus Christ, and shall tell men that without the shedding of blood there is no remission of sin ? Is it possible that these men, who are carriers by nature, shall bring these glad tidings, converted in your homes, in your churches and mine, and go out for the Lord Jesus Christ ?

Friends, what shall we call such a work as this ? Shall we call it home mission work because the men were here converted ? Shall we call it foreign mission work because they go to the uttermost parts of the world ? Ah, friends, there is a chance here for the spread of the kingdom that we do not realize. There is an opportunity here that these men may be transformed by the grace of God into men who shall be saviours of others in the name of Jesus Christ. Perhaps we have in times past considered that common which God has not considered unclean.

Oh, the transforming power of the blood of Jesus Christ, which cleanses ! If it were possible for me to relate to you some incidents, you would find that the old lives of Bunyan and of Carey, those lives which were so far away from God in blasphemy, are repeated now and again in usefulness across the face of the waters.

We ask you, friends, to consider whether there is a possibility for the Christian Endeavor societies to here take up a line of kingdom work which has not been adequately touched upon in the past.

How about the harvest from these fields? My friends, in the old time when Christ was on the earth, and after his departure, it was not success which was looked after, it was the heralding of the news; it was not the counting of the gains. And there was no man that followed the word of the Master, and no one who was faithful, that looked forward to the immediate results in the time of his life. And so, perhaps, it may be for us. The business of this world is to save men and to bring them back. As Christians, it is our part to be energetic, and to so take in the whole world, as our Saviour took it in. Not only was he talking to Martha, but, broader yet, was he taking in Jerusalem. And, broader yet, there were sheep in the outside world to be taken into the fold, and his love gathered them all in.

Dear friends, our denominations have great opportunities in spreading the work of the kingdom. Oh that we might have Congregational societies who should have their own missionaries because of their own converts in this land of ours, sending them abroad to other lands and there heralding the gospel! Oh that we might have Presbyterian missionaries!

Young men, how about that mission started at Nagasaki? Was it of any importance to the world that that young man was converted on the United States ship *Charleston?* Was it of any importance to the world that in that Japan port there should be a light-tower located there to speak of Jesus Christ?

There is an opportunity in this line that perhaps we do not realize, nor the ease with which it started. What does it mean to you who are in port cities? It means simply, the Bible in hand, going on the ship with melody in the heart for the Lord. It means that we want to get the melody into your lives and bring it to the lives of others. And these men who go out to other shores give them the melody that they may gladly take the news of the kingdom to others.

I wish that in these few minutes I have I might recite some of the incidents that have occurred as the word of the kingdom has been spread from shore to shore. I might tell you, perhaps, of the Word of God going to the Gilbert Islands. There were missionaries and men who wanted to be saved. Christian Endeavor brought these men into the kingdom, and Christian Endeavor sent these missionaries out, heralding the kingdom to those who knew not of it.

Have you no desire that God's Word shall go out from your society? In case there is a better organized work in the future, from England, from India, and from other lands, in this way there shall be systematic work. Will you of the inland hold the hands of those who are standing for the Lord in the port service?

After the address, Dr. Blakesley Little and his sister, Miss Little, of Palo Alto, Cal., sang the duet, "Whiter than Snow." This was so much enjoyed that they repeated it.

Then followed one of the most interesting half-hours of the whole Convention, in which the State secretaries spoke in symposium upon the topic, "How Can We Make the Committee Work in Our Local Societies More Effective?"

Symposium by State Secretaries.

Mr. F. F. Tucker (Nebraska): The only thought, it seems to me, in our committee work is that it is *you* who are to do the work. Remember that whether *you* are a part of the committee or not, *you* have a part to do. If your committee does not meet weekly (and I do not mean w-e-a-k-l-y), see to it that the chairman calls your committee, or that *you* meet weekly and do the work. In one word, remember in all of *your* planning, whatever it is, that

Christ is to be the foundation, and that whatever *you* are planning to do, do not plan to have a good report at the end of the month, or do not plan to have a fine showing at any time financially unless you can show that the work has been done for Christ. In short, plan to do the work and plan to see to it that Jesus Christ is the foundation of it all, because you love him, and then *your* work will be well done.

MISS CARRIE A. HOLBROOK (Minnesota): We can do our best work by emphasizing the thought that we are laborers together, grouped together as committees to do personal work for the Master; also remembering that the only way we can work for the Master is to work for his children; strongly emphasizing the thought that no duty is a small duty in the sight of God; strongly emphasizing the thought that no work is unimportant that has God back of it.

MISS JESSIE CALVERT (Washington): The most effective aid to the committee work of the local societies in our State was found in a list of questions sent to each society to be answered and returned to the State secretary. I will give you the list sent to the Prayer-meeting Committee:

Have you a Prayer-meeting Committee?

How many members?

How often do you meet?

Do you meet for prayer with the leader before the regular Sunday evening prayer-meeting?

How many leaders have failed to report on the evening of the meetings?

These questions give an idea of what should be done by the committees, and serve as an impetus for better work for the Master.

MISS CARRIE PARSON (Michigan): Open and close the committee meetings always with prayer. Conduct the Lord's business, as we would have our agents conduct our secular business.

REV. F. F. LEWIS (Vermont): To make committee work effective, we must have regular committee meetings. At these meetings we plan definite work for each member. Each member carries out his work and the report is made at the regular business meeting of the society. Each county convention offers a banner for the best set of monthly committee reports from any society within its borders. Our State convention offers a banner to the local union that presents the best set of written reports from any society within its bounds. The State secretary visits the county conventions and explains the committe work in detail, answering all questions, and impressing upon them the necessity of earnest, powerful, systematic committee work, if their society is to do its best for Christ and the Church.

"CALEB COBWEB" (Professor AMOS R. WELLS), Managing Editor of *The Golden Rule:* If I had lungs of leather and a throat of steel and a tongue of brass, and could talk for ten minutes instead of three-quarters of a minute, to every Christian Endeavor society in Christendom, I would use one of those minutes in saying this: Emphasize the executive committee meeting. A society without regular executive committee meetings is like a train without a schedule. I know that comparison will appeal to all of you. Have regular times for your executive committee meetings; have a regular place of meeting — the president's home, perhaps. Hear from every other committee in turn; have the best present whenever you can; open the meeting with prayer, continue it with prayer, close it with prayer. Spice the meeting occasionally with lemonade or apples and a pleasant game.

Miss Lida Clinch sang "Jerusalem" with fine effect, and the audience responded to the rendition with hearty applause.

The chairman emphasized the importance of the work which the trustees of the United Society were doing, and the value of the suggestions that they might offer. As he introduced these leaders in Christian Endeavor, they were accorded a warm reception.

Practical Suggestions by the Trustees.

Rev. Wm. Patterson: Christian Endeavorers, I think there is one thing that spoils a great many Christian Endeavor meetings, and that is having a leader who does not announce the hymns in such a way that the people can hear them. I think it is essential to have a leader who will announce the hymns, and any portion of Scripture that may be read, so that all can hear.

In our societies there is another thought,—that we ought to open the meeting and close the meeting on time.

One thing we have found very helpful, and that is to have a ten minutes' intermission, and to have that before the meeting closed. If it is to close at nine o'clock, say ten minutes before nine have the intermission, and then before you go home have a song and a word of prayer. If the intermission came at the close, many would go home without waiting for the little social part. And in large districts, have the society meet on a week-night; have that night as sacred as the weekly prayer-meeting; let nothing interfere with it. I represent a society that has prospered summer and winter over eight years. We give to that society Tuesday night. Nothing is allowed to interfere at the church with that meeting, and to a large extent that Tuesday night meeting has been instrumental in helping the society along.

Rev. W. H. McMillan, D.D.: I am persuaded that in all our societies there is a timid brother who is prone to forget his pledge to take some part in the meeting. I think the Prayer-meeting Committee has a great deal to do in the direction of encouraging the timid ones, giving them suggestions as to some part that they may take; and when they are persuaded to come forward to the discharge of their duty, give them a word of encouragement, because we know that when a person first attempts to lead in prayer, Satan will be there to say to him when he is finished, "Now you have made a fool of yourself; don't do it again." And we ought to head off Satan by showing that person that we think he has done well, and that the Lord thinks so.

Rev. M. Rhodes, D.D.: I think that one of the very effective things of our great movement is the power of testimony. It is God's ordination that the voice of testimony to his existence shall never cease to be heard throughout the whole world. So we have all got the sun, and you have got the ocean, and all of us more or less — you a little more — have the flowers. And now, here is a consecration, universal, unceasing, world-wide, in testimony of Jesus Christ's fundamental truth. Just as well might the evening zephyrs try to break down and pulverize the pyramids of Egypt as to attempt to deny that truth.

Bishop Samuel Fallows, D.D.: The most practical suggestion that I can give these Christian Endeavorers is the suggestion which was a living illustration of a very great and important truth. On a car which for ten days and ten nights was on its way, and not on its way to San Francisco, there were twelve sections, twenty-four berths, fifty women and five men. The porter of that car never lost his temper from beginning to end. In the midst of all the dust and the perspiration, on one particular occasion, somebody asked him the question, "Well, John, how do you feel?" He said, "Before the Lord, I am almost dead; but I try to keep as sweet as possible." Now, simply try to keep as sweet as possible in all the work of Christian Endeavor, and take as your motto, "To provoke to love and good works."

Rev. W. J. Darby, D.D.: Give unceasing attention to the circulation of good literature,— your own church literature; your own church paper, along with *The Golden Rule;* the history of the church in general, and history of your own church in particular; biographies of great reformers, great leaders in the history of the church; biographies of leading men in your own church. In short, literature that is solid, pure, wholesome, uplifting and inspiring; that is not simply for a day nor for a week,— as much as we love the weekly paper,— but literature that comes to us in solid form, that will enter into your own nature for solid results, and will furnish you a solid foundation on which to build a Christian character.

Rev. E. R. Dille, D.D.: You have poured a mighty torrent here like Niagara and the Mississippi and the St. Lawrence, enough to start a great dynamo of enthusiasm. And the practical suggestion I have is, What good is a dynamo unless it is hitched on to something? I trust that this great consecration which begins in this grand Convention is not to end here, but that this mighty power is to be hitched on to all our activities. Hitch it on to the prayer-meeting. Hitch it on to the temperance society. Let it be the mighty propeller of the floating society. Hitch this dynamo on to a great steam puller to pull the saloons out by the roots. Make your consecration intensely practical. Let this enthusiasm be carried out into every department of church life and work.

Rev. M. M. Binford: Christian Endeavor has succeeded in abolishing two things. First, the idea that all good children die young; second, the kind of piety that made good children die young. It has substituted for that conception of Christian life a recognition of the fact that young people can be as sincere, and that their religious capacities are as great, as those of older people. Its effectiveness lies in the fact of its recognition. Christian Endeavor has succeeded in abolishing the narrowness of religious life. I once heard of a man who was given to exaggeration, and his friends often rebuked him for it. One time, in remarking on something, he said he had seen a house that was half a mile long. Then he thought that that might seem an exaggeration, so he would make it all right, and added, " and five feet wide." We have no exaggeration in the Christian Endeavor work, and all narrowness has been abolished in religion by Christian Endeavor. Christian Endeavor has also been effective with us in the church in the intensifying of the missionary zeal. I believe that three-quarters of the missionaries from my own denomination who are in the field to-day have gone out from Christian Endeavor societies at home.

Bishop B. W. Arnett, D.D.: I have only this suggestion to offer to you as Christian Endeavorers. First, let us be true to our Bible. Let us see that every Christian Endeavorer has a Bible. Second, let us inculcate denominational loyalty. Third, let us have personal consecration to the great work that is before us. I was taught my denominational loyalty when I was a boy. Before we had any Moody and Sankey hymn-books, we used to sing the old hymns, and this is one : —

> " My Saviour's name I'll gladly sing;
> He is my prophet, priest, and king.
> Where'er I go his name I'll bless,
> And strive to live a Methodist."

On the next Sunday we had another verse : —

> " A better church cannot be found;
> Our doctrine is both broad and sound.
> One reason which we give for this, —
> The devil hates a Methodist."

When Dr. Hill presented President Clark, the multitude arose *en masse* to greet him.

Rev. Francis E. Clark, D.D.: I think the best story I heard at the Christian Endeavor Convention in Liverpool a few weeks ago was this. Two men met on New Year's Day. One lacked an eye and the other an ear. The man without an eye said to the man without an ear, " I wish you a Happy New (Y)ear." " Oh, indeed," said the man without the ear, a little touchy, " I wish you a Happy New Eye."

Now, I think what we want in our Christian Endeavor societies is a new eye and a new ear — a new ear to take in all the good suggestions, a new eye to see everything that God would have us to do. We ought to pray for the open ear, the open eye, and the open mind, so that the very best things that come along shall be grasped by us for the development of our society.

Two things I would say. First, keep out of ruts. There are new developments every year ; better ways of doing old things, better ways of keeping our society's life fresh ; and it may be a better way simply because it is a new way, and has not been tried one thousand times before. Try some of the new committees. Have an Information Committee; have a Pastor's Committee and a Pastor's Sermon Committee; have a Whatsoever Committee; have a Music Committee. Try some of these ways, and see if they will vivify your society. There is great power in the Information Committee. Give five minutes at every meeting to information from the wide field of Christian Endeavor work all around the world.

Another thing is this: Not only keep out of the ruts, but keep in the ruts. That is quite as important. The principles of Christian Endeavor we can never depart from safely. The idea involved in our covenants, in our pledge, in our consecration meetings, — these things are absolutely essential to a Christian Endeavor society. You can do the old things in old ways, and you can do them in new ways, but do not forget the old principles. In all my experience in sixteen years, I have never known a society to fail, except some that have been destroyed by ecclesiastical authority, that lived up to the prayer-meeting pledge. I have never known a society to succeed that did not live up to the prayer-meeting pledge.

Often the young people ask me, " What shall we do to make our meetings more interesting? " They think they must have something new, something startling, something sensational. No; keep in the old ruts. Keep to the pledge. Make every effort to live up to the pledge and the consecration meeting, and you will succeed. In India a little while ago they started a society without the pledge. William Carey, the great Baptist missionary in that field, says that they utterly failed. Then they reorganized and adopted the pledge, every line of it, our American pledge, — church attendance, church loyalty, prayer, participation in the meetings, — every word of it, and from that moment the society took on new life. The movement is spreading there. Sixty unions have been organized. So keep in the ruts. To this extent keep out of the ruts, in regard to the methods and unessential principles. Keep in the ruts in regard to fundamental principles.

At this point Dr. Hill introduced a feature which proved to be fruitful in suggestion.

Rev. J. L. Hill, D.D.: I want to know how many persons in this company are connected with the Sunday-school either as pupils or as teachers or as committee workers. Will you manifest it by rising? (The majority of the audience rose.) That is a beautiful sight.

There is another expression I want to have made. Somebody was telling about that hymn, " Blest Be the Tie that Binds." It seems that in some churches they have the abominable practice of giving out a hymn to be sung when they take a collection. And in one of those churches there was a good old deacon who had his hand in his pocket fishing out a nickel that looked all right, but which street-car men didn't want, when the minister gave out the hymn, " Blest Be the Tie that Binds Our Hearts in Christian Love." Just as the deacon got his hand on the right nickel came these lines of the hymn:—

> " When we asunder part, it gives us inward pain;
> But we shall still be joined in heart, and hope to meet again."

Now, I hope that is not the feeling we have when giving to missions. I am going to ask for another expression. If there is anybody in the house that during the last year has read one book on missions, biography of any missionary, or a volume of any kind on missions, I want to shake hands with him when we get through. How many persons in this society are on the Missionary Committee? How many have made some contributions to missions? I am not talking about your old clothes. What have the missionaries done that they should wear your old clothes? They won't be fit for missionaries or any one else when you get through with this trip. The hymn I would sing if I were a missionary and were given old clothes would be, " Your (Travel-stained) Garments They Have All Put On." Now, will all those who are interested in missionary work manifest it by rising? (Nearly the entire audience rose.) That is good — we are rising.

Now, we want to hear from any one who has a thought to contribute to the good of the society. Each one wants to take home some suggestion. Give us your methods that have been most effective in your own society. Speak right up, anybody.

A DELEGATE: The most effective method in our church in Austin, Texas, has been a general contribution levied of one-tenth of our income. From our little church of two hundred and fifty members we give about four hundred dollars a year to support foreign missions.

A DELEGATE: Since we first organized a society and elected a chairman, secretary, and committees, we have held our regular committee meetings once a month without fail.

A DELEGATE: We have sent a missionary into the foreign field and support him with our prayers and our means, and are interested in missionary work.

A DELEGATE: We have a society of forty members, supporting a Chinese missionary entirely.

A DELEGATE: We have a missionary of our own. He is responsible to us, and we are responsible to him for his support.

A DELEGATE: We take up missionary collections in our society each month.

A DELEGATE: We build a country church every year, and, besides, support a missionary in a foreign field, and give instructions to those who come to the Sunday-school, and our prayers and supplications to the mission work.

A DELEGATE: The method we have taken in our society is to appoint a Missionary Committee. The chairman of that committee goes round to each Endeavorer in the society and asks him or her, whichever it may be, to contribute two cents a week to missionary work. We generally give only about half what he asks, though, because we poor Oregonians cannot afford any more. But what we can afford, we give, and our chairman of the Missionary Committee makes his report at the end of each month.

REV. J. HEMPHILL, D.D.: The most effective method we have adopted in the church I represent is to hand over the conduct of the monthly concert of prayer for missions to the Young People's Society of Christian Endeavor. For two years and more they have given us about the best missionary meetings I have ever attended anywhere.

A DELEGATE: We have a membership of thirty-seven, and give one-tenth of our income to missions.

A DELEGATE: One-third of all that is taken in our collections goes to the work of Jesus Christ in the foreign field.

A DELEGATE: In our society we levy an assessment of two cents a week on each member to be sent to our missionary in India.

A DELEGATE: We follow the Student Volunteers' plan for missionary study, besides contributing money through the Woman's Board.

A DELEGATE: Conduct a missionary study class whose leaders shall be volunteers for the foreign field.

A DELEGATE: The most interesting and effective work is done through the Prayer-meeting Committee. Get a chairman that is afire for Christ and the Church. On your Missionary Committee get a chairman who is afire for missionary work. And get them to give of their means for that work. And the more you give, and the more people you have working for missions, the better society you will have. The two-cents-a-week plan is the best possible to get your committee to work, and if you will adopt that you will be very successful.

A DELEGATE: We find that the weekly pledge from all of our members, and the maintaining of that pledge, is the best thing possible.

A MISSIONARY: Our girls in China have enthusiastic missionary meetings' and send their collections to the missions in India, Africa, and different parts of Asia.

A DELEGATE: Our society in San José, in the Santa Clara Valley, welcomes strangers into our midst to work with us. Some of us will go forth as mission-aries, and high above our heads we will unfurl in the breeze the colors of the Christian Endeavor Union, and go forth to save those in foreign lands.

A DELEGATE: The two-cents-a-week plan is all right to start with, but it is too small to last. At least, that has been our experience. We have raised $800 and sent out a missionary to India last year.

A DELEGATE: We gather the boys and girls into an Intermediate Society, and they gather other boys and girls. And we put them all to work.

A DELEGATE: Fifty per cent of our society belongs to The Tenth Legion.

A DELEGATE: We are keeping our young men out of the saloons by making the church more attractive.

A DELEGATE: The best thing in our church has been the organization of a Christian Endeavor Society in the State Penitentiary, where we have sixty members connected with the movement, thirty-five of whom are now active members.

A DELEGATE: The society that I represent, with less than one hundred members, gives about $250 for missions. We raise the money on a systematic pledge plan.

A DELEGATE: Our society observes a week of self-denial, in which we do without some necessary thing, and give the amount saved to missions.

A DELEGATE: Our society is the Soldiers' Home Christian Endeavor Society, formed in the Soldiers' Home by the men who fought in the last war. We give toward the missionary work in the merchant marine service.

A DELEGATE: I have the pleasure of representing a church that has in it thirteen Christian Endeavor Societies, averaging about sixty members each. The threefold mission of our church is the healing of the sick, the preaching of the Word, and the education of the people. The influence and power of this is solely due to its missionary spirit. God is sending out his missionaries. Glory to God.

A DELEGATE: I think we need more missionary work than most any other people among the sea-going men, the sailors. Do not forget them in your mission work.

A DELEGATE: In our society in Boston many of us belong to The Tenth Legion, and the one-cent-a-day mission. Last year we gave over $200 in a society of 200 members.

A DELEGATE: We are using our influence in the abolishment of the saloons and in gaining converts to total abstinence.

THE CHAIRMAN: Right there I want to ask that as many persons as are committed in their personal lives to abstinence from intoxicants, and so far as they have opportunity are working individually and through their societies against the saloon, will manifest it by rising. (The entire audience rose.)

A DELEGATE: There is a saloon-keeper in Oakland who contributed $10 to the Convention fund, and now he is disappointed because the Endeavorers do not support him.

A DELEGATE: In Ohio we believe each member of the Endeavorers should give an amount weekly to be divided among their missionary enterprises; that that is in the Baptist denomination.

A DELEGATE: An Ohio Endeavor society raised $500 to build a mission chapel, and they conduct mission services there every Sunday afternoon.

A DELEGATE: I try to impress upon the young men of our society and of our community that if they would save the money they now spend on cigarettes and cigars, our missionary box would be overflowing.

A DELEGATE: The Endeavorers of Southern California raised over $1,000 this year that was sent to the relief of their foreign missions.

A DELEGATE: We have just organized a committee to go each Sunday and preach the gospel of Jesus Christ on the streets. We have also organized a pulpit committee, to fill the pulpits of churches too poor to support pastors; also a committee to send flowers to the suffering ones, thus giving an opportunity to make converts and bring souls to Christ.

A DELEGATE: In our society every member is on some committee. The Floating Committee lately visited sixty ships. Our Social Committee does not allow any one to leave the church without a handshake with some of its members.

Many misconceptions regarding the office and practical value of the United Society of Christian Endeavor were cleared away by the next address, upon "The United Society of Christian Endeavor; What It Is, and How It Works," by Mr. William Shaw, treasurer.

Address by Treasurer William Shaw.

The United Society is a providential development of the Christian Endeavor movement. It came, not by the will of man, but by the purpose of God.

The first society of Christian Endeavor was born, not made. Like little Samuel, whom we may consider a type of Christian Endeavor, it was born in answer to prayer. From the first, it made its home in the temple of God, and was in training for his service.

As the knowledge of the success attending the work of the first societies was spread abroad by newspaper reports and in other ways, requests for information came by the score, and then by the hundreds, to Dr. Clark and others of the early friends of the movement, and leaflets and letters were sent in reply, at their own expense. They were all busy men, and the burden of correspondence became so great that they were unable to bear it longer. So, in 1885, the United Society of Christian Endeavor was incorporated under the laws of the State of Maine, and the next year its headquarters were established in Boston, and the Society was incorporated under the laws of the State of Massachusetts.

The membership of the United Society is made up of individuals, as required by law. Local societies, as such, could not be united in a legal corporation. The membership required is the payment of $1 for annual, or $20 for life, membership, and election by a two-thirds vote of the members present at any meeting of the corporation or the Board of Trustees.

The purpose of the corporation is "to promote earnest Christianity amongst the young people, and to make them more useful in the service of God."

Its necessity sprung from the fact that some central organization was necessary that could lawfully hold the funds, and be held to strict account for the expenditure of the same for the purpose for which they were secured.

Individuals may come and go, but the corporation is permanent.

THE EXPENSE.

The expenses of the United Society have ranged from $2,000 to $18,000 a year. The average for the last eight years has been about $13,000. The first four years the funds were furnished by the voluntary contribution of the societies and friends of the cause, but from the beginning the trustees had for their ideal a self-supporting organization. This ideal was realized in 1889, and since that date the United Society has received no contributions from local societies or unions. Through the co-operation and help of *The Golden Rule*, a printing department was opened, and by the receipts from this department, and the sale of our badges and other publications, we have been able to meet all our expenses. This has been made possible through the co-operation of local societies that have favored us with their printing orders, so that whatever profit there might be on them should go to the extension of the movement, instead of into the pockets of private individuals.

ITS FRUITS.

Organizations, as well as individuals, have a right to demand that they be judged by their fruits.

The United Society has not escaped the shafts of criticism. Some have thought it was doing too much, others too little. But most of the critics belonged to the school of the prophets. It was not what it had done, but what it might do under certain imaginary conditions, that they feared.

What have been some of the fruits of the twelve years of work performed by the United Society? In 1885 there were reported 253 societies; 1886, 850;

1887, 2,314; 1888, 4,879; 1889, 7,672; 1890, 11,013; 1891, 16,274; 1892, 21,080; 1893, 26,284; 1894, 33,720; 1895, 41,229; 1896, 46,125; 1897, 50,700; with a membership of 3,000,000.

In 1885 the movement was confined almost wholly to the Eastern States; to-day it belts the globe. Then only a few of the denominations were represented; to-day, more than forty are included in our fellowship. In 1885 the movement was without an advocate among the religious papers of the country; to-day it has, in *The Golden Rule*, the best young people's paper published, a large number of monthly and State papers, and a regular department in nearly every religious paper, and also in many secular papers.

The United Society has stood for loyalty to Christ and fidelity to the local church and denomination. It has stood for spiritual fellowship among the young people of our evangelical churches. It has exercised no authority over the local societies, but as a bureau of information and a bond of union it has tried to advance the Master's kingdom through the Society of Christian Endeavor.

It has contributed thousands of dollars through the State and local unions and foreign organizations for the advancement of Christian Endeavor. By its aid the work in Germany, Sweden, India, Japan, Africa and other lands has been carried on. It has stood as a barrier between the societies and those who would use them for their own selfish purposes and plans.

It has never usurped the authority of the local church and denomination, but rather has supplemented and reinforced them in all their efforts to develop a sturdy, spiritual manhood and womanhood in the members of the societies.

It has stood ready to co-operate to the fullest extent with the publication houses in their efforts to supply their own young people with literature and supplies.

It has modestly but earnestly tried to help the pastors to win the young people of the world for Jesus Christ, and train them so that they may become in the church " workmen that need not be ashamed."

It has demonstrated to the world that it is possible for an organization to develop and foster a world-wide movement which students of religious history declare is unparalleled in the history of the church, to promote a spiritual fellowship that is the completest answer the world has ever seen to our Lord's prayer "that they all may be one," and to conduct its affairs in such an economical and business-like way that no financial burden for its support is laid upon the societies it has formed and fostered.

It has been peculiarly fortunate in winning the life's devotion of officers whose consecrated abilities have, under God, made the movement what it is; who, by unwearied toil at their desks, by inspiring addresses at conventions innumerable, by journeys up and down this great country and across the ocean into every land, by many a book and magazine article, by their best thought and unceasing prayers, have lifted Christian Endeavor upon its present high plane of service for Christ and the church.

But splendid and successful as has been the work of the past, the United Society does not propose to live on its memories. Its face is toward the future. The development of the work has made changes necessary, and they have been made according to the best wisdom of those who loved this cause and sacrificed for it, and who have best understood the difficulties and obstacles to be overcome. At the present time still further changes are being considered, by a committee, with a view to broadening the denominational and geographical representation on the Board of Trustees. The membership fees can also be reduced to a nominal sum, as funds from this source are no longer needed.

In all such changes there are questions of law as well as sentiment to be considered. But we believe that He who has guided us in all the plans and purposes of the past will continue to lead his people, and that the future of Christian Endeavor and the United Society will be fuller of power and blessing to the cause and church of Jesus Christ than the past has been.

The session closed one-half hour earlier than usual, that the delegates might attend the open-air demonstrations, on Van Ness Avenue, in the interest of patriotism. At Dr. Hill's request the audience left the pavilion singing "At the Cross," carrying the words and melody into the streets and avenues adjoining. The effect was strikingly illustrative of the real spirit and service of Endeavor.

Woodward's Pavilion.

"Christian Endeavor enthusiasm welled up and bubbled over at the morning meeting at Woodward's Pavilion;" so said a San Francisco paper. And so it did. Everybody who came had a distinct aim: to give and to receive for the sake of the cause of Endeavor. Rev. Ralph W. Brokaw, of Springfield, Mass., one of the United Society trustees, presided. The session was profitable, and the parts of the program distributed in such a way as to secure the co-operation and interest of the audience.

Mr. E. Meredith, of Oakland, directed the singing. "Sunshine in My Soul" was a favorite, as usual, in that sunny land. The exercises of devotion were conducted by Rev. William C. Clark, of Keeler's Bay, Vermont. Mr. Brokaw introduced the first speaker, Miss Cora B. Bickford, of Biddeford, Me., to present "The Mothers' Society of Christian Endeavor."

Address by Miss Cora B. Bickford, Biddeford, Maine.

A young professor was trying to explain to a little girl the process by which a lobster changes its shell. Finding it rather a difficult task, the learned man finally said, "My dear, what does your mamma do when you have outgrown your frock? She gets you a new one, does n't she?" "Oh, no," replied the little miss, with considerable *esprit,* "she just lets down the tucks." Christian Endeavor is much like the little girl's frock; it is long enough to meet the individual needs of all humanity, — of the young, the middle-aged, and the old. We have only to let down the tucks, and it covers the work with the Juniors, Intermediates, Seniors, and Mothers.

One peculiarity of Christian Endeavor is the rapidity of its growth. In this it is much like a healthy baby — one fed on California wheat and sunshine — and, with its growth, it is continually developing new phases of life; for the different branches of Endeavor are not, as many suppose, separate organizations of the whole, each of a different kind, and the Mothers' Society is not a new movement, but a development of the original growth. What is the Mothers' Society? Just what its name indicates, a society of mothers pledged to the noblest endeavor in Christ's name. Its object is, first, to stimulate mothers to raise the standard of the Christian home. It could not have a higher aim, for the home is the greatest institution in this land to-day, and out of it are the issues of life, civic, social, physical.

A young Sunday-school teacher, who had a large class of little girls, was very anxious that they should all be present on a certain Sunday in June. He urged this upon them for several weeks, but when the Sunday came, one pupil was absent. Meeting the child upon the street the following day, he stopped to ask, "Why were n't you at Sunday-school yesterday, Jennie?" "Oh, sir," replied the child with eager apology, "my hat was n't clean." "But, Jennie," said the young man, "don't you know that God does n't care for the outward appearance? It is the inner — the heart that he looks at." "Yes, sir," replied the child, feeling that she had the right of it, after all, "but the lining was n't clean." The home life is the lining of the world's life. Keep it pure and wholesome; guard it from every foe that would assail its peace and hinder its divine mission; set the seal of Christly love upon it, and then its life will be of the truest sort, and because such a home exists, all life will be made purer, the world better.

The home is the greatest of the world's institutions, and the mother is the most potent influence in that institution. She possesses a quiet power for the like of which kings would gladly sell their birthright ; a power of which she ofttimes little dreams.

Childhood associations cling to us longest. The boy and the girl never forget mother's life, mother's love. We may drift as far from home as the East is from the West, but earth is not wide enough, heaven is not high enough, to allow us to drift from the remembrance of mother.

Life's changes may vex, its discords stun, its glaring sunshine blind us; and yet in the midst of toil and turmoil will come to us the picture of a dear face bending over us, while we seem to hear again the echo of a sweet lullaby : —

> " Hush, my babe, lie still and slumber,
> Holy angels guard thy bed;
> Heavenly blessings without number
> Gently falling on thy head.''

We dream until the angel part is a reality, and peace and quiet have taken possession of our souls.

Mothers, does it never come to you with overwhelming reality, the thought that your work is the training of human souls?

In testimony to the dear mother back in the old Pine Tree State, the mother who has been my inspiration, intellectually, patriotically, spiritually, I would say that next to Christ in the divine influence stands the true Christian mother.

What shall be the world's future? In the coming years, who shall be the civilians, patriots, and statesmen but the boys and girls who are to-day learning lessons of trust and wisdom in the homes?

On the morrow these will sit in chairs of state, wield the editor's pen, fill our pulpits, and mete out judgment from the bench, but rarely will their standard of right be higher than that raised for them in their childhood home. The home is the training-school of the nations, and here should be taught the principles of good citizenship, the truest patriotism, the highest ideals, in all lines of Christian ethics. Mothers, will you not give to the world the best when you give your boys and girls?

And, secondly, the object of the Mothers' Society is to pray for aid to help in their Christian life the children, especially those who belong to the Junior Society of Christian Endeavor; and these boys and girls, Juniors and otherwise, need your older strength to help them stand against the influences that surround them. Not so many months ago a pastor of my city started from his home to attend a business meeting in another part of the city. It was evening, and as he passed along one of the principal thoroughfares he was approached by a party of boys, not one of them over ten years of age, yet each carried in his mouth a lighted cigarette, and in his right hand a toy pistol. As the boys drew near, they formed in line directly in front of him, and, taking the attitude of firing, said in the most highwayman-like tone they could command, " Hands up !" The man hesitated, then was about to pass on, but the boys drew together in a yet more compact line, and, again taking the attitude of firing, repeated the command in a tone even more brigandish than the first, " Hands up !" And this in Christian Endeavor Maine!

Not your boys or mine? No, mothers; thank God for that! Not my brothers or yours? No, my sisters, and for this, too, we are thankful; but somebody's boy, somebody's brother, and your boy and my brother must meet such influences as this if they go out into the world, and one cannot live with evil without being contaminated by it.

What can be done? Form a Mothers' Society, and by banded prayer and concentrated effort strive to fortify your Juniors against every such evil, and do not forget the boys and girls who need to become Juniors. Form a society, if there is only one other mother to join you. Strive particularly to interest the mothers who are bowed beneath the thought: What shall I do for my boy or my girl? Bring in every other mother. Throw into the work all the enthusiasm there is in your heart when you think about the future of your child. Enter into all the lines of Junior work; give the children your support, your symthy, your comradeship. Every Mothers' Society should be a body-guard to the Juniors.

As motherhood is the crowning glory of womanhood, so the Mothers' Society is the crowning glory of Christian Endeavor. Every community needs such an organization; no church is complete without it.

May the Mothers' Societies multiply, grow, wax strong, until the earth shall be girt about by a welded bar of mother love!

The symposium by the State presidents was spirited and valuable in suggestion. The topic was, "How Can We Interest the Pastors and Churches in the Organization of Junior and Intermediate Societies?"

Symposium by State Presidents.

REV. W. J. McKITTRICK (President New York Union): Well, dear friends, one way to interest people, including pastors and church-members, in anything, is to talk with them about it. Talk to them kindly, and lovingly lead them into the church, or patiently and gently ram the truth into them. This, however, is something which the State presidents have very little opportunity to do. Most of our time, apart from our regular church work, is taken up going up and down, through and across, the State, writing lots of letters, and making a great many speeches. But what does count in this work is the Junior superintendent.

In our State of New York we have a lady Junior superintendent and two lady assistants, and these are the ones who, going through the State, make this question which we ask on the program to-day the chief sum and substance of their talk. We thank God that they are women who carry on this work in the State of New York. There is not one man out of ten who knows how to shake hands with a little boy or girl. The man takes the boy's hand and holds it as a pair of scales holds a pound of sugar; but a woman shakes the hand of the little boy, or the little girl, with her fingers and her eyes, and with a smile upon her lips, and with every wrinkle on her cheeks. Dear friends, womanhood is so near to childhood — as near to it as the earth to the flower which blooms on its surface; as near to it as the stream is to the little boats that float on its bosom; and out in New York State, I thank God for the Junior Endeavor societies that have been formed by our consecrated women Junior superintendents.

Then, another way to work is through the church officers, especially in the country towns. You go into the country towns, and in most of them you will find that the people are active in the Sabbath-school, but not active in Junior Endeavor Societies. Now, invite them to come in and see the Juniors, have them attend a meeting, and this will have a tendency to interest them in this work. I tell you, dear friends, you will find it of great advantage to found a Junior Society in your own church.

REV. W. K. SPENCER (President Michigan Union): People down in Michigan are very soft-hearted and very hard-headed. It is a great deal easier to touch their emotions than to pound facts into their heads, and therefore the great need in Michigan in regard to Junior and Intermediate Societies is information.

I had one of the keen, straight, solid business men of my town say to me, with tears in his eyes, when I was telling him that the church wished to elect him as an elder, "When I was a boy I didn't have a chance; they sat down on the young people, and now to-day I could not make a prayer in public if I was to try. Although I would like to be an elder, I could not discharge my duties in that position." That is the situation throughout the churches. One-fifth of the people do the religious work, and the other four-fifths all ride. Now the need of Christian Endeavor work is fully illustrated by this reply of my brother, that he did not have a chance when he was a boy; he was not trained to speak, not trained to do any active work; he was not trained to do anything but to unite with the church and to sit still in the meeting, and go to sleep, or chew caraway seeds. We need to train children when they are young. In Michigan we used to wait till a colt was four or five years old before we broke it, and then we had a terrible time in breaking it; but now we begin to break our colts when they are six months old. So we want to begin to break the children into the work of Christ in early years, and not wait until they are sixteen or eighteen years old when they unite with the church. The Junior Society is what does this. That is what many of our ministers and a great many of our church-members do not understand. They think the Junior Society is a kind of primary department of a Sabbath-school. It is nothing of the kind. It is just as different as the primary department of the Sabbath-school is from the Thursday night prayer-meeting. The Junior Society is where you teach the children there is a work for them to do, and how to do it. The Junior Society is a place where the children are taught their duty toward God by practice; taught to pray by praying; where they are taught to have confidence by doing work, and where they are taught to do work on committees by giving them work to do.

MR. CHARLES A. FORSE (President of Missouri Union): My friends, I have had some experience in the extension of Christian Endeavor work, and my experience has taught me this: first, show the churches and the pastors the need of Christian Endeavor work in all its branches; second, we need to show them the benefits derived from this work; third, we need to overcome indifference; fourth, we need to overcome opposition. We want to show the great necessity of this work among young people, and that the church cannot get along without it.

We find in our churches young people, and they are ready to be used. We find there is need of their service, that there is work to be done; and if we can get the pastors and the churches to see this it will help us in the extension of Christian Endeavor work.

What is more blessed in the sight of the Master than young people interested and active in religious work? What we want to do is to bring the young people into the service of the Lord Jesus Christ, and use them, and make their lives bright in Christian work, and then, when we bring them up in the Christian Endeavor Society, and prepare them for the duties of the church, which will fall upon them in after-life, their efforts will be crowned with abundant success.

I sometimes find that there is much opposition, because the work is not understood. Some think that it will disturb the harmony of the church to attach this work to it. They do not see any need for the work, or the benefit to be derived from it. The work devolves upon you as much as upon others, and every one who is interested in it should individually do what they can to show the church and the pastor the need of this work, and in this way you will be doing your share of the extension of this work. Each individual Endeavorer in this land must be faithful, must be active, and must earnestly labor for the upbuilding of Christ's kingdom. If we do our share, then the pastors and the people will see the need of the work, the opposition will be overcome, the indifference will be overcome, and then we will be on the road to success in Christian Endeavor extension.

REV. RALPH LAMB (Indian Territory): I come to you from a territory that is altogether out in the cold in every sense of the word, Christian Endeavor and otherwise.

I have come up to this Convention to try and learn how to interest our people of the Indian Territory in Christian Endeavor work. I have tried to do what I could, and have followed the plan I use in my own work, and I have succeeded to some extent. We have a Junior Society, although we have no Intermediate Society. About the only way is to go to work as individuals, and first get ourselves interested. If we do this, I think the rest will surely follow. That is the way I am trying to extend Christian Endeavor work.

MR. H. A. GILE (President of Oregon Union): I perceive that you have been hearing from the pastors this morning on this subject. I am going to represent the business side of it. In Oregon we believe that an ounce of prevention is better than a pound of cure. Hence we believe in Junior work. We do not think it is necessary for the boy to go down the scale into the depths of sin and vice. We believe in leading the boys and girls gently from the infant class of the Sabbath-school into the Junior Endeavor Society, and then into the Intermediate and Senior.

How are we going to interest our pastors and our churches? I believe by agitation.

I believe in making our Junior and our Intermediate Societies prominent. We have been very successful with our Junior work in Oregon. We have very active Junior workers in our State. I will just give you a little illustration. Perhaps you have heard that on our special train coming down from Oregon, we came very near running into a burning bridge. This delayed us, and while stopping at a little town, one of the Junior workers, a little girl, went quietly around through the little town, and we noticed that she had gathered around her a nice little band of children. They were following her around the street, and she told me that she was going to organize a Junior Society before she left the town. That is the kind of workers we have in Oregon. With a few of these people scattered here and there throughout our State, we hope to interest, not only our pastors, but our church-members in the Junior and Intermediate work.

MR. LYLE A. DICKIE (President of Hawaiian Union): A few years ago a Junior Society was started in a church in the suburbs of Chicago. I was one of its first assistant superintendents, and in my first enthusiasm over the matter I wrote a letter to mother in the Hawaiian Islands. That letter was the cause of starting a Junior Society in Mowaii.

My suggestion is to use ink. Whenever anything occurs that will arouse enthusiasm in Junior work, anything new and good, spread it about, and do it quickly before there is a chance for the enthusiasm of the writer to grow cold. Junior extension spread from Chicago to the Hawaiian Islands in two months. If it may go that distance in two months, how quickly may it not go in a State, if the writer is full of enthusiasm and works quickly?

In the Hawaiian Islands there are only three Junior Societies, but we hope to greatly increase this number in the future.

MR. JOHN P. HARTMAN (Washington): I have discovered that when a builder is about to erect a large building, he first places upon the ground a derrick, and then he uses a steam-engine, and great ropes, and machinery to take up the material and swing it around to the different positions, and the building gradually rises from its strong foundation. Over in Washington we are trying to erect in the church a derrick; and when we have done that, we are going to fire up the steam-engine, and take the best timber we have in the church, and we are going to handle this derrick and swing it around over the home, and pick up the Juniors, and then swing them around into the church, and fill them with sunshine and glory, and transport them back to the home, so that they can tell about these things at home, and thereby interest their fathers and mothers and relatives. But we are not going to stop with that. We are going to keep track of the Juniors. We are going to keep the derrick in good order, and keep it at work transporting the Endeavorers from one individual to another.

We have about twenty-seven in the Intermediate Society in our State that we have started out in this work, and with the energy and vim from the training that they get in the Junior, then the Intermediate, and finally in the Senior, they will be well equipped for excellent service. We remember that we are going to, make them our successors, and that we are going to step out of the harness, and that upon their shoulders will fall the work. We are going to take the weak, the puny, and the dull from the walks of life where they are doing no good, and make them bright, happy, sunshiny, glorious Christian men and women.

REV. C. H. PHILLIPS (President of North Dakota Union): I came here with these instructions: "Tell the rest of the United States that North Dakota is alive." I suppose that those who formulated these instructions had an idea that the rest of the world had been learning from. the twin city papers of our snowbanks last winter, and that the rest of the United States would have an idea we were all snowed under; that we were cold and frozen up.

Now Minneapolis, as you know, has the best flour that is made in the world, —" Pillsbury's Best,"—but it could not manufacture '• Pillsbury's Best " if it were not for North Dakota back of it. It has the best soil under the sun for the raising of wheat, together with its intense cold, and its ozone. It turns out an article that is unsurpassed. From the twin city papers you would think that we would have to dig down about twenty feet from the snow to get to the top of the windmills during the winter. The deepest snowbank last winter was about sixty feet, but that had melted away before I left home.

In North Dakota we have ministers that are very much alive, and there you will find no trouble with this question of how to get the ministers interested in the Endeavor Societies. Once in a while you will find a man who does not know the great value of using young people through the Junior and Intermediate Societies. I think one of the troubles with such a man is this: In the first place, he likes to hear himself talk too well to give the· children a chance. We preachers have the reputation of liking to hear ourselves talk, so I took the precaution not to come here with my pulpit coat, so that the chairman could not pull my coat-tails and choke me off. The minister also appreciates the fact that he can talk, and he thinks the children cannot.

Here the speaker was interrupted by the chairman telling him that his time had expired.

MR. C. N. HUNT (President of Minnesota Union): While in Chicago I was looking over the papers to see what the services would be at the different churches on the Sabbath, and I saw that one of the subjects that was an-´ nounced was this: "The Fool in a Fix." I was stopping with a good old lady, and I said to her, " What do you suppose that pastor is going to talk about Sunday morning?" She said, as she looked at me very sweetly, "Why, don't you know?" I said, " No, I cannot guess." " Why," she said, " he is going to talk about himself."

Now I am not going to talk about myself, for the North Dakota fellow has already done that. The subject, I believe, that we are to talk of is, "How To Interest the Pastors and the Churches in Junior and Intermediate Societies." The very backbone of all of the Christian Endeavor movement is the Junior Society. as it is the source of all our life and strength. One time, after I had been talking to the Juniors, a little fellow five years of age came and sat down beside me on the sofa; and he said, " Brother Hunt, I remember all of your sermon yesterday. ' In the first place,' you said, ' you are to love Jesus. In the next place, you are to trust Jesus, and in the next place you are to pray to Jesus,' and then I kind of forget, but in the fourthplace you said 'monkeys.' " Now the fact was that. in making an illustration, I had referred to monkeys, and he had forgotten the point, but had got the illustration. In the first place, I think it is necessary to get into sympathy — I mean for the president, the secretary, and the Junior superintendent, and those who are trustees and secretaries of the local societies, to get into sympathy with the pastor. If I were to express that in the language of to-day, I would say, " Get into touch with the pastors. I tell you they are not such hard-hearted fellows as you think, and the churches are not as cold as you think. Just go and have a quiet talk with them. Do not criticize the pastors, nor the church. Assure them that the society which you wish to organize is not to be greater than the church, but that it is to be a help to the church, and that it is a part of the church.

In the second place, bring, if possible, before the pastors and before the members of the church, say fifty or sixty of the young people, and then tell them what is to be done, and I am certain that they will be inclined to establish a Junior Society.

Rev. F. L. Nash (President Nevada Union): You have all heard that Nevada is a fighting State. Some of us are not prize-fighters, but we are trying to fight the good fight of faith. We came down here, not for the purpose of speaking, but to listen and learn more about your methods, and know what you are doing in other portions of the world, and then to go home and spread your enthusiasm among our own people.

I thought that Nevada was a very bad State until I came here and heard the speech this morning of this lady from Maine, who tells you that there are boys going around in Maine with pistols in one hand and cigarettes in the other. Our boys are not quite as bad as that. But there are portions of our State that are very needy, and we require a great deal of help, and the sympathy of God's people, and their earnest prayers. We have places where there is a great deal of religious destitution. A missionary told me of a place way off in the eastern part of the State where he went into a family and talked and prayed with the people, and a boy who was present afterwards said to his father, "There was a man that got down on his knees, and he cussed and cussed and cussed." He had never heard anybody use the name of God except in profanity, and he did not understand the language of the prayer. So you see that we are in need of earnest help, although our people are not so bad as they are way up in Maine.

But we are willing to help and do all we can, and to carry on the good fight of our Lord and Saviour. We are represented in three classes. The other day a friend of mine said that he rode in a stage coach and they asked him which class he was in. He said that he was not in any class, only that he had paid his regular fare. He found there were, however, three classes, but at first he did n't understand what they meant. When they came to the foot of a hill the driver said, "The first-class passengers may keep their seats; the second-class passengers, get out and walk; and the third-class passengers get out and push." We are ready to take hold and push and help all we can.

Rev. T. G. Langdale (President South Dakota Union): As I noticed the question that is given us, "How shall we interest pastors and churches?" there came home to my mind what I heard on the train a great many times, "Who are we, who are we? The presidents of the Y. P. S. C. E." The question is, Shall the presidents interest the whole State in Junior Endeavor without the co-operation of the societies that have no Junior Endeavorers? Let us get some one in our Endeavor Societies all afire with enthusiasm for Junior Endeavor, and then you will find your pastors and your churches interested in this question.

This is a very vital question just now. It seems a very strange thing that we should have to consider the question of how to get our pastors interested in the children; it seems strange that we should have to stir up the churches, and prepare the church for such a work. My friends, it seems preposterous to say, How shall we interest our churches in those persons that are dependent upon them? They are those who in the future are to be its support and its stay. It is time that we were waking up to this question. Who are we going to wake up first? You know it is sometimes necessary, when a party are going to start on a journey early in the morning, for some to be awakened by an alarm-clock; and then that person goes around and wakes up the rest. Now let us have the Young People's Society of Christian Endeavor awakened by the alarm-clock of their conscience, and then let us go around and wake up the pastors, and let them wake up the churches.

Rev. S. H. Woodrow (President Rhode Island Union): I have the honor of coming from a State that is so small that, when a commission was appointed a short time ago to straighten the State line, one of our Boston papers facetiously remarked that "great care must be exercised, or the little State would be wiped out of existence." But there is some advantage in being small. In Rhode Island we have our Senior Societies quite well and thoroughly organized. We have Junior Societies well organized and under a competent superintendent. I think the great need in Rhode Island is, as I believe it is in other places, an Intermediate Society. Most of the talk to-day has been about Junior Societies. We have, as I said, Junior Societies; but we are coming into that condition where our SeniorSocieties are very much like the old-fashioned prayer-meetings. It has been some years since these societies were organized, and we have all been growing old; the result is that our Senior Societies have people in them that are thirty-five and forty years of age. They have been well trained, and they are competent workers, but there are younger people, from twenty-five down to eighteen years of age, who do not work as well in those societies as they otherwise would if there was an Intermediate Society. I believe in the Intermediate Society, for it fills the gap which exists between the Junior and the Senior Society. I think that this work should not be left to the pastors. I believe that our pastors are thoroughly interested in this work, and that they will do all they can. We want the Intermediate Society to carry on the Juniors to the Senior Society, and in this way, I think, they will all become active members of the churches.

Rev. W. A. Humphrey (President Oklahoma Union): While *en route* to this Convention, in the City of Leadville, while engaged in conversation with a gentleman on the street, I was asked if I was a business man. I said "Yes." He said, "In what business are you engaged?" I said, "I am trying to preach the gospel." I believe that this is largely the solution of the question confronting the church and confronting the Endeavor Society,— simply to be about the Lord's business. and in business ways. I think we may be as wise in planning, as faithful in executing, as men are in business and in political life. There is an inspiration in a new voice, there is an inspiration in numbers, in Endeavor songs. and in Endeavor conventions,— in our district conventions, and in our State and Territorial conventions,— and in these conventions we ought to be able to secure the attendance of pastors and churchmen in general. I want to state one thing that is well to consider in arranging these conventions: let us arrange them in such a manner, with reference to the Lord's Day, that the pastors will not be compelled to return so quickly that the Convention will not reap its full benefit; neither to offer any excuse to persons who might otherwise be in attendance, but remain at home in order that the work may be well kept up in their home churches. Much can be accomplished in every way by workers coming together so that they can counsel with other workers, and where they may see and hear of the benefits that have been derived from the Junior Society. I think that pastors generally are favorable to the work, and will do the best they can. Churches are willing to be led, if the pastor in charge is able to direct the forces. The great difficulty is in securing the leader. One way to enlist interest is to call upon the United Society for literature, and to place in the church *The Golden Rule* and other religious publications covering the same ground.

Mr. A. A. Reed (President Colorado Union): You will all agree, I am sure, that if we interest our pastors and churches in Junior and Intermediate work, we must have the right kind of pastors and the right kind of churches. The quality and ability of the pastor will be determined largely by the church itself. If the individual members of the church, and of the Christian Endeavor in the church, is worth anything at all, I think it will be interested in Junior and Intermediate Societies.

I have in mind a Presbyterian church in Colorado where there is an eldership of eight individuals. and out of these five are young men, four of whom are very active members of the Christian Endeavor, or graduates therefrom, and the executive officer of the trustees is an active member of the Christian Endeavor Society, and the Board is nearly all composed of active Christian Endeavorers. If you find in your church, or in your pastor, a lack of interest, you need not look outside of your own ranks for the reason. I pray you that you examine your own heart, and your own conduct, and look there to rectify the mistake which maybe you have made.

Colorado is interested in the education of the young. We have a public-school system which is second to none; but our interest extends not only to the education of the intellect but to the education in our churches of the soul and of the spirit within. And so I say here and now. in this public place, that I pay a tribute to the ministers of Colorado, who are almost without exception deeply interested in the cause of the young people, in the Junior Society, and from that up to the Senior Society.

MR. M. M. SHAND (District of Columbia): Perhaps I can more practically answer the question by telling you how we do it in the District of Columbia. So I will substitute "do" for "can" in the question. We have done a great deal of work in the line of organizing Junior and Intermediate Societies in the city of Washington. We have more than sixty Junior and seven or eight Intermediate. We have Lookout Committees in both classes, and they both act together along these two lines. We try to interest the pastors and the churches. We have a list of every church and mission and religious institution that has not a Junior or an Intermediate Society, a Christian Endeavor Society, or a young people's society, and we bring all our forces to bear upon these places. In the first place, we try, in each of these places, to find at least one person who is interested in it, and get them to work, and have them bring all the influence they can to bear upon the subject. We use the literature of the United Society very much. We have personal interviews, and letters are written by our committee, and thus, in several ways, we try to interest one person of a church or society, or several persons, in this work. And then we try to bring an influence to bear upon every pastor. We have personal interviews with the pastors, and we also give them literature,— a great deal, if necessary, — and a great deal of pressure — love pressure — is brought to bear upon them, especially if they do not seem to be very much interested in the work. I am very happy to say that most of our pastors are.

In regard to this Junior movement, it is well to remember the little girl's rendition of a very familiar passage in the Bible: "Suffer the little children to come unto me, and if you won't hinder they will come."

MR. F. T. VINCENT (President Kansas Union): I suppose this meeting would not be complete without a man from Kansas — a long man with a short speech. I am specially glad to be here this morning. In my blessed Christian home, which was in the grand old Buckeye State, I remember that we did not all sleep in the same bed; but the baby had a cradle, and Johnny, he had a trundle-bed, and the rest had a narrow bed in the front room, in the back room, and other parts of the house. You can imagine the condition if grandfather and grandmother, and father and mother, and all the children, had gotten into one bed. Their heads would be hanging over the headboard, their feet over the footboard, and their arms over the side. It would not fit. And I want to say that there are some churches that are doing very much the same thing. They make up a great big bed in the mid-week prayer-meeting, and they say, " Let the old folks, and the Seniors, and the Intermediates, and the Juniors come in and go to bed with us." Now, it don't fit. We have found out that the little people, with their simple hearts and their childish feelings and sympathies, are different from the old, hard-headed, and hard-hearted people, and they ought to have different things. And so we have, in the Christian Endeavor, a Junior Society. If you were going to convince a man that beefsteak was good for him, you would not take him over in a corner, with a club, and say, "Beefsteak is good to eat;" but you would go and get a nice, tender piece of beefsteak, and, after cooking it, bring it to him steaming and hot, and then its sweetness and tenderness would convince him that it was a good thing for him to eat. And so it is, dear friends, that if we are full of the love of Jesus Christ, we will go home, and in a kind and gentle way organize the Junior Endeavor Society, and lift it up before God for his blessing. If we go about it in the right manner, the churches and the pastors will become interested in this important work, and carry it forward.

MISS CORA B. BICKFORD (President Maine Union): You ask how we shall interest our pastors in the Junior and Intermediate work. There are some pastors you can never interest, I am sure; but there are others that can be interested, if we use the tact and grace that God will give us The latent energy will come forth when we wish to call it forth.

The first thing that I would do to interest a pastor in a Junior Society, if he did not have a society in his church, would be to get together every Junior, or would-be Junior, in that church for some kind of exercise, and just fill his church with them. He would be so glad to see those empty pews filled up — a thing, perhaps, that he has never seen before — that he would be glad to enlist in the Junior cause.

And then I would just go out after the mothers, one at a time, visit them in their homes, and I would try to interest them, and I would get one mother to bring her own child, and when she has done that she will bring somebody else's child, and every Junior, and every Intermediate, with a mother and the pastor back of them, will go out after another Junior and another Intermediate.

MR. H. H. GROTTHOUSE (President Texas Union): You know that in Texas we have lots of room. There are some pastors in Texas that I would try to interest by throwing upon them a 200-horse power arc light, so as to make them shine. There are some churches in Texas which ought not to have an Intermediate society just now, but ought to commence with a Junior Society.

I would say, from my individual standpoint, that I would first send them literature, and I would try to reach them by letters, and bring to bear upon them every power that I could. These influences can be used there, but some of the methods cannot be employed to the same advantage in Texas as they are in other places. What I would do would be to *shine*. It might be by letters, it might be by literature, it might be by talking, it might be by personal influence, but I would SHINE.

REV. A. D. KINZER (President Iowa Union): Iowa is the birthplace of Junior Endeavor. So, of course, we are very fond of the children. In a word, I will try to tell you how we do it over there. One reason why we have not more Junior Societies is because we have not any more children. But we have a great many young people, and the prospects are very hopeful for the future.

We have our State Junior superintendent and twelve district Junior superintendents. We also have county superintendents, and if that is not sufficient, we are going to have a superintendent in every school district, and we will carry the work on in this way until we reach every school and every home in Iowa, and by and by we will have all the churches converted to this movement, and when we get the churches converted, there will be no need of this question.

REV. J. W. COCHRAN (President Wisconsin Union): It seems to me that this discussion, How we shall interest the pastors and the churches in Junior and Intermediate Societies, is very much like asking how we are going to interest the mill-wheel in the water that runs it, how we are going to interest the steamship in the ocean upon which it floats, how we are going to interest the windmills in the wind that drives them; because there is no church unless there are children; there is no pastor unless there are young people. I believe that the trouble with a great many pastors is that they are neither married nor engaged. I would not give much for a church that selects a pastor who is neither married or likely to be very soon. (I am married.) I believe that this is a great home question, and that these ministers who are bachelors must understand that it is necessary for them to get into the hearts of the children. When I went through Wisconsin a little while ago. I was in the home of a boy named Jack. He was the jolliest kind of a boy, and I said to him, "Who is your best boy companion?" He said, "Don't you know?" I said, "No." He said, "It is my father, and he is the jolliest boy I ever knew. We have got a big arm-chair, and father and I sit together in it, and we talk together, and have such a good time." We want this kind of pastors. They want to be the jolliest boys in the congregation, the jolliest boys in the neighborhood. We also want such for Junior superintendents.

We not only want to send literature to the pastors who are not interested in this work, not only write letters to them concerning Junior and Intermediate Societies, but we need to bring every influence to bear upon them.

The hour was late when this discussion closed. The next number upon the program read, "Practical Suggestions from the Trustees of the United Society of Christian Endeavor and from General Secretary

Baer." That the audience might adjourn in time to attend the open-air services, this feature was cut short.

REV. H. B. GROSE: I want to make a hit, but I do not want to make a base-hit, and so here are three strikes, and then we are all out.

The first is, if you want to interest your pastor, find your work, organize your Junior and Intermediate Societies, go earnestly at work, succeed at it, and keep at it. You will convert your pastor if you keep at it in the right way, but you must *keep at it*. Our young people are bound to be busy at something. Every one of our young people are something like Daisy, the flower in our home. She is just a good girl, — because all girls are good, — she is full of vim, and when she goes to church it takes about all her mother's time to look after her, so that she does not hear very much of the sermon. I said to her one Sunday morning, "Don't you think Daisy, that for Mamma's sake you could try and sit still?" She looked up at me, and she said, "Papa, do you know I would like to; but I guess when God made me he forgot to put any sit-stiller in." Get at it, succeed at it, and keep at it, and your pastor will be with you in the work.

SECRETARY JOHN WILLIS BAER: I think, sometimes, as I study the relationship between the older and the young people, that we are really responsible for the lack of Junior and Intermediate Societies in our churches. Instead of putting this upon the pastors, I prefer to place it upon myself for one as an individual. I do not believe that there is a pastor of a single church that would be antagonistic to Junior work if those who proposed it would assure him that they would *stand by it sincerely, honestly, and faithfully*. So, fellow Endeavorers, God speed the day when you and I will appreciate *our* particular part in widening God's kingdom, by bringing the boys and girls into this organized effort, — the Junior and Intermediate Society.

If there is one thing I see in Christian Endeavor that seems more bright than any other, it is the fact that the Junior movement is growing very fast, and the Intermediate Society is also going along very rapidly; and in these two societies I see the flower of the whole movement. As I remember my two little "cubs" to-day way back in Massachusetts, I feel like bending every energy of my life to building up these young societies, that your boys and girls may be workers for Jesus Christ, and that I may expect from you in return your sympathy and your prayers for my boys. This is a co-operative work. You who have not boys and girls, but who pretend to have a wonderful love for the children of the church, I would have you stick so close to that first love that, after you have organized your society, you will not say six months after that *you* were tired of the society, that there was lack of interest, and that the pastor was indifferent. See to it that *your* interest is constant and steadfast. Don't blame the pastor.

These are not the pleasantest words in the world, but situated where I am, I see a great deal of the unpleasant side of our work. And, friends, when the *right time* comes for a Junior Society in every church, I don't believe the pastor lives that will stop it. Do not say that you cannot organize one. Think it over; think it over. I pledge you that the very best work God ever let me do in Christian Endeavor when I came away from the Minnesota State Convention a number of years ago to my home in Rochester, Minnesota, was to gather the boys and girls together in my home church into a Junior Society. If you will engage in the work, you will love it. I beg of you not to hang back on the outside, but to take an active part in the movement.

The Convention was then dismissed by Rev. Nehemiah Boynton, D.D., of Detroit, Michigan.

SATURDAY NOON.

Open-Air Services on Van Ness Avenue.

There were 14,000 people in attendance upon the patriotic meetings held in " the open " on Van Ness Avenue. They were not upon the more fashionable quarter of the street, and were removed by a considerable distance from the business portion of the city. Thus viewed, the gathering was large. If you speak of Boston with 40,000, and Washington with 75,000, gathered under similar circumstances, these figures seem small. But as one of the city papers expressed it, " San Francisco is not Boston." Doubtless, it would have added, " nor yet is it Washington."

The inspiration of the theme, " Our Country," was upon the speakers, and awoke an enthusiastic response in the audience. Four stands were placed, one block apart, and the national colors floated over them. From Mechanics' Pavilion 8,000 Endeavorers marched in line to the song, " Onward, Christian Soldiers." The sight was impressive. Dr. Clark led the van, accompanied by a standard-bearer. The first speaker's stand was at No. 309. Here Dr. Clark presided. The music was directed by Mr. Charles E. Day, of Los Angeles.

This service opened with prayer. Rev. Matt S. Hughes, D.D., of Minneapolis, was the first speaker. He made an earnest appeal for conscientious voters at the polls. Bishop B. W. Arnett spoke of the past and future of the country, closing with the words : " There is room beneath the banner for every one except a slave. We now demand our just and equal rights. We have been emancipated. Now the Christian Endeavor hosts are going to try to emancipate the white men. We are going to emancipate them from intemperance and all the other evils."

The Bishop then led the audience in three cheers for the country, the flag, Dr. Clark, and the Christian Endeavor host.

Rev. Dr. Silas Mead, of Adelaide, Australia, spoke in honor of American womanhood, saying, " They should have citizenship rights, because they are the best representatives of the people. We know that they do not get them because wicked men are afraid they would use their power against the saloon. ' Our Country!' Yes, I want it to be one Christian country that shall hold us all. Let us hope our great Christian Endeavor movement will make us all the citizens of one country."

The service at this part of the avenue closed with a brief address by Dr. Clark. After the Mizpah the strains of " America " supplied the music for their return march to the pavilion.

MEETING NO. 2. 409 VAN NESS AVE.

Mr. Rolla V. Watt, of San Francisco, presided at this service. Mr. J. J. Morris, of the same city, was the musical director. Rev. L. G.

Garber, of Grass Valley, led in prayer for " Our Country," and then the national hymn was sung.

The first speaker was Rev. H. H. Russell, LL.D., of Columbus, Ohio. Among other helpful things he said : " The greatest work of the church has been in the direction of better government. For the twentieth century, ' reform ' will be the cry. The Christian Endeavor movement has done much to prevent the farming-out of public offices to the saloons and the rough element. An honest man is the noblest work of God, but an honest politician is the scarcest. We have registered our vows that we will see that Christian conduct, whose right it is to rule, shall be carried into our public life. Bad citizenship wins to-day because its votaries are more ready to pay the price of success. It has discovered that the way to rule is to dominate the inside movements of political parties. So we shall never have an honest country until honest men dominate as politicians.

" Let our pastors act like Parkhurst in New York, and help to lead us in all Christian citizenship movements ; then we can take off our hats and cheer, as I want you to do now, for better citizenship, for Parkhurst, and for the pastors to lead us."

Rev. William Patterson, of Toronto, was next introduced. He said in part : " When a man settles down in a country he ought to do everything for it. When a man leaves his father and mother and takes up a wife, it does not do for him to tell her too often what father and mother used to do when he was a boy. So when he leaves his native land he can still retain his love of country, yet all his best endeavors should be put forth for the good of the country in which he is making his home. Some say his country owes every man a living; I say it owes more a hanging.

" I was asked by a gentleman recently from England why in Canada we did not have a leisure class called ' gentlemen.' I looked at him for a moment, and turned around to him and said, ' Why, we call that gentry here " tramps." ' "

Rev. Josiah Strong, D.D., of New York, was the last to address this meeting. He paid a graceful tribute to California's hospitality, and spoke of the pleasure of his journey from the Atlantic to the Pacific. He compared the States of Connecticut, Colorado, California, and Texas with the countries of Europe, and said : " Remember, bigness is not greatness. Only a people can make a country great. What use are broad acres unless dedicated to the service of God and the use of man ? What if our country be noble, if our people be selfish and be led around by demagogues ? God has made our country vast. It is ours, with God's help, to make our country good."

Musical Director Morris concluded the service here by singing very acceptably, " Throw Out the Life-Line."

MEETING NO. 3. 515 VAN NESS AVENUE

At this service Secretary Baer presided. O. M. Vesper and Charles Robinson conducted the singing. " Just as I Am " and " Onward.

Christian Soldiers" were sung, after which Secretary Baer invited an officer of the Salvation Army, Major Brengle, to lead in prayer; then Rev. Robert Johnston, of London, Ontario, was introduced. He spoke of the advancement of Christianity among patriotic men and women. Among other things, he said: "Americans are the result of the best strains of people from out the world. Love of liberty and their flag is no stronger than it has been since birth was first given to our nation, but the love of God and the hope of a home beyond are becoming greater and greater as time goes on. American people represent in government and religion more than any other nation of God's beloved children."

Rev. George F. Pentecost was next introduced, and said: "Never before in the tide of times has there arisen a generation of men like our Puritan fathers, who laid deep and strong foundations for a free and glorious country, and a religion which teaches that God is all powerful. I am afraid there has been a tendency to lose sight of God, merely dazzling our eyes with earthly things; but in late years, gospel teachings are the foundation upon which all other great and good things are done."

Rev. E. L. Powell, D.D., of Louisville, Ky., said: "We have one flag, one land, one destiny, and one God. How beautiful is the thought that we are God's creatures, and that we have been promised a home beyond, where we shall know no sorrow, nor have a want! Blessed are the words of our Saviour, for upon them rest all things with which we have to do."

The meeting closed with prayer by Secretary Baer.

MEETING NO. 4. 609 VAN NESS AVENUE.

Here Treasurer Shaw, of the United Society, presided. Mr. Robert Husband led the singing.

Mr. Shaw opened the speech-making with a few appropriate remarks, and then introduced Rev. Cortlandt Myers, of Brooklyn. Mr. Myers said: —

"As I was out in the Park this morning and saw the monument to Francis Scott Key, all thoughts of San Francisco and of my address were crowded out of my mind by the refrain of the 'Star-Spangled Banner.' It is glorious to die for one's country, but what this country needs now is for men to live for it. That, at the present, is the right way to express patriotism. There are all sort of remedies for our social and political evils; but it is not a question of money, of tariff, or of free trade, but the salvation and perpetuity of the country depends upon righteousness.

"As the American land goes, so goes the world, and it is incumbent upon this Western Hemisphere to bring more of the decalogue into political affairs and drive the demagogue out. God pity the man who gives up principle for party, or who, in the associations of politics, shakes hands with Judas Iscariot."

The speaker closed with an impassioned appeal to put the principles of the Christian Endeavor above those of party and concentrate the force of the society toward exterminating the saloon.

Rev. J. C. R. Ewing, D.D., of Lahore, India, was the next speaker, and among other things he said: "I have looked at America from a distance for eighteen years, and rejoice in the fact of our splendid American people and American government. The one thing that has occasioned me, as an American citizen, anxiety and distress is the fact that the best people are not taking an active part in the affairs of state. It is not the respectable element that is guiding the politics, particularly of the large cities. It is too late to think of reconstructing the old people, but the remedy lies in educating the young people to the necessity of abolishing jingoism and jugglery in politics."

Dr. B. B. Tyler, of New York, was then introduced by the chairman as the "grand old man of Christian Endeavor, but the youngest in spirit."

He said: "I want you to know first that I am an American because I am a Christian, and no man can become a Christian who does not love his country. A man should love his country with the same earnestness as inspires him to attend communion. This love must be practical and active. It should be surrounded with such zeal as will cause him to participate in the primaries, even though the prayer-meeting should happen to fall on the same night. You must give the parties to understand that if they want your franchises it is necessary for them to first plant themselves on the eternal principles of righteousness. There are a great many political doctors, but they don't know what ails the patient; their remedies don't begin to touch the case. But we have reached the beginning of a new era. Electricity and steam have revolutionized the world, and there is a new factor which will accomplish the same for politics. The new issue is the question of woman's suffrage. In this country there are five million women wage-workers, and in New York alone there are seven thousand women who support their husbands.

"The introduction of these women into politics means progress and reformation. It is not going to spoil women to have the ballot, but it is going to do the men a world of good. The American people are never more deeply in earnest than when a moral question is involved. The issue was slavery once, and now it is the saloon in politics. We must make our politics a part of our religion. I have never spoken from a political platform, but I preach politics in the pulpit every Sunday, because it is identified with my gospel. Good Christians are good citizens; and when the three million young people enrolled under this banner understand the practical meaning of their pledge, it will work a readjustment of our political affairs."

Chairman Shaw closed with an appeal, urging the male members of the audience to take an active interest in having men nominated for office who will represent the Christian sentiment of the country instead of mispreserenting it.

The meeting ended with a fervent singing of "My Country, 't is of Thee," and a benediction by Dr. Tyler.

SATURDAY AFTERNOON AND EVENING.

Probably never before in the history of Endeavor Conventions did the attraction of the Convention city and surroundings appeal to so large a proportion of the visiting delegates as in the Convention of '97. Yet, though many delegations arrived twelve, twenty-four, thirty-six, and even fifty-four hours behind schedule time, and great companies of Endeavorers were obliged, owing to the limits of their vacation periods, to turn their faces homeward immediately after the adjournment of the Convention, the meetings did not suffer because the delegates were off sightseeing. Of course, not every Endeavorer attended every one of the five or six different services held every day. Good sense as well as physical limits forbade that, but the greatest amount of sightseeing and excursions was reserved for Saturday afternoon, when there were no meetings, and for the days following the closing of the Convention.

There was much in and about the city of absorbing interest that could be caught on the fly, so to speak, when there was a half-hour or more that was free for such a purpose. The museum containing relics of the days of '49 was right on the thoroughfare to the Convention halls, and was visited by throngs, as was also Golden Gate Park.

Saturday evening, following an afternoon of sight seeing, brought the delegates around to the great social event of the Convention, the State rallies and receptions. These were held in a dozen or more of the prominent churches, the local society taking upon itself the care of providing for the arrangements. The songs and speeches were all of a jovial nature, strongly flavored with high praise for the royal welcome which California, through its chief city, had extended with bountiful hand to all visiting delegates. With sunshine in their souls and California ozone in their lungs, the songs and cheers of the delegations went with a will.

For the first time, various States from the same section of the country joined together in a common jubilee and exchange of friendly greetings, instead of holding separate rallies for each State. Many were the souvenirs provided by the societies serving as hosts, as well as attractive tables handsomely decorated and spread with such refreshments as might be expected from Californians anxious to give the strangers within their gates the very best they had. The meetings were all crowded, and afforded a fitting close to a week filled with matters of more serious moment.

OHIO, MICHIGAN, AND INDIANA.

The Endeavorers from these three States were delightfully entertained by the society of the First Congregational Church. President Littlefield of the society presided. A gracious word of welcome was spoken by the pastor, Rev. Dr. Addams, to which each of the three State presidents responded. After a pleasant social hour spent in the parlors of the church, the guests were speeded on their way, each being presented with a beautiful souvenir of the happy occasion.

MASSACHUSETTS, CONNECTICUT, MAINE, RHODE ISLAND, VERMONT, NEW HAMPSHIRE.

In the Plymouth Congregational Church, before a crowded house, the following program was carried out : Music by the orchestra was followed by the hymn, "Onward Christian Soldiers," and then prayer was offered. Rev. C. R. Brown, of Oakland, gave the address of welcome. Rev. F. E. Clark and wife were warmly greeted.

Responses by the guests followed. For Maine, Miss Cora Bickford, president of the State society, responded, likening the warmth of the welcome received to the golden-hearted poppies of the State. Rev. S. H. Woodrow replied for Rhode Island, while Connecticut's claims for recognition were presented with much humor by Rev. Henry Upson. Rev. O. C. Sargent for New Hampshire, Rev. Benjamin Swift for Vermont, and Rev. James L. Hill, D.D., for Massachusetts, expressed their appreciation of California's welcome.

Rev. E. W. Shurtleff, of Plymouth, Mass., presented the Young People's Society of Christian Endeavor of the Plymouth Church with a piece of old Plymouth Rock. With the response by the local president, this was a pretty feature of the evening's program.

Treasurer Shaw made a brief address, after which the company adjourned to the vestry, where refreshments were served. Other brief speeches were made by Rev. H. B. Grose, Rev. E. L. House, and Rev. Warren P. Landers, of Massachusetts.

IOWA, MINNESOTA, WISCONSIN, NORTH DAKOTA, SOUTH DAKOTA.

At the Third Congregational Church the rally from Iowa, Minnesota, Wisconsin, North Dakota, and South Dakota took place, with the pastor, Rev. William Rader, presiding. He welcomed the delegates in an amusing talk. Rev. A. D. Kinzer responded for Iowa, and then " Fair Iowa," by the Rev. N. A McAuley, was sung, after which Miss Anna Egenhoff recited " The Famine," from " Hiawatha."

Rev. Mr. Phillips responded for North Dakota. He said he had been trying to think what the monogram " C. E." signified in this part of the world, and gave it three significations : " Cordiality Everywhere," " Charming Entertainers," and " Cold Eatables."

The Rev. W. P. Langdale, replying for South Dakota, referred as a special feature in Endeavor work to the Indian Endeavorers.

Norwood Stratton sang a bass solo, and Samuel Booth read an original poem descriptive of the "Gathering of the (C. E.) Clans." Evangelist C. N. Hunt, of Minneapolis, addressed the meeting, and was followed by a tenor solo by Harry Hanley, the Iowa State song, and a quartette from Minnesota. An adjournment was then made down-stairs, where was a flower-booth filled with bouquets for distribution to the delegates, while in the larger rooms four tables were loaded with fruits, cakes, and lemonade.

COLORADO, ARIZONA, NEW MEXICO, INDIAN TERRITORY, OKLAHOMA.

Bethany Congregational Church was crowded by delegates from the Christian Endeavor societies of Colorado, Arizona, New Mexico, Indian Territory, and Oklahoma Territory. The church presented quite a pretty picture, decorated, as it was, with flowers and bunting The services were opened with prayer by Rev. W. C. Pond, pastor of the church. The speakers who followed came in no regular order, the meeting being more of an impromptu gathering than a regular church service.

In reply to the address of welcome made by Dr. Pond on behalf of his church, addresses were delivered by leading representatives from the various States and Territories represented. Solos were sung during the evening by Misses Mary Cook and Nellie Partridge, and when the meeting had adjourned refreshments were served in the parlors of the church by the young ladies in attendance. The Market Street Congregational Church of Oakland also assisted in the entertainment of the visitors.

KENTUCKY, MARYLAND, TENNESSEE, VIRGINIA, WEST VIRGINIA.

The First Presbyterian Church, on Van Ness Avenue, was the gathering-place of the visitors from Kentucky, Maryland, Tennessee, Virginia, and West Virginia. The Endeavor societies of the Mizpah Presbyterian Church, African Methodist Episcopal Zion, Centennial Presbyterian of East Oakland, First Presbyterian Volunteers of Oakland, and the Presbyterian churches of San Rafael and Temescal united with the Endeavorers of the First Presbyterian Church in giving the reception. The rooms were tastefully decorated, and each guest received on his entrance a dainty souvenir,— a bit of highly polished orange, manzanita wood, with " C. E., '97 " in gilt on the face.

Rev. E. H. Jenks, the associate of Dr. McKenzie, welcomed the delegates. Short addresses were made by Rev. J. B. Arrick, of Kentucky, H. D. Boughner, of West Virginia, Dr. B. F. Wilber, of Alaska, Miss Katherine P. Jones, young people's secretary of Home Missions in New York; W. L. Noell, State president of Tennessee, and Rev. Ira Landrith, of Nashville, Tennessee. The Sunday-school orchestra rendered some pretty selections, and a quartette from Alameda sang several times.

PENNSYLVANIA AND DISTRICT OF COLUMBIA.

The delegates from Pennsylvania and the District of Columbia were entertained in Calvary Presbyterian Church. The hymn " Blest Be the Tie that Binds " was sung, with Robert Cleland as leader. The address of welcome was delivered by Rev. John Hemphill, D.D., pastor. The hymn "And He Has Made Me Glad " was sung by Mrs. Beatrice Priest, Mrs. Sedgly Reynolds, and the Messrs. Lawrence. An address on behalf of Pennsylvania was delivered by Rev. A. B. Philputt, D.D., of Philadelphia. Among other things he said : "Many welcomes have been given to Christian Endeavor, but the welcome by California will never be outdone in America nor any part of this vast world. The word 'welcome' has rung in my ears since I first entered the borders of California. 'Let peace be o'er all the earth' seems to have been obeyed, for harmony, truth, welcome, and song greet us on every hand."

Miles M. Shand spoke for the District of Columbia. He said : "Words of praise are upon all lips for California. Welcome and welcome yet again has echoed and re-echoed throughout homes and wherever we may happen to have been. 'For Christ and the Church' is our motto, but we must deviate from the banner a little and sing the praises of California."

George P. McDougall, president of the Calvary Young People's Society of Christian Endeavor, delivered an address on behalf of his society. After singing the hymns "Banner of the Cross" and "Keep Step with Thy Master," all adjourned to the church parlors for refreshments.

NEW YORK.

The Trinity Presbyterian Church was the scene of the New York State rally. State President Rev. Wm. J. McKittrick, of Buffalo, presided, and the program included "California's welcome to New York" by Rev. F. S. Brush, of Alameda ; "Addresses by New York State Officers," under which head President McKittrick, Secretary A. E. Dewhurst, Treasurer H. A. Kinports, and Committeemen H. F. Remington and Jno. R. Clements spoke briefly.

"Remarks by pastors of New York" was the announcement for two-minute speeches by Rev. Dr. Geo. F. Pentecost, Rev. Dr. Park, of Gloversville, Rev. Dr. J. L. Dickson, Rev. Mr. Lyle, of Millbrook, Rev. Dr. Wylie, of New York, and Rev. F. P. Arthur, of Rochester.

The singing of the State song, "We Are Soldiers of Jesus," brought the very interesting exercise to a close ; then the San Francisco Endeavorers invited their guests to the basement of the church, where a series of tables, placed to represent the Endeavor monogram, all profusely decorated and amid surroundings of tropical beauty, were laden with tempting delicacies to which every one did large justice. A social hour followed, and the evening closed with singing "God Be with You Till We Meet Again."

NEW JERSEY AND DELAWARE.

The New Jersey and Delaware delegations were entertained at the First United Presbyterian Church by the Christian Endeavor societies of the Stewart Memorial Church, the United Presbyterian churches of Alameda, Newark, and Alvarado, and the Friends of West Berkeley. Rev. E. M. Thompson, of New Jersey, presided. After a prayer by Rev. M. M. Gibson, pastor of the church, Rev. J. M. French, of Oakland, delivered the address of welcome. Short addresses were made by Rev. Dr. Tinker, of Wilmington, Del., and Rev. L. R. Dyott, of New Jersey. After the program refreshments were served in the parlors of the church.

ARKANSAS, ALABAMA, FLORIDA, GEORGIA, LOUISIANA, MISSISSIPPI, NORTH CAROLINA, SOUTH CAROLINA.

Several hundred delegates met at Howard Presbyterian Church to participate in the joint rally of Arkansas, Alabama, Florida, Georgia, Louisiana, Mississippi, North and South Carolina. Purcell Rowe, president of Golden Gate Union Society, presided, and the program was of unusual excellence. Miss Blair rendered a violin solo, Miss Decker a contralto solo, Mrs. Susie Hert Mark a soprano solo, and the California Quartette gave one of the best selections from its extensive repertoire. Arthur M. Currie, president of the local Endeavor Society, addressed the gathering, assuring them that the Convention would bear rich fruit for this city, and, indeed, for the entire Western country; and every one was then requested to adjourn to the lower floor, where light refreshments had been provided.

Canadian Reception.

CANADA.

The reception for the Canadian delegation was held in Westminster Presbyterian Church, which was most elaborately decorated for the occasion, two Union Jack banners meeting over the Stars and Stripes on the platform. The first few minutes of the evening were spent in making acquaintance, after which a very spicy program was placed in the hands of Mr. B. H. Barker, who very ably filled the position of chairman. An address of welcome given by Mr. T. M. Sherman, touching the Jubilee of Canada's Christian Queen, Toronto's Sabbath observance, made the delegation feel very pleasant. Rev. Mr. Gandier, of Halifax, responded for the Maritime Union, humorously touching upon the " Blue Noses " and the Christian Endeavor work in the East. Rev. C. W. Finck, of Cookshire, responding for Quebec Provincial Union, said : " We Canadians are justly proud of our Christian Sovereign, and are truly loyal, and we know you are loyal to your superior officer ; but we join hands to-day under the King of kings, and the tie that binds us in Christian Endeavor will never sever. Rev. Robert Johnston, of London, spoke for the Ontario Union, and drew a happy comparison between the United States and Canada, and hoped for the most pleasant relationship ever to exist between them. Rev. W. C. Dodds represented the British Columbia Union, and touched forcibly on the industries of British Columbia.

Music for the occasion was supplied by Miss F. Smith, Miss Emma McCormick, Miss Daisy Cumming, who sang solos, and the California Male Quartette, consisting of Messrs. G. F. Graham, R. W. Smith, C. L. Gage, and E. McBaine, who rendered several selections. There were 208 delegates from Canada.

MISSOURI, KANSAS, NEBRASKA, AND TEXAS.

At the Central Methodist Episcopal Church delegates from Missouri, Kansas, Nebraska, and Texas were received. Rolla V. Watt opened the meeting with the hymn, "Sunshine in My Soul." The address of welcome was delivered by Rev. E. R. Dille, D.D., pastor, and was followed by a baritone solo by J. M. Robinson. The response on behalf of Missouri was made by C. A. Forse, who said : " It is with feelings of intense gratitude that I stand here this evening. A welcome such as we have received in California is enough to fill the soul with gladness. Welcome, and welcome only as we have seen can be given by California, is at all times gratifying ; but when it is given in the interest of Christ and his teachings it is increased twofold."

After a soprano solo by Miss Grace Davis, a response was given on behalf of Kansas by F. T. Vincent. A. D. Harmon, of Nebraska, spoke for his State, saying : " We have been welcomed in a way not soon to be forgotten. The gold and purple are on all available space. Even the saloons have hoisted words of welcome." H. H. Grotthouse, speaking for Texas, said the welcome was glorious, but if he thought the climate and fresh air in California would fill him out sufficiently to wear Chairman Watt's clothes he believed he would stay — welcome or no welcome.

OREGON, WASHINGTON, ALASKA.

At the reception to the delegates from Oregon, Washington, and Alaska, given by the young people of the First Baptist Church, a pleasant song service was held while the company was gathering. The program was in charge of Mr. J. A. Wilson. Prayer was offered by Dr. A. B. Banks, of Sacramento. Rev. M. P. Boynton, pastor of the church, gave a welcome to the audience in behalf of the San Francisco churches, and Mr. J. A. Wiles voiced that of the societies. H. S. Gile responded for Oregon, John P. Hartman for Washington, and B. K. Wilber for Alaska.

Charming music and readings varied the exercises, and an impromptu speech from the Christian Endeavor Mayor of Seattle, giving a word of encouragement to Christian citizenship work, closed the formal exercises. Refreshments, and an all-too-short social gathering, followed in the parlors of the church.

UTAH, IDAHO, MONTANA, WYOMING, NEVADA.

At the West Side Christian Church were held the joint rally and reception of Utah, Idaho, Montana, Wyoming, and Nevada, with over a thousand persons present. R. H. Walker, president of the West Side society, delivered an address of welcome to the visitors, and it was responded to by Mrs. Shepherd, of Salt Lake City, and others, in behalf of the States mentioned. Rev. William A. Gardner, pastor of the church, supplemented the welcome in a brief speech Mrs. Cutting, of Carson, Nev., sang a plaintive Scotch ballad, and Miss Hines recited effectively two selections. Refreshments were served in the Sunday-school room attached to the church building.

CALIFORNIA.

The Tenth Annual Convention of the State was held on Saturday evening. Not since the Convention started has there been a more enthusiastic crowd than those who formed the one that rallied round the California banner in the galleries of the pavilion. Every one had a smile for his and her neighbor; every one had a kind word to speak, and genuine heartiness marked every movement. At each of the county headquarters the delegates gathered and extended a welcoming hand to their fellow Endeavorers, and so the minutes flew.

Hardly had the last anthem been sung before the galleries were crowded. There was a jam at once, but every one was good-natured and took the attendant pushing and jostling as a matter of course, and rather enjoyed the novelty of the crush. Suddenly some one started up one of the familiar hymns. Then, by one after another, the refrain was taken up, and soon the whole gallery was filled with song. One after another was rendered, a line was formed, and round the headquarters they marched until the first warning bell, announcing the hour for closing the hall.

Los Angeles dispersed lemonade at one end, Santa Clara souvenirs at another. As a foil to Placer's fruit, Alameda County gave away its choicest blossoms from Oakland's gardens. Tulare's sequoia-bark pincushions were in great demand, as the bunches of moss tied with yellow ribbons which were San Mateo County souvenirs.

A series of four-minute addresses on "Advance Lines of Endeavor Work" was opened by C. Z. Merritt, of Oakland, the first president of the California Christian Endeavor Union. His topic was "Sabbath Defence." Rolla V. Watt made a short, bright speech on "Systematic Giving." The Rev. E. B. Hays. of Modesto, spoke of "Missions." Dr. E. E. Kelly spoke on "Fellowship," and Giles Kellogg on "Floating Work."

The Rev. R. F. Coyle, D. D., of Oakland, made an eloquent address on the work in California, and the Rev. F. E. Clark, D. D., presented the greetings of the United Society to the California Christian Endeavor Union.

The reports from all departments were most encouraging. The grand total membership was given as 34,645.

ILLINOIS.

The First Christian Church entertained the Illinois Endeavorers at their rally. The church was filled to overflowing with 500 enthusiastic Illinoisans, who sang the praises of their State in speech and song for about an hour, after which their entertainers served them with refreshments.

Judge Dewey, of Cairo, State treasurer, presided in his usual felicitous way, the pastor of the Christian Church, Mr. Ford, welcomed the visitors, and Rev. H. Stough, of Oak Park, responded for Illinois.

The other speakers were Miss F. LeBaron, Junior superintendent for Illinois, A. E. MacDonald, president Chicago Union, and Bishop Fallows, trustee of the United Society from Chicago. Miss Edna Luce rendered a piano solo, Mr. McGuirea, cornet solo, Mme. Waltz sang "The Cradle Song," and Miss F. Luce recited "A Buffalo Hunt in Chicago," which was thoroughly appreciated by the Chicago contingent.

The occasion was a very enjoyable one and will be remembered by us of Illinois because of the spirit of fellowship engendered and the added reason for friendship to the California Endeavorers, which our hearty welcome induced.

Colorado, New Mexico, Oklahoma, Arizona.

The combined rally of Floating Societies with Colorado, New Mexico, Oklahoma, and Arizona, was not among the least enjoyable, though small. Miss A. P. Jones, Falmouth, Massachusetts, and Mr. Makins, of Tacoma, Washington, were speakers.

A solution of the apparent intention of former and present convention committees was brought out in the remark of one speaker that doubtless the intention was to combine the *dust* of these States and Territories with the water of the *ocean* and so make a mammoth *Christian Endeavor mud pie.* The *sailor* and the *cowboy* received Christian interest, though *none* of the latter were present, and but three active sailors in uniform.

THE CONVENTION SUNDAY.

PREPARED by the inspiring words of the preceding days, the delegates at the international gatherings entered upon the Convention Sunday with open hearts and obedient wills. The impress left by the sermons of that day is multifold.

They are preparatory, too. The consecration service was to be held the night following. The Lord's Day supplied a "quiet hour" in which to review the life, to make determinations calmly and honestly. In the midst of so much to clarify the vision, one could have conceptions of the meaning of consecration more nearly adequate to the demands of Jesus when he called his disciples to be in the world, yet not a part of it.

The preachers of the Convention sermons of '97 seemed to feel the significance of their position. That day they were to be pre-eminently teachers. Immense audiences thronged the churches of San Francisco and vicinity. Those whose business had kept them from the Convention sessions improved the opportunity to hear its voices Sunday.

An insight into the character of the sermons can be obtained from some of the texts : " For our Gospel came not unto you in word only, but also in power ; " " Go, ye, therefore, and teach all nations, baptizing them in the name of the Father, and of the Son, and of the Holy Ghost ; " " So much as in me is, I am ready to preach the Gospel to ye that are in Rome also ; " " Sir, we would see Jesus ; " " I am come that they might have life, and that they might have it more abundantly ; " " He leadeth me beside the still waters."

Churches everywhere were filled to the brim, with scarcely standing-room left, even half an hour before the opening of the service. It was a new experience for the city, and made a deep impression on the non-churchgoing citizens. That the throng was an Endeavor crowd was plainly manifested by the freedom with which they sang the popular Convention hymns before the opening of the services. Even in some of the largest churches it was necessary to arrange for an overflow service in the vestry, and in several cases three overflow services were held.

SUNDAY AFTERNOON.

Mechanics' Pavilion.

The attendance at the meeting held in the Mechanic's Pavilion on Sunday afternoon in the interests of the Lord's Day proved Endeavor's loyalty to the Sabbath. Long before the opening of the service the doors were closed and no more could enter.

Musical Director Husband said, as he announced the first hymn, "This is distinctively your service." The response of the audience showed its appreciation of the opportunity to praise God on his holy day. President Clark was chairman of the session. Rev. A. D. Kinzer, of Lyons, Iowa, selected scripture and offered prayer in keeping with the purpose of the gathering.

Dr. Clark took occasion to say in introduction, " I trust that the reputation of this day will be upheld by all delegates, and that not a single one of them will be seen in any place where the badge of the Society should not be carried. California has won the Sunday observance banner, and I hope that the effort to increase the observance of the Lord's Day in this State may be even greater during the coming year. And I trust that this spirit may sweep to the East and cover the entire country." He paid a tribute to California's Endeavorers which the audience indorsed with applause.

The first speaker was Miss Mathilda Kay, of New York City, upon " Woman's Part " in preserving the Lord's Day.

Address of Miss Mathilda Kay, New York City.

A great arrest has been made. Have you heard of it? If not you must hear of it, for it occurred on the Lord's Day, and you and I are concerned in it.

One Sunday noon in one of the central cities of our country there stood at the door of the post-office a man; he was the Secretary of the Young Men's Christian Association. Church services were over, and to the post-office hurried throngs of people to get their Sunday mail. Silently the man at the door handed each a card. Every man and woman looked at his card, and read : —

" Remember the Sabbath Day to keep it holy.
" Six days shalt thou labor and do all thy work ;
" But the seventh day is the Sabbath of the Lord thy God : in it thou shalt not do any work, thou, nor thy son, nor thy daughter, thy manservant, nor thy maidservant."

The arrest had taken place. No fettered prisoners were there; no clanking of handcuffs on the captives' wrists, but swiftly and surely thought was arrested, and indeed this was no trifling event.

Do you know what an arrest of thought means?

" More ill is wrought by want of thought,
Than e'er was wrought by want of heart."

The president of the World's Christian Temperance Union has used the white ribbon to bring about this " arrest of thought," as she termed it, in temperance work; and this afternoon I hold up my warrant for the arrest of your thought, the same warrant used by the Secretary of the Young Men's Christian Association that Sunday afternoon on the steps of the post-office: " Remember the Sabbath Day to keep it holy. Six days shalt thou labor and do all thy work."

Of all those people who came to get their Sunday mail how many do you suppose ever thought before of the man at the general delivery window and the woman at the stamp window as their manservant and their maidservant? God Almighty had forbidden them to work on the Sabbath. Do you ever think of them as your servants? Shame on us that we need this arrest of thought!

We Sabbath-lovers of New York State point with pride to-day to a city in which the Christian Endeavorers have awakened to a sense of shame, and which now has no need of a silent secretary with the Fourth Commandment on a card to remind people that it is the Sabbath Day, but confronts them with the closed and barred doors of the post-office. And yet for fear you may think no more arrest of thought is needed in New York, truth compels me to tell you of a city up the Hudson where one who was once the president of the Christian Endeavor Union said, "We tried to stop the church dress parade in our town, but we could not." What was the church dress parade? Church-members, dressed in their best, going in throngs to the post-office on Sunday because it was kept open for only one hour on that day. Nineteen members of his own church were counted by the silent secretary, as he stood that Sabbath noon on the post-office steps with his warrant in his hand. Take the same warrant. Stand on the steps of the post-office in your town. How many of your church-members will you count?

But I am not here to tell you what Christian Endeavorers have done, are doing, or ought to do for the Lord's Day; I am here to tell you woman's part in furthering Sabbath observance; I firmly believe her part is to make this arrest of thought.

> "The bravest battle that ever was fought,
> Shall I tell you where and when?
> On the maps of the world you will find it not—
> It was fought by the mothers of men."

Here is a battle to be fought. Social customs and a growing indifference to the claims of others are arrayed against the "Remember" and the "Thou shalt not" of the Lord. Woman can win in this contest. Who but woman decrees very largely what shall be done in social life? A woman in high social position arrested the thought of another; the latter, stopping to think, said but a few words to her husband — the result? The Sunday dinner, planned for prominent officials, was not given.

Woman can do what man cannot. Every man before me nods his approval at that, while every woman is conscious of this truth. Did you read "The Summer Girl," a booklet published by the Woman's National Sabbath Alliance? In it, Rosamond Ellis, by her influence, leads the summer boarders, gay young men and the jolly girls, to surprise the country parson by filling his pews on Sunday. Perhaps a young man could have done that, but I never heard of one who did.

"It does me good to be with her," said a young man of a young woman to whom he had been talking. Rest assured he would have said the same thing had she pleasantly refused to sell him a postage-stamp on Sunday, as a girl whom I know once did; or even if she had pleasantly refused to take a long journey on Sunday night to hear a noted preacher.

Why shall woman be the one to make this arrest of thought? Because woman, above all, needs the day of rest. All over our land countless women work from daylight till dark on the seventh day, and work harder than on any other of the six.

"The preacher means me," sobbed a servant-girl in church, as the minister accused church-members of not attending church services. "Yes, he means me; but there is a big dinner to get on Sundays; and when Sunday night comes I am so tired I just creep up to bed and go to sleep." "But suppose I get you a place in a Christian family, then you can go to church?" "Oh, they are Christians! They all go to church, and they say their prayers every morning; they are good enough to me," was the reply.

Listen to another voice that tells the story of thousands of girls: "When would you have me get my dress ready for Monday morning?" Who said it? A girl who worked all day Saturday and the greater part of the night in a dry-goods store. Her visitor was shocked to find her sewing her gown on Sunday morning.

A second reason why women should further Sabbath observance throughout this land of ours — because man needs it. Said a returned missionary lately, speaking of some dreadful customs in the country from which he came, "Whatever degrades man degrades woman;" and no truer word than this could ever be spoken with regard to the custom of desecrating the Sabbath.

Out among the mountains in New York State was an old homestead; here lived a hard-working farmer with his family grown up about him. No dainty hand-painted calendars hung up in his log cabin, but the old man marked each day by a "chip in the stick." One morning all were working as usual in a field, when a neighbor, driving home from church, cries out, " Mr. Davidson, you working on Sunday ? " In surprise the old man cries, " Is this Sunday ? " Yes, he had forgotten to make a chip for one day. The day passes and the next dawns. The men start for work, but the old man stops them. " There 'll be no work to-day : bring out your books ; we 'll keep Sabbath this day." And a Sabbath quiet reigns, though Sunday is past.

Long years pass by, and another Mr. Davidson takes the place of this Sabbath-keeping man. He has grown old and feeble ; his mind is weak ; he wanders about like a restless child. One Sunday he goes to the barn ; something needs to be done for the horses. " But, pa, this is Sunday," reminds a sweet voice ; and the long years of Sabbath-keeping show their influence, and the old feeble man is contented to rest because it is the Sabbath Day. Another Sunday he sees some stones in the pathway. The stones must be cleared away, and the old man commences to work, but the sweet reminder tells him of the day, and pretty soon, lying at rest on the pillows, he enquires feebly of his son, " Why did n't you tell me it was the Sabbath ? " " Why, you have n't been breaking it, have you, pa ? " " Well, I guess I 've pretty well cracked it," said the old man.

Again the years pass, and the old man's grandson, a little boy of six, visits with me his sister living in a distant village. Sunday morning comes, and the little child questions, " Why are the wagons rumbling along filled with milk-cans on Sunday ? "

This is the story of four generations, and as usual the woman's part is hidden, but it needs no keen insight to point it out. Think you the Sabbath would have been kept on Sunday if the mother had not aided and helped ? Did you notice that it was the voice of a woman who reminded the old man of the return of the Lord's Day ? And who was it led the little boy of six to see the difference between one day and another ?

" Our nation is doomed if we keep not the Sabbath," said a thinking, reasoning woman.

In one of the salons of Paris was hung a wonderful picture. Look at it with me. The name strikes you,— " Toward the Abyss." And now the picture. You see a dry and barren hillside. Down it moves a long procession of human kind, of every age and sex. On they come. They trample each other in their haste, though blood stains the way, and some rise no more where they fall. Old men are on their knees. One man is being dragged under foot by the crowd rushing onward. A blonde-haired maiden, robed in tenderest green, clings to her neighbor as she falls. Who leads in this dreadful downward course ? Look at the figure in the foreground. It is a woman. A woman leads " Toward the Abyss." She steps lightly over the rocky soil, while others, her followers, stumble and fall, and are crushed to the ground.

Only a picture in Paris, you say ; but what is a picture in Paris may become a reality in the United States, for woman will lead, and whether toward the abyss or toward heaven depends upon the woman.

Said a French woman to me the other day. " I have been asked to translate a paper that is to be read this summer before the Sunday Rest Congress in Brussels." In it the writer said, " Foreigners coming to the United States are impressed with our quiet Sabbaths." She said, " I wrote him that was true twenty-five years ago, but it is not true to-day. Think of it ! Twenty-five years ago ? What a work we have to undo ! Are the women of America making any efforts to bring back the Sabbaths of twenty-five years ago ? "

Gathered in a hall in New York City, a little over two years ago, were eighteen Christian women, representing various religious denominations. This meeting was the outcome of many prayers. The object of holding it was to inaugurate a movement to bring about a better observance of the Sabbath. The ladies present took this pledge : —

"We, women of America, recognizing the American Christian Sabbath as our rightful inheritance. bequeathed to us by our forefathers ; as the foundation of our national prosperity ; as the safeguard of our social, civil, and religious blessings ; as the conservator of the rights of the wage-earner ; do hereby pledge ourselves to resist, by precept and example, whatever tends to undermine Sunday as a day of rest and worship,—such as the Sunday secular papers, Sunday social entertainments, and Sunday driving and traveling for gain or pleasure; and we further pledge ourselves to use our influence to create a right sentiment on all aspects of the Sunday question, especially in reference to traffic of every kind on that day."

This was the origin of the Woman's National Sabbath Alliance.

It is only one way of saying, "We Christian women of America have seen the thoughtlessness regarding the observance of the Lord's Day, and we are determined to 'arrest thought.'" In 1895 eighteen women were pledged to do this. In 1897 there are several hundreds of women who have taken this pledge. Many of these are members of the Alliance, others are members of auxiliaries to the Alliance. The secretary of our auxiliary in Washington, D. C., wrote: —

"A delegation of our society met the District Committee in Congress, to urge the passage of a Sunday rest bill, in the District of Columbia. By calling the attention of the public to the necessity for action, a marked decrease in Sunday entertainments has resulted."

And the secretary of our auxiliary in Atlantic City, N. J., writes: "Send me some literature for our work here. Our women have decided to put up boxes in places much frequented on the Sabbath, and intend keeping these boxes well supplied with literature bearing on the Sabbath question."

Does your town need any work of that kind? Could you not do it if you had a well-selected committee representing the different churches?

The Woman's National Sabbath Alliance has an office in the Presbyterian Building, on Fifth Avenue and Twentieth Street, New York City. The recording secretary invites you now, each one, to come and see her in room 711 on any Tuesday afternoon after the 15th of September, and we will have a good talk about the Auxiliary you are going to form; or, better still, "Uncle Sam" will carry your letter for the small sum of two cents, and we will arrange to have our field secretary make one of her convincing addresses before your society. As I look at you I am reminded of Charles Kingsley's words: "I have a great desire to do something, God only knows what!" For I believe you are looking me in the face and saying, "We have a desire to do many things, but 'God only knows' which of the many we can do." Do not leave this undone, this work of the Sabbath. Think for a moment, and you will see how it underlies all the rest.

Do you know why the work of the Woman's Christian Temperance Union will endure? It is because of the "Y's," — the young women's divisions they have organized. The members of our Alliance are longing for such a band of young women workers to stand behind them to take up the lines of work they are planning, and to carry them forward with youthful persistency. News has reached the Alliance of the Lord's Day committees formed amongst Christian Endeavorers, and most heartily have we endorsed and commended these efforts.

A little girl closed her evening prayer as follows: "And I saw a poor little girl on the streets to-day, all ragged, and cold, and barefooted; but it's none of our business, is it, Lord?" That is just what people are saying with regard to Sabbath desecration. It is true that these dreadful things are taking place on the Sabbath, "but it's none of our business." And so an organization is needed to shoulder responsibility, individuals think! You claim you have no time for more organization, even though it would call for but few meetings during the year. Then will you use your own personal influence to bring about a better observance of the Lord's Day?

Standing on Boston Common to-day, opposite the State House, is a monument in memory of a young man who wrote home in a letter before the Civil War, "I do not see how one man could do much against slavery," and yet what Colonel Robert Shaw did has inspired sculptors, painters, and poets.

What can one woman do in this battle for the Sabbath? One woman arose in a meeting and read this pledge: "For the well-being and comfort of the many who need the advantages of a Saturday half-holiday, I promise not to do any shopping on Saturday after 12 o'clock, save in an emergency, and as little as possible at any time on Saturday."

She alone had secured the name of about fourteen hundred women to this pledge.

Said one woman: "I have quietly taken the Sunday newspaper and put it in a drawer, so that it was not easy of access. It is no longer taken in my house." Said another woman: "We will take two copies of the Saturday *Tribune* in our home, if that will aid in securing the proprietor's promise not to issue the Sunday edition."

Instances of individual work might be multiplied, but you have already heard enough.

The American Sabbath will be rescued if each woman in America will sacredly observe the fourth commandment.

There was recently exhibited in London, on Bond Street, a most magnificent ornament. It was a cord of pearls about a yard long; it was made of fifty or sixty strands of tiny pearls threaded together and rolled into a rope of more than half an inch thick. Said a woman writing of it, "It is one of the most exquisite ornaments the heart of woman could desire." Of greater length and of far more intrinsic value than this cord of pearls is the cord that is yours and mine to-day. Each year there are woven in it three hundred and sixty-five jewels, and one in every seven shines pure and white, a lovely pearl. How have you kept your pearls? And how will you keep them?

Once, at Stockholm, Jenny Lind was requested to sing on the Sabbath at the king's palace on the occasion of some great festival. She refused, and the king called personally upon her, in itself a high honor, and as her sovereign commanded her attendance. Her reply was: "There is a higher King, sire, to whom I owe my first allegiance," and she refused to be present.

Said Victor Hugo of Rosa Bonheur: "As a creative artist I prize her works above those of all other women, because she listened to God and not to man." May that be said of every woman here. She listened to God—and remembered to keep his day holy.

The voice of Rev. W. H. G. Temple, of Seattle, Washington, was next heard upon the "Modern Forms of Sabbath Desecration." After a highly commendatory introduction by President Clark, Mr. Temple said :—

Address by Rev. W. H. G. Temple, Seattle, Wash.

Mr. Chairman and Christian Friends :— The last thing that a speaker ought to be called upon to defend in this Christian country is the Christian Sabbath. And yet we have to stand guard over it with drawn swords lest some new form of iniquity shall put its hoof upon its sacred pathway and defile it. I would not return to the Puritan Sabbath of our ancestors, because it seems to me that the best time to pass from the week into the Holy Day is when the world is lost in unconsciousness,— that going to sleep on a week-day we may wake up with the golden glory of the Sabbath all about us.

But do not make the mistake of thinking that I would advocate that there should not be some preparation for the proper observance of this best day, this joy day, of all the week. So I would place back at the sundown of Saturday night the proper preparation of every Christian mind for the glorious Sabbath that shall follow.

I deprecate the idea that business should be in such a rush to make profit that it must force its industries close up to the opening of the golden gates of this golden day. I would have the Saturday evening spent around the fireside, with the hush of the anticipation of the Sabbath in it, the whole family one, unbroken by the absence of a single member living, that thus together they might anticipate the glorious privilege that with the sunrise shall be theirs.

There are many mothers in this audience this afternoon,— there are many bereaved mothers, for I see the black among the garments that are before me,—

and I call upon you to witness that the grandest moments that you have ever spent during any day of your life have been those when, having undressed your little ones, you sat by the bedside, had them kneel by you, and closed their little hands together, and they repeated their childish prayer that your own lips had taught them. And then, when the prayer was over, and you had tucked them into their little cots, and had kissed them with the mother's kiss, which is the sweetest kiss that ever comes to human lives, and let them ask those queer, those strange, those deep questions that little children love to ask at such an hour,—that surely then it had seemed to you that heaven and earth had met around that little cot.

Oh, tell me what night in all the week is so sweet and tender to you as that Saturday night, after the industries of the week are passed, after the school and the play for the week are over, when you can talk to them a little more about God and heaven, and prepare their little minds for the blessing that shall surely belong to every child of faith through the wide, wide world on the holy Sabbath Day. Mothers who have lost your children, as you go back over the years, I challenge you to give me a moment when it seemed as though the communion of heaven and angels came as near to your heart as when you thus prepared your little ones for the splendid simplicity of our true American Sabbath.

So I appeal to you to-day, is it not better that we give a little time and preparation on that day that shall be so infinitely blessed to us on this earth that it can be a type of the eternal Sabbath that shall follow, and then, when the dawn comes, and all its golden splendor fills the inner recesses of the soul, let it be a day to you long to be remembered through the week of struggle and of sacrifice. Sit about your breakfast-table a little differently from the way you generally sit on other days. Let the meal be almost as sacred as the communion; let the solemn hush of the day find a response in your own heart, as you think of the tender truth that shall be preached to you, and the holy influences that shall be shed about you, and the glorious aspirations that shall be awakened in your hearts as you hear the Word of God read and the glory of the life and death of Jesus Christ depicted to you as you gather in the sanctuary. So may it be that you shall feel God's breath blow gently on you out of the golden East in the morning, into the golden West of eventide, and find its harborage in the bosom of Almighty God.

This Sabbath is threatened on every hand. There are those who are ready to destroy its peace, and its purity, and its influence. There are several hands that are reached out after it. It would be impossible for me to-day in this presence to mention the list of all the evils that are threatening the sacredness of our day. Therefore, I must classify them.

The first hand that threatens the peace and the beauty and the glory of the Sabbath is the hand of rationalism. There is a rationalism which may not be altogether godless — I am not speaking of that; but of that which blots God out of heaven, as well as takes the crown from the brow of Christ, and demands that human liberty shall not be interrupted in enjoying every day of the week just as it pleases, no matter whether it interferes with the rights of its fellows or not. There is a godless rationalism that blots God out of the heavens, and starts man as a mere creature of self-existence and resistless force. God is not the father of man, and there is no God—only matter, only force. These are godless evolutionists, because they do not believe in the creation of the world as an act of divine will. Some time ago I remember hearing or reading that some one had given a scientific paraphrase of a part of the fifth chapter of Genesis, taking out the word "man," and putting in the words "primordial germ." I do not remember who it was, that I may give acknowledgment to him for the idea. I claim, however, the right to present an interpretation of this verse in this light. Let me read it to you, as it seems to me a Godless evolutionist would like to have it read: —

"This is the book of the generations of the primordial germ. In the æon that mighty self-existent force evolved the primordial germ, in the likeness of the primordial germ evolved in it. Male and female evolved it then, and called their name the primordial germ in the æon in which they were evolved. And the germ life for 100,000,000 æons evolved a monad; and the monad evolved a radiate; the radiate evolved a brachiopod; and the brachiopod evolved a gasteropod; and the gasteropod evolved a cephalopod; and the cephalopod evolved a worm; and the worm evolved a crustacean; and the crustacean evolved a fish and reptile; and the reptile into the bird, and the bird into the vertebrate, and the vertebrate became a mammal; and then a monkey, and then a man."

While man was a plastic monad he was obedient to the force; but after a time he began to become mighty independent, and then he took a wild leap across a chasm that has always seemed to us impossible, and put on a swallow-tailed coat,—and I presume that was a trace of the bird-stage through which he had gone,—and a very high shirt-collar,—and that was probably a lingering essence of the giraffe in his nature,—and then he defied both God and the rights of his fellows. I presume this mighty independence must have been owing to his bright ancestry, for I notice that they who rule God out of the heaven as the creator of man generally take their own destiny into their own hands. Talk to such an one about the holy Sabbath, and he will laugh you almost out of countenance. If you suggest to such an one such a thing as prayer, he will scoff at the very pronunciation of the word.

But let me put over against all that humbug the glorious statement: "And God said, Let us make man in our own image, in our likeness. And God breathed into the clay, and into the nostrils of the clay, and it became a living, aspiring, immortal, eternal soul."

Oh, shall we not plead that our God shall have his Sabbath, your and our Sabbath, observed according to his law, because that is our highest law, and seeks his glory in the highest possible usefulness and best interests of his creatures?

Again, the hand of greed is placed upon our Sabbath. I believe thoroughly in a spirit of ambition and in a spirit of industry. But there are some hereditary nonentities that have come within the borders of the United States which we have to consider. It has been the glory of our American civilization that in this country there are self-made men. We point back to the beginning of a man who seemed to give no promise, and we follow him up, step by step, till we find him standing in important positions, and he has come into notice, as well as the nation to which he belongs. The self-made man is rightly the proudest man that dwells on the face of the earth. Obstacles—what cares he for them? When he started in his successful career, he knew that with the leverage of his hands, and the power of his brain, he could accomplish the end he had in view. He had a clear head, and two hands, and he knew he could make his way, even though it was impeded with oppositionists. What cared he for them? He had a great soul within him, and he felt that he could conquer. I believe that every man forms in his mind a picture of what he intends to be, if he is to be successful. I will make one or two illustrations here. If he starts out to be a merchant, suppose he puts his tide-line at $50,000; as he nears that line, he moves it on to $100,000; and almost when that golden tide washes the shore of his ambition he puts it forward and makes it half a million. Or, if he is a politician, he is looking out in the political world, and he begins in the council of his own city, and then he is not satisfied and he goes on toward the State Legislature. No sooner elected than he looks forward to Congress, and then toward the Senate, and then toward the presidential chair; and then when he becomes the occupant of the White House, he begins to plan for a second term. This is only the spirit of our industrious and ambitious Americans. I think we should glory in such ambition. But, if we are going to succeed, we have got to get up pretty early in the morning, and put on our seven-league boots, and work until we are almost ready to drop of exhaustion, if we are going to win these prizes, either in business or in the political field. But let not man drive his team from Monday morning until Saturday night so fast that they cannot stop when God shuts the gates of the Sabbath against all unholy feet. This race for gold is a magnificent race, and we pat any man on the back who undertakes it. May you all before you die be worth a million. But in making this race, look out that you do not win the prize through loss of principle or desecration of the holy Sabbath. All businesses are bad enough on the Lord's Day; all stores that are open for the sale of wares, whether they be fruit-stands, or clothing-stores, or hardware establishments, or any other kind of store — or even a drug-store, if it sells soda-water and cigars.

But one of the very worst forms of business that desecrates the Sabbath is the American saloon. It is never satisfied; it has an insatiate maw. It has swallowed farms, firms; it has swallowed whole families, whole characters — it will not be satisfied until it can swamp and swallow everything that is good and glorious in this nation, including our Sabbath. It is determined on this Pacific Coast not to shut its doors, even during the night or during the Sabbath. When I was in Boston, I used to be proud to say that every saloon in the city of Boston was by law shut up at 11 o'clock at night, and not opened until, I think, 6 o'clock in the morning. When I came out to this great and glorious Northwest, and began my work in Seattle, Washington, I found that the first vice I had to resist, and the first influence that I had to use, was for the protection of the American Sabbath against this leprous hand of the American saloon. They destroy our homes, our civilization, and now they are seeking to destroy our Sabbath. O Christian Endeavorers, to-day make a solemn vow to God that, God helping you, as long as you have a voice to raise, or any influence to use, or a vote to cast, you will use these three mighty engines of power against that saloon, and in favor of our American Sunday.

Another hand that is placed upon our Sabbath is the hand of unsanctified pleasure. The poor, dear, working people, who are shut up in tenements five stories above ground, two or three stories below ground, two or three families in one room, with hardly a curtain hung up between them — the dear, poor people must have their recreation. I think I sympathize as much with these down-trodden classes as any man. I lived in the midst of the great city of Boston for seven years, and I came in contact with many of that class of people, and I trust I have never ceased to have a sympathetic heart for every man who is shut up in a factory cellar, or in a factory garret, six days of the week, and only has a chance to get out in the sunshine and breathe the pure air on Sunday. I am willing to turn him out loose in the field, and let him enjoy nature, and let the fresh air blow through his poor tired body; or, if he wishes to go into the public library and read, if he cannot afford to have literature at home; that he shall go into the museums and learn something concerning the structure of animal life, and something concerning the geological world, if it will do him any good. But he must have the purest motive in so doing. But I do regard as dangerous these excursions on steamers and on trains, such as they have in Boston, New York, Chicago, San Francisco, and in other large cities, which are merely for the purpose of pleasure, and turning Sunday into a gala day; against this I hold up my hands in solemn protest.

Then there is the theatre — which is bad enough on any day of the week — that gives Sunday concerts, sacred concerts so-called, for the delectation of the people. I protest against that. Go into one of these sacred concerts, and you will see half-clad ballet-girls, and some one made up as a colored minstrel will stand up and sing "Old Black Joe," and probably think that the audience may be so ignorant that they will think it is a selection from the "Messiah." Our Boston Sunday concerts have been our disgrace, down even unto to-day. I learn that some of the actors and actresses in England are opposed to these Sunday concerts, and their reason is because of the degraded nature of the audiences to which they are called upon to play. And when an average actor in an average theatre begins to talk mellifluously and sniffifulously about depraved character, some of us, I think, might be permitted to smile.

Dear friends, believe me, if you desecrate the Christian Sabbath, whether it be for greed or for pleasure, you strike immediately at the foundations of the American nation. This nation was founded in prayer. This nation in infancy was bulwarked by faith, and the wise men came and laid their treasures at its feet; the star of empire moved west from its cradle, and it grew in favor with

God and man. It was intended to be a saviour of nations. You, the American people, are responsible for the character of the nation to which you belong, because the government has been committed into your hands. Make the most solemn vow that you can take that you will preserve the integrity, as well as the entirety of this nation, and see to it that it shall have a Sabbath that shall come with a holy hush upon its great multitudes, as though God himself had spread his hands in mighty benediction over this whole land.

Our life is very much like the seven days of the week. In the earlier part of it we are infants, merely, about our mother's knee, sometimes looking into the light to see what the world is. Then we reach the middle of the week in our manhood, and then the responsibilities begin to fall more heavily and seriously, our burdens become more hard to bear, our joys take on a higher and more ecstatic service; then our responsibilities begin to grow still more serious before our eyes, until we almost tremble before them. Then we go on and it draws near the close of the week, and we are like an old man traveling down the last hillside, leaning upon our staff, with nothing apparently but the grave in front of us. Then comes Saturday night. O the hush of it! O the darkness of it! We call it death. But then bursts the glory that God has promised all those who are faithful unto him until the end, and then we realize that the eternal Sabbath of God has come.

A continuous whirlwind of hand-clapping greeted the announcement that the San Francisco Police Glee Club would sing. These "finest of the force" rendered some selections that were among the musical features of the whole Convention. Under the leadership of Mr. Robert Lloyd they sang "Throw Out the Life-Line" with wonderful effect. The audience rose in a body and gave the silent Chautauqua. The demonstration continued until the officers of the peace returned and sang in response, "Still, Still with Thee." Satisfaction did not reign even then, but Dr. Clark restored quiet and said : —

"We have been indebted to the police for many great favors in the pavilion, on the streets — in fact, everywhere. Never has a convention been favored as we have this afternoon by their singers. When California gets a Sabbath law these guardians will help enforce it."

The well-known author of "Our Country" was then introduced, Rev. Josiah Strong, D.D., of New York City. He delivered an address upon "The Civil Sabbath."

Address by Rev. Josiah Strong, D.D., New York.

Mr. President and Fellow Christian Endeavorers: — I think if we had some hundreds of thousands of such policemen scattered through our country as those to whom we have just listened, our Sabbath laws, where they exist, would be better enforced. In the absence of such officers of the law, I believe that the best hope of becoming a bulwark against the inflowing tide of Sabbath desecration of which the speaker who just preceded me has spoken is the living wall of human wood built by these Endeavorers — built also by the Epworth Leaguers, by the Luther Leaguers, and by the other organizations of young men and young women throughout the country pledged to Christian work and Christian reform.

Fellow Endeavorers, if your efforts in behalf of workable Sabbath laws and the enforcement of those laws are to be intelligently made, we must understand that we observe two Sabbaths, which are quite distinct in their origin, their authority, and their character. One of them is divine in origin and authority, and sacred in character. The other is human in origin and authority, and is what we call secular in character. This later Sabbath is the civil Sabbath, of which I am to speak to you briefly.

The fact that these two Sabbaths are co-existent in point of time leads to their being confounded, leads to much misunderstanding as to the real character and value and strength of our Sabbath laws; and we find, as a matter of fact, that the opponents of those laws have viewed them on a wrong basis, and the defenders of those laws attempt to defend them on a wrong basis. We find here some such debate as this. The opponent of those laws says, "Your conscience forbids your going to the theatre on the Sabbath; mine does not. You obey your conscience and I will obey mine. Why should you, simply because you are in the majority, force the dictates of your conscience upon me, in this land where we profess to have freedom of conscience and religious liberty?" And the defender of Sabbath laws, which he supposes to be based upon the sacredness of the day, replies, "The word 'Sabbath' is a divine institution, and obedience to the Sabbath is not a matter of opinion; it is required of us by the sacred Scriptures." The other answers, perhaps, "Suppose I do not admit that your Scriptures are authoritative. And even if I do, Shall the State forbid and punish everything which the Scriptures forbid? The Scriptures forbid covetousness and worldliness. Shall the State forbid everything that is covetous and worldly?" "Oh," replies his opponent, "Sabbath-breaking violates the common laws of morality, while worldliness does not." "Very well," says the other individual, "envy and lying violate the common code of morals. Shall the State therefore forbid them?"

I am afraid that about this time the defender of Sabbath laws based upon the supposed holiness of their character says, "Very well; this is a Christian country, and if you don't like our institutions you had better go back to Europe, where you belong."

Then probably this opponent says, "I shall not go until the laws require me to go; and meanwhile I shall use my liberty and regard you as a bigot and your Sabbath laws as oppressive." Thus we see that much bad blood is engendered because of the failure to distinguish between the civil Sabbath and the sacred Sabbath.

It is true that in Colonial times, when there was a union between Church and State, the laws required attendance upon the church services of the Sabbath; and in Virginia the third offence against the law was punishable by death. But after the adoption of the Constitution of the United States no such law became possible. All of our Sabbath laws now are of two characters: one forbidding labor on the first day of the week, excepting works of mercy and necessity; the other forbidding certain forms of amusement. Let us look at the first for a few minutes.

Laws forbidding labor on the Sabbath are based upon the right of every man to enjoy a day of rest; and it is the duty of the State to secure to him that right. The right to rest on the Sabbath comes from the necessity of rest on the Sabbath. It has been scientifically determined by different lines of investigation that the strength exhausted by the day's labor is not fully renewed by the night's rest, so that those who do not observe the weekly rest-day are drawing upon their physical capital and gradually undermining their strength and shortening their lives. No hygienic fact, no physiological fact, is better established than this. And this necessity of rest constitutes for every man his right to rest. So I say it is the duty of the State to secure to every man that rest.

Most toilers are employees, are in the control of employers, who, in most instances, are at liberty to discharge them. The desire to accumulate, emphasized by the sharpness of competition, leads the employer to get all that he can out of his men. Thus it becomes necessary for the State to step in and limit the number of hours of the day's work, to prevent overwork for six days in the week. For precisely the same reason it is necessary for the State to step in and forbid the employer's compelling his men to work seven days in the week under pain of being discharged.

But some one says, "Perhaps I wish to work on the Sabbath. Has the State any right to limit my industries, and, therefore, my income?"

As a matter of fact, Sabbath laws do not limit earnings or income. It has been demonstrated over and over again that men can do more work by resting one day in seven than by working 365 days in the year. During our late Civil War, when the government was very anxious to secure arms as fast as possible, an order was issued in the Springfield Armory to work seven days in the week. Several men who had conscientious scruples against working on the Sabbath asked permission to rest on that day. They secured it. It became apparent in the course of a few weeks or months that those men actually did more work than those who worked seven days in the week.

But further: The liberty of rest to all can be secured only when there is a law of rest for all. In a town of New York all of the barbers in the community once petitioned the City Council for an ordinance closing their shops on the Sabbath — all save one. That one made a law compelling the closing of those doors necessary. If all others were closed and his doors were open, of course he would draw customers from the other men. These other men had a right to demand that the law protect them from that injury. Therefore, I say the liberty of rest for all can be protected only by a law of rest for all.

Now, my friends, there is no age of the world that has so needed such a law of rest as this feverish age in which we live. This is the age which cuts canals across isthmuses; which tunnels mountains; an age in such haste that it cannot go around, it cuts across lots. This is the age of hypothenuse. This age, as no other, needs the day of rest because of its feverish activity. And if this is true of modern civilization, which rides with whip and spur, it is especially true of American civilization.

A friend of mine went as a missionary to Constantinople. He told me that when he arrived he was met on the dock by a young man from the Bible House to conduct him to his lodgings. As he passed by a group of Turks on the dock, they exclaimed, "Ea wash." As they proceeded, passing another group, each man exclaimed, "Ea wash." And as they went along, more and more of them said the same thing, only more emphatically. He at length inquired of his companion, "What is the meaning of that? Are they swearing at me?" "No," said he, "they are all saying, ' Go slow, go slow ! '"

I heard a Bohemian say once that the very first words which his people learned as they came to the United States, and probably the first time they heard it was going down the gang-plank, were, " Hurry up, hurry up ! "

These two expressions are typical of Eastern and Western civilization. In Turkey the working proverb is, " Never do to-day what you can put off until to-morrow; " while every typical American is sorry he is n't twins — he has two days' work to do in one. But if this is true of our American people as a whole, it is pre-eminently true of these Western people, whose very air is a wine which stimulates us to the highest activity. So, my friends, if there is a State in all our Union which needs a Sabbath law, it is the State of California.

Now turn, my friends, for a few minutes, to this other class of prohibition under our Sabbath laws; namely, the prohibition of certain forms of amusement. This rests upon the duty of the State to protect the leisure of the day from such uses as will prove detrimental to public morals. There are forms of amusement indulged in upon the Sabbath Day which are not by law prohibited, and which should not be by law prohibited,— forms of amusement which we, as Christian Endeavorers, could not indulge in conscientiously. But if they are to be suppressed, it should be, not by law, but by an educated public opinion and a quickened popular conscience. Hence the responsibility laid upon us to exert a right example.

But there are other forms of public amusement, or popular amusement, which should be prohibited by law because they are detrimental to popular morals. We must remember, my friends, that the law of self-preservation is the first law, both for the individual and for the State. If a State has a right to exist at all, it has a right to provide those conditions necessary to its existence. Now there are two conditions necessary to the existence of every republic. One is popular intelligence; the other is popular morality. When the average citizen falls to a certain level, the dead line of ignorance or the dead line of vice, popular institutions must perish. Hence it becomes the right of the State to forbid ignorance and to forbid vice. It must do it in self-defence.

This is the ground on which our public-school system rests. The State has a right to take money out of your pocket and educate my child, if need be — not because education is good for my child or that it will be a good business proposition for him, but the State has a right to tax you to educate my child because the ignorance of my child is a dangerous thing for the State. Hence, our compulsory education laws. You may want your boy in the field on the farm, or at the bench in the shop. Notwithstanding that, the State interferes with your liberties and with his liberties, lays its hand on that boy's collar and puts him into school, and says, " You must learn." That is right, because the ignorance of that boy is dangerous to the State.

Now in like manner, immorality is dangerous to the State. Intelligence and virtue are as necessary to the life of the republic as brain and heart are necessary to the life of the individual. Therefore, if there are public amusements which tend to corrupt popular morals, it becomes the bounden duty of the State to forbid and to suppress such amusements, because they are detrimental to morals which are absolutely essential to the life of the State. But in so doing it may interfere with the liberties of those who are indulging in those amusements. Now, in like manner, there are certain amusements which are hostile to morals because these amusements are hostile to a religious observance of the Sabbath Day. A holiday Sabbath has been found to be subversive of religion, and therefore subversive of morals, because religion is the tap-root of morals.

As has been said by Mr. Blackstone, a corruption of popular morals usually follows a profanation of the Sabbath. Washington said, I believe, that reason and experience both forbid us to expect that national morality can prevail in exclusion of religious principles.

Those amusements which entice the youth away from the church, away from the Sabbath-school, and away from the home — which places are where morals and religion are taught — are therefore detrimental to morals, and may under our Constitution be forbidden by law — not because they are detrimental to religion, but because, being detrimental to religion, they are detrimental to morals, and morals are essential to the life of the State. That is the ground on which laws against popular amusements detrimental to morals are constitutional. And this ground is absolutely defensible — has been held so again and again by the Supreme Court of our various States.

As a matter of fact, Sabbath laws are the front and the bulwark of popular liberty. How much popular liberty is there in the world outside of Great Britain, her Colonies, Switzerland, the United States, and Canada? And these are the countries in which you find the Sabbath most sacredly observed. For years France has been struggling for popular liberty, and her failures came when France had no Sabbath. In recent years France is planting her free institutions on firmer bases, and it is a significant fact that in these recent years there has been a profound revival of religion in France, not encouraged by her religious leaders, but encouraged by her patriots because they recognize the fact that France cannot be free unless Christian. It was Mirabeau who said, " France needs God as well as liberty." But neither France nor America nor any other country can turn its face toward liberty while she turns her back upon God.

I think it was Hallam who said, " A holiday Sabbath is the ally of despotism."

We must recognize the fact, my friends, that our popular liberties are bound up with the civil Sabbath. I have been looking at the work done by the California Endeavorers the past year in behalf of the Sabbath, and I want to congratulate them upon the efficiency of that work. I trust it will provoke other organizations in other States to emulate your example — not only other Christian Endeavor Unions, but all young people's organizations.

My friends, I believe that it is in the power of these young people's organizations to transform public opinion in the United States and educate the popular conscience of the United States along any needed reform. And it is the hope and aim, the present plan, of the Evangelical Alliance of the United States to secure the co-operation of all these young people's organizations to that exact end.

In Pennsylvania recently there has been an effort by the Bakers' Union to secure a law which would enable them to have their Sabbaths to themselves. A clergyman of Philadelphia told me he had received a pitiful letter from the secretary of that union, begging the clergymen to help them to get that law. Yet he could do nothing — nothing more than write a letter in its favor. If, now, such an organization as the Evangelical Alliance is attempting to perfect were accomplished, it would be practicable for these young people to sow seed throughout the length and breadth of these United States that would bring forth the greatest value physically, intellectually, socially, and spiritually for Sabbath observance, and so prepare the minds of the people to circulate a petition to be given to the Legislature so powerful that it would bring to us through their mediation a law protecting the civil Sabbath.

We have only begun to appreciate the value of organization.

Here is a little snowflake falling falteringly down, almost as light as the air, and utterly powerless in itself. But when millions upon millions of those snow-flakes are massed, they make the mighty avalanche which fairly shakes the earth on its downward plunge. Your influence and mine alone may be as light as air; but with these young people massed together, every young people's or-ganization in the United States brought into one grand organization, we will have a power that will shake the continent.

After singing "All Hail the Power Of Jesus' Name," Dr. Clark presented to the audience Rev. Robert Johnston, of London, Ontario, to speak upon "The Claims of God — Keep It Holy."

Address by Rev. Robert Johnston, London, Ontario.

When the Pilgrim Fathers on board the *Mayflower* came in sight, after a tempestuous journey of nearly five months, of the shore, the long-looked-for shores of this new land, they found that they could not land without bringing their labor into the early morning hours of the Sabbath. They therefore cast anchor in the lee of a little island some distance from shore. There in the clos-ing hours of the week they landed, and there they kept their first Sabbath in this new world, quiet and sacred to God in worship and in praise. Amid the storm they sang, and the stars heard and the sea, too, and the distant aisles of the dim woods rang with the anthem of the free. Free men they were, and lovers of freedom, those brave souls who, on the 22d of July, 1620, embarked at Delft Haven and turned the prow of the *Mayflower* toward the setting sun. But free they were because, loving the service of God's law so well, they hated man's tyranny so utterly. There never can be love of freedom without love of service to God; not liberty without God. But having God, we have liberty; and those who eulogize them to-day for their love of liberty, for their courageous daring in leaving native land and well-loved shores, in daring tempestuous and untried seas, in braving a king's displeasure and coming to an unknown shore where they might unfurl the standard of conscience unchallenged to the breeze — those who eulogize them for their courageous as well as high thought, should not fail to eulogize them also for their reverence to God's laws and their loyalty to his day. And those who rejoice in the grand inheritance left to us of this great land of the West should not fail also to rejoice in the grander and greater inheritance of Sabbath observance, love to God, loyalty to principle, which they have bequeathed to us as well. Better that we surrender our land; better that we surrender every broad prairie, every mountain steep, every smooth-flowing river, and every mine with its illimitable wealth rather than that we surrender the greater inheritance they have left us and the better example or privilege of keeping God's law, — the privilege of resting one day in the seven, and observing the Sabbath Day to keep it holy.

There are two institutions without which no nation can grow great — these are the family and the Lord's Day. And just as God in the Garden of Eden started this world on the right lines, so we find in the Garden of Eden these two institutions laid down as the foundation of all social living and religious living. The family, consisting of one husband and one wife,— that shuts out laws of divorce. That shuts out all impurity. That shuts out legalized and licensed vice. The family, consisting of one husband and one wife,—God's idea of the social structure, and that lying at the foundation of all the social system,— he established when he created this world and started it well and fair on its way.

The other foundation which lies at the base of all religious life is the Sabbath, one day out of seven, which he also established in that garden when he rested on the seventh day and hallowed it. And it is recorded that on that day he rested, and sanctified its use. You will remember that Jesus Christ summed up the law in these words: " Thou shalt love the Lord, thy God, with all thy heart, and with all thy soul, and with all thy mind; and thou shalt love thy neighbor as thyself." Now, regard it. The one table of the law looks manward. The family is the keynote of all society. If you let the thought of the family go, you cannot rectify it in the superstructure above. No more can the orchestra, if they get off the key-note struck, rectify the mistake when the flood of sound is pouring on. Can you and I, by the shortening of wages, the lengthening of the hours of labor, rectify the social evil if we lose the idea of the family.

So with the other law, the law that looks Godward — the law of man's religious life, the law of worship. God laid the foundation of that when he separated the Sabbath Day from the others and kept it holy for himself. My friends, religion goes if the Sabbath goes. The church is lost if the Sabbath is lost. You cannot retain your Bibles if you do not hold on to the Sabbath. One day out of seven — a day when man can forget the world and the earth toward which his eyes are so continually cast, and when he can lift his soul up to God, and get a breath of heaven's air, and a sound of his Creator's voice.

The Sabbath lies at the root and foundation of the religious life of the individual, the religious life of the church, and the religious life of the nation.

God, by his example, by his precept, by his command, emphasizes the thought that the Sabbath was to be kept holy unto himself — by his example in Eden. Again that example was repeated when he withheld the manna from the people on the seventh day while he gave it to them on the other six days of the week. And then, again, over and over again through the prophets has he exhorted his people to keep this day holy, reminding them that it was a sign and a seal of their covenant to be his. Then came the Messiah. Jesus Christ, though he did away with much of the ritualism and the traditions that had surrounded it, yet never by word or deed or inference did he detract from the holiness and sacredness of that day as a day that was to be the Lord's. Then the disciples and apostles, by their example and precept, continued on the same line; and so all down from creation, all through the ages of the Old Testament and the New, we have one line of testimony running throughout all this time, as if God used every avenue he could to reach man's soul; as though he would write these words on his heart, " Remember the Sabbath Day to keep it holy."

We may all be agreed on this, and yet there are many who will say, " What is it to keep the Sabbath for God? What is it to obey the command of God in this respect?" It seems to me that in God's example, in God's precept, in his commandment, it is made very evident what God would have us observe in the keeping of that day holy unto himself. He rested from all his work; he retired from his creative activity, in contemplation of himself and of the work that had been flung forth by his word. It was the expression of his own nature and character, and in contemplation of himself and his work he kept the day and separated it from common purposes.

And then, in the commandment, "Remember the Sabbath Day to keep it holy," occurs this further command: " and do all thy work, for the seventh day is the Sabbath of the Lord thy God. In it thou shalt not do any work." He commands us to cease from activity, to rest, to rest in God, rest in contemplation of himself — in a word, the Sabbath is to be kept holy by looking upward and not earthward.

That is all I know about Sabbath observance. Whatever lifts my soul up to

God, whatever opens my soul to receive God, whatever helps me to get a clearer view of my Creator's face, whatever blesses me, whatever leads me to understand myself and him, that is Sabbath-keeping. Whatever degrades that day to common purposes, to labor and toil, and to pleasure, as we have heard, that is Sabbath desecration and Sabbath destruction. The Sabbath is to be separated from all common uses. He who degrades the Sabbath, he who takes the Sabbath to use it for the purposes of business, of pleasure, and mere recreation is desecrating the Sabbath. I cannot see any difference between a picnic on the trolley and the mental picnic of the museum ; I cannot see any difference between the physical picnic out in the green fields and the mental picnic in the art gallery. We want to remember that we are God-men; we want to remember that while for six days we are laboring for our physical needs, we have a soul, which is more than these bodies, which is a part of God, and on the seventh day we want to make such use of it that it will lift us up to himself, that he may fill, satisfy, and refresh our higher nature.

Oh, let the man, and let the nation, beware, lest in their robbing God, and his fellow man, and himself, he be like the eagle that stole the consecrated meat from off the altar and carried with it the fire, which set in flames its nest on the mountain-top, and consumed itself, the nest, and the birdlings! They who take the Sabbath from God take with it the seeds of their own destruction and death.

Just one word further: How is the day to be kept? What can we do to preserve it more and more for God? I am in sympathy with all that I have heard; I am in sympathy with civic legislation; but to-day I believe my message to the church is that it must save the Sabbath to the world. The State cannot do it ; the civic power cannot do it; the church of Jesus Christ itself must be true to God's day, and true to the purposes for which God's day has been given. My friend said that he did not want the puritanical Sabbath. I hardly know what that was, but I do long oftentimes for the old Sabbath of the Scott hills, — the boots blacked on Saturday night, the wood-box all filled, the little ones all bathed, everything done so that nothing would be left to do on Sunday,— the pies baked, the roast cooked, so that even a fire might not be lit. Oh, I long for the old Sabbath, the day kept sacred to God, the day when the church doors were thrown open and we listened with joy to the words of the man of God, because we had prepared ourselves to hear him.

We have been celebrating the glorious sixtieth anniversary of our Queen, not so much as a woman who has honored every position in life, but because of the constitutional liberties that have been vouchsafed to our people. Those liberties are founded on the great charters of British liberty. But woe to those who, under misguidance, would seek to overthrow those charters of liberty ! If this should be attempted, by tens of thousands the people would rise to the service of their country, to preserve the foundation principles of British liberty. And if men should be so misguided and so unwise in this land as to seek to overturn your Declaration of Independence, on which the superstructure of your glorious country rests, there is not a State represented by the stars on your banner but would sacrifice men and money for the preservation of the liberties under which you live and under which you rejoice. The mighty Rockies that form the backbone of this continent are like the Sabbath Day, which is the foundation of the liberties of the world. The Sabbath Day is God's best gift to a world all too ready to become earth-worn, soiled, and entirely worldly. It is his gift to save the souls of men, who otherwise would be corrupted by the world. Therefore, friends, I summon you in your churches, in your societies, to preserve this day. Do not let our churches give the Sabbath to the world. In so far as our sermons become mere lectures, in so far as our music becomes mere entertainment, and in so far as we degrade the pulpit by not preaching the blessed gospel of Christ, and make it a place for the discussion of the ordinary topics of the day, in so far as we make the Sabbath a mere day for the entertainment of our congregations, just in so far do we give the Sabbath over to the world, and set the world an example to take it and use it for other purposes. Members of the Christian Endeavor, hold on to the Sabbath Day. I summon you, in the name of the Lord of Hosts, to the defence of our life, our liberties, and our existence as a nation, against all the powers of corporations — soulless corporations — strong in the power of wealth; against all the encroachments that are continually crowding upon it; against all the iniquitous vices of the world; and remember that the foundation of all our liberties rests upon the observance of God's law. Fellow Endeavorers, I summon you to-day, in God's name, to the defence, to the protection, to the preservation, of the Lord's Day as a day holy, holy unto himself.

The session closed with the benediction pronounced by President Clark.

Evangelistic Meeting for Men — Woodward's Pavilion.

This service has been of special value whenever held in connection with the Conventions. This year it was no exception. The service was inspiring, the messages from the preachers helpful. The sight of so many thousands of men from youth to age was uplifting. What a power was there if consecrated to the Lord Jesus Christ!

Several appropriate hymns were sung in opening, under the direction of C. E. Lloyd, of Oakland.

Rev. Dr. Chapman, of Philadelphia, presided, assisted by Rev. Ford C. Ottman, of Newark, N. J. As introductory Dr. Chapman said that many of the people in the East had always heard that San Francisco abounded in two classes; that many of the best people in the world resided here, and that all the criminals and evil-doers did not live in Philadelphia and Pittsburg.

"But I have never found," he said, "in all my travels a city where the police department boasted of a grand chorus. We are now to have some songs by the Police Jubilee Club, and as they march on the stage I want you to give to them three cheers and the Chautauqua salute."

For three minutes the audience complied with all its male strength. The guardians of the peace then sang "Throw Out The Life-Line." There were three encores before Dr. Chapman placed a period. A unanimous vote of thanks was passed the officers.

Rev. J. W. Cochran, of Madison, Wisconsin, offered prayer for the police of the city, not forgetting others in municipal and State authority. Mr. Ottman was then presented. He took for his text that part of the 27th chapter of Acts which contains the parable of the headstrong sailors who put to sea against the warning of Paul and were nearly drowned. He said life had been compared to a voyage across the sea, but he believed a Christian life was more like a ship riding at anchor in a quiet harbor. No storms could ever come, he said, to one who had an abiding faith in the Word of God and the power of Jesus Christ to save. Great stress was laid by the speaker upon the value of faith. Religious belief could not always be based upon reason, because God's ways are inscrutable and man's range of vision limited. He told how the waters of Jordan parted when the priests of Israel touched the soles of their feet to the stream on their way to the land of Canaan. The waters were not parted by any law of nature, he said, but in obedience to the will of God, who had promised that those who believed in him should pass over the dry bed of the river and pursue their journey in safety.

The speaker then made an urgent appeal to all men to forsake the paths of sin. He said that he never knew a case in his life when a man was ready to break his anchorage from Jesus Christ but that the devil had a soft south wind conveniently near. He urged men to resist temptation and seek the only salvation which promised a perfect future.

When Dr. Chapman rose to address the men, he was greeted with a storm of applause. His subject was "Dissipation, Infidelity, and Morality."

"I want to ask you to repeat with me the fifth verse, twelfth chapter of Jeremiah : ' How wilt thou do in the swelling of Jordan?' Now our other friend has been talking about a sea. I am going to tell you something of a river. You all know how the children passed over the river into the promised land. That is the very way to salvation. There was never a man stepped on the platform of God's salvation without finding that for which he sought.

"Now I am going to tell you something about religion. It is good to live by and good to die by. The river Jordan, as you know, overflows its banks, along which are many caves, occupied by wild animals. The waters drive these animals out, and just that far it furnishes a parallel for me to-day. Every man in this world to-day is in some kind of a cave. There is the cave of drunkenness, the cave of gambling, the cave of licentiousness, or some other caves equally as degrading.

"Any man who has in his makeup the smallest particle of sin is carrying death about with him. I want to talk about drunkenness for a moment. I do not believe that drunkenness is the greatest sin. I had a thousand times rather take the drunkard into my home and give him all the advantages I might have there than to take the man who passes this drunkard by and says, ' I thank God that I am not as other men.' Deliver me from these whited, lecherous men, whose very souls reek with filth and vileness!"

The speaker then recited several pathetic incidents illustrating the ends to which the drinker will go. He continued : —

"I want to say something about gambling. I never gambled in my life, but I have seen its evil effects. I knew a Harvard graduate who staked his two and one-half-year-old little girl and lost her. He then pulled out his revolver and sent a bullet crashing through his brain. He had been brought to this by strong drink, which robbed him of his senses.

"I want to say just a word about licentiousness. I shall say nothing but what any woman might hear. My wife, I know, draws her skirts to one side when she passes a fallen woman ; but mark you, my friends, there is not a fallen woman but that somewhere in this great world there is a fallen man who should go with her."

Dr. Chapman then turned to infidelity. He said that the greatest minds of the world acknowledged the Christ. He went on : —

" The man who is in·the cave of morality is not by any means a Chris·
tian. I look out on this sea of faces and I know that some of them
are lost. I would not be true to myself if I did not give you an invitation to turn over a new leaf. Men, God seeks you; boy, Christ is
looking for you. Everybody who wants me to pray for him please
stand up."

At this request the entire audience rose and remained standing while
Dr. Chapman offered a most fervent prayer touching various phases of
sin, and asking God to seek out each one.

Cards bearing these words were distributed : " Desiring to commence
the Christian life, I here and now give my heart to God, and pray for
his grace to help me to lead henceforth a consecrated Christian life."
Upwards of 150 were signed.

The meeting then adjourned.

Evangelistic Meeting for the Boys and Girls.

The First United Presbyterian Church was attended by nearly one
thousand children.

Secretary Baer conducted the service. The singing was led by
George H. Corfield, of Jersey City. Masters Harry Abbott and
Leland Cutler played cornet accompaniments.

After prayer by Miss Bell Nason, of San Diego. State Junior superintendent of California, Mr. Baer introduced one who had spoken to
boys and girls in nearly every land, Rev. G. F. Pentecost, D.D., of
Yonkers, New York.

Dr. Pentecost talked from the words, "My son, give me thy
heart."

He spoke upon the promises that have been given us who shall obey
the Word of God, and try to do to others as we would be done by. He
said, " My son, give me thy heart and soul and follow my teachings and
you shall have everlasting life and happiness ; but stray from the path
which has been shown you by your precious Father and everlasting
death will be the result. The little boy who stole the fruit from his
neighbor's yard not only punished himself and made the Lord think
that he was straying from his fold, but also made his father suffer when
he thought that he had raised a boy who would grow up to be a menace
to the community and a hopeless addition to the devil and his cause.
Parents are made to suffer more from one wicked deed committed by a
son or daughter than they would care to tell. A good deed in the eyes
of God and man cannot help but call for praise from all who have
profited from the teachings of the Gospel. Try and be like Jesus ever
so little, and our good works and thoughts will be recorded on the book
above, which is worth more to us than wealth or health. God has died
for his children, and why should we not follow his teachings and
endeavor to do good for the world which our Saviour has given us. The
footprints of Christ are the only ones to follow. They are everlasting
and are not erased by time nor even by the ceaseless beatings of the

tide, as are those made by insignificant man. Follow the way of Christ and he will lead us to eternal life and joy unspeakable."

The children then enjoyed a solo by Mrs. G. L. Hanscom, of New Hampton, Io.

Mr. Baer then presented Mr. C. N. Hunt, president of the Minnesota State Union.

Mr. Hunt's address, "Try and be like Jesus," was attentively listened to. In part he said : "It is not so hard to try and be like Jesus as it is to strictly follow out the teachings of his words. Any one may say that he is trying to be like Jesus ; but those who succeed in doing deeds one-tenth part as perfect and self-denying as those of our Saviour, Lord Jesus Christ, are hard to find, and still harder to keep on in the same path as that in which they started. When we are young we are taught the blessed words of God by our mothers ; but as we become older we meet young men and women who scoff at our religious teachings and ideas, and in this way, through a false shame, we are more or less apt to become scoffers ourselves, and lose the love of our parents and our hope in God and become as heathen children who have not even heard the slightest sound of our Saviour's blessed name. This is what we have to guard against ; for a backslider, as we call those who have lost the grace of God, is more to blame and is more in danger of hell than those who know no better, and are traveling in a darkened and treacherous path. If little boys and girls will follow the teachings of their mothers they will be almost sure to be placed in the path of righteousness, for all parents wish that their children may be placed in the straight and narrow path. A mother is a child's best friend, and God watches over all ; so when you try to do what you are bid, do not lose sight of the fact that God is everywhere and knows when wrong is done, even though your trusting parents believe that you are doing what you should do, if you may happen to be committing some forbidden sin."

The children then sung, "Blessed Assurance," and Mrs. Hanscom rendered "Tell It Again," much to their delight.

Secretary Baer closed the service with a brief address and led the boys and girls into a consecration service.

At the close of the meeting Mrs. Hanscom sang "Anywhere with Jesus."

Evangelistic Meeting for Women — First Congregational Church.

"It was a meeting by women, for women, and about women." Mrs. Francis E. Clark presided over the session, which, in a peculiar way, was the "woman's hour."

While the meeting was in the main evangelistic in its aim, there was a missionary coloring to the addresses. The music was in charge of Miss Lida J. Clinch, of Sacramento. After a hearty song service, Mrs. Henley rendered a solo entitled "Come To Me."

In her introductory remarks Mrs. Clark said : —

"Since I came to San Francisco I have been asked if I thought the

Christian Endeavor was likely to become a distinctively woman's movement. To this I will say that I have no hope or expectation of anything of the kind. I do not want the Christian Endeavor to become a distinctively woman's movement. It is for all, and there is work in it for every one — for the brothers as well as the sisters, for the fathers as well as the mothers. There are too many departments in the Christian Endeavor for it to hecome distinctly a woman's movement. Yet there is much for the women to do. I believe the Lord has a special work for each of us. We women have come here this afternoon to ask God to lift us up, and to reach our hearts; to ask him just what he would have us do. Will all who are for Christ and willing to do his work please rise?"

In response about nine-tenths of the congregation stood up. When Mrs. Clark asked those who desired to lead a Christian life to rise also, nearly every one of those who were seated arose.

Mrs. C. Rice then offered prayer, and Mrs. Scott F. Hershey, of Boston, led the devotional exercises.

Mrs. Clark introduced as the first speaker Dr. Kin Eca da Silva, of Alameda, California, whose topic was, "How To Reach the Hearts of Oriental Women." She said, in part: —

"On the faces of Oriental women you will see stamped stolidity, sensuality, and gaping curiosity. It is worse than in an audience that cares nothing for God, for in the Orient they do not even understand the Word. There you see the curse laid upon Eve. In a sense that you cannot understand, her husband is her lord and master. Her sole hope is through her motherhood. Among the women of Japan there is the deepest reserve. There is a barrier between your own warm soul and the heart that is so hungry But once she is touched, let us see what is before her. You all know Pundita Ramabi. She is the highest type of Oriental womanhood. See what she has done for the poor child-widows in India — a work in which you have had the privilege of assisting.

"Think what it would mean if the Empress of China were a Christian — she who is a model for all the women of her empire. Will you not pray as never before that God will send his spirit to women in Oriental lands?"

A solo was then rendered by Miss Clinch.

"The Awakening of the Afro-American Woman" was the topic upon which Mrs. Victoria Earle Matthe is, of New York, spoke vigorously. We quote the following: —

"During the last double decade a race has awakened after 250 years of self-effacement and debasement No one can estimate this debasement. The auction-block of brutality has been transformed into the forum of reason. Time is as necessarily an element as opportunity in the uplifting of a race. The women of the United States and of the world know almost absolutely nothing of the joys, hopes, and ambitions of the black women. What a caste was ours! There was no attribute of womanhood which had not been despoiled, desecrated. Imagine, then, what it meant when the pen of Lincoln and the sword of Grant set these women free, the arbiters of their own will and the owners of their own persons.

"They had lost more than the men. They had no past. They had but the future. And these creatures were expected to make homes for four million and a half of people. No Spartan mother had a harder task. The marvel is not that she has succeeded so well ; the marvel is that she did not fail. She had no rights that a white man was bound to or did respect. These women are the arch of the Afro-American churches. They have given to the world 25,000 trained and educated school-teachers, who are the hope of the race. The educated daughters of these slave mothers have banded themselves together to help their race where it is meet.

"The awakening of the Afro-American is one of the wonders of the nineteenth century. I think I have shown that we deserve the help of the entire sisterhood of women. As long as the marriage of black and white persons is forbidden, there will be illegal unions, to the degradation of the black woman and the disgrace of the man. A slave regulation should not be allowed in a free land."

Mrs. Matthews made a stirring appeal against unjust marriage and divorce laws, against separate cars for negroes in the South, for reformatories and a better system of prisons in the Southern States.

Miss Katherine M. Jones, of New York, spoke on "One Woman's Power."

"What we can do as a body amounts to very little," she said. "What each woman can do means a great deal. Do you ever think of the misplaced enthusiasm in this world? Enthusiasm, they say, is conviction on fire. If all the misplaced enthusiasm in this gathering could be brought together there is almost no evil that could not be overcome. We need first self-preparation, to know what is to be done. We meet together, talk together, are pessimistic as to conditions in our own or other lands, and never do one practical thing. We need self-consecration. We must be willing to give — not only money. Money is such a cheap thing to give. Self-consecration means giving everything. Christian Endeavor means continual exertion. Each year the work grows. It takes more of self and time. We need, too, self-confidence. If you do not fill your place in the world it is never going to be filled. If you and I are not willing to put our shoulders to the wheel we are keeping the world back."

Mrs. George W. Coleman, of Boston, had for her subject, "Our Reasonable Service."

"Our first reasonable service," she said, "is to give ourselves to God. We cannot give ourselves to others as long as we are self-centered. It is a logical thing that is asked of us. It is a living sacrifice that is asked of us. The second service is ministry to others. How free we are when we once enter in the service of the Lord ! The other characteristic of service is joy. Christ first, others second, self last — that covers the terms of reasonable service."

After the meeting, which filled every one of the two thousand seats in the church and crowded the aisles, many of the ladies crowded forward to grasp the hands of the various speakers.

One incident in the meeting must not be omitted from this report. The event was in no wise intended to be spectacular,— merely a lesson in Home Missions, a concrete illustration of what America has to do within her own borders.

A little Chinese girl was placed by Mrs. Clark upon the reading-desk as a living protest against the customs of her people. It was a living appeal also to the Christians of the land. "Unless this little girl is rescued," Mrs. Clark said, "she will be sold as a slave. Her life will be one of hardship and degradation. Her fate seems almost too dreadful to contemplate." Mrs. Clark's voice choked. She made several attempts to go on, and then she stopped. Hundreds of eyes filled with tears and a thrill of horror ran through the great audience when a realization of the child's peril was fully grasped. "A prospective slave girl, and in America!" was the whispered exclamation all over the house. It was a new experience for the Eastern women. They were somewhat bewildered. It was no novelty for the Californian women. They bowed their heads in grief.

Mrs. Clark went on to say: "When Christ said: 'Go out into the world and preach the gospel,' were not his instructions for his disciples to begin at Jerusalem? I believe he meant us to begin at home, to work for him at home. There are sisters in foreign lands who need our help and our sympathy, but we must remember that there are sisters at home who need us quite as much. Some of them who are in the darkness of heathenism and who are bound down by heathen customs were born in this country. 'Begin,' Christ said, 'in Jerusalem.' Perhaps that means beginning right here in San Francisco."

The sight made a deep impression upon the entire audience. Mrs. Clark's words intensified the effect.

MONDAY MORNING, JULY 12.

Mechanics' Pavilion.

SEVEN THOUSAND people were in attendance when Mr. C. M. T. Parker, of San Francisco, began the praise service. Every circumstance was auspicious. So far as appearances could indicate it might have been the first instead of the last day of the great Convention. There was no noticeable weariness, no lack of appreciation in applause, and the fervor of the speakers was as marked as on any previous day.

The topic of the morning session was "Christian Endeavor a Missionary Force." One of the trustees, Rev. Dr. M. Rhodes, of St. Louis, presided. In introducing Rev. W. H. Scudder, of Tacoma, Wash., to conduct the devotional exercises, Dr. Rhodes said: "It is a great thing to come up on the Mount and be with the Lord in the morning. I am glad to see so many of you here. As a general thing ministers and visitors are tired after the Sunday work and are consequently slow in turning out. The presence, therefore, of such a vast concourse of people, this the last day of the Convention, shows that the spirit of God is abroad. Now let us make this the banner day of the Convention of '97."

Mr. Scudder then read from the sixth chapter of Ephesians. The congregation joined him in the Lord's prayer.

One of the brightest addresses ever given upon the "tithe" was then presented by Professor Amos R Wells, managing editor of *The Golden Rule*, Boston. Professor Wells's topic was the new and energetic "Tenth Legion."

Address by Professor Amos R. Wells, Boston.

Some men pray for the millennium and don't give a mill toward its coming. Endeavorers, the chariot wheels of the millennium are made of consecrated dollars.

"Go ye into all the world," we say to our missionaries. "Stay right here in my pocket-book," we say to our greenbacks.

We take an interest in missions — but we keep our money on interest!

"Thy kingdom come," we pray. Ah, we must send our money to fetch it.

The Lord will judge this nation, Endeavorers, not by its prayer-books, but by its account-books. And how do the account-books of our nation read? I want to show you a line of shameful totals. (Here the speaker stretched a cord between the platform posts and hung upon it, as each item was mentioned, a pasteboard symbol. These represent a bottle, a pipe, a loaf of bread, a bicycle, a wooden gate, a shoe, a molasses jug, a chair, a Bible. The first was very large, the rest successively smaller, the last being very small.)

Our annual strong-drink bill is one billion dollars. The tobacco that Uncle Sam's pipe burns up every year costs $625,000,000. We buy more tobacco than bread, yet even the bread costs us $600,000,000. For things we make of iron and steel — chiefly bicycles, nowadays! — we pay $560,000,000. What we make of wood — not including nutmegs — costs us, for sawed lumber alone, $495,000,000. Our boots and shoes, with the corns thrown in, cost us every year $335,000,000. Our annual bill for sugar and molasses is $225,000,000, and still not every one is sweet. Our rocking-chairs to be lazy in, and our other furniture, costs us yearly

$175,000,000. And for foreign missions, for the spread of the kingdom of God over the earth, we pay yearly only $5,000,000. The missionary Bible is so small you can scarcely see it. It makes me feel small to hang it up. Now is n't that a pretty washing for Christendom to put out to dry?

Why, Endeavorers, every year the United States pays twice as much for corsets to squeeze the life out of folks as can be squeezed out for foreign missions. We, the salt of the earth, pay more every year for salt than for foreign missions. Yes, we spend more yearly for safes to put our money in than we take from those safes for foreign missions. We pay twice as much for the trunks for our yearly travels as to send the gospel traveling, and twice as much for umbrellas to keep off the rain as to keep the heathen from the devil's fires. Why the gloves for American hands cost twice as much as those hands put into the contribution-box for foreign missions, and American pocket-books cost half as much as those pocket-books give to the heathen, and the new mirrors in which Americans smirk each year at their benevolent faces exceed in value all their gifts to foreign missions.

Endeavorers, what is to be done about this?

Mr. Amerman, president of the New York City Union, knew what to do. With Christian Endeavor directness he wrote a pledge. Then he' signed it. Then he got others to sign it. And the pledgers promised to pay to the Lord's work one-tenth of their incomes.

Thus in the year 1896 was formed the Tenth Legion. Cæsar's valiant and trusty Tenth Legion rendered unto Cæsar the things that were Cæsar's. This Tenth Legion takes for its motto: "Unto God the things that are God's." It may easily grow more famous in history than that splendid Tenth Legion of the Romans, and infinitely more useful and noble.

The New York Union cared more for God's glory than for their own; and so, in April of this year, they handed over the Tenth Legion to the United Society of Christian Endeavor for its more powerful advocacy. That action. great in its modesty, was worthy of Greater New York. All honor to the New York Union!

Since that day the Tenth Legion has grown at the rate of more than one hundred members a week. Many a union, many a local society, has held meetings to advocate tithe-giving. To encourage others, those already tithe-givers are enrolling, and scores of converts to the principle are made every week. May the number receive a magnificent addition at this Convention! Blank application-cards have been distributed. Secretary Baer will furnish these free, in any number, if you want to work up the plan in your society or union. Sign them and send them to him, and he will send you, without charge, a neat certificate of enrolment. To withdraw from the legion at any time you need only to notify Secretary Baer; but you won't want to withdraw. Oh how much blessedness to the world is implied by every new name!

And now does any one think a tenth too much to give to the Lord's work? Look at this circle; it stands for your income. (The speaker hung on the line a large pasteboard circle divided into ten sections, each of a different color, and one of them — the white one — removable.) Here is the Lord's tenth. I set it aside. What have you left?

Well, there's one-tenth for your head, to provide a roof to cover it. (As the several particulars were named appropriate pasteboard symbols were hung on each of the nine sections, — a picture of a roof, a little book, the picture of a picture in a frame, a bar of music, a bottle of perfume, a pie, a necktie, a gold ring, a bicycle.) There's one-tenth for your brain, and books to feed it; one-tenth for your eyes, and pictures to delight them; one-tenth for your ears, music to hear; one-tenth for your nose, perfume to smell; one-tenth for your mouth, something to eat — including pie; one-tenth for your body, something to wear; one-tenth for your hands, a ring, and all it implies; and one-tenth for your feet — a bicycle, to be sure, with arnica and court-plaster thrown in.

And now what depends upon the Lord's tenth? (The speaker hung upon the detached section, in a lengthening chain, fitting pasteboard symbols — a church, an "S. S.," a "C. E.," a ship, a mission church, a Bible, a lily, a red simitar, a loaf of bread, a broken chain, an electric light, a globe.) The church depends upon it. The Sunday-school depends upon it. Christian Endeavor work depends upon it. On it depend the ship of foreign missions, the mission church at home, the distribution of Bibles, the cause of temperance. Upon this tenth hangs safety for the persecuted Armenians, food for the starving Hindoos, freedom for the slaves in Africa, enlightenment for the superstitious of China; yes, hope and happiness and life for all this sinning, suffering world.

Look at the burden of the nine-tenths and of the one-tenth. Is the tenth too much for you to give? I have read of a man with a soul so small that you could take the little end of nothing and whittle it down to a fine point, and with it punch out the pith of the invisible hair and draw that man's soul through the hole. Such a man might call a tenth too much, but surely no Christian Endeavorer.

And how near do we come to this standard? Watch these ribbons (unpinning rolls of ribbons of various colors whose lengths represent the figures named). The denomination that gives the most gives each year for foreign missions only forty-five cents a member. The denomination that makes the next largest contribution gives $1.09 a member. The next gives $1.39 a member. The fourth gives seventy-one cents a member. The fifth gives fifty-six cents a member. The other denominations bring down the average so that the gifts to foreign missions of our rich nation's Protestant churches do not average forty cents a member.

Now the wealth of this country is in the hands of Christians. Their average income surely exceeds $500 a year. If they gave one-tenth to the Lord, and only one-fourth of that tenth to foreign missions, the average gift from each Christian would be increased more than thirty times, and would be represented no longer by these petty four inches of ribbon, but by this magnificent purple streamer three yards long.

Less than forty cents a year for foreign missions, Endeavorers, from each Protestant in the United States! ¶I want to burn that figure in upon your memory: Only forty cents a year!

When our ever-living Saviour passed away from earthly eyes,
Sounded forth this great commandment from the eager, opening skies:
"Go ye, go ye, teach all nations; boldly teach them and baptize."

So they went, those men anointed with a power from on high;
So they went, to sneers and hunger, to the mob's vindictive cry;
Went to suffer racking tortures and triumphantly to die.

All their life was but one purpose — that the life of Christ should be
Spread abroad among earth's millions as the waters fill the sea.
So the heroes died, and, dying, left their task for you and me.

Children of the saints and martyrs, with all peace and plenty blest,
What obedience are we giving to the Saviour's last behest?
What desire, what self-denial, thought, and prayer, and eager zest?

In the stead of what the martyrs bore through many a conflict drear,
In the stead of homeless wanderings, bitter fightings, cruel fear, —
Ah, the shame! — we modern Christians give — just forty cents a year!

Forty cents a year to open all the eyes of all the blind!
Forty cents a year to gather all the lost whom Christ would find!
Forty cents a year to carry hope and joy to all mankind!

Worthy followers of the prophets, we who hold our gold so dear!
True descendants of the martyrs, Christ held far and coin held near!
Bold co-workers with the Almighty — with our forty cents a year!

See amid the darkened nations what the signs of promise are,
Fires of love and truth enkindled, burning feebly, sundered far;
Here a gleam and there a glimmer of that holy Christmas star.

See the few, our saints, our heroes, battling bravely hand to hand,
Where the myriad-headed horrors of the pit possess the land,
Striving, one against a million, to obey our Lord's command!

Mighty is the host infernal, richly stored its ranging tents,
Strong its age-encrusted armor and its fortresses immense,
And to meet that regnant evil we are sending — forty cents!

Christians, have you heard the story, how the basest of men
Flung his foul, accursed silver in abhorrence back again?
" Thirty pieces " was the purchase of the world's Redeemer — then.

Now — it 's forty cents in copper, for the Saviour has grown cheap
Now — to sell our Lord and Master we need only stay asleep.
Now — the cursed Judas money is the money that we keep.

But behold ! I see the dawning of a large and generous day;
See the coming of a legion; read its banners, " Pray and Pay ; "
And I see the palm of triumph springing up along its way.

These are they of open vision, open purses, open heart,
Free from Mammon's heavy bondage and the serfdom of the mart,
Where the woe is, where the sin is, come to bear a hero's part.

They have beaten out their coin into weapons for the fight;
Glows the gold and gleams the silver in this legion of the light;
Selfishness and sloth behind them, onward now for God and right !

Lift your banners, loyal legion ; swell your ranks from every clime !
All the powers and throne in heaven strengthen your resolves sublime !
Build the kingdom of your Captain on these latest shores of time !

" Foreign Missions " was the subject of an address by Rev. Dr. J. C. R. Ewing, of Lahore, India.

Address by Rev. J. C. R. Ewing, D.D., Lahore, India.

If I were asked under what sky the human mind has most richly developed some of its choicest gifts, most deeply pondered upon the great questions of human life, and rendered solutions of them which may well engage the thoughtful attention of those who have studied the philosophies of Plato or of Kant, I would mention India. Henry Martyn once said, " If ever I see a Hindoo converted to the Lord Jesus Christ, I shall see something more nearly resembling the resurrection of a dead body than anything I ever witnessed." These words were uttered less than a hundred years ago, and yet there are to-day in that India of which I speak nothing less than 2,284,000 native Christians.

The question is sometimes asked, " What is Hindooism ? " No possible definition for that can be given here, or even by those of us who perhaps know most about it, in any conceivable language or time as reckoned by our own standards. But there are one or two things in this great social system which I will speak of.

Some one has said that there are two points of doctrine upon which all Hindoos agree. The first is the depravity of woman, and second, the sanctity of the cow. These are principles which are universally accepted, I believe, from north to south and from east to west. To the Hindoo all that is is God's, the sun, the sky, the man, the woman, the ox, the bee — all that is, in all its manifest shapes, is but a manifestation of the great God; and all the great philosophical systems of the people aim at one thing, and that is to inculcate the idea of absorption back again into the great spirit of Deity from which they come. As the spider weaves its web from its own body, as the sparks fly from the heated iron, so this universe, with all that is in it, is but God, the Great Spirit. Those who fail to realize this practical absorption back into the Deity are compelled to go through numerous stages after this one, and this may reach 33,000,000 in number to the ordinary individual if he is not careful. For example, the man who steals fruit is liable to be born in the next life as a monkey; the man who steals corn is apt to be born in the next life a crocodile; and the woman who is a good woman in this life may hope to be born a man in the life to come.

A catechism was recently published in that country by an English educated gentleman, and seriously proposed for acceptance by the Educational Department. The first question he asked was, " What is the greatest hell," and the answer was, " A man's own body." The next question was, " What is the chief entrance to that hell ? " The answer was, " Woman." " What is the greatest of all evils in the world ? " " Woman." " Who is the wisest man ? " " The man who has never been deceived by a woman."

Into this country have come representatives, so-called, or self-styled, of the Hindooism of to-day. It is my duty and my privilege, I take it to-day, standing before this great audience, to say that Hindooism, as it is to-day, as it has been for more than four thousand years, has never been presented before audiences in this country but by men who have not absorbed the truth of the Sermon on the Mount. In the mission and government schools throughout the country, they have taken it into their very life blood and imagined they were teaching Hindooism. But the Hindooism of to-day can only be understood by us who have lived among the people and seen how very low those are who are without the Lord Jesus Christ in the world.

Among the objects of worship in that country, the most common one, the one before which millions of those people bow down every day, is an obscene one. I wish you could go with me into the temples and see those grinning, hideous idols. You could never imagine those great monsters, with eyes of fire, and teeth projecting, as objects of worship.

One day, some years ago, as I stood in that great crowd at Allahabad on the banks of the Ganges, at a great fair, where there were said to be 100,000 people, there were present ninety-two men who went to the British officers and asked permission to worship God according to the dictates of their own conscience; and then, that being granted, clad in nothing but their nakedness, two by two, they went down through that great crowd to the bathing-place, at the junction of the two rivers, and as they passed by in all their hideous nakedness, the women and little children looked upon them; they were worshipped by the people; and those standing by rushed after them when they passed, and greedily caught up the dust in their hands and ate it—the dust that had fallen from their feet as they walked along. You should see those who practise self-torture. I have seen them with their finger-nails grown through their hands, protruding through the back of the hands. One day a man was advancing on the public road, when he was seen to throw himself down and make a line upon the sand. Then retreating a few steps, he advanced again to a certain point, threw himself down again and made another line upon the sand. This he continued along his journey. I said to him, "Whence have you come?" He answered, "I have come from Hardwar." "Where are you going?" He said, "To Gaya." This was no less than a distance of from six to seven hundred miles, which distance he was marching in this strange way in obedience to a vow.

The most interesting and important part of the work we have to do in Hindoostan to-day is that of meeting the necessities of the new class that has risen up in that country. Educated men and women, dismiss from your minds for a moment the fact that there is a great class of uneducated people in India, and fix in your mind this: that there are in that land no less than 5,000,000 of our fellow beings who can read and write and speak this English language of ours about as well as we can—not so rhetorically, perhaps, but so that they can be easily understood. Their mistakes are idiomatic, but their speech is grammatical. As an illustration of the strange idiomatic mistakes that are made, I will relate the following incident. An address was given to a missionary who was about to leave for his native country, and in the address these good brethren said—and I tell it, not that you may laugh, but that you may understand the difficulties under which they labored—"We recognize in you, sir, a successful Mason, stuffing us with useful knowledge, and polishing it highly smooth."

These people constitute to-day, I believe, the greatest call, the greatest necessity, of the age. There is, in a special sense, a crisis upon us in that land. These 5,000,000 of people, bright, enthusiastic, able, possessed it is true of a wonderfully fascinating and unsubstantial philosophy, with a whole pantheon of ridiculous Deities which they have long ceased to worship, having lost their faith in them, are looking out upon the great Christian world and asking what we are going to do about it. It seems to me that the one message I wish to bring to you from my Christian brethren, from my heathen brethren, my Mohammedan brethren, my Hindoo brethren, and all the others in darkness there, is, send to them, in all its purity and power, the message of the gospel of

Jesus Christ. For, side by side with your missionaries in that country to-day are the emissaries of the evil one. A man said to me there, "I have read your Bible; I know a great deal about it; but I have found a book that is far more satisfactory." "What may it be," I said. "It is called 'The Mistakes of Moses,' and is written by the greatest living American; and I have found the book eminently satisfactory."

The atmosphere of that country is filled with many leaves, but they are not all leaves for the healing of the nation. In that land to-day there is a call for us, because, leaving the old Hindooism of the past, they are rising like a giant in his strength, looking out on the world, wondering what is to happen, longing for light and truth, and I believe many of them are longing for Godliness.

Some of the best men in that land to-day do not recognize Jesus Christ as divine; but the purity, the morality, of the Christian faith is by them inculcated. They are going into atheism, into materialism, into scepticism — not into idolatry. And I believe that within the next ten years the opportunity will be gone from us to save them to our faith, the opportunity which we have to-day of winning great multitudes of them for our King; for with faith and prayer and love, you and I can go forth and do that which we find to do.

I believe that in the Christian Endeavor Convention, in the great body which is represented here to-day, there are few, if any, who now utter the cry, "Charity begins at home." For you and I know so well how true it is that charity that is always talking about beginning at home usually, if not always, ends at home.

Amongst these English educated people there is a magnificent opportunity for the preachers and the teachers among you to labor. You know we have had a Pentecost and a Barrows and a Clark, and we thank God for these great men above, standing as they have done, day by day, before great audiences of educated Hindoos and Mohammedans. One of the speakers on this platform, and whom you all know well, for three long weeks stood in the town hall at Lahore, preaching the gospel of Christ to a daily increasing audience, for which there was not room. And we thank God for it. And we thank God again for the splendid testimony uttered by Dr. Barrows. And no less do we thank God for the testimony and the life and the work inaugurated by your beloved president during the last winter. Send out to Hindoostan the brightest and the best you have. Send out to that country those who know, down deep in their hearts, what God has done for man. Send out to that country those who know, down deep in their hearts, the fact that there is a power of the Holy Ghost, a promise to every one of us in these latter days, to make us efficient and effective servants of our King.

There is in the Gulf of Naples a little island called Capri, much visited by those who go to see its beauty, and flowers, and verdant foliage, but most of all for the sight of the blue grotto. Entering that place in a little boat, only two at a time, and being compelled to lie down as the boat enters, the visitor finds himself in a strange, weird place. Everything is transformed and assumes a most grotesque and hideous appearance. The oar, as it flashes in the water, is of a bright silver. The body of the boatman, as he swims by the boat, is of the hue of bright silver. Suppose there were people who lived all their lives in a place like that. What would you do? Would you not go in and say to them, "Come out, you have got light here, but your vision is distorted. Come out and live in the bright sun which we enjoy outside."

Christian Endeavorers, shall not you and I, sitting in the light of the Lord to-day, say to those sitting in darkness, cry out to them, "Come out! We have got the true light. You know something of God, but we have seen the light of God in the face of Jesus Christ." Let that be the work in the Christian Endeavor Unions, and our work shall never fail.

It seems to me that we can see the time coming on fast when we shall be able to see, with the old Peter the Hermit, — not the new Peter, but the old Peter the Hermit, even as the modern one has begun to do, — "God wills it." With all the open doors, with all the magnificent opportunities for service open to us, does not God will it?

The people in that land are a missionary people. Six or seven hundred years before Jesus Christ came into the world, strange things happened over all the world. Pythagoras did strange things in Greece; Zoroaster in Persia; Confucius in China, and Buddha in India. Buddha gathered about him a great mass of people, for his godly state, for his pure morality, his spotless purity; gathered about him in increasing numbers that great army of people that made its way down southward, across the sea to Siam and Burmah, and the borders of China, then away up into the mountains into Thibet. We think we see to-day signs of the time when there shall be a similar movement, led by our King, away over the plains of India, into Ceylon and Thibet, and into China it may be, with leaders who are being raised up,—magnificent men, specimens of the power of the grace of God, such as we have upon our platform to-day from that missionary work; men who will lead the hosts of God, and will go forth conquering and to conquer. " None but Jesus Christ deserves to wear the glorious diadem of India." So said one who never more than touched the hem of our Saviour's garment. None but Jesus deserves to wear the diadem of India, and Jesus shall have it, shall he not?

Dr. Rhodes said, in introducing the next speaker, that "prayer, work, and giving constitute the great trinity of forces in successful religious progress." Rev. Dr. John R. Davies, of New York, then spoke upon " Systematic and Proportionate Giving to God."

Address by Rev. John R. Davies, D.D., New York City.

Different periods present the church with different problems. In the fourth century it was the divinity of Christ; in the eleventh, the crusades; in the sixteenth, the reformation; and in the nineteenth, among the many difficulties which are pressing us for a solution, stand very prominently the question : How are we to raise the money necessary for the Church of Christ to carry on its ever-widening work at home and abroad, and thus be enabled to enter and occupy the world-wide field which now is whitening to the harvest as never before since time began ?

Now the only solution of this problem is that which is given to us so clearly in the teaching of God's Word; and to that teaching we now turn to find in the first place that it is the duty of all of God's people to give toward the support of God's work.

God never does for us what we are able to do for ourselves; and while Israel was unable to furnish the food necessary for the wilderness journey they were able to provide the material necessary to build the Tabernacle, and therefore each individual was given an opportunity to make some contribution to this important work. In like manner the obligation to give rests upon us because we are abundantly able to furnish the financial strength necessary to prosecute with growing and successful energy the great work entrusted to our care by Jesus Christ.

Consider our wealth. The mere statement of it looks more like a chapter from " The Arabian Nights" than a page out of some national ledger. Crœsus, whose wealth has been the astonishment of centuries, is supposed to have been worth about $8,000,000. But nearly ten years ago, according to a writer in the *Forum*, it was possible to select seventy American estates that would average $35,000,000, while ten could be found to have possessions which would reach $100,000,000. If this was the case a decade ago, we must be far richer now, because money makes money, and with it growing power. Thus we have every reason for the statement that never before in any nation in the world, that never before in any age of human society, has there been such a vast accumulation of wealth as that which we see to-day in our country; and, mark you, a large proportion of this wealth is under the control of the Christian Church, so that we are able as never before to do the Lord's work.

But Israel was not only able to give, but because it was the continual recipi-

ent of the mercies represented by God's house it was under every obligation
to give toward the support of that house. Thus we who enjoy the unspeakable
mercies of the Christian Church are bound by every consideration of righteousness and revelation, by every legal and moral obligation, to do all in our power
for the financial support of that church which for ages has been the world's
redemption, and which to-day more than any other institution holds in its hands
the fate of the future. God by a direct miracle could keep the ecclesiastical
treasury from shrinking as he kept the widow's cruse from failing. But this he
will not do. He knows that giving to the support of his church is one of the
most important duties, one of the most sacred privileges, of his dear children,
and with this Magna Charta of the believer's life he will not interfere, though
Christian altars are deserted and Christian work be neglected by those who, as
beneficiaries of that work, will, under bonds most binding, give it their fullest
and most loyal support.

At the coronation of Queen Victoria the Duke of Norfolk presented her
majesty with a glove for her right hand as a recognition of the fact that he held
certain lands and titles at the pleasure of the crown. So Jehovah was to Israel
not only the Creator, the Preserver, he was also their King, whose authority
and generosity touched and blessed every life; and therefore each individual
was required to make some acknowledgment of such a gracious sovereignty,
and one of the ways in which this allegiance was expressed was by the firstlings
of the flock, the first fruits of the fields being laid upon the altars of the Lord's
house. And any obligation which may have rested upon Israel in that direction is a thousand-fold increased for us who enjoy the more blessed privileges
of the new dispensation, in which we not only live and move and have our being in God the Father, but in Jesus Christ his Son we find our King, who from
the Throne of the Cross in the spheres of the seen, and through the spaces of
the unseen, is ever ordering all things for our greatest good. Therefore with
authority does Paul speak when, writing to the Corinthians, he says: "Upon
the first day of the week let every one of you lay by him in store as God hath
prospered him." And in the spirit of this command we present our offerings
before the Lord. We not only recognize the Kingship of Jesus Christ, we not
only make some return for mercies received, but we also discharge in part the
solemn obligation resting upon every child of God to give for the financial support of God's house.

In the second place we find that it is the duty of God's people to give for
the support of God's work according to their ability.

In the building of the Tabernacle there was a great variety of material demanded, and those who could not give gold for the lamps were invited to
contribute something toward the oil, and those who could not give fine fabrics
for the priestly garments were invited to contribute something toward the
coarser material which covered the roof; and thus the whole congregation,
according to its several abilities, entered into the work and shared the divine
blessing. The same rule obtains to-day. According as the Lord has prospered
us are we to give; and in thus making room in his hearing for the offerings
of rich and poor, we have an illustration of the wisdom with which God has
planned his work, making its support dependent, not upon the favors of the
few, but upon the means of the many. Thus God gathers about the church
the sympathies of a vast multitude, and where this law is ignored, when this
law is ignored, when the church is supported, controlled, by a handful, then
it departs from the divine ideal; and one of the reasons why the Protestant
Church is not found in closer touch with great multitudes of our population
is found in the fact that we have made of small importance the offerings of
the very class to which, by the teaching and example of our Divine Master,
we are especially appointed to preach.

But some one says, "I know that the gifts for the building of the Tabernacle
came within the reach of the poorest; I know that Christ called special attention to the widow's mite; but I am so poor that really my offering can be of no
value whatever." There would be force in such a remark if upon us rested not
only the privilege of giving, but also the duty of investing. But that is not our

concern. We are simply the depositors, and God is the banker. Some time ago a business man calculated the increase of a dollar at compound interest for 240 years. He found that it amounted to more than $2,500,000, and then he asked the significant question: "Cannot God make a dollar given to him grow as rapidly by the laws of grace as it does by the laws of trade?" The largest, the most helpful, bequest ever given to the Christian Church was the widow's mite; and why? Because it was coined in the mint of self-sacrifice; because Christ stamped it with a special benediction; and while nations innumerable in the meantime have called in bank-notes and golden coin by the billion, this mite is still in circulation, and its influence is being felt to-day by every member of the church of old. Therefore, let none, because of the smallness of the offering, be ashamed to approach the Lord's treasury; for if that gift be the offspring of self-sacrificing love, God will invest your mite, and with such efficiency that when the secrets of eternity are unveiled the ends of the earth will rise and call you blessed.

More than a century ago the great question which was agitating the State was: taxation without representation. To-day one of the questions very seriously troubling the church is: representation without taxation. That is, the husband gives for the wife, the father for the family, so that thousands have no personal part in the offerings of God's house; and then in all our churches there are religious mendicants who, like the woman that found it cheaper to move than pay rent, find it cheaper and also meaner to flit every Sabbath, rather than settle down in some church and face the financial responsibility which Almighty God has placed upon them. A poor, half-witted lad being reproached for the meagerness of his life replied, "God does not seek what he does not give." True, but he does seek what he does give; and if Christian people would grant to this great truth its proper consideration, what a revolution it would work in the motive and manner of our benevolences! Instead of this giving by proxy, instead of giving by impulse, instead of subscribing because some one has subscribed something, we would take an inventory of our resources, and then, according as the Lord hath prospered us, we would endeavor to discharge our financial stewardship, knowing that in the great duty our responsibility is no more transferable than is that which soon will rest upon us at the judgment-seat of Christ.

In the third place, we find that it is the duty of God's people to give for the support of God's work systematically.

In writing to the Corinthians, Paul says: "Concerning the collection for the saints, as I have given order to the churches in Galatea, even so do ye. Upon the first day of the week let every one of you lay by him in store, according as the Lord hath prospered him;" and there is good reason to believe that this was the financial plan which Paul proposed to all the churches under his care. The apostle knew that little could be accomplished without system, for order is heaven's first law. By means of it tides ebb and flow, suns rise and set, seasons come and go, and all the vast machinery of the universe moves with the precision of the most delicate mechanism. The same is true of the commercial world. Look at the immense corporations which to-day are transacting business in every part of the globe. You marvel at such stupendous operations, and you say, "How can such millions of capital, such volumes of trade, be handled?" In many respects much easier than the old-fashioned corner grocery, because everything is systematic and reduced to a mathematical precision. And the more you think of human life the more you will see that success is very largely dependent upon the method, so that every moment and every power may be safely guarded, properly guided, and used to the best advantage.

In this day of trusts and combinations, when we are so dazzled by the aggregation of immense sums, we forget the power of accumulated littles. The snowflake may seem a very insignificant thing, but yet he and his fellows have paralyzed the business of a metropolis, and overwhelmed mighty armies upon the march. The coral insect may attract but little attention, and yet from his labors there rise islands in whose harbors great ships anchor, and upon whose plains populous cities are built. Immense exertions are made every year in the communion that I represent to raise the money necessary to support our foreign missions; all sorts of legitimate expedients are resorted to, and then we frequently fail. Now if each one of our 900,000 members could be induced to give two cents per week to this cause for which Jesus Christ gave himself, we would have at the end of the fiscal year a handsome surplus in our treasury. And our church authorities are beginning to realize the immense possibilities which are enfolded in this systematic idea, and in our denominational papers, our ecclesiastical courts, our religious services, the subject is being presented with growing frequency and increasing favor; and these are signs of hope, not only because of the financial power it must give the church, but also because it brings us back to the scriptural method of giving.

The Jew was not permitted to appear before the Lord without an offering, each being commanded to give according to the blessing of God rested upon him. This teaching Paul recognizes when he says, " Upon the first day of the week let every one of you lay by him in store;" and while these words may not directly and positively command an offering upon the Sabbath, we know that very shortly after they were spoken the church chose this day upon which to make its offerings. And what better time could be selected than the Lord's Day, the memorial of the crowning miracle of Christ's redemption? And when the offering is made in the proper spirit, in what better way can we honor him who, though he was equal with God, yet humbled himself, and became obedient unto death, even the death of the cross. And the sooner we get back to this apostolic method, the sooner will we roll from our burdened churches the debts under which they are staggering, and give to them an opportunity for that enlargement of work which to-day is so imperatively demanded by the cries of human need and the voices of God's providence.

The audience then arose and sang two verses of "Onward, Christian Soldiers" with soul-stirring effect.

Dr. Rhodes said: "The roll of honor in all college exercises, at the schools and in the churches, always proves to be the most interesting feature." He then introduced The Right Rev. Edward Rondthaler, D.D., of Salem, North Carolina, to unroll the "Missionary Roll of Honor."

The Roll was borne by two ushers. Upon it were inscribed the names of more than 10,500 societies contributing $10 last year to the cause of missions. The scroll was upwards of 600 feet long; about 60 feet were exhibited.

Address of The Right Rev. Edward Rondthaler, D.D., Salem, N. C.

Fellow Endeavorers : — it is an inspiration to feel your numbers and to look into your faces — hundreds behind me, thousands before me, multitudes in the galleries, like witnesses on every hand; reporters beneath, sending the message of this great Convention to the millions of our land wherever the English tongue is spoken. Missionaries. brethren who have hazarded their lives for the Lord Jesus, like Paul and Barnabas did, all around me. It is a joy simply to stand among you and look into your faces and feel that, though there is but one man making a speech on the rostrum at the time, you really are all making it with him, because there is one heart and one soul in all this matter that unites us in a great Christian Endeavor Convention.

I say again, it is a joy to stand among you and look you over on every side, and from my heart say, God bless you all.

On Saturday I was out at the Cliff House, and for the first time in my life looked out upon the Pacific Ocean. I was watching the seals on the rocks, and was very sorry that I had forgotten my opera-glasses. By and by a young lady turned to me, and of her own accord asked me if I would not use her beautiful glasses. And when I thanked her for her unexpected courtesy, she simply said, " Oh, I am glad to do it." And I thought to myself, This dear young lady, in a single sentence, has voiced the whole secret of the success of the Christian Endeavorers thus far.

The society consists of those who, whether in little kindnesses or in great services, are glad to do something for the dear Master who died to wash away their sins.

I went down on Saturday in amongst the wilderness of trunks and valises at the foot of Market Street to look for my own. I found a white-and-gold-capped Endeavorer there — God bless the white caps and gold caps all through this audience. He had been on his post there for two days amidst the dust and fret connected with looking after lost and intermingled baggage, and he was as glad when my valise was found as if I were his father and he my own son. It was willing service he was rendering. And when I look at the white-and-gold caps all through this audience, I thank God for the free-hearted, willing Californians who are illustrating by their service the spirit of the whole Christian Endeavor Society.

Now I want to say, my brethren and sisters, as long as this spirit of glad service continues in the Christian Endeavor Society, so long it must grow and flourish and succeed. No power of man or authority or devil can make another course than that. But if there ever comes a day when the pledge is simply kept because it must be kept, when the committee work is done because it must be done, when emergency services are rendered grudgingly, not willingly, — if there should ever come a day like that, which God forbid, then the Lord Jesus Christ will look upon this great movement, and will say, as he said to the church of Ephesus, " I have somewhat against thee because thou hast left thy first love." Then it will not be necessary for man to oppose the Endeavorers, because the society of Endeavorers will die of itself, like a candle at the open casement put out by the blowing of the wind.

But as long as the joy of the Lord is the strength of this great movement its banners will be planted onward and still onward, and there is no such thing as going back in this great work.

Now I have been appointed — it is as if you all were doing it with me, dear Endeavorers ; let us do it together — I have simply been appointed with you to unroll this roll of honor in connection with this great missionary movement.

(The roll was unrolled amid great applause.)

There are the names of 10,500 societies on this great roll, each one of which has given to the Boards of its church $10 or more for the cause of foreign missions during the last year, aggregating the sum of more than $200,000 for the spread of the gospel among the heathen. In the course of the present Convention as many as 600 societies have desired to be added to this great roll. So that the gift can amount to no less than $250,000. The society that stands first in the roll gave $1,000 during the past year for the cause of foreign missions. A society in this city of San Francisco, which has welcomed us so heartily,—a noble society,—has given $700, and besides that, supports a number of workers in a Chinese field.

A quarter of a million of dollars for the spread of the gospel among the heathen! It is a great sum, and yet it is but the acorn-seed of what is coming through the giving of our dear young Endeavor people throughout all this great land. And I am quite sure they are doing it in the same spirit in which the young lady gave me her opera-glasses on Saturday afternoon. They are not giving because they must give, they are not giving from a vainglorious motive, to have their society's name enrolled upon a roll of honor, but because they are glad to give to Him to whom they first gave their hearts because he first died for them.

I might say a great deal more, dear friends,— my ten minutes are not quite up,— but I think I have said enough. One more thought only, and that is to plead with you just for one moment that you may not, by any neglect, by any unwillingness on your part, allow your name to be unrecorded upon the Master's final roll of honor, when he comes in his glory to reward those who have freely and gladly served him. This roll is but a picture of that final roll which

Jesus himself will unroll amid the admiring throngs of heaven. Oh that your own individual name may be there! And Jesus will gladly acknowledge what you have gladly done for him, as he did the service of Mary of Bethany long ago, when he said, "She hath done what she could." God bless you all. Amen.

Introduction of Visiting Missionaries.

Secretary Baer then introduced the following missionaries, who were greeted with tremendous applause by the audience: Mrs. Raymond Taylor, India; Miss Rose Webster, Utah; Rev. and Mrs. Gulick, Japan; Mr. and Mrs. Sage, West Africa; Rev. R. N. Craig, New Mexico; Mr. Wilson, Utah; Rev. Mr. Fowler, Utah; Miss Ella J. Newton, China; A. V. Soares, Hawaii; Mrs. Jones, Utah; Dr. Wilbur, Alaska; Rev. Ralph J. Lamb, Indian Territory; Rev. Mr. Green, Washington; Miss M. E. Maguire, Japan; Rev. K. Brown, Washington; Rev. D. J. Wolseley, New Mexico; Dr. and Mrs. Condit, Japan; Dr. Harris, San Francisco; Rev. Mr. Wineland, San Francisco; Miss Mattie White, Idaho; Rev. Dr. Yunacks, India; Mr. and Mrs. Thomas C. Wynne, Japan.

Mr. Wynne responded on behalf of the missionaries present in an earnest speech, reviewing the work of the missionaries in all parts of the world. He thought that the term "foreign" as applied to missionary work should be used only in a general sense, because labors of this character should have no restrictive appellations.

"Home Missions" was the theme of the next address. Dr. Rhodes presented Rev. Nehemiah Boynton, D.D., of Detroit, Michigan, as "the one best able to speak on the topic." Dr. Boynton spoke clearly and eloquently.

Address by Rev. N. Boynton, D.D., Detroit, Mich.

When George Romanez used to go to see Charles Darwin, the great scientist, Darwin always introduced his conversation with the young man whom he supposed to be his scientific successor with the words, "O George I am so glad you are young!"

As I look out over this splendid audience this morning, I feel like putting a religious spirit into the scientist's words and saying to you, I am so glad you are young. For the history of heroes is the history of youth, and good resolutions with us, as with Jacob of old, come in the dawning of the day.

The reason why the topic of "Home Missions" has special suggestion in a Christian Endeavor Convention is because we are young, in the morning of our lives, with a young republic in which to live, and with all the glorious hopes and realizations of our land beyond us in the near and the not distant future. I wish I could make you feel this morning, deep down in your souls, what it is to be an American, for I cannot talk upon home missions from the standpoint of an Englishman or from the standpoint of a Japanese. If I am to talk about home missions at all, I must talk about them from the American standpoint, and my brethren from other countries must remember that I am simply giving an American application to the spirit that lives in their own lives.

A friend of mine was saying to me that not very long ago he was in the city of Constantinople, looking out upon the sea, and there was a great naval demonstration there. The ships of nearly all the countries of the world were gathered there and manœuvering, and he looked at the topmasts of them all and failed to see the insignia of his own native land, Old Glory. There was not an American war-ship there. But there was a little bit of a Yankee schooner which caught the spirit of the air, and this Yankee skipper, realizing that America ought to be represented somehow in that great naval demonstration, had simply hoisted Old Glory to his masthead, set his foresail and his mainsail, his jib and his gaff topsail, and was doing as well as he could with a light breeze to follow around those sea dogs under steam. And my friend said to me that although the guns were frowning from the quarterdecks of those magnificent war-ships, and although they had all sorts of streamers flying from their mastheads, still that little Yankee schooner, with the torn and tattered Old Glory at its masthead, meant more to him than all the rest, and if he had been a betting character, he would have bet that that Yankee fisherman could have cleaned out the whole fleet. And he said that tears of joy and pride rolled down his cheeks in that far-away country because of all that simple flag spoke to his soul as he saw it there upon the masthead of the simple Yankee schooner.

If I were going to make a great endowment (and had the money) I would make a fund, by virtue of which a certain number of young people every year should go away from America over the sea, that they might lose sight for a little while of their dear old flag, in order that when they meet Old Glory in Constantinople or in Venice, or in any other city of the Old World, they may have their souls filled with the same sense of thanksgiving and gratitude to God for their dear country in the same way that every American heart overflows with humble gratitude when he sees his stars and stripes in the uttermost parts of the earth. And if I were an Englishman, I would do the same thing for the English boys.

There are three things that I want to say to you about home missions, American home missions, to you who are young, who are in the morning of your lives; and the first is this: that the fundamental characteristic of virile home missons is an appreciation of your own native land. The man who has not a good opinion of his own country is fit to be only a man without a country. And I have sometimes thought that in these days, when we join with all the world in giving our generous criticisms of this land of the free and home of the brave, that some of us have gotten the idea that we cannot make a speech in relation to America unless in a polite way we condemn her. I would like to be understood as saying this morning that with all the faults of our native land, there are glories which put those faults absolutely into the shadow. I would like to be understood as affirming to-day that the liquor-saloon and the gambling-den and the brothel and other evils do not comprise the entire inventory either of America's possessions or of America's perils; that this land which you and I boast to be our own has certain qualities and characteristics of its own which must be estimated and approved and emphasized, if we lend the influence of our young strength to the solution of our home-mission problem.

Rudyard Kipling was writing some of his poetry the other day, about the American spirit, and he got the idea that I want you to have. He was thinking of the new American who is being made on our shores,—a conglomerate of all the blood in the world, and therefore destined to be the superior human being in the world because of that. He says the Celt is in his head and heart, the Gaul is in his brain and nerve.

> " Lo, imperturbable he rules,
>   Unkempt, disreputable, vast;
> And yet in spite of all the schools,
>   I, I shall save him at the last."

What did he mean? He meant that there was a spirit which was noble and true and royal in our land, which was at eternal war with the spirit which is low and vile and base; that the spirit which makes righteousness utterly, absolutely, inevitably powerful will conquer this fair land, hand it over body and soul one day to the One who is King of kings and Lord of lords.

I say to you young people that if you have a small, petty, pessimistic idea of your native land, you cannot contribute one iota to the solving of our missionary problem.

The second thing I wish to say is this: if you and I would contribute to the solution of our home-missionary problem, it is absolutely necessary that we make the highest and greatest resolutions. Youth is the time when resolutions are dared and when resolutions are performed. And the great need of America to-day is a company of young people who have resolved the highest and the noblest for the land of their birth and of their pride.

What is the great peril that looks us in the face? Is it not the peril of mammonism and materialism? "In all things," says Mrs. Browning, "we are too materialistic, eating clay instead of Adam's fruit and Noah's wine — clay by the handful, clay by the lump, until we are filled up to the very throat with clay; until we become the very color of that on which we are feeding."

O materialistic world, we need to-day a company of young people who will resolve before God that no personal advantage shall stand between them and the interests of their fatherland.

What has happened in all our newer States? Take the State from which I come, and which I am happy to represent here, the State of Michigan. What has happened there? People have come from one part of the country, and from the other, and they have cut off our forests, and they have worked our mines, and they have enriched themselves from the resources of our State, and then, when they have become millionaires, they have gone to New York and Boston, and left the State from which they obtained their riches to help itself as best she could without them, and without the resources from which they have gathered within her borders. And what is true of Michigan is true of every other new State in our country,—that there have been scores of people who have come and used the resources of the State and country simply and purely for the materialistic purpose of enriching themselves; and when they have filled their coffers, they have departed with their wealth, leaving the State to its own struggles, its own endeavors, and its own salvation.

Now we want a company of young people in Michigan, and in every other State in our country, who will rise to the situation, and nobly resolve that no personal advantage shall stand between them and the weal of their native land; who will not only be willing to take not only the vow of chastity, but also the vow of poverty, in order that the religion of Jesus Christ may be enshrined within their borders.

We want, in the third place, a splendid consecration on the part of the young. My heart has been moved, this morning, as I have seen these noble missionaries stand here to receive your congratulations. Not one of them could have been here but because of somebody's consecration. These missionaries have counted not their lives dear unto them that they might be near Christ. Can you tell me any reason why the same spirit of consecration which rules their lives should not rule yours and mine? I remember a minister who, as he entered upon his parish, fell upon his knees and said to God, "O God, I promise thee that I will give to thee my strength and my life; I am willing to endure hardships, I am willing to be poor, I am willing to undertake any arduous endeavor, if only thou wilt give me success in my profession." And he had the success he prayed for. A man said of him, "He is a consecrated man." Can you tell me any reason why a minister should be consecrated any more than a missionary, any more than a merchant, or manufacturer, should be equally consecrated? Do you know any reason why one religious principle should reign in the heart of the elect, and should not reign in the heart of the multitude? We talk about saving our youth, about giving to home missions, about purer politics and statesmanship. The root of it all is the individual character in your heart and my heart, your life and my life.

Upon whom does home missions depend? Upon you, and you, and you. Thirty years ago and more, when our fathers were boys, they marched to the front, and as they went they had this for the motto of their lives: "Sweet and pleasant it is to die for fatherland." And some of them did die. But for you and me to-day there needs another slogan: "Sweet and pleasant it is to live for fatherland in the spirit of Jesus Christ,"—to live nobly, heroically, resolutely, consecratedly. And those home missions which are near the hearts of us all. I am sure, shall receive an impetus from the consecration of your life and my own which shall take it out to meet the splendid possibilities, the immense responsibilities, which wait upon your actions here, and bring to our land all that it needs to help it to become absolutely, what it is to-day potentially, Emmanuel's land.

When Dr. Boynton had concluded his address, " How Firm a Foundation " was sung by the multitude. The Committee of '97 then passed along the front of the platform, each one warmly grasping the hand of General Secretary Baer, and by him being introduced to the audience.

Presentation of the Committee of '97.

The audience gave the Chautauqua salute, and cheered repeatedly, and then Mr. Baer expressed the grateful appreciation of the treatment accorded, and the substantial aid given by the members of the committee, in words that came straight from the heart. His glowing, sincere words touched his hearers to the depths; the pent-up emotion of the past week, nourished and encouraged by each succeeding day's exercises, proved too much for the audience, and in an instant a thousand handkerchiefs were raised to twice as many eyes, heads of old and young, hoary-headed men and mature, gentle-faced women, were buried in their hands, and sobs broke out from all parts of the pavilion. The wave of feeling, the outpouring of hearts which offered up their noblest sentiment to Him in whom their faith had been renewed, began to spread. Mr. Baer himself, with tears in his eyes, his voice faltering, stopped suddenly in his talk, and with an effort recovering himself, raised high in air the banner presented by the United Society to the Golden Gate Union. In behalf of the United Society of Christian Endeavor he thanked the " Committee of '97 " for their labor of love and started to speak further, but words failed him, and he contented himself by bringing Chairman Rolla V. Watt to the front.

Mr. Rolla V. Watt Replies for the Committee.

Mr. Watt, who labored so assiduously to make the Convention the most successful ever held, said that neither he nor his associates on the Committee of '97 could claim any credit for their work in behalf of the Convention, that their object had been a purely selfish one, because they wanted the people to come here, and that they were certain that their efforts to entertain them and aid them in this great Convention were given with the most absolute cordiality and good will, and that if the opportunity to repeat them ever came, as they sincerely trusted and hoped, they would not be found reluctant nor averse to lending their best energies to such an exceedingly pleasant duty.

At the conclusion of Mr. Watt's remarks the doxology was sung by the audience, and Rev. George F. Pentecost, D.D., of Yonkers, N. Y., pronounced the benediction.

Woodward's Pavilion.

The largest Convention audience that had gathered in this pavilion met there on Monday morning. The prevailing thought throughout the session seemed to be to make this day a fit closing to the wonderful meeting. Enthusiasm abounded. Under the careful direction of Dr. Clark the session proved helpful and inspiring.

Mr. A. T. Sutherland, of Berkeley, Cal., conducted the music. The Rev. H. Mosser, of Reading, Penn., led the devotional exercises.

"Christian Endeavor an Evangelistic Force" was the morning topic. The prelude was in the form of an address upon "The World's Prayer Chain." When Dr. Clark presented the speaker, Miss Lilian Staples Mead, of Adelaide, Australia, the Convention greeted her with great heartiness.

Address by Miss Lilian S. Mead, Adelaide, Australia.

Mr. President and Fellow Endeavorers: — We have heard a great deal during this Convention about the Jubilee bonfires that blazed all over England, and from there to Gibraltar, and Malta, and Cypress, and then to India, and then down to the land that we call home, on to Hong Kong and Canada, until the bonfires were blazing all round the world. It has seemed to me that this was something like the World's Prayer Chain—only the light of the fires of this Jubilee were kindled in England, and this Prayer Chain in America. But this light was shown in more countries than even the Queen of England reigns over. While there is a likeness, there is also a difference. Their bond is that of a great empire; ours, to the country of Him who rules over all, and whose kingdom endures forever and forever. Theirs is a bond to a great Queen; ours is the closer bond of those who are bound to God, the King of kings, our Father.

This is the only bond that is asked from those who belong to this World's Prayer Chain. It is not that we need to be Christian Endeavorers, not that we must subscribe to any particular creed, but it is that we shall be faithful, and trust in Jesus Christ, and look to him for strength, and that we will pray every day for this great movement, and that he will use us to do his will, and to guide it and fulfil the purpose for which he called it into existence.

And further, that we might pray each month for the subject which is specified to us generally through the pages of *The Golden Rule.* I will not say anything about the reflex influence upon ourselves of the Prayer Chain. It will not lift us out of our own circle of work, but it will broaden and widen our sympathies for the whole world.

Each part of the world has its own special needs. For India we pray for the downfall of caste; China, that foot-binding shall be abolished. Then there are other needs which are common to all the world. Take thereof these, which are specified for the next six months. We are asked to pray for our homes, and is this not a prayer that we should all engage in? Think of what the result would be if we should all pray to God that he might be honored in all our homes throughout the world.

We are asked to pray for our schools. That means a different thing in different countries. Here in America it means a different thing from what it does in Australia, and it means a different thing in Persia and Turkey, and a different thing in England. We are to pray all over the world for our schools, and that teachers and scholars may teach and learn in the schools lessons of the great Master.

We are asked to pray for increased liberality in the Christian church. This is indeed needed, when at the present moment each Christian is giving but one cent a year for missionary work in heathen lands. You may say that this is impossible with all the expense that we have of our homes and of the schools. All the wealth of Christians should be given to Jesus Christ. When the Queen was leaving her palace to enter upon that splendid procession through London, she pressed an electric button that sent a message of love and gratitude through the whole world. Was it because the hand that touched the button was so strong that it was carried so far? No, the hand is old and feeble, but it touched a mighty power that was unseen but irresistible. So it is not that our individual prayer might be of such value, but it is that when we pray we link ourselves on to the Arm that moves the world. And shall we not look for answers to these prayers of ours? I heard a story since I came to the Convention about a little girl who prayed to God that the family might collect a sum of money that was due them, and which they needed very much. At last the money was paid, and she went to her mother and said, "Is it all right, mother?" And the mother said, "Yes; your prayers are answered, although it has been quite a long time." The little girl said, "Well, after we have thanked God for a little while, then we will start in with something else." That is the spirit in which we should offer these prayers, and if we pray in this spirit we shall receive answers from God, and the time shall come when this whole world is bound by these chains to the feet of God.

The object of the World's Prayer Chain is to try and lift up the world, with all its needs, and bring it into connection with Him who rules over it, and who can bring all these things to pass. Shall we not, each one of us, become links of this great Prayer Chain, and may we not each pray

> "O thou by whom we come to God,
> The life, the truth, the way,
> The path of prayer thyself hast taught;
> Oh, teach us how to pray."

Rev. Charles Roads, D.D., of Chester, Penn., was the next speaker, upon " City Evangelization Outside of the Churches."

Address by Rev. Charles Roads, D.D., Chester, Penn.

A great city is the brightest spot in Christendom, her most intense life, her richest resources and mightiest power. It is a commoner utterance and equally true that a great city is the worst of civilization. Æsop, the old philosopher, was asked to prepare a dinner of the best he could buy, and brought tongues, "the sweetest, brightest, wisest, most helpful and greatest power in man's possession." When asked to get the worst he could, he again presented tongues, " also the most hurtful, venomous, stinging, deadly of man's powers."

So is the great city the tongue of civilization, both blessing and cursing, babbling, slimy, forked, fiery, threatening, or stirring, inspiring, instructing, comforting, and full of sublime promise. It is a vast aggregation of forces, good and evil, powers of darkness and armies of righteousness, all charged with the city's energy, liberality, indomitable spirit.

We must save our cities or all Christendom perishes. We have at last come to believe we can save them by turning over their best side upon worst in Christlike evangelism and Christian citizenship. What can Christian Endeavor do for comprehensive city evangelization? Leaving Christian citizenship, now let us ask this great question.

We must be loyal to our churches, but we cannot save either our churches or the city unless we work outside. But if Christian Endeavor can, indeed, save San Francisco, Denver, Chicago, Philadelphia, New York, Boston, she will have lighted up the whole continent, and will have taken long great strides toward saving the whole world.

Heretofore city missions have been prosecuted largely by earnest workers independently of the churches; and pastors and church workers naturally are fearful of Christian Endeavor enthusiasm toward it, lest it should alienate harmfully from church work. Undenominational bands have labored in little rooms and halls, Young Men's Christian Association, Salvation Army, Gospel Wagons, and street exhorters all more or less in sympathy with the churches, but entirely apart from that of Christian Endeavor. These others have been greatly blessed of God, and we earnestly continue to pray for them; but has Christian Endeavor no call of God to the great city—The dark, the terrible, the fearfully corrupt, yet the grand, live, and powerful city?

1. I hold from long practical experience with outside rescue missions, as one of the very few pastors who has labored regularly in many of them, and

now in contrast from blessed experience with Christian Endeavor city missions, under church auspices, that the city can be saved only by the Christian work of the churches. It must be outside of their walls, but leading directly into them.

Disabuse yourself of the notion that the unsaved cannot be reached as well by the organized church people as by the undenominational workers. The fact is remarkably proven that they can be reached far more effectively by the church bands. There is an impressiveness to the unwashed and degraded in the great church coming to visit them, in well-dressed and cultivated singers and speakers interested in them. The pastor, too, whose name they may have seen in the newspapers is regarded with respect, and the pastors are our most acceptable speakers in the darkest slums. The best singing by the finest soloists and chorus is not lost.

There are two kinds of people in the morally submerged of a great city,—those who were always down, and those who fell from high places. A hand-to-hand experience with penitents in slum missions will surprise you with the large number fallen from the better classes. Here is an intelligent school-teacher in a bawdy-house, a minister's daughter in another, wrecks of once prominent physicians, lawyers, merchants, and so on. Such are the people actually picked up, and to them the cultured and gentlemanly pastor, the splendid singers, and the regular church band are most powerful.

2. It would be a grave mistake, however, for the church company of evangelistic workers to devote themselves wholly to the slum mission, so as to withdraw from their own church activities — a misfortune for the mission itself, which needs, above all, a vital connection with the church. The men and women who are saved must be taken into the. church, and will become valuable members under wise care. We could name a dozen who recently came out of the lowest depths and are now modestly, but most efficiently, serving as trustees, choir-leaders, Sunday-school workers, and spiritual leaders in great churches. One is an eminent singer, another a masterly orchestra leader, another a foreign missionary, still another an evangelist, and so on. Pastors will get more work for their own church out of city evangelistic Endeavorers than from any other class of workers, and a unique quality of deeply spiritual services. These pastors, if great-hearted and wise as many we know, will add many thus saved to their church forces whose enthusiasm and love for Christ will be contagious to the whole church. For the sake of your church, send out evangelistic workers; and for the sake of the mission keep them also at work in the church.

3. What kind of evangelistic service can be undertaken by these church companies? I will tell you what has been done. We are occupying several street-car sheds once a week. The motormen and conductors crowd the meetings, take lively part in the singing, and some of them who are Christians testify for Christ. A pastor is called in to address them, the Endeavorers testify, sing, and pray, and invite the unsaved to accept Christ. How the hands go up for prayers — six or eight in a single meeting!

We go to police-stations and hold wonderful meetings there every week, with many conversions. Other church companies rent a vacant room or small house, and hold weekly meetings, or twice a week. Such was a mission by a cultured band of young Presbyterians, whose enthusiasm and Christlike spirit deeply moved the people in what was known as the " Devil's Pocket " in Philadelphia. The reflex influence on their own church was fully as remarkable. Their pastor was from the first an enthusiast in such outside work.

Prison meetings, open-air services on street-corners, the church gospel wagon, and factory meetings are other forms of work tried with great success. We could give touching illustrations of their effectiveness.

4. City evangelism requires the parish responsibility. The young people are trained to feel that for several blocks in every direction from their church they must assume special care for souls; that they are directly called to that field. They visit from house to house in this territory and direct families preferring other churches to the nearest one, while seeking to win all to Christ. They

aim to substitute a spiritual parish idea for the lack of parish divisions. We believe it possible, and have made great progress in that direction in Philadelphia, to put every street and every house under the pastoral oversight of some earnest body of workers. What pastor does not recognize the immense value to his church of such a spirit among his young people?

5. The final object must be no less than fully-comprehensive or all-inclusive evangelism of the whole city. And this by consecrated bands from all the churches. Every street-car shed, every police-station, every hospital, prison, street-corner, every available room in dark quarters, nay, every motorman and conductor, every policeman and fireman, every sick man or criminal, every man, woman, and child, regularly reached by gospel influences and Christly contact. Somebody to feel responsible for every one down to the last soul in the largest of great cities. It can be done by Christian Endeavor thoroughly organized. Our C. E. stands for comprehensive evangelism! We will be inspired to do some really effective Christian citizenship work when we once come to see the awful worthlessness of our city government in darkest quarters. City evangelism will become an earthquake under the City Hall. The Law and the Gospel will join hands to save the city in the spirit of Robert Ross and Dwight L. Moody united.

6. The church atmosphere must become evangelistic. The saved soul must not come from the warm mission into the chilly church. House-to-house visiting will fail if it sends people simply to be received in the church without heartiness; to be taken into services dull, cold, and formal; and to be held aloof by prominent members. Some of the people will go back to their sins with an additional bitterness against all churches and professing Christians. Build a warm fire in the open grate for your church guests; get them socially around it into an evangelistic atmosphere. There is joy in heaven. Lift up the standard then with city evangelism, Christlike and comprehensive: —

1. By the churches and toward the churches.
2. In every open place preach Christ.
3. Give us parish responsibility.
4. Every man, woman, and child in the city for Christ.
5. The local church evangelistic and warm.

The city must be saved. It can be saved. The vision of holy cities is our inspiration. The forces of Christ are adequate in any city to redeem it. Organize, energize by the Holy Spirit, evangelize with Pentecostal faith and power, localize every worker in a definite field, centralize results in your own church.

Very appropriately followed an address upon " Deepening the Spiritual Life Inside Our Churches." The speaker was a Convention favorite, the Rev. J. Wilbur Chapman, D.D., of Philadelphia, Penn. Dr. Chapman said in part: —

Address by Rev. J. Wilbur Chapman, D.D., Philadelphia.

We are living in the dispensation of the Spirit. He is the Vicar of Christ, and the life of the body, which is the Church. The lesson may be taught by contrast. That which does not grieve the Spirit deepens the spiritual life. That which is to be avoided is the cause of his being grieved.

Of all the epistles that ever came from the heart of the great Apostle Paul, this letter to the Ephesians seems to me about the sweetest and best. It is the epistle in which we find " the heavenly places " mentioned so many times; it is the epistle in which we find so many different names applied to our Father in Heaven; and I suppose it is the letter in which we find the very highest spiritual truth presented in all the Bible. But while we find the very highest idea of spiritual things, we also find the Apostle Paul turning to give us instructions concerning the most ordinary affairs of daily life. Some rules are here concerning Christian conversation. Some suggestions are made touching the relation which the husband sustains to the wife, and the wife to the husband.

Indeed, if one should live in the spirit of this letter to the Ephesians, he would do nothing less than live what has been called by some "the life of surrender," and others "the victorious life," but which Paul calls "the life in the heavenly places." Paul makes all these different suggestions, and then adds: "And grieve not the Holy Spirit of God," as if he could be grieved by a wrong atmosphere in the home, or by a wrong use of the lips; and this is true.

First of all, the very fact that we may grieve him proves by inference his personality. You cannot grieve an influence. It seems to me that we may grieve the Spirit by even stopping to prove that he has a personality equal to the Father and to the Son, for it is so self-evident.

In the second place, the fact that we may grieve him proves his sensitiveness. In John 1. 32, it is said, "I saw the Spirit descending from Heaven like a dove." The dove stands for all that is sensitive in the family of birds.

This idea of sensitiveness presents to us the thought of his love. If I do not love you, you cannot grieve me; but just in the proportion that I love you, you will find it easy to grieve me.

1. We may grieve him by disobedience. Disobedience of children always raises a barrier between them and their parents. There may be ever so much love in a father's heart, and he may have ever so much desire to pour forth that love, but he cannot do it so long as there is this barrier of disobedience between him and his child.

What does Paul mean when he says, "Be not drunk with wine, wherein is excess"? We take that to be a command. "But be filled with the Spirit" is the rest of the same verse, and that is just as much a command as not to be drunk with wine. The only difference between the first command and the second is that one is negative and the other is positive. Are you filled with the Spirit? If not, you have disobeyed God's command, and there is a barrier between you and him.

2. Again, we grieve the Spirit by failing to keep our hearts clean. The late John MacNeil, of Australia, said that a new heart is not necessarily a clean heart; but many of us have been thinking that it was. David committed a great transgression, and was pardoned, and prayed: "Create in me a clean heart, renew a right spirit within me." Paul says: "He is faithful and just to forgive us our sins, and to cleanse us from all unrighteousness."

3. Then we may grieve the Spirit by practically denying his Word. Was there not much of pathos in Jesus' words when he said: "Why do ye not understand my speech?" Christ has promised to be with us "alway, even unto the end of the world" — with us even in disappointment and trial. Some one has said that a Christian should spell disappointment with an "H" in place of the "d," and make it His-appointment.

But we grieve the Spirit more, perhaps, in matters of doctrine than anything else. We grieve him in our lack of assurance. John says: "This is written that ye may know ye have eternal life." and yet Christians are continually praying, "Save us at last." Do you not think that grieves the Spirit of God?

One word in closing. In Ephesians iv. 31, the apostle says, "Let all bitterness, and wrath, and anger, and clamor, and evil speaking be put away from you, with all malice." This is a practical thought with which to close. Paul would seem to indicate that we grieve the Spirit by yielding to any of these things. The Spirit of God is grieved whenever we allow our old nature to triumph over our spiritual nature; for God has promised in his Word to set us free from the law of sin and death.

Banner for Best Progress in Promoting Proportionate Giving to God.

The presentation of the banner for the best progress in the past year in promoting systematic and proportionate giving to God was the occasion of one of those outbursts of State patriotism which has been one of the features of some of the previous Conventions. The banner has been held for a year by the New York City Union, and was presented to it again. This is the union in which The Tenth Legion originated, and it is in this union that its greatest progress has been made during the past year.

Presentation Speech by Rev. E. L. House, Attleboro, Mass.

Mr. President:—On the eve of April 15, 1861, Abraham Lincoln issued his call for seventy-five thousand volunteers. The news was flashed over the wires to the great cities of this country in the North and West. In the city of New York and the city of Philadelphia this question of the call of Abraham Lincoln was discussed. But in the city of Boston, when the telegram came, the Governor upon receiving it sent forth his commands, and the Sixth Massachusetts Regiment reported at once. On the morning of the 18th, early in the morning just as the sun was kissing the east, the city of New York, that had been discussing this great question as to what they ought to do in connection with the presidential call, were aroused by the sound of fife and drum; as they threw up their windows and looked out, lo and behold, marching down Broadway was the old Sixth Massachusetts Regiment going to the front, going to help the President and sustain him in his work. The whole city of New York was aroused with enthusiasm, and at once they also began to march forward toward Washington. In Philadelphia the same scene was repeated; in Baltimore the same. On the night of the 18th the Massachusetts Sixth Regiment reached Washington, and looking up into the face of the President, they said to him, "We are here." And the President, looking upon them, said, "Thank God!"

A little later "It is not a question of men," said Abraham Lincoln, "but it is a question of finances. How shall we sustain these men?" The Secretary of the Treasury spoke of this matter to a New York banker, and some of the great financiers of the city were called together in a meeting to talk over the question. The city of New York said, "Call upon us for fifty millions of dollars, if need be." The city of New York gave one hundred million dollars within one year to sustain the army that had gone forward.

A greater than Abraham Lincoln has issued His call. It is not a call for war; it is a call for peace. He has asked his soldiers to come forward that they may go forth in the mighty conquest of winning the world to peace and to righteousness. It was not in Massachusetts, not in the city of Boston, but in the city of New York, this time, that young hearts heard the call of the Great Commander; and as they heard the call of the Great Commander, they not only gave themselves thirteen hundred strong, but they also said, "We not only give our hearts, but we give our pocket-books to sustain our Commander in his great work." As this Tenth Legion has gone forward in its great work, their steps have been heard around the world, arousing enthusiasm in the great centres and in the hamlets; and all over the country Endeavorers have caught the inspiration of this Legion, and they are rallying around the banner and marching forward to save the world for Christ.

It is right that we should give ourselves and all that we have to the Master, for he has made this world, he has made man and put him in the world, and he only asks that we shall give that which he has given to us.

So to-day, let us young Endeavorers catch the inspiration that God wants not only our hearts, but also the consecration of our means.

After one of the battles of the war, when the soldiers were lying sick, and means were wanted to supply them with care and attention and those things which would relieve their suffering, a telegram was sent to one of our great cities asking if it could be called upon to furnish ten thousand dollars at sight. When it had been presented to the Chamber of Commerce, they telegraphed back, "Call upon us for sixty thousand dollars if necessary." Let that be the spirit of the Christian Endeavorers of the world. Let us have ten thousand soldiers of The Tenth Legion this year who will say, "Call upon us, not only for ten thousand dollars, but for sixty thousand dollars — nay, call upon us until every loyal Christian Endeavor heart has become a member of the great Tenth Legion Regiment, that shall send its joy and its good will the world around, until all men shall know that Christ is Lord."

To the New York City Union, who have this last year gone on to greater heights and to greater consecration, in behalf of the Trustees of the United Society I present this banner. May it stimulate you to still better service, may it arouse you with enthusiasm, and may you go on to accomplish greater things.

And let us who see this banner given to them say in our hearts that we will also be aroused by it, and, realizing that it is the best and grandest banner of all, we will strive to get it from them in the year which is to come, that we may also be able to say, "We have done our work well."

Harry A. Kinports, vice-president and treasurer of the New York State Union responded. He said: "The figures have been canvassed, and the column has been added, and the banner is ours."

As he received it from the hands of Rev. Mr. House, the New York delegation, which had assembled over a hundred strong in one of the galleries, arose and greeted it with a salute and sang a paraphrase of the familiar song "My Bonnie Lies Over the Ocean," to the melody of that favorite. At the same time another member of the delegation seated on the platform unfurled the blue banner of the State and waved it during the singing : —

> Last night, as I canvassed the figures,
> Last night, as I ciphered till dawn,
> Last night, as I added the columns,
> I dreamed that my banner was gone.

CHORUS.

Bring back, bring back, bring back my banner to me, to me, etc.

> Oh, roll ye cars over the Rockies,
> Oh, roll ye cars down to the sea,
> Then hasten over the prairies,
> And bring back my banner to me.—CHORUS.

> It echoes from ocean to ocean,
> Glad tidings from New York Cit-ee;
> The delegates homeward have started,
> And brought back our banner to we.— CHORUS.

> Oh, wait till we gather at Nashville,
> Till we greet yóu at fair Tennessee ;
> For surely next summer's Convention
> Shall bring back my banner to me. — CHORUS.

Mr. Kinports continued : —

When at Washington last year we took this banner back to our hotel amid shouts and huzzars, we never dreamed that we should come to this Convention under such favorable circumstances, and receive it again.

We love this banner to-day more than we ever loved it before, because during the last year while it has been in our possession The Tenth Legion has been steadily gaining, and it has become known world-wide, and that New York

City deserved the credit of the formation and organization of this work. Therefore, as long as we see this banner, so long as we follow it, so long will be the idea of the formation and organization of The Tenth Legion associated with it. I assure you, Mr. President, that we shall go back to New York filled with zeal and with renewed courage to do greater things for Christ and for his church.

During the last year we gained four hundred tithe-givers in our local union. I do not know how many we shall gain during the coming year, but we assure you that we shall neither rest or slumber, but shall press forward and onward and upward to win tithe givers for Christ and for his church. We trust that when we meet you at the next Convention the banner shall again be ours, and that we shall have not only thirteen hundred tithe-givers, but two thousand in the New York City Union of Christian Endeavor.

And so, Mr. President, this means a great deal to us and our work for Jesus Christ. It means systematic endeavor for him. It means also that the churches of New York City are going to be quickened more and more; for as the young people of that city give one-tenth of their income to the Lord Jesus Christ and to his service, more and more will the churches feel its influence and power, the more they will be quickened, more and more will the entire City of New York, the entire nation, and the entire world feel this influence for Christ and for the church.

And so I thank you, and accept this banner in the name of the New York Union of Christian Endeavor, with the honest determination of all our Christian Endeavorers to press onward and upward for Christ and for his church.

Apropos of the giving and receiving of this banner was the last address of the morning, on " Some Spiritual Returns for Missionary Investments." This topic was considered by Rev. Thomas O. Crouse, of Baltimore, Maryland.

Address by Rev. Thomas O. Crouse, Baltimore, Md.

There is nothing novel or modern in the principles which lie at the base of the missionary and evangelistic movements, which have engaged the thought of this Convention this morning. The chief motive and the supreme and undying inspiration to world-wide evangelization must be obedience to our risen Lord. The Master Missionary is our Lord Jesus Christ, and his word, "Go ye," is our permanent and plenary authority; his word settles the obligation. If no other reason could be given for the aggressive work to which we are being called to-day, this would be enough.

But this utilitarian age is likely to ask concerning any enterprise in which it is invited to invest, " Does it pay? Will our investment yield any returns?" This question is sometimes asked concerning missionary work in the spirit of selfishness and commercial policy. Men often give more thought to the returns and recompense in the way of material and temporal advantage than is consistent with the spirit of the Gospel. To these it may be sufficient to reply, as Dr. Pierson suggests, " It always pays to obey authority, especially when authority is supreme."

But there is a sense in which this question is a lawful one. On one occasion, you will remember, the disciples asked: "Master, we have left all and followed thee; what shall we have therefor?" Some may cry out against their question as a selfish one; many say that it betrays the spirit of the hireling. Our Lord, however, did not rebuke it; he answered them, "Every one that hath forsaken houses, or kindred, or lands, for my name's sake, shall receive an hundred-fold in this life, and in the world to come life everlasting."

We are often called to look upon this work of missions at home and abroad from the standpoint of the people in whose behalf it is prosecuted. We hear of their need of the Gospel, of their spiritual wretchedness and woe, their sin and sorrow; and by these appeals to our humanity and Christian benevolence we are stimulated to an interest in the cause of missions. It may be we have not thought as much as we should of this work from this standpoint of the worker; what the work of missions does for the workers. It is to that phase of the subject I am to direct your attention. My message is a very definite, simple, and practical one. I have no time to consider in its broadest sense the reflex influence of missions. I must pass over in silence what commerce and science owes to Christian missions; I cannot stay to discuss the large contributions the brave and intelligent men and women on mission fields have made to the sum of useful and curious knowledge. These are fruitful and interesting topics, and one who studies them will have a higher respect for the intellectual worth of missionaries, and be impressed with the conviction that the world owes a debt of gratitude to Christian missions far greater than is generally recognized.

But to my theme: I want to lead the minds of the young people who are before me to think of the spiritual returns that shall come to them as they give thought, sympathy, prayer, money, personal service and sacrifice to the divine work of world-wide evangelism. Hence it is true in the highest and most blessed sense: "Give, and it shall be given unto you."

My first thought, then, is:

1. Missionary investments yield a sure return in the development and enrichment of character. You aspire to the largest, grandest Christian manhood and womanhood. The enlargement and enrichment of the new nature born in you of the Holy Ghost is the goal of your desire and ambition. But how shall you attain this? You will not think I undervalue the study of the Word, attendance upon ordinances and prayer. Far from it. But I am only reminding you of what you have doubtless learned long since: the man who seeks to cherish and develop a higher spirituality and a manly Christian character by private devotions and by attendance upon religious meetings alone is making a fatal mistake. A vigorous and symmetrical piety is not the product of the cloister. Growth is not simply a matter of taking in, but of giving out. The act of respiration, by which our life is sustained, is a twofold process,— inhaling and exhaling; the one as important as the other. Money grows by wise investment, not by miserly hoarding. Physical strength is conserved and increased by judicious exercise. Intellectual possessions are made more truly ours by imparting to others what we have learned.

It is profoundly true in every sphere of life that using is an essential factor in gaining. The religious life, like the intellectual or the physical, needs work for its full-rounded development; yes, even for its continuance. "There is that scattereth and yet increaseth; and there is that withholdeth more than is meet, but it tendeth to poverty. The liberal soul shall be made fat; and he that watereth shall be watered also himself." This law is nowhere more sure and imperative in its operation than in the realm of the spiritual life. So in our aspiration to make the most of life, to develop a sturdy, vigorous, beautiful, Christian character, we must not forget the great paradox that we get by giving. However strangely that may sound to the carnal, selfish worldling, there is divine philosophy in it. "He that loseth his life shall find it." Loving service ior others reacts in ourselves, and we find in our growing spiritual health abundant reward for our sacrifice. The principle holds both in individual and in church life. Just as we reach out with holy enthusiasm to serve and to save others we shall be enriched and strengthened in all the qualities of Christian character. The law of self-preservation and of growth demands that you invest in missionary work. You cannot reach the highest development of Christian personality unless you live and work for others. You dwarf and repress — nay, you smother your spiritual life as you limit your sympathies and labor to a little circle of which you are the centre, and those bound to you by the ties of family are the circumference. Selfishness is stagnation, atrophy, paralysis, death. Give yourself to a noble cause that calls out the best that is in you; that puts faith, love, hope, and sacrifice into exercise; and there will come back to you in largest measure moral strength, grace, and beauty.

It has often been remarked that missions have been vindicated and glorified by their reflex influence upon the personal character of those who have engaged in them. From the days of Paul until now the annals of missionary labor have been glorious with the sublimest heroes the world has ever seen. Theodore Parker rose from the reading of the life of Adoniram Judson to declare that if missions had produced but one such hero, all costs were amply repaid. Judson was a hero; but he was only a type of an evergrowing galaxy.

The church only lives and grows as it cherishes and cultivates the missionary spirit. The church that merely holds its own will soon lose its own. Neglecting the people, the people will neglect it; leaving the lost to die without the gospel, it invites, insures, and justifies its own decay. Attention has been called to the fact in vegetable life that the light, heat, moisture, and nutrition which are so necessary to growth where life exists, actually promote and hasten decay where life is not. Dr. Pierson remarks: "It is a corresponding fact in spiritual experience that the most abundant blessings become only curses where they are not used for the ends which God designed, and the peril of our souls and of the churches lies in the very conditions which, if we are faithful, insure prosperity." You and I are called to give the gospel to those who have it not,—not only that they may live, but that we may live.

2. Missionary investments yield a rich return of truest spiritual joy.

There is, first of all, the joy of obedience to our risen Lord. His command is, "Go ye;" and with this, as with all his commands, we find "in keeping it there is great reward." The way of obedience is the way of delight. Love can ask no higher motive than the will of the beloved; so it can know no greater delight than the sense of pleasing him. With the pierced hand of Him who redeemed us with his precious blood pointing to the great world-field, and the voice that brought peace to our souls as it whispered within us the welcome invitation, "Come unto Me" now saying, "Go ye and tell others of my power to save," can we be happy if we linger in selfish ease, or seek to find some excuse for our neglect of the perishing souls about us? Only as we go or help others to go preaching everywhere the gospel of the kingdom are we obeying the word of our Saviour; and the sure recompense of this work for him is closer fellowship with him and deeper draughts of his own peculiar joy. We make the Saviour more really our own as we seek to give him to others. "You will catch new gleams of his gracious heart in the very act of commending him to others." Have you noticed how closely linked with the command, "Go ye into all the world," is the promise, "Lo, I am with you alway"? Only as we obey the command can we claim the promise. You all remember the old legend which Longfellow has embalmed in his sweet verse of the monk who had prayed long and earnestly for a vision of the Christ. But let the old story illustrate again our present thought.

You remember how, in answer to the old man's prayer, Jesus stood revealed before him. The radiant joy of the Saviour's presence filled his cell with golden light; the heart of the saint was thrilled with ecstatic delight; his eyes feasted on the vision, and he cried out in rapture: "The joy of my heart has come at last; mine eyes behold the face of Jesus!" But while he gazed in awe and rapture on the vision, the bell rang — the bell which summoned the unfortunate poor to receive their evening meal from the hands of this very monk. "What shall I do?" he cried; "if I go I shall miss the vision; Christ may never come back to me." But the bell kept ringing, and the good man went away from his cell to serve the poor, who needed him. His errand done, he turned back to the cell, thinking, "The Master will be gone now, and I shall see him no more." But, lo, the cell was more radiant than ever; the vision was clearer and more beautiful; and he heard the words: "If thou hadst stayed to feast thine own eyes I must have gone; but because thou didst thy duty to my brethren, I remained." No man can expect to taste the deepest joy of salvation, to behold the face of his Lord, and hear his approving voice, if he is content to sit down in solitary meditation and selfish concern for his own soul, caring not for the starving world that unconsciously, but none the less truly, pleads for the bread of life. The man who sits down to enjoy his religion, satisfied with the ecstasies of devotion, will soon find his joy expiring. The "delightful services" of the prayer-meeting have been a failure, so far as you are concerned, if they have not impelled and fitted you for service.

The true conception of a church is not a land-locked harbor where each man may sit in his little craft as it lies on the placid waters and sing and shout all day long over his deliverance from the tumultuous waves and cruel reefs outside, but rather a life-saving station from which brave and living souls go out to rescue other storm-tossed and sinking mariners. And just as we accept this conception of our relation to the world, and in the spirit of our Master go to seek and to save, shall we know the real joy of Christian experience. A godly pastor writes: "There was a period in my ministry marked by the most systematic effort to comfort my serious people; but the more I tried to comfort them the more they complained of doubt and darkness. At this time it pleased God to direct my attention to the claims of the perishing heathen; I felt that we had been living for ourselves, and not for their souls. I spoke to my people as I felt. They wept and wondered at my and their past neglect. They began to talk and to pray about missions. We met and considered what could be done. We prayed much for the heathen, and money was collected and devoted to this cause. While all this was going on the lamentations I had heard ceased. The sad became cheerful and the despondent calm. No one complained of a want of comfort. They were drawn out of themselves, and God blessed them while they tried to be a blessing." That is just the story that has been repeated in thousands of lives. The perfect flower of Christian joy will not bloom in the chilly atmosphere of selfishness, but in the warmth of sympathy, sacrifice, and service for others. A story is told of Alexander to this effect: On a hunting-trip his attendants had been left behind. As he rode through the forest alone the king heard a groan, and, following the pitiful sound, he came upon a wounded man. Quickly dismounting, Alexander staunched the flowing blood, chafed the temples of the fainting man, and did his utmost to restore him. When his retinue found him bending over his reviving charge, the king looked up and greeted them with the cry, "Oh, this is the happiest day of my life! I have saved a man!" His military triumphs, his royal honors, the obsequious homage he had received from courtiers and conquered kings, had never given him such rare and real pleasure as his service to this distressed fellow-man.

We sometimes hear much said about the surrenders, privations, and hardships of the missionary life. I thank God this does not come from the missionaries themselves, but from other people who undertake to speak for them. Turn to the letters and journals of the missionaries themselves, and you will find them instinct with the spirit of peace, praise, and devout thankfulness. They are happy in their privilege to tell the story of redeeming love to people who never heard it before, and to whom the story comes as good news from a far country. Mary Moffat wrote to her parents from South Africa: "You can hardly conceive how I feel when I sit in the house of God, surrounded by the natives. Though my situation may be despised and mean in the eyes of the world, I feel an honor conferred upon me which the highest of the kings of the earth could not have done. . . . . I am happy, remarkably happy, though the present place of my habitation is a vestry-room with a mud wall and a mud floor. It is true our sorrows and cares we must have, and in a degree have them now; but is it not our happiness to suffer in this cause?"

You may not be called to go to distant mission-fields; but give yourself to service for the salvation of others, do something to spread the tidings of great joy, and you shall find your investment yielding you a rich return of purest spiritual joy. You may or may not be able to invest much in this work of missions; your service and sacrifice are not estimated by the greatness of the one or the dignity of the other, but by the motive that inspires them. The perfection of the fruit is not its size, but its flavor. Some one has said, " Though Noah could not boast of many converts for his long years of preaching, he could at least enter the Ark with a clear conscience and the happy sense of duty done."

3. Missionary investments yield a return in practical Christian unity. When the spirit of missions animates a community of Christians, and the needs of the unevangelized and unsaved are laid on their hearts, there is neither time

nor disposition for bigotry, bickering, controversy, or mutual coldness. The spirit of missions is the spirit of Christ, and like purging fire it consumes pride, prejudice, personal ambition, greed, and apathy, and fuses the heart of the church into blessed unity. We get near to Christ in mission work; and the old colored brother was right when he exclaimed, "Christianity is like de cart-wheel; Christ am de hub, and we am de spokes; and de nearer we gets to de hub de nearer we are to each other." There is such a thing as the old deacon described when he said that the church to which he belonged was, after years of wrangling and divisions, united at last; and, when asked how this unity had been brought about, he replied, "We are frozen, frozen together from top to bottom." The spirit of missions does not bring about that kind of unity, but the unity of a common devotion to our Lord and Saviour, a common purpose, a common sense of responsibility, and a common faith and hope. At Trafal-gar Lord Nelson learned that there was an alienation between two of his sub-ordinate officers; calling them to him on the flag-ship *Victory*, he pointed them to the combined fleets of France and Spain, and said: "Gentlemen, there are your enemies; we can have no divisions and jealousies among ourselves. We have only one great object in view: annihilating our enemies, and getting a glorious peace for our country." In quite another spirit the Church of Jesus Christ stands facing the awful darkness of heathendom and the spiritual destitution of even much of so-called Christian territory, and she can have only one object in view: to obey her marching orders, to publish the gospel to "the uttermost parts of the earth," and to achieve a victory for the Captain of her salvation.

MONDAY AFTERNOON.

The Junior Rally. — Mechanics' Pavilion.

One of the most inspiring sights upon which one could look in the sessions of the Convention was the myriad children gathered in Mechanics' Pavilion on the afternoon of the famous Junior rally. What possibilities! Benjamin Franklin would have been obliged to doff his hat ten thousand times! The hall was filled with the bright and interested faces. They watched every movement of the program and often rent the air with their shrill applause. It was difficult to sup-press them, doubtless because there were many of them "Young Americas." But the company was still cosmopolitan,— numerous Chi-nese, here and there an Indian, and many children of Africa.

Rev. John Rea, of Oakland, led the spirited singing, which every child enjoyed. Such songs as "Our Junior Band," "Onward, O Junior Endeavorers," and "Sunshine in My Soul," were rendered with a will. The effect to the on-looker was delightful.

Rev. Mr. Dawson offered prayer. The following telegram was an-nounced, and the Juniors assembled gave an enthusiastic response : —

The Nutmeg's Telegram.

New Haven, Conn., Junior Union to our little Western brothers and sisters, the Juniors of California, greeting.

Dear Friends : —Although we are separated by more than 3,000 miles and have never seen each other's faces, yet we know that we are all brothers and sisters, because we have the same Elder Brother whom we all love and serve. We can-not all be at our great Convention — we wish we could, but we shall think of you and pray for you that you may have a very happy time, and may receive so much blessing and enthusiasm that you will not only be better Juniors, but better Christians all your lives. We also hope that you will think of us and pray that this same blessing and enthusiasm may flow across the land even as far as our own little State of Connecticut, so that we, too, may be inspired to serve Christ more faithfully. With much love, from your friends

THE JUNIORS OF THE NUTMEG STATE.

The chairman of the session, Rev. J. H. Bomberger, of Ohio, made a felicitous speech, in which he declared himself still a Junior.

The introduction of the Chinese Quartette was another opportunity for the children. The "flaky salute" did not quite suffice; cheers could only express their feeling. The quartette was composed of Jung Guy, Edgar Chee, Lem Sent, and L. S. Chee, all from the Presbyterian mission. They responded to the encore.

It was when Mrs. F. E. Clark was presented that the children really found their vocal and palm powers. Certainly Mrs. Clark was welcome. When quiet was again the rule, she said : —

Greetings from Mrs. F. E. Clark, Boston.

" I thank you, boys and girls, from the bottom of my heart for this greeting. It is the prettiest I have had since my return home. I want you to think of me this afternoon as one who comes merely as a messenger. I bring to you greetings from all over the world — from Salt Lake City, from Minneapolis, from Boston, and across the waters. I bring messages of love and good cheer. Some weeks ago, when I was in England, I attended a meeting of the Junior Endeavorers. There were two American boys present, and I wish you could have heard the three British cheers when those boys got up to speak. It resembled thunder, and if you heard it over here you must not think it was thunder, for it was only the outpouring of those loyal young hearts.

"I bring to you greetings from Germany, from Italy, from China, from Japan, and from many countries of which some of you have never heard. If these people could be here, they would greet you in a manner that would be at once peculiar and strange, but none the less hearty and true. Some of them would appear clad in fine raiment, while others would come with no clothes at all. Some would shake hands with themselves, while others would rub their brown noses against yours ; but whatever the manner of greeting, it would be honest and sincere. Now, my greeting to you is that you help other boys and girls in other lands to lead a true Christian life."

The Chinese choir from the Presbyterian mission then favored the throng with a Christian song. There were twenty members in the choir. On the very edge of the platform were four little tots. After the singing by the others, they rendered a selection in which each swung a candle as they sang " Jesus Bids Us Shine with a Clear, Pure Light." This feature was followed by a recitation. Then the smallest one voiced a patriotic verse which ended with the words, " Hurrah for these United States ! " Uproarious applause from the Junior audience greeted these efforts.

" Sunshine in My Soul To-day " was then sung by the myriad. Mr. Bomberger next introduced Rev. Robert F. Y. Pierce, of Philadelphia, who gave a most delightful chalk-talk to the children upon " The Song of the Heart." Mr. Pierce, cheery of face and of speech, quite won the hearts of the children. His talk to them was crowded — doubtless too much crowded — with good things. We can here give only an outline of the series of pictures he drew and the illustrations he used.

A big circle appeared on the board. It represented the Junior Society. A spoke was added. That means you. Another spoke. That means *you*. Many other spokes. In goes a hub. It is changed to a cross. Jesus must be the hub of all our Christian Endeavor work. All our life-work must be centred in Jesus. A spoke must be fastened to the felloe of the wheel, but it must also go down into the hub. Christian Endeavorers must be fastenened on the one side to the institution and on the other to the institution's Christ. Now all you Juniors that will promise to be good spokes in the Junior wheel hold up your hand. Hold up *both* hands.

Two candles were shown, one a common affair, the other covered with gilt; but it appeared that they gave equal amounts of light.

Another pair of candles was brought out, — one very large, the other very small; but, when both were lighted, it was discovered that the little one gave the bigger light.

"Ragged Jim" came forward, — a very disreputable candle, all broken and crooked and dirty. But he was lighted by a missionary candle, and straightened up, and cleaned off, and lo! he was as good as any one.

A staff of music. Seven notes put upon it. They mean, "In thy presence is fulness of joy." The dark cloud of sin appears above, and from it flashes a red stroke of lightning. The music parts, and the joy note falls out, being transferred to the bottom of the board. A heart drawn around the ruined staff of music completes the lesson.

A field of daisies, drawn one after the other. "Daisy, what is your name?" "My name is joy." "Daisy, what do you tell us of God?" "God is love." So the daisies were named,— Daisy Mercy, Daisy Charity, and the rest. But what are the daisies saying? Let us draw telegraph-wires along and see if we can hear. Let us put in the poles to support the wires. The daisies are seen to be notes on a musical staff, and the notes make the tune, "Praise God, from whom all blessings flow." Then the great audience sang the doxology.

The bad use of good things. A beautiful sheaf of rye stood on the platform. Suddenly Mr. Pierce felt down in its depths, and pulled out — a bottle of whiskey! He showed by pouring it over an egg in a bottle how alcohol "cooks" the egg-like substance of the brain. But something better comes out of the rye Mr. Pierce pulled from the sheaf a load of rye bread. He broke off a piece and ate it with relish. "How many of you children would rather have the rye bread than the whiskey?" And in response to the torrent of "I's." Mr. Pierce broke off bits of the bread, and threw it here and there among the laughing children.

A great Y was drawn on the board. It stands for *You*. The left side is broad, for the broad way; the right side is narrow, for the nar-

row way.　Mr. Pierce drew hands from the two arms, pointing in opposite directions.　At the dividing of the way, you must choose.　"Remember thy Creator in the days of thy youth."　All say it together.
Why choose the narrow way?　On the left the speaker drew a stormy
sea, a wrecked ship.　On the right he drew a peaceful sea, a lighthouse,
with the light flashing from it, ships sailing safely,— and some of them
very little ships,— the birds flying cheerily over all.　He made the
lighthouse red.　He transformed it into a scarlet cross.　"Choose ye
this day whom ye will serve."　Now say it all together, Juniors:
"*Choose ye this day whom ye will serve.*"

The main feature of the afternoon was then given.　It was an exercise entitled "The Junior Garden."　The words of this very pretty
composition were written by Prof. Amos R. Wells, of *The Golden Rule.*
The music was composed by Mr. Charles S. Brown, of Boston.

The effect of the varicolored costumes and profusion of flowers was
beautiful indeed.　The outline of the exercise was as follow : — "Christian Endeavor," represented by Miss Lottie J. Graeber, shows her Junior garden to new members of the society.　These are Miss Florence
Graeber and Master Cass Downing.　Their curiosity aroused as to
what is done in the garden, Christian Endeavor promises to show them.
First nine boys with spades marched in and sang a song in which the
words "dig, dig, dig" formed the refrain.　The sowers, twelve little
girls dressed in white and yellow, appeared and pretended to scatter
seed, which they designated in their song as "may-I-help-you seed,"
"thank-you seed," and "laughter seed," and these were followed by
twelve boys with watering-cans, wearing green sashes, who sang a rain
song.　The sunshine girls came next, twelve colored girls, dressed in
white and yellow, carrying suns in their hands, and they gave a chorus
effectively.　Weeds were then discovered in the garden and a corps of
weeders, twelve boys carrying hoes, went through the movements of
removing the obnoxious growths from the pretty garden, accompanying
it with a song.　These intruders in the garden of happiness and content were termed "Obstinacy, Laziness, Anger, and Hatred."

The beauties of the garden were then shown by the Junior flowers.
First, the lilies, twelve little girls in white, carrying bunches of that
flower ; then twelve more, in white and purple, carrying violets ; then
eighteen girls in yellow, wearing great bunches of poppies ; and then
twelve girls in white, with pink sashes, carrying bouquets of roses.
Each group sang a chorus as its members marched across the platform.

Christian Endeavor then asked the flowers to greet the two new members, and this was done by the rendering of a chorus of welcome participated in by all.　A grand march followed, and many intricate movements were executed.

Everybody in the audience heartily joined in the three cheers and
the "silent Chautauqua" for the authors of the beautiful and instructive vision.　The exercise was presented under the direction of Miss
Myrtle Simpson, of San Francisco, who deserves great credit for the

careful training given to the children, and for her successful conduct of the hour, one of the most attractive in the Convention.

The boys and girls had an opportunity to greet President Clark and to listen to his pleasant words. Dr. Clark introduced the first Corean Endeavorer, Ye Seung-ku, son of the Minister of Foreign Affairs. He has come to this country for his education.

Miss Newton, of Foochow, China, was next presented, and she handed to Father Clark a silk banner with an inscription on it in Chinese, meaning, "Come to China and help us." Miss Newton said that she offered it as a gift from the Endeavorers of that part of the world to the United Society, and Dr. Clark thanked her in the name of that organization.

A flashlight photograph was then taken of the children on the platform who had taken part in the "Junior Garden," and the annual rally of the Junior Christian Endeavorers was at an end.

Woodward's Pavilion.

Greater crowds! More enthusiasm! More practical results! Most certainly the new manner of considering the principles and methods of Christian Endeavor in this Convention was eminently successful. It was what it was advertised to be : "A Practical School of Christian Endeavor Methods and Ways of Working." This was true of the Convention as a whole; peculiarly true of the Monday afternoon session in Woodward's Pavilion.

Everybody could not attend the Junior Rally. The Juniors themselves must go. Others got into the Mechanics' Pavilion, if they could. The rest crowded Woodward's and were well repaid.

Secretary Baer presided, and to his efforts is largely due the value of the session. After the praise service, conducted by Mr. J. J. Morris, of Oakland, Mr. Baer offered prayer

The Chinese quartette sang "Be Glad In the Lord," and the audience cordially applauded.

The first paper presented was upon "The Lookout Committee," by Mr. A. E. MacDonald, president of the Chicago Christian Endeavor Union.

Paper by Mr. A. E. MacDonald, Chicago.

Each Christian Endeavor committee is the most important one. Paradoxical as this may seem, nevertheless it is true, or ought to be true, that each Endeavorer believes that the committee of which he is a member is the most important one, and uses every effort to make his work so effective that others will agree with him in this opinion. What the society is along the line of fidelity, earnestness, and efficiency depends largely upon the Lookout Committee. It goes without saying that this committee should be composed of the best material in the society. Its members should possess common sense in large measure, tact, plenty of unselfish energy, a deep and earnest consecration, and an ambition to be used of Christ for the advancement of his cause.

I would emphasize as its most important work the admission of new members. How can we manage to admit only those who will prove faithful and zealous? I am afraid members are sometimes admitted carelessly. In our desire to swell our numbers, we are sometimes not careful enough about finding out if the candidate is ready to take upon himself the responsibilities membership involves. I believe the candidate ought to meet with the committee and have the pledge carefully explained, and then be questioned as to his desire and purpose to keep prayerfully all of its requirements. And to this end I believe the committee should have a weekly meeting, and have it understood when and where it is held, so that the entrance door to the society may be always open to receive any who are willing to enter. If this plan is followed, no one can become a member ignorant of what membership means, as I fear it is now sometimes the case.

Proper care about the admission of members does away with much of the work necessary to be done in looking after the members when they are carelessly admitted, and this duty of looking after members is second only in importance to that of their admission.

This, you know, is a delicate and difficult task. The constitution says that any one absent and unexcused from three consecration meetings should be dropped from membership. But don't wait till he is absent from three consecration meetings, or from three regular weekly meetings; but go and see him after he is absent from one regular weekly meeting. He will see you are interested in him, and you may be able to save him to the society by preventing him from drifting away; but if after faithful, prayerful, earnest effort on the part of the Lookout Committee a member persists in absenting himself from the meetings, drop him from membership. You have not severed the connection; he has done it by his unfaithfulness, and it is better for your society and its influence to have it known that such persons are no longer members. You must not, however, relax your efforts in his behalf, but rather increase them.

The Lookout Committee's duty toward associate members is to see that they attend regularly the meetings, and ever keep in view and continually work for their conversion and transfer to active membership.

Societies which do not have a regular form of admission of members neglect an opportunity, which no society can afford to do, of impressing upon those received and all present something of the responsibility of the step taken, by a brief but impressive service led by the president, the candidates standing in front and answering a few questions as to their desire to become members and their purpose to assume the duties of membership.

The Lookout Committee should aim to secure from every active member some participation in every Christian Endeavor meeting. An impossibility! you say. No, not if you have been as careful about admission as I have indicated, for if you have been they will all want to participate and be prepared to do so.

The "open parliament," which followed the reading of the paper was conducted by T. J. Grant Shields, of Philadelphia. Mr. Shields asked for suggestions from those present, and the answers came from all parts of the building, from gray-haired fathers and mothers, and from some of the youngest delegates present. The first question put was "How to get rid of unworthy members?" And an answer came quickly from a young man, "Convert them," which raised a hearty cheer. "What is the best plan to convert them?" asked Mr. Shields, and a lady in the gallery replied, "Hold prayer-meetings." Other suggestions were "By praying," "Embrace Jesus," "Give them the Gospel," and many to the same effect. Another question was, "Where shall we draw the line in taking in new members?" and the replies were of all characters. Other questions were, "How to keep ex-presidents interested in the work?" "What shall we do with young people who don't attend the meetings?" "How can we secure punctuality in starting meetings?" to which the delegates who answered told of the modes in vogue in their various societies.

"The Prayer-meeting Committee" was the subject of the next paper, presented by Miss Lillie M. Dieter, Sedalia, Mo.

Paper by Miss Lillie M. Dieter, Sedalia, Mo.

Our Christian Endeavor Societies exist for the purpose of making strong, well-developed, serviceable Christians for the cause of Christ. The Endeavor mission is soul-winning. Though in one sense the conversion of souls is all God's work, in another sense it is our work as well, and we are unfaithful to our trust, unmindful to our duty, unless we do our part. The prayer-meeting is the people's opportunity. Dr. Goodell has said, "It is a place for replenishing the daily losses of the soul." Since the prayer-meeting is like a fountain of refreshment, it is imperative that the Prayer-meeting Committee be composed of the most earnest and devout members, who are constantly endeavoring to make this fountain the source of true spiritual growth.

The duties of the Prayer-meeting Committee may be considered under two heads; namely, General and Special.

General Duties. To select leaders and topics. The leader should be chosen with the greatest care, for spiritual blessings cannot be expected when the leader is a Christian Endeavorer in name only.

To see that each meeting is a good one.

To help new and timid members take some specified part. Notify them in advance of the meeting, and encourage them at every opportunity.

To appoint a number of subordinate helpers. It shall be the duty of these helpers to instantly follow the leader with remarks; to attend each meeting with definite grounds of assurance that participation shall not lag; to keep a list of names of all the persons whose voices are never heard in the prayer-meetings.

Special duties. Assign individuals to individuals. (Do not make this known outside of your own committee.) To the heart of every one there is some open highway or quiet byway, if we can only find it. The active member should not rest contented until the one specially committed to him has had every good influence thrown around him which may bring him to Christ.

Do something. Pray, testify, quote Scripture, read short articles on the topics, read from the Bible, and sing. Forget self and be used simply as a "vessel meet for the Master's use."

Take a front seat. Collect the coals together and they will make a heap, while scattered they die out. It always enthuses the leader to have you close to him.

See that the meeting does not drag. If there is an indication of a "depressing weight," be quick to call for a verse of some familiar hymn, or a chain of sentence prayers for some particular thing.

Pray. Ask others to pray. Pray in private, pray in public, pray always. Live a life that is worthy of example — a pure, unselfish, godly life. Our best life should be brought into the prayer-meeting, that it may be made the register of all the best thoughts and feelings, struggles, and triumphs of each week.

Care must be exercised that the prayer-meeting is not made a literary meeting. Its object is spirituality. A recitation is a good thing if it is recited "in the name of Christ." Uniformity becomes monotonous and irksome, and interest soon begins to wane; but with the tact and ingenuity of the Prayer-meeting Committee, spice may be added to the service.

The one question above all others that is ever before this committee is, "How can we make our meeting an ideal meeting?" "How can we make our meetings more effective?" It is only through variety that our ideal meeting is created, for the ideal prayer-meeting *never happens;* in other words, it is not a thing of chance. If it is a good meeting, some one has put prayer and thought and work into it.

The laws of grace are as rigid and as reliable, too, as the laws of nature. "Heaven may be had for the asking," says the poet, but the ideal prayer-meeting cannot. The ideal prayer-meeting has an object as well as a subject — a definite object, never to be forgotten by the leader or committee. What is that object? It is not simply to have an interesting or a lively meeting. A service may be interesting, lively, and even vivacious, and yet be so devoid of spirituality as to suggest only "some sounding brass and tinkling cymbals." Then what is the real object which the Prayer-meeting Committee has in view? Why does it strive so hard to raise the standard of its meetings? Is it for self-praise or the plaudits of men? No; emphatically no. Our Society badge, the little pin formed of the two letters "C.E." reveals the secret of our committee's desire for our ideal meeting. Some, perhaps, see nothing in this wonderful little monogram but the letters "C.E." Others interpret it "Christian Endeavor;" but to the consecrated, earnest Prayer-meeting Committee it has a higher and a broader meaning; to the members of this committee it means Christ Exalted. The model Prayer-meeting Committee must exalt Christ in the prayer-meeting, and thereby win souls to him.

"And if I be lifted up, I will draw all men unto me." The Prayer-meeting Committee is working for Christ, not for self. A sculptor, one of the old masters, whose touch transformed into beauty and almost priceless worth the cold, hard marble, wore ever, while at work, a tiny lamp in his cap, that no shadow of himself might fall upon his work. If the light of Christ be upon the Prayer-meeting Committee, self will sink into insignificance, and no shadow of its own shall mar the work it is doing "for Christ and the Church."

The "open parliament" on the paper was conducted by John H. Cary, of Baltimore, Md. He suggested that, instead of delegates telling of the troubles that existed in their committees on prayer-meeting, they suggest the best means how to do the work which was the duty of that committee. He called for experiences which had helped the work of the committee. Some of the suggestions were : " Preliminary prayer-meetings ;" " Make every one read *The Golden Rule ;*" " Hold a prayer-meeting with the leader of the committee before the regular meeting ;" " Be ready to follow the leader at all times ;" and " Hold open-air services."

Mr. Chas. A. Forse, St. Louis, Mo., presented a paper upon " The Social Committee."

Paper by Mr. C. A. Forse, St. Louis.

Some time ago my sister, whose hobby is Social Committee work, received a request from Mr. Baer for this paper; but, as she could not be with you, I bring her message to you.

For many years it has been a problem with church workers how to reach and interest those who do not attend regular services — how to get them into the society of the church-members. They remain away because they feel nothing in common with churchgoers. They have different amusements and different tastes for amusements. If they can be interested in the amusements of the Christian part of the community, one point is gained. To cover this, the church societies and church workers must make their church home attractive. To my mind, one of the most important of all the committees in the Endeavor Society is the Social Committee. The members of this committee have such a grand opportunity for doing good! The very brightest and most talented, as well as the consecrated and sensible young people in the society, are needed to plan and execute the work, if the social life is to be a well-spring of joy and good. The chairman of each committee is practically responsible for the young people of her committee, and should not fail to secure the co-operation of every member of it. The greatest harmony is necessary for success. Self must be forgotten in order to do anything on this committee. But some one objects to serving on this committee; it means so much hard work. Did not our Master set us the example of tireless, loving, enthusiastic endeavor to reach men and keep them? And is not this the work of the Social Committee? Put upon the Social Committee at least one person who is large-headed and large-hearted enough to appreciate the magnitude and possibilities of good which may be done, so that the committee will be inspired with the condition that they may, if faithful, do in this way Christ's work as really as in the prayer-meeting.

The first work of the newly elected Social Committee is to see that all members are personally acquainted, attending to new members and associate members especially, and welcoming, if possible, each member every Sunday evening with a smile and a handshake, and be in truth what our dear Dr. Clark so aptly calls us, "The Smile 'em Up Committee." Another very important duty of the Social Committee is to plan and conduct the periodical socials. If they do these things well, they have their hands full. Young people need and will have some sort of social life. It is not wicked, it is not injurious, but right and healthy and good for us to enjoy so much society, so long as we do not abuse our privilege, and for this reason I believe in having church socials and in having them often. Don't have all your socials money-making schemes. Don't let outsiders think they have to pay to go in every time the church door is open. Spend a few dollars now and then for a free social — you won't lose by it when you do charge. To raise funds is not the only point to be gained. The renewing of acquaintances, the formation of new friendships, the introduction of strangers, and the mingling together on a common social footing are deserving of the greatest consideration and attention, and certainly, without these features, financial success would be impossible. Genuine sociability is another important factor. To get people to come is one thing; to have them glad to be there and anxious to come again is another. Have a cordial greeting, and a word of welcome, for all, especially those who may feel neglected and strangers. We need not confine ourselves to concerts, lectures, and dull amateur debating meetings, but open the way for something better, at least for a change. Show outsiders the devil hasn't all the good things of this life. Pure, wholesome, laugh-producing or instructive entertainment is always at hand if we will only make use of it.

Once in two or three weeks is not too often to have a church social. Your success will depend, not so much upon what entertainment you decide to give, but upon the enthusiasm and push you put into it. If you are determined to make it go, and work faithfully and unitedly in that direction, you cannot fail. If, on the other hand, you don't believe it will be a success, for this reason, or that, or the other, you need have no fear but that it will be a complete failure.

In large churches or societies, where socials are frequently given, it is well to make an alphabetical division of the membership, thus dividing the work and responsibility, and at the same time making each one feel that they have a special part in the social work. Thus the A, B, C and D's give the January social, arranging the program, and serving the lunch. The E, F, G and H's give the February social, and so on, until the alphabet is exhausted. This causes each one to feel individual responsibility for success. Do not be discouraged if some evenings your gatherings are small. Look up the reason, and correct the fault. If the church were only as anxious to give the young men social food as it is to administer spiritual food, there would be little need of asking, "Where is my wandering boy to-night?" Where does the social power of the saloon and billiard-hall lie? Is it the liquor alone, or the game alone, that attracts the young man? It is not difficult to see that many a man frequents these places almost solely on account of the social enjoyment he gets there. Few young men drink in the privacy of their rooms as compared with the vast multitudes that throng the saloons.

The social problem is one that the church must grapple with.

Young men who frequent saloons will not desert them for religious services merely. The church must give them something to take the place of that which they have left. They are asked to give up good company, gaily lighted rooms and entertainment, and they must be given something to replace these. It is the mission of the church to do this. Sunday and week-day religious functions alone will not suffice. Once in perhaps every three months have an entertainment on a large scale, in your church or some hall. Give an honest return for all you get, and conduct everything in a business-like manner. Never let the price of admission bar any one from attending, remembering that those to whom the price is no object always have the privilege of making extra contributions if they wish.

Avoid all objectionable features,—chances of all kinds, fish-ponds, grab-bags. There are enough bright, innocent, and attractive features, without employing any of these methods to increase the funds. A competent person should be placed in charge to direct the work in general, and to whom all important matters may be referred.

It should be understood from the beginning that no questionable feature will be tolerated, and that honest, which means moderate, prices for everything must prevail; that to buy is optional, the same as when dealing with any business firm. There is no better or cheaper way of advertising a church entertainment than by selling tickets. Many will purchase, desiring to aid in the work, who are unable to attend.

This, however, must always be pleasantly and courteously done, remembering that to buy is not obligatory, and that all who wish to, have the privilege to decline. When the importance of these things is understood, and the principle applied, entertainments of this kind will receive a more liberal patronage, and will be anticipated with pleasure by many who would not otherwise attend.

In conclusion, dear fellow-workers, remember that the way to be sociable is to be sociable.

An "open parliament" followed the reading of the paper and was in charge of W. H. Lewis, of Seattle, Wash. Many suggestions were made as to the best means of helping the Social Committee. Among the suggestions were: "Have a committee to be at the doors to welcome all;" "Have one at the doors to say good-night;" "Be sociable at the meeting, and not after it." Much laughter was caused by one young lady asking the question, "What can we do to get the young men to attend a social — we never have enough to go around?" None of the delegates seemed able to answer the query.

After Clement Rowan had sung "The Handwriting on the Wall," the congregation joined in singing "The Banner of the Cross." A brief prayer service followed, under the direction of Mr. Baer.

The paper then presented was upon the mission and work of "The Missionary Committee." The speaker was Miss Frances B. Patterson, Chicago, Ill.

Paper by Miss Frances B. Patterson, Chicago.

A live Missionary Committee should take for its motto, " Prayer and pains, through faith in Jesus Christ, will do anything."

Its object. The awakening of an intelligent missionary enthusiasm in every member; an earnest, prayerful determination, either to go and carry the glad tidings of a loving, personal Saviour to those who know it not, or to send those who will go.

Sometimes our enthusiasm is of the soda-water kind — a great deal of fizz and that 's all. We want an intelligent enthusiasm that will accomplish something for the Master and his kingdom.

To attain this object, have regular, wide-awake missionary meetings. Make free use of maps, charts, object-lessons, etc. Always throw part of the meeting open for general discussion. Plan to get independent thought and study. Keep out of ruts. Meet the need of the hour. When the attention of all the world is directed toward famine-stricken India, that is the time to have a meeting on India, and tell how our missionaries are carrying the Bread of Life to the people. When our hearts are wrung by the sufferings of our Armenian brethren, that is the time to bring our members in touch with our heroic missionaries in Turkey. When our sympathy goes out to Cuba, struggling, bleeding, dying for liberty and truth, that is the time to study and present the need in Papal lands. In every meeting have a definite purpose, and expect results. " If ye ask anything according to my will, ye have the petition ye have desired of me."

Start a missionary library. Begin with a few live books, such as " Life of John G. Paton," "Life of David Livingstone," " Bishop's Conversion," " Neglected Continent," " Murdered Millions," " Rule of the Turk," " Retrospect," " New Acts of the Apostles," " Our Country," and " By Canoe and Dog-Train." Get them read. Have speakers refer to them in missionary meetings. Place a bulletin-board in your prayer-meeting room, and refer to chapters of books and recent magazine articles. Follow constantly by personal, persistent, prayerful work. Never give out a book or leaflet without earnest prayer that God will use it for his glory. It is impossible to estimate the results in prayer, time, money, and lives given to the Master's work in all the world.

In one county in Illinois, the county-seat took the Missionary Extension Course. Missionary Campaigns were carried through the county, the large societies started missionary libraries, and the county officers bought a library and circulated it through all other societies. In one year gifts to missions increased one hundred per cent in that county, and its president gave his life to the work.

Aim to have every member of your society enrolled in The Tenth Legion. " Render unto God the things that are God's." The tenth is but the low-water mark of Christian giving; and yet if all the Christians of these United States gave only one-tenth; the gospel could be preached to every creature in this generation. This is a crisis time. The missionary advance has been checked at home and abroad. Our Master calls us to larger service. Our Chinese brethren here in the First Congregational Mission put many of us to shame. Oh, let us be more faithful to the great trust the Master has committed to us.

One little country society at North Hume, Illinois, meeting in a schoolhouse, with only twenty-two members, eleven of them so poor they could give nothing but their prayers, have for three years given $300 per year to support their own missionary in inland China. Do you wonder they write much of spiritual blessing received?. The day is coming when not a church or Christian Endeavor Society in this land will dare to sit under gospel privileges here at home, and not support one of their own number on the foreign field. Will you hasten the coming of that day?

Lastly, remember that all methods of work, even the best and brightest, are simply useless and worse than useless — just so much dead machinery — unless the Spirit of the Living God breathes into them life that is life indeed. Look to him for guidance every step of the way. His promises are not thin ice, but solid rock under our feet. Let us step out upon them, and trust him for the result. Do not say, " Oh, we are just a weak society — we can't do very much." Dear friends, we can do just as much as we are willing to let the Lord Jesus Christ do through us. He is saying to each of us here to-day, " My grace is sufficient for thee, for my strength is made perfect in weakness." Oh, let us put our weakness into his strength and let him work through us for the glory of his kingdom. With every tick of the watch one soul passes from Time to Eternity, without knowing the love of Christ. Awful responsibility ! With every tick of the watch one soul is born into the world who will never know the love of Christ unless we tell them. Glorious opportunity ! It comes but once. Once only to live in a world of sin ; once to suffer ; once to tell the story ; once to hold a stewardship ; once to pray ! " The night cometh when no man can work." The day is still ours. What will we do with it ? Will we let him live in us ? Think of it ! " Christ our Life,"— our life of prevailing prayer, our strength, our humility, our love and joy. He will speak through us, love through us, live through us. Why be discouraged with him for our life? Why suffer defeat if he dwells within? What is here that we cannot do in him? "The things that are impossible with men are possible with God." "All things are possible to him that believeth." Oh, "that your faith might not stand in the wisdom of men, but in the power of God."

H. N. Lathrop, of the Clarendon Street Baptist Church, of Boston, led a ten-minute open parliament on "Ways of Working." His society, he said, led on the missionary roll of honor, and it did it by changing its method of collecting from quarterly to monthly and then weekly. They made it a point to take up a collection at every meeting. Fifteen per cent of the money raised was used for the expenses of the society and the other 85 per cent was given to home and foreign missions. Where it was possible he advised that there be separate committees for home and foreign missions, as where one committee was in charge of both, one or the other, and usually the home missions, was apt to be neglected. He asked how many present were members of societies that had separate committees for these two branches of the work. Nearly half of the audience rose, as indicating that their societies thus divided the work. Fully fifty rose as indicating that they belonged to societies that supported a missionary in the field. "Now I want you to tell me," he said, "how to raise money for missions." "Get your hand under your own money and lift" was the immediate response from a man in the gallery, which raised a laugh all over the hall.

"The Other Committees" was the topic of a paper by Mr. Miles M. Shand, of Washington, D. C.

Paper by Miles M. Shand, Washington, D. C.

Christian Endeavor reaches out in many helpful ways of service, and so in every large society at least, many other committees than those already mentioned here to-day find abundant opportunity for doing good. It is absolutely necessary for the full development and prosperity of a large society that its work should be many-sided, and that so far as is possible, every pathway opening up should be trodden by willing feet, and every inviting field should be cultivated.

With but a single exception, all the committees I shall speak of exist in the society of which I have the honor to be a member. They are these. First, the Executive Committee, whose meetings are the cabinet meetings. All matters of importance should first be considered by the Executive Committee, and the unanimous result of its careful and prayerful consideration should be presented in good form to the society for its action. It seems to me that then all unseemly debate would be avoided, and everything done decently and in order, and with heartiness.

The Sunday-school and the Christian Endeavor Society should be very closely connected, and the Sunday-school Committee may assist in bringing this good thing to pass; and so I think that whenever it is possible there should be a Sunday-school Committee.

One of the most important committees is the Music Committee. Yet it is painfully true that the great field for usefulness for this committee is not always appreciated, nor its opportunities improved. Do we not come together in our meetings to worship the great Creator, our Heavenly Father? Surely, the hymns we sing, and the manner in which we sing them, have much to do with making our meetings worshipful; and it has been my prayer, "O Lord, send us a revival of hymnology."

Allow me to give you a little personal experience in that line. I have within the past two years led more than sixty regular prayer-meetings in more than sixty different Christian Endeavor Societies, and in the large majority of those places we have used simply the old standard hymns of the church. And again and again and again have the audiences been delighted and surprised — surprised that we used these hymns, and more surprised that there were such hymns, very often.

Then there is the Flower Committee, the members of which take God's thoughts woven in pansies, and roses, and violets, and other beautiful flowers, to the sick and suffering ones, with a pretty card or a little visit, when, if possible, God's Word is read and prayer offered. This is one of the loving services which I think is most acceptable to our dear Lord.

The Relief Committee, in many societies, is a prime necessity. In Calvary Church this committee works directly with the deacons and our Sunday-school missionary. Let me mention two phases of its work which are most important. We have a large storehouse in which are kept clothing and articles of food, which may be dealt out as needed all through the winter months. Another feature is giving car-rides and carriage-rides to the sick and suffering little ones, especially those who otherwise could not get out of their homes; also having little picnic parties for them.

Culture for service is a demand. The Lord ought to have the best there is in everything. The Good-Literature Committee may help in this direction of culture in various ways. It may make many a desert life to blossom as the garden of the Lord as the intellect is led captive and the young man or woman, the boy or girl, is made to feel the necessity for intelligent service and to improve the mind.

Then there is the Calling Committee, who have the special duty of calling on strangers, newcomers, and others.

There is also the Strangers' Committee, whose special duty should be to look out for strangers, invite hotel guests and all visitors to the church.

Then there is the Good-Citizenship Committee, which has a great place in these days, and I need not emphasize its importance. Washington has a peculiar government, and our Good-Citizenship Committees in the various Christian Endeavor Societies have, during the past year, been operating with outside Good-Citizenship Committees in anti-saloon work, and in the endeavor to prevail upon Congress to pass several laws which we believe are imperatively demanded from all over the country. Petitions have come universally for the enactment of these laws, and being upon the ground, we have kept in close touch with Congress, and have done all in our power to hasten the day of righteousness, which, may it please God, may soon dawn upon us.

Then there is the Denominational Committee, whose influence, wisely exerted in a Christianlike spirit, may help very much for Christ and the church.

There is also the Information Committee, which is very important. Its province may be to bring to the attention of the young people many wonderful things happening in the kingdom in these days.

The Press Committee is a very important one, which will let the world know, through the secular papers, some of the best things that are being done for Christ. Its members may also edit and publish church papers, and perhaps take charge of all the printed matter issued by the church.

And now let me mention, as the last committee, what is, in my opinion, the most important line of work in which the church ought to be interested in these days,—the Committee on Systematic Beneficence, or the Tithing Committee. The great need of the Christian Church to-day is that the pocket-books of the Christian world may be unloosed. The great need of the church and world is the blessing of the Lord. Listen. Thus saith the Lord: "Bring ye all the tithes into the storehouse, that there may be meat in mine house, and prove me now herewith, saith the Lord of Hosts, if I will not open the windows of heaven, and pour you out a blessing, that there shall not be room enough to receive it." If it be true that our greatest spiritual uplift, and our greatest spiritual blessings, shall come along the lines of our giving, don't you think that this committee, which ought to be in every Endeavor Society in our land, is the most important committee? I think it will be, if it is not now.

So, as our societies go out into all these and other avenues of service, in the name of him whom we call Lord and Master, his blessing shall ever be upon us, and we will be gladsome, bright, and happy Christians.

In the enforced absence of H. A. Kinports, of New York, Treasurer William Shaw, of the United Society of Christian Endeavor, conducted the "open parliament" upon this paper in his customary clear and vigorous way. In ten minutes he drew forth from the audience many and various helps following the direction of the paper.

Dr. Little then sang two stanzas of "In the Secret of His Presence." The closing remarks were by Mr. Charles T. Studd, of London, Eng., upon "The Source of All Power for Service." This source he indicated as in God, and that real power comes only through entire consecration.

After the benediction, adjournment was taken until evening.

MONDAY EVENING. — CLOSING SESSION.

Mechanics' Pavilion.

If the Christian could summon together in his mind the mounts of the Scripture whereon the disciples heard the Sermon, saw the Transfiguration, and beheld Jesus "lifted up," if he could draw from these their inspiration and lessons, he would be able to form some adequate conception of the significance of the closing scenes of the Convention of '97. In those sessions the later disciples of Endeavor heard the voice of Jesus speaking to them of conduct and service, they saw him in glorious apparel, they perceived Christ on Calvary for the sins of men, and were taught self-sacrifice and forgiveness. It was no idle hour. The Holy Spirit was there; his presence was felt. Until "the books of the Judgment Day unfold" none can estimate the power and influence of the occasion. God never neglects his opportunity to strengthen the souls of his children, and to fit them for the most effective service.

The pavilion was thronged. Every space was taken. The air was laden with expectancy. The hymns and prayers were preparatory to the consummation. All who led the thought of the multitude were under divine direction. The thousands that responded moved under the power of the same unseen Spirit. Pre-eminently, it was God's time.

Dr. Clark presided and conducted the consecration service. The singing was led by Mr. A. M. Benham, of Oakland. The vast company were seated by States and countries.

After the praise service Rev. J. W. Beckett, of Baltimore, sang a much-appreciated solo.

Dr. E. R. Dille, of San Francisco, then read by request the Platform of Principles of Christian Endeavor adopted by the trustees of the United Society of Christian Endeavor.

Platform of Principles.

We reaffirm our adherence to the principles which, under God's blessing, have made the Christian Endeavor movement what it is to-day.

First and foremost, personal devotion to our divine Lord and Saviour, Jesus Christ; the Bible, the inspired word of God, the only rule of faith and practice.

Second, the covenant obligation embodied in the prayer-meeting pledge, without which there can be no true Society of Christian Endeavor.

Third, constant religious training for all kinds of service involved in the various committees, which — so many of them as are needed — are, equally with the prayer-meeting, essential to a society of Christian Endeavor.

Fourth, strenuous loyalty to the local church and denomination with which each society is connected. This loyalty is plainly expressed in the pledge; it underlies the whole idea of the movement, and, as statistics prove and pastors testify, is very generally exemplified in the lives of the active members. Thus the Society of Christian Endeavor in theory and practice is as loyal a denominational society as any in existence, as well as a broad and fraternal interdenominational society.

Fifth, we reaffirm our increasing confidence in the interdenominational spiritual fellowship through which we hope not for organic unity, but to fulfil our Lord's prayer, "That they all may be one." This fellowship already extends to all evangelical denominations, and we should greatly deplore any movement that would interrupt or imperil it.

Sixth, Christian Endeavor stands always and everywhere for Christian citizenship. It is forever opposed to the saloon, the gambling-den, the brothel, and every like iniquity. It stands for temperance, for law, for order, for a pure political atmosphere; in a word, for righteousness And this it does, not by allying itself with a political party, but by attempting, through the quick conscience of its individual members, to permeate and influence all parties and all communities.

Seventh, the Society of Christian Endeavor stands always and everywhere for the rescue and preservation of the Lord's Day, and is unalterably opposed to all forms of Sabbath desecration.

Eighth, that all moneys gathered by the various societies of Christian Endeavor for the cause of missions be always sent to the missionary boards of the special denominations to which the particular society belongs.

And also Christian Endeavor officers and societies are affectionately reminded that appeals to them for money should come through their pastors and the officers of their churches, and when such appeals are addressed to the societies directly they should be referred to the pastor and church officers for their approval before being acted upon by the society.

Also, that the causes to which the societies give should be those approved by the denominations to which the societies belong. Thus the societies avoid recognition and support of independent and irresponsible movements.

Ninth, Christian Endeavor has for its ultimate aim a purpose no less wide and lofty than the bringing of the world to Christ. Hence it is an organization intensely evangelistic and missionary in its spirit, and desires to do all it may, under the direction of the churches and the missionary boards, for missionary extension the world around.

These objects it seeks to accomplish, while it remembers that it is an influence rather than an institution; that its united societies and its State, provincial, and local unions have no legislative functions; that they can levy no taxes and control no local society, which is always and only under the control of its own church. The duties of these unions are limited to matters of information, inspiration, and fellowship.

We rejoice in the growing friendliness of Christians and in the fact that more and more as the true spirit of Christian Endeavor is understood in every evangelical Protestant denomination the world around, with but one or two exceptions, our fellowship is constantly growing larger.

We believe that for the sake of Christian fairness and courtesy in all denominations and all over the world the Christian Endeavor principles should go with the name, and the name, either alone or in connection with a distinctive denominational name, should go with the principles.

For the maintenance of these principles of covenant obligation, individual service, denominational loyalty, and interdenominational fellowship we unitedly and heartily pledge ourselves. _____

The following resolution was unanimously adopted at the Minneapolis Convention, and is reaffirmed at San Francisco : —

Resolved, That, as from the beginning, we stand upon an evangelical basis (meaning by "evangelical," personal faith in the divine human person and atoning work of our Lord and Saviour, Jesus Christ, as the only and sufficient source of salvation), and we recommend that, as in the United Society, only societies connected with evangelical churches be enrolled on the list of State and local unions.

The registrar, Dr. E. E. Kelley, then presented the statistics of the Convention. He stated that the figures more nearly represented the actual number of Christian Endeavorers in attendance than previous reports had done. It should be added that the number of visitors in the city coming upon Christian Endeavor trains — but not registered Endeavorers — would raise the total to upwards of 40,000. As the names of States having large attendance were called, a generous applause came from the assembly. This was also true in reference to foreign lands.

Statistics of the Convention of 1897.

STATES REPRESENTED.

Alaska .	3	New Mexico	.	29
Alabama	20	Mississippi .	.	31
Arizona	20	Missouri		566
Arkansas .	35	North and South Carolina		13
Colorado . .	243	Nebraska . .	.	288
Connecticut . .	276	New Hampshire		109
Delaware	24	New Jersey .	. .	329
District of Columbia	95	New York . .		596
Floating Societies .	29	North Dakota	.	23
Florida .	10	Ohio .	. . .	814
Georgia .	23	Nevada		53
Idaho	46	Oklahoma		36
Illinois .	1,083	Oregon . . .		505
Indiana	479	Pennsylvania		859
Indian Territory . . .	6	Rhode Island .		51
Iowa .	920	South Dakota .	.	57
Kansas .	366	Tennessee		57
Kentucky .	100	Texas		133
Louisiana .	19	Utah . .		69
Maine .	74	Vermont .		57
Maryland . .	124	Virginia .		79
Massachusetts	523	Washington	.	265
Michigan .	289	West Virginia		81
Minnesota	261	Wisconsin		284
Montana	63	Wyoming .		12

FOREIGN DELEGATES.

Hawaii	20	Japan	4
Canada	222	China	1
Scotland	2	Australia	3
France	3	South America	1
England	4	India	2
Palestine	1	Ceylon	1

TOTALS.

OUTSIDE OF CALIFORNIA	11,260
CALIFORNIA	12,694
JUNIORS	2,500
TOTAL	26,454

The evening's devotions were conducted by Rev. A. H. Harshaw, of Junction City, Kansas. At his request Rev. John Thompson, the oldest missionary present, read the scripture lesson. Mr. Harshaw offered an earnest prayer.

Dr. Clark, in opening the service, said : —

" I hope our friends who happen not to be Christian Endeavorers or who are without badges will consider themselves thoroughly welcome. It has been impossible to supply all with badges, so great has been the rush. I have made a careful calculation, and I am satisfied that 40,000 at least have journeyed to this great city. I also find that between 300,000 and 400,000 have attended the meetings here and elsewhere.

" But now we come to the closing exercises. It is proper that we should thank those who have helped to entertain us. These are hospitable people, these San Franciscans, and I hardly know where to begin. If I leave any one out I want it understood that it was not intentional. The pastors have thrown wide open their doors. The Committee of '97 has done wonders, while the ushers and the committees on hall and music have helped in a way which can only earn our lasting and heartfelt gratitude. The policemen at the doors and on the streets have been uniformly courteous. The newspapers have published exhaustive accounts of our deliberations and, in my opinion, they are the best in the world. The hotels and the clerks and the motormen and the porters and the conductors — who shall I leave out? — have all been kindness itself. Our hearts are overflowing with love and thanks to those who have helped to make this Convention what it has been.

" Now, my friends, we have come to the closing scene, to the last hours, when I think we can best serve God by absolute quietness. Let this show our appreciation. When we leave here let us feel that we have been face to face with God. In conclusion, I take pleasure in introducing to you Dr. George F. Pentecost, of Yonkers, N. Y."

Sermon by Rev. George F. Pentecost, D.D., Yonkers, N. Y.

Dear Christian Endeavorers: — It seldom falls to the lot of a man to have the privilege and responsibility of speaking to you such words as I am bidden to speak to you to-night, and upon such occasion as this. I hope that whilst you give me your attention you will also be silently lifting up your voices to God, that I may be helped in the message that I shall attempt to bring to you, and that that message may be accompanied by the Holy Ghost sent down from heaven, without which accompaniment all my words would be as sounding brass and tinkling cymbals.

My text is found in the 13th chapter of the gospel according to St. Mark, the 34th verse: " The Son of Man is as a man taking a far journey, who left his house and gave authority to his servants and to every man his work, and commanded the porter to watch." The particular words in this brief, beautiful, and suggestive parable which I have chosen for my text, are these: " And to every man his work."

I have been profoundly impressed, as no doubt all of you have been profoundly impressed, by the magnificent cumulative force of such a vast gathering of picked and representative Christian young men and women as have been gathered in this city during the past week. And we doubtless have thought that if we might take this meeting, and project it into every city of the United States, throw its combined force as a convention against all opposing forces of sin, and use its combined power for the uplifting and the furthering of every good cause that we have at heart, what mighty results might be accomplished !

But another thought has been possessing my mind during these last few days. To-morrow we shall begin to scatter; we shall go back to our homes; we shall sink, as it were, our autonomous character into our individual characters. And the message that I have to bring to you to-night bears upon the individuality of our responsibility to God as Christian Endeavorers. The measure of the work which the Christian Endeavorers shall accomplish in time to come will be the measure, not of a great aggregation of men and women in a society, but it will be the measure of the faithful performance of the work which Christ has given each one of us to do.

To every man his work. It is one of the fundamental principles and teachings of the Gospel that there is no salvation where there is no service. " Come unto me, all ye that labor and are heavy laden, and I will give you rest." But the text does not end there: " Take my yoke upon you and learn of me, and ye shall find rest unto your souls."

We are told that in that great day when we are summoned to appear before the judgment-seat of Christ — not the great white throne where the godliest shall appear, but the judgment-seat of Christ, where the Christians will appear — that every man must give an account of his work to God.

The Christian Endeavor Society as such is probably not known in the judgment records of our Lord Jesus Christ. No particular church is known as such, I believe, in heaven. The records of that great day will be the records of individual lives, not of the society lives of each one of us, or of the society doings; not of churches or ecclesiastical organizations. But one by one, as the individual servant of Jesus Christ, each one must give an account of his or her stewardship to him. This is a solemn, and it ought to be an inspiring, truth to every one of us. Just as we were called into the kingdom of God, not by masses — not by hundreds, or by fifties, or by tens, or by twos — but one by one, as the word and the spirit of God came to our individual hearts, so one by one, notwithstanding our association into societies and into churches, we must take our individual way through this world, and each one of us must do his individual work.

My first suggestion, then, is the individuality of our relation to Christ, both for salvation and for service, and the individuality of our responsibility as Christian Endeavorers. The second thought that is suggested to me as I pass briefly, without elaborating them, is that work is the supreme characteristic of the Christian man or woman. Our Lord Jesus Christ, when he stood, a little boy twelve years of age, in the temple, with the consciousness of who he was and what his relations to his Father were, and what his relations to his human mother and his foster-father were, and what his relations to all the world were, turned in sublime utterance and said to the mother and the father who chided him for absenting himself from their company on their way back to their Nazarene home, " Wist ye not that I must be about my Father's business?" And from the time Jesus was a little boy, during all those years which have been covered by the silent record, I believe that Jesus Christ was occupied with the great thought of the work which God had given him to do. When he sat by the well-side and talked to that poor Samaritan woman, and his disciples wondered that he had not been concerned about his food, he said, " I have meat to eat that ye know not of. My meat is to do the will of him who sent me, and to finish his work." Again, and again, and again he reminded us that we must work while it is day, "For the night cometh when no man can work." And our Lord Jesus Christ crowded every day, and every hour, and every moment of his waking time with conscientious, sincere, exhaustive work for God. " My Father worked hitherto, and I work."

It is delightful to indulge ourselves in the sweet emotional experiences which come to us as Christians. It is delightful for us to gather ourselves together in such assemblies as this, and to give expression to our enthusiasm in tears and in songs. But, after all, the important concern with each one of us, following the footsteps of our Master, is to be about our Father's business in this world. The world is waiting not only for experimental, emotional, and enthusiastic Christians, but for a vast host of individual Christians who realize their personal relations to God and to his Christ, and their personal responsibility for the great work which he has left us to do. In the spirit of Paul, each one of us must say to himself, " I bring up in my body and I bring up in my life, with my hands, with my time, with my talent, with all my abilities, that which remains of the work of our Lord Jesus Christ." In the great redemptive work he was alone. He trod the winepress alone. No man was with him. In the great salvation work, following upon that redemptive work, while our work comes together in a common stream at the close of time, it must be characterized by the individual rivulets which you and I contribute to the magnificent and the grand consummation of the kingdom of God.

I was told the other day by a pastor here, that for six years he lived up in these Sierras, by the side of a beautiful lake, over whose broad bosom there were occasional flocks of geese, and in whose deep, pellucid waters there were many beautiful and game fish. That lake, he said, was simply for years a place to him where he could shoot a few ducks and catch a few fish. But it seems that the conception came to some one to utilize that vast body of beautiful water, sleeping there under the skies, by turning its waters into a great fertilizing and power-generating channel. Now, the lake that for centuries lay there, only the home of the wild fowl and of the fish, is sending forth a stream of power hitherto wasted by misdirected and undirected force; is sending forth a stream of power that is estimated to amount to four millions of horse-power, for the generation of electricity, besides the spread of its waters through ten thousand different channels, over the arid plains, and through the rich, unfertilized valleys.

So, my friends, there is in you and me a lake of unutilized force. The thing for us to do is to make a channel for the outflowing of those forces, to harness and direct those forces, and turn them into streams of power, and into channels for the fertilization of the country around about us. Out of you shall flow rivers of living water. See to it that these rivers of living water are not dammed-up lakes in your lives. Apprehending our individual responsibility to Christ and the vast potency of the spirit of God in each and every one of us who have been brought by that spirit to a knowledge of Jesus Christ, let us make our work count in the great cause of our Master.

The apostle said in the conclusion of that magnificent chapter, the 15th of the First Corinthians, where he has guaranteed to us, through Jesus Christ, resurrection, and therefore life and immortality. " Wherefore, my beloved brethren, be ye steadfast, unmovable, always abounding in the work of the Lord, knowing that your labor is not vain in the Lord."

I wonder if you have ever thought that the only welcome that we have any knowledge of, to be extended to us as we pass through the pearly gates of yonder portal, will be, not to us as children of God, but to us as servants of Jesus Christ : " Well done, good and faithful servant, enter *thou* into the joy of thy Lord." It is not to the Son but to the servant of God that that abundant welcome is given. Just as Jesus was introduced to the world once as the beloved Son of God, so he was introduced to the world from heaven as the beloved servant of God : " Behold my servant, my beloved, in whom my soul has delight." God had delight in his Son as his Son was his great servant, meting out his grace without stint to the world whom God loved, and for whom he gave his Son Jesus Christ a ransom.

Now let me pass rapidly to the application of these two principles : individuality of the Christian life, and the individual responsibility of the Christian for service. If every Christian man and every Christian woman in our churches in America — if we were realizing what is one of the desires of the Christian Endeavorers, and that instead of one-tenth of the communicants in the Christian churches in America being workers, nine-tenths were workers, there would be no way of estimating the vastness of the results which would accrue to the honor and glory of Jesus Christ.

But there are so many saying, " I am but one. It does n't matter if I fall out of the ranks of workers. It does n't matter much if I am not included with those who have given themselves to conscientious service for Jesus Christ. What would be the result of my little work in this world ? If I should do all that I could, and give myself without reserve to Christ, what would be the result of my individual work ? What can I do toward the bringing-about of the consummation of God's purposes in this world ? "

I wonder if any of you have ever taken the pains to ascertain what the result of a single honey-bee is in the course of a·year ? If you are like me, you are very fond of honey. I like a good, heaping tablespoonful of it on my hot cakes in the winter-time, or my biscuits, or even bread and butter ; and I have often dipped the spoon into the honey-dish, and dished out a dessertspoonful, or even a tablespoonful, of the delicious sweetness. But what is the work of a single honey-bee, starting in May — I am speaking from the Eastern standpoint, not from a Californian — and working from morn till dewy eve through all the days until the end of September or into October, traversing thousands of miles, visiting ten thousand flowers, and sucking the honey from a million petals and stamens. How much honey do you suppose one honey-bee sucks in the course of those weeks and months, all those miles of fields traversed, and all those tens of thousands of flowers visited and sucked dry ? A little more than one-quarter of a teaspoonful. Think of it ! And yet, California alone exports hundreds of tons of honey. What is the secret of it ? It is that of the two hundred or three hundred or four hundred or five hundred thousand of bees that are massed together in the hives, each is contributing his quarter of a teaspoonful, and the aggregation is the splendid mass of dewy sweetness for the world. No single bee can afford to draw out of the hive, because, after all, his contribution is only so small. No smallest or least Christian can afford to draw out of the great army of workers because, looking at his work individually, it is so small or so insignificant.

But some have said to me, " I have tried Christian work, and have not succeeded. I taught a Sunday-school class ; I have tried testimony ; I have tried individually to win some soul ; I have done this and that, and being discouraged because I had no success, I have fallen out of the ranks." Some years ago I was walking down the streets of the City of Brooklyn, which was then my home, and I was attracted by a stonemason, who was laying up, with some others, the great foundation-walls on which was to rest a great warehouse. He had a block of stone weighing about one hundred and fifty pounds, I should say, before him, and with his hammer was trying to break it. He struck it a blow, and the hammer flew up ; and another blow and the hammer flew up ; and another blow ; and the stone rang its resentment ; and up went the hammer and down it came with a thud ; up it went and down it came ; up again and down again, and the contest went on, until, stopping for breath, the mason wiped his brow, and took a little dust broom and brushed away the little dust he had knocked up on the top of the stone. I took advantage of the pause, and ventured to say to him, "Well, I don't believe you will break that stone with that hammer." He looked at me rather scornfully, and perhaps catching sight of my white tie deepened the scorn, and he replied with quite a brogue — for he was an Irishman — "Shure, sir, that's all you know about breaking stone." And then he turned the stone over, put a little fulcrum under it in the shape of another small stone, and took his hammer and down it came and up it flew; and down it came and up it flew; and down it came and up it flew. He went at it and kept at it until at last I thought I detected a little change in the ring of the stone, and I thought the hammer didn't fly up quite so far. And finally, perhaps for the hundredth time, the hammer came down with a dull thud, and the stone broke into two pieces. And then Pat turned to me with triumph in his face, and said, "Would yer honor answer me one question?" I said, "I'll try." "Well, then, would your honor tell me which one of those blows it was that broke the stone?" Desiring to get a little information, I assumed a knowledge that I did not have, and said, "I suppose it was the last blow." "There," he says, "yer wrong, sir. It was the first one, and all the middle ones, *and* the last one."

My friends, that first blow that seemed to be without success had as much to do with the disintegration of those tightly knit particles as the last blow. So many of us strike a blow, and another blow, and still another in our early enthusiasm, but because the stone did not lay open in one or a dozen or a hundred efforts, we gave up. Turn it over, my friends, and hit it again. Keep at it, and even if you never see the stone broken, you have contributed to its disintegration, and somebody else will come along and hit that a blow, and perhaps somebody else still will strike another blow, and the stone will finally lay open. Never be discouraged with your work. It may be mine to hit the last blow here to-night on a stone which has been hit a hundred times before. It may be mine to hit a middle blow which will be followed up by some other of the Master's workers. But never let us be discouraged. Keep at it till the stone breaks. The scientist tells us that every blow of that hammer started a wave of motion through every particle of that stone, and under the place where the impact of that hammer first fell there began to be the work of dissolution. Let us remember that if we strike in the name of God and strike again and again, even if we only live to see a little dust knocked up on the surface of the stone, we are disintegrating that stone, and contributing to the final success of the work.

I have two other things to say, and one of those two things is this: I have heard Christian workers also say, "It is not that I am discouraged, but I am so weak; I have so little power. Why, if I should strike at a stone it would not make the least impression. What would it matter if I, with my little strength, if I, with my meagre and commonplace talents, should fall out of the rank?" I will tell you what I saw in a great gun factory. I was being shown through one of the great gun factories of the East by the superintendent, and, passing through one room, I saw suspended by a delicate chain of steel wire a cylinder of solid steel, weighing perhaps two or three hundred pounds. "What is that for?" I asked. The superintendent said, "We have been trying some experiments." I said, "What experiments?" He said, "The experiment called the superimposition of motion." I have n't the remotest idea of what that meant, but I did n't tell him so. I said, "That is the very experiment I am most anxious to know about." Hanging beside this great steel bar weighing two or three hundred pounds, and about three feet from it, hanging by a little cord of silk, was a common bottle cork, weighing perhaps half an ounce. The experiment was to see if the impact of that cork would set that two or three hundred pound steel bar in motion. I said, "Well, I can tell you right now without any experiment that it won't do it." He laughed and said that in half an hour he could demonstrate to me that it could. I said, "I will give two hours to see that." He took the little cork and lifted it with his finger and let it fall against that steel bar. It touched it as if a zephyr had touched it perhaps. He lifted it again and let it fall; lifted it again and let it fall; lifted it again and again. Five minutes seemed a long time, ten minutes seemed longer, and that bar of steel was as stolid and as immovable as the first instant the cork touched it. But he lifted it again and let it fall, lifted it and let it fall. Presently, at the end of possibly fifteen minutes, I walked up close to this bar of steel and looked at it carefully, and I thought I detected a suggestion of a shiver — as if it had a slight attack of the ague. And presently, as the cork fell again, there was just the suggestion of a movement; and before twenty-five minutes had passed, that great steel bar was swinging like a pendulum to the utmost length of its tether. That little cork did the business by its constant impact.

My dear brother, my dear sister, let me tell you that there is no mass of humanity so inert, no steel force so great, opposed to us, but that if you and I will let the Master take us in his hand and lift us up and let us fall with the strength of God in our hand, with the blessing of God behind our willingness, soon we will see the great supposedly resistless mass moving at our touch.

There are Christian Endeavorers enough on this Pacific Coast, there are Christian Endeavorers enough in all our States from which representatives have come here, and if we will lift ourselves, or let God lift us, and fall again and again and again, patiently, hopefully, believingly, we will see everything in motion under the impact of a consecrated heart and a consecrated life, however small, however insignificant, that heart or that life may be, measured by our human measurement.

Now I will use my last four minutes in this other suggestion. I have not been able to argue the question; I have only tried to leave a few pictures before your minds. And the other is this: In our work we need not only continuity; not only consecrated use, as the bee uses his time; not only the courage of hopefulness in view of our willingness, and our smallness, and our weakness; but, above all, we need to throw into this work of God all the enthusiasm we can gather from heaven. And if I were asked to-night for a definition of what the baptism of the Holy Ghost was I would not describe an experience, I would not suggest an emotion; I would say it was a great baptism of enthusiasm,— the pouring out of heavenly enthusiasm upon us like a fire to kindle everything there is in us to a flame of usefulness for Christ.

I will give you one little illustration out of many that I think of, of what enthusiasm is. In 1864 or 1865, when Mr. Moody first came back from England, in dear old Boston, in that old tabernacle so replete with memories unto this day, into the inquiry-room in Dr. Gordon's church, packed as it was with inquiring souls, empty as it was of willing workers, a poor woman came, who had walked all the way over the mill-dam from Brighton, to come to the tabernacle meeting. She had brought her babe in her arms, and all through the services the babe had slept upon its mother's breast. But when she rose to go into the inquiry-room, smitten by the word of God, she carried her babe with her. The little thing was disturbed, and began to cry. Dr. Gordon looked around the room for a worker to go to this poor woman. He could not find one, and finally, his great, tender heart full of compassion, he sat down beside that poor woman and spoke to her of the need of her soul. But you can understand how difficult it was to talk to a woman of salvation who was trying to hush the crying of a little baby, and you can also understand how hard it was for her to listen. Presently a splendid Christian merchant in Boston, who had never done any Christian work openly that any of us ever knew of, but who had crept in there to steal a word for his own hungry soul, was noticed to stand up. Dr. Gordon had asked him to speak to the woman, but he had declined, saying he knew not what to say. But now he came forward and said, "I am ashamed to say I don't know how to tell this woman how to be saved; I want to know it better myself. But if she will let me take the baby while you tell her how to be saved, I will try and hush the baby and care for it." And I saw that splendid merchant take that little baby in his arms and press it to his heart, and hush its crying, and walk up and down the hallway with it for an hour, while Dr. Gordon talked to the poor woman. Now that is what I call enthusiasm. If you cannot talk to a hungry soul, if you cannot teach the Bible Class, if you cannot lead the Endeavor meeting, or do a great work in God's name, hunt up a baby somewhere, take it in your arms and nurse it, and hush it to sleep, while some other skilled worker does the work you have not been able to do.

Let me take my text and burn it deeply into your hearts. Our Master has gone into a far country to get a kingdom and return. In the meantime he has given command and authority to his servants, and to every man his work. And he has commanded the porter to watch. When he comes may he find us at work in his service, each one in our own place, regardless of the other, remembering what Wesley's great motto was, "All at it and always at it." And before another half-century comes to this world, India, and China, and Japan, and the islands of the sea, and South America, will be covered with the flags of triumph, telling the story of the victorious work of Christian Endeavorers

At the conclusion of the sermon, which held the audience in closest attention, Mr. Robert Lloyd sang "The Holy City."

The Service of Consecration, Led by Dr. Clark.

This service was opened with the hymn, "I Will Tell the Wondrous Story" by the audience. Mr. Beckett then rendered "Saved by Grace."

President Clark then asked for a moment of silent prayer. Ten thousand heads were bowed while he repeated "Just As I Am, Without One Plea."

Words of Introduction by President Clark.

And now we come to our closing hour of consecration service. We have tried to have at this hour the most perfect stillness possible in this vast audience, because, though God can hear us and we can hear God's voice in the rush of the busy world, yet we are more apt to hear his voice, more sure to hear it, if our souls are quiet and at peace. And what we want this evening is to hear God — not simply these State delegations that shall be called before God — speaking to us as we dedicate ourselves to him. It is in the still, solemn voice that we must often hear God, rather than in the excitement of enthusiasm and applause. And this is why we are here together at this last meeting, in this quiet hour, in this quiet frame of mind.

Dear friends, the only thing for us to consider, it seems to me, comparatively speaking, is our sincerity. We shall consecrate ourselves by the thousands standing here together sometimes, sometimes two or three of us, sometimes only one man or woman speaking for a vast territory. But no matter whether *en masse* or individually, it must be an individual thing if it means anything. And it must be sincere. O Endeavorer, think of this. If five hundred stand with you, no matter if one thousand stand with you, or if five thousand, as when California is called — if that number stand together, no matter. It is your individual consecration that God will hear. Be sincere when you sing these songs. Sing no word that you do not mean. Say no familiar verse of scripture that you do not mean. Speak with your hearts to-night as well as your lips, and God in heaven, his dwelling-place, will hear and will answer you.

And now, dear friends, let us join in a moment of silent prayer before I begin to call the roll. And after we have prayed silently for a moment, let us still, with bowed heads, sing our prayer, "Just as I am, without one plea but that thy blood was shed for me." Sing it very softly, with your heads still bowed, and I hope every eye will be closed and every head in this vast audience bowed. Let us pray for God's peculiar pentecostal blessing. We need not pray for his presence — he is here. He has been with us all these blessed days. Pray for a special pentecostal giving of the Spirit to each one to-night. Let us all pray.

The Consecration of the Hosts.

After Dr. Clark's earnest words the multitude participated in the service.

Alaska came first on the list, and thankfully told how "they that sat in darkness saw a great light." Alabama prayed, "Create in me a clean heart." Arizona's delegates knew whom they had believed. Colorado would lift up her eyes unto the hills. Connecticut, mindful of the great cloud of witnesses, would run her race with patience. Little Delaware prayed that the words of her mouth and the meditations of her heart might be acceptable. The District of Columbia delegation took up again the motto of last year's noble Convention, "Not by might, nor by power, but by my spirit, saith the Lord." Georgia would acknowledge God in all things, that he might direct her paths. "Gem of the mountains, Idaho," raised her State song, "that God may reign in Idaho." God bless the pioneers!

Illinois's great host sung, " I consecrate my life to thee, my Saviour and my God," and then Dr. Coyle, of Oakland, offered an earnest prayer for our associate members, that they might be led into the fullest confession of the Lord.

Indiana, "saved to serve," would not "be ministered unto," but would minister. The Indian Territory would do Paul's "one thing." The hundreds of Endeavorers from Iowa, "steadfast, unmovable, always abounding," promised, in their beautiful State song : —

> " For the State our hearts have learned to love
> We will labor with a will."

Kansas was "crucified with Christ," and Kentucky, who could "do all things through Christ," sung blithely her State hymn : —

> " Our blest Endeavor band
> In the Old Kentucky home, far away."

The Endeavorers of the Pioneer State of Christian Endeavor would "win the State of Maine for Christ, their King ;" and Maryland's beautiful song was heard as usual : —

> " Shout, shout for joy the glad refrain,
> Our King shall gain his own again,
> Maryland, my Maryland."

Massachusetts, being justified by faith, was sure of peace with God. The rising of those hundreds of young people from his own State suggested to Dr. Clark to call for prayer for the dear ones at home, and this prayer was tenderly offered by Dr. Dickinson, of Boston.

Michigan Endeavorers, whether they lived or died, would live or die to the Lord ; and the large company from Minnesota sung of that "fair land of lakes," and vowed to win it for their King. Montana would "lay aside every weight," and New Mexico rejoiced in the sowers' promise of sheaves, while Mississippi hoped for "the peace of God, that passeth all understanding."

Missouri's hundreds sung sweetly : —

> " Missouri for Christ!
> Our watchword, let it ring!
> Missouri for Christ!
> Our State for our King!"

South Carolina would labor "not by might, nor by power," but by God's Spirit; and the North Carolina representatives pledged them-selves to evangelistic work, asking our prayers. Nebraska : "Not that we loved God, but that he loved us." New Hampshire sung a beauti-ful adaptation of "The Old Granite State." New Jersey, looking back to the Atlantic, was confident that God should "have dominion from sea to sea."

Then came a male double quartette that sung a magnificent anthem, raising in our minds the solemn question of eternity. And then New York's legion prayed, "Create in me a clean heart, O God, and renew a right spirit within me." North Dakota prayed for "the mind which was in Christ Jesus." Ohio's motto for the year was, "If any man be in Christ, he is a new creature."

Nevada, mindful of that shameful prize-fight, pledged itself to "fight the good fight of faith." Oklahoma fittingly reminded us of its great fields white to the harvest, and prayed us to send forth laborers. Ore-gon's many delegates expressed their gratitude for the great Convention. Rev. Raymond C. Brooks, of that State, the first boy to sign the Junior Christian Endeavor Constitution, offered prayer; and then Oregon State song was sung : —

> " In the name of Jesus we work and wait;
> We will labor early and labor late,
> Till from end to end of our noble State
> He is King whom we sing to-day."

Pennsylvania's regiment pledged itself to seek a deeper spiritual life, a more fervent loyalty to the church, and greater zeal for souls. The Rhode Island Endeavorers re-consecrated themselves, that they might "know God more perfectly, love Christ more fervently, and obey the Spirit more faithfully, and thus do better service for Christ and the Church." The South Dakota band were certain that they could do all things through Christ, their strength.

The Tennessee cohort, that is to entertain us next year, expressed their belief that Christian Endeavor is divinely guided, and that all its International Conventions are held where God would have them held, and therefore took courage to claim the same promise with South Dakota.

Texas sung : —

> " This is our burden, this is our plea:
> 'Texas for Christ,' our motto shall be."

Utah had a similar prayer for the basis of its State song.

Vermont's motto was the quaint one : "I cannot be everywhere, but

I can be somewhere; I cannot do everything, but I can do something; what I can do I ought to do, and, by the grace of God, I will do." Virginia Endeavorers, "few in number, but loyal in spirit," prayed, "Search me, O God, and know me, and lead me in the way everlasting."

Washington had sent down an astonishingly large delegation, and they sung with a will their State song, "Washington for Christ, the Lord." The West Virginia Endeavorers would let their light shine, "till from every hilltop of their mountain State shall flash forth the light that shineth more and more unto the perfect day." Wisconsin repeated that great sentence of the Christian Endeavor pledge, the "whatever" sentence, and Wyoming would work the works of God while it is yet day.

Then came Canada's goodly delegation, who bade us, whatever things are true, honest, just, pure, lovely, of good report, to think on those things. And then Canon Richardson, of Canada, prayed that God would cement the ties that unite these two lands.

There were present many Floating Endeavorers, — more Christian Endeavor sailors than attended all other International Conventions combined; and the appropriate motto of these was, "Though I take the wings of the morning, and dwell in the uttermost parts of the sea," etc.; and their appropriate hymn was, "Throw Out the Life-Line."

Never before, either, had there been present more than one delegate from Hawaii; now there were twenty. Their motto was, "Be thou faithful unto death, and I will give thee a crown of life," and they followed this with a song in their native tongue whose sentiment we could all feel, though we could not understand the words.

Japan's prayer was to be fervent in spirit, serving the Lord. China quoted, "These shall come from the east, from the west, from the land of Sinim," and begged, "Brethren, pray for us." Australia's representatives fittingly reminded us of the heavenly host, "the voice of a great multitude, the voice of many waters." India took comfort in the promise, "I am come that they might have life, and that they might have it more abundantly." Syria was represented by two Christian Endeavor girls in native costume, who sung a beautiful song.

"And now, California," asked Dr. Clark, "what is your desire, after God has blessed you and us with this great Convention?"

Ah, what a mighty host then arose; and with what joyful acclaim they repeated their consecration verse of hopeful onlooking! "Bring ye all the tithes into the storehouse, that there may be meat in my house; and prove me now herewith, if I will not open the windows, and pour you out a blessing, that there shall not be room enough to receive it." "May God grant that to you abundantly, dear Californians!" said the leader.

Then the sweet singers, the great ranks of the choir arose: "The ransomed of the Lord shall return, and come with singing to Zion. They shall obtain joy and gladness and sorrow, and sighing shall flee away."

Then Dr. Clark called upon the ministers to rise, and surely every one was astonished to see how many hundred pastors had accompanied their young folks to the great assembly. Their consecration motto, repeated after Dr. Clark, was, "Let a man so account of us as of the ministers of Christ." And may all of those pastors be able to lead their Christian Endeavorers into green fields and beside the still waters during the year to come!

Then all members of Lookout Committees, a wide-awake host. Their verse: "I have made thee as a watchman unto the house of Israel; therefore hear the word of the Lord."

The Prayer-meeting Committee: "Pray one for another; for the effectual, fervent prayer of the righteous man availeth much."

The Missionary Committee: "Bear ye one another's burdens, and so fulfil the law of Christ."

Then rose a glorious company of Junior workers, — far more, many times more, than could have been found a few years ago. Their year's motto: "Inasmuch as ye have done it unto one of the least of these my brethren, ye have done it unto me."

The Social Committee: "Whatsoever ye do, do it all to the glory of God."

All the men then rose, and what a magnificent sight it was! Who could have faint heart concerning our gospel after witnessing that uprising of men? And their consecration verse — may it be a prophecy — was, "I have written unto you, young men, because ye are strong. Be strong in the Lord, and in the power of his might."

Finally, the women, young and old — and now, in turn, the hall seems full of women. Their verse: "The Lord gave the word. Great was the company of women that published it."

And now comes the great moment of this marvellous meeting, — the greatest meeting, as we think, of all yet held under the auspices of Christian Endeavor. First the active Endeavorers were called upon to rise. Nearly every person of the ten thousand arose. Then all who were Christians and were in sympathy with the movement were urged to stand with us. Many an eye was wet, and certainly not a few souls in that moment made their first public profession of faith in the Lord Jesus. It was with hesitation that some rose, but only a very few remained seated.

Then solemnly we all made our great consecration: "Trusting in the Lord Jesus Christ for strength, we promise him that we will try to do whatever he would like to have us do." Every hand is raised in the solemn silence. "This for me, this for me," we repeat together, as the grand old Romans were wont to speak. A few words of heartfelt prayer, the Mizpah benediction, the Apostolic benediction, and the blessed hour is over. It has been an hour with God. May it draw those thousands of lives closer to him. Amen.

But has the Convention of 1897 closed? No, it has just begun! Throughout the year — beyond the years — will its power extend. By it one more bond of union cements the States and Territories of our home land. By it has been forged new links to hold as one the nations of the earth. Through it peace has received new inspiration, brotherly love a new meaning. Christianity has been interpreted for our Christian youth — as demanding both personal life and service and a tithe of God's bounty.

Such a convention God will honor.

Woodward's Pavilion.

Not less impressive was the last session of the '97 Convention held in Woodward's Pavilion. It was an hour in which to commune with God. It was a time in which to remember the emphasis of the pledge, to gather up the personal messages of the Convention, and to resolve upon a more sacrificial life.

The multitude assembled sat like the disciples before Jesus on the Mount. And he spoke to them. The Holy Spirit revealed the purposes of Christ unto them. For the Convention it was "the day of Pentecost . . fully come." There was divine power manifest. There was a baptism of the Spirit for life and service.

The pavilion was crowded. But none of the vast concourse broke in upon the real aim and mission of the hour. The hymns and sermon united to uplift the thought into the realm of consecration. Applause was absent. The ear and heart were sympathetic. The multitude awaited the voice of their Master.

The praise service was conducted by J. J. Morris, of San Francisco. The Clara Schumann Quartette rendered "Still, Still with Thee" and "Then Shall the Light Shine Forth" in an artistic manner, and was followed by the California Male Quartette. The devotional exercises were conducted by the Rev. John V. McCall, of Mineral Wells, Texas, who asked the blessing upon the work which was about to end.

Secretary Baer's Introductory Remarks.

The General Secretary, John Willis Baer, presided. Before introducing the preacher of the sermon, Mr. Baer asked all present not to applaud during the evening, but to spend the last hours of the present Convention in quiet with God. He then stated that the officers of the Convention desired to extend their thanks to every one who had taken part in making the visit of the delegates a pleasant one, and included the police, the fire department, the railroad and street-car companies, the hotels and boarding-houses, and the press.

The Rev. Robert Johnston, of Toronto, Canada, then invoked the blessing on the audience, and for the work which they had come to the city to carry out.

The Secretary then introduced Rev. J. Wilbur Chapman, D.D., of Philadelphia, Pennsylvania.

Sermon by Rev. Dr. J. W. Chapman, of Philadelphia, Pa.

TEXT: "*And when the day of Pentecost was fully come, they were all with one accord in one place.*
"*And suddenly there came a sound from Heaven, as of a rushing, mighty wind, and it filled all the house where they were sitting.*
"*And there appeared unto them cloven tongues like as of fire, and it sat upon each of them.*
"*And they were filled with the Holy Ghost.*" — ACTS ii. 1-4.

And thus the dispensation of the Spirit was ushered in ; the Church of Christ, called in some places the house of God, in others the Bride of the Lamb, and in still others the Body of Christ, was born. But this ⬛ a day not to be experienced once and then forever to pass into a memory ; for Pentecost is believed by many to have been just a specimen day of what may be repeated times without number.

We certainly need another Pentecost, and the need is always a prophesy of the coming of that which would meet the longing. The Church needs it. We behold people to-day utterly forgetting the place of the Holy Ghost in the government of the Church, substituting man-made power and methods for his power and direction, stooping to all sorts of methods for the purpose of raising funds to carry on the work of the gospel and the advancement of the Kingdom, almost completely marking out the line of demarkation between the Church and the world.

In the light of all these things, I say without hesitation the Church needs another Pentecost—when the money-changers shall be driven from the sanctuary, when hypocrisy shall be cast out of the house of God, when the Holy Ghost shall be given the place of the vicar of Christ, and when the fire of cleansing and of power shall burn in us from morning till night, and from night till morning. God, send the church another Pentecost. As individuals we need a Pentecost. We have on every side men and women who undoubtedly are saved. If they were to die they would certainly go to heaven ; but God save us from the feeling that the Lord Jesus Christ is simply an insurance against hell. Such people are weakness itself ; they amount to nothing as a prayer force or a work force. They have the name to live, but they are dead. If all the church were like them it would amount to almost nothing. They are like Lot in Sodom ; it is true, as Lot teaches us, that one may gain something by being worldly ; Lot certainly did. He became a man of great wealth ; he gained an official position in the city ; his daughters married into the highest social set of Sodom. All this a man may gain and still be worldly ; but it has its attending loss, too. Lot lost his influence over his fellow-citizens, for they mocked him, and would have killed him ; he lost his influence over his own household, for they laughed him to scorn ; he lost his influence with the angels and with God. It costs too much to be worldly, and no sensible man can pay the price. We have in our possession, many of us, what would give to the world another Luther, a Calvin, a Wesley, a Moody ; but God cannot work in us against our wills, for we are what we will to be as a rule. As individuals we need another Pentecost.

It is said that when you enter Mr. Edison's studio the figure of a young man rises to meet you as you cross the threshold. He salutes you by saying "Good morning." He takes out his watch and tells you the time of day ; but it is not a man at all, but simply a creature of springs, and an illustration of Mr. Edison's marvellous mechanical skill. But wonderful as the figure is, there is something more remarkable still, and that is Mr. Edison himself. But the difference between Mr. Edison and his creation is not greater than that between the man who is born of the Spirit and knows nothing more of the work of God in his life, and the man whose whole nature, spirit, soul, and body is surrendered to God, and this for his honor and glory. God send to us as individuals a Pentecost.

We have but to read the account in the book of Acts to understand clearly what steps must be taken in order that we might have a repetition of Pentecost. We read in the first verse, "They were all with one accord in one place." The place is nothing, for a man might just as easily expect the outpouring of the Holy Ghost upon a meeting held in the streets as in the most costly cathedral, or just as readily look for the manifestation of the power of God in the Rescue Mission as in the stateliest of churches. Indeed, it would seem sometimes as if the preference might be given to the outdoor meeting of the mission ; still, I repeat the statement, "The place is nothing, but the accord is everything." A man may never expect the outpouring of the Holy Ghost upon himself in power for service until his mind is in accord with the mind of God and his will submitted absolutely to him.

When the 120 had met this condition and had tarried through the ten days, we are told that there appeared cloven tongues, like as a fire. We may look at the fire in two ways; first, as a power. This is the secret of success of one man beyond another; the difference between man is the difference of heat; the difference between one reader and another is the difference of fire, and the difference between one preacher and another is the difference of fire. There is a difference between being Spirit-filled and Spirit-driven. The latter expression applies to the majority of Christians. Here is a man who preaches from a sense of duty; he is Spirit-driven. And here is another who teaches a Sunday-school class because he thinks he must do something, and this is the easiest form of service in his estimation. That is being Spirit-driven. Here is another who reads the Bible because he is afraid not to read it. That is being Spirit-driven, also. It is a low order of service when compared with the man who counts it his highest joy to preach, the greatest blessing of his life to teach in the Sunday-school, and his meat and drink to study the Word of God. Let us not be Spirit-driven men, but Spirit-filled, delighting to do his will.

The other way in which the thought of fire may be used is in its cleansing or purifying power, and this certainly is necessary before we may expect the outpouring of the Holy Ghost. God needs no golden vessel, no silver vessels, but clean vessels. Many a man is having the experience in his business life that is entirely foreign to the mind of Christ, and that must be regulated before Pentecost may be repeated. Many a home circle is being rent and torn because of the inconsistency of some of its members, who profess to be followers of Christ, and that must be made right. Many a member of the Church is so entirely out of touch with him who is in the Word Head of the Church, and with the Spirit, who is its right, that even though God waits to bless us he cannot do it while the wrong is not righted. Many a church-member has sought to cover his sins and to hide his iniquities only to find to-day that he that covereth his sins shall not prosper, and there can be no Pentecost until the awful wrong is righted.

And as a result of all these things above noticed, we would be filled with the Holy Ghost. I know very well that there are those who are opposed to what may be called the blessing of the infilling of the Holy Ghost; but, as for myself, I am perfectly willing to let it rest upon a clear statement of the Word of God. Did he not say to his disciples, "Now ye are clean, through the Word which I have spoken unto you?" Did he not say, also, "Rejoice that your names are written in heaven?" And unto these very disciples he said, Acts i. 5 : "For John truly baptized with water; but ye shall be baptized with the Holy Ghost not many days hence."

The power of God waits for our apprehension and possession, and we may have it if we will. There are but three conditions : the first is that the blessing is possible. I am absolutely certain that God is more willing to give the Holy Spirit than earthly parents are to give good gifts unto their children.

Second, we must be in right relations with God, and we likewise must be in right relation with our fellow-men.

Third, on the ground of redemption and by faith in God now we must claim the blessing. We need not pray. We need not wait. We may have it if we will.

The consecration service followed directly upon the delivery of the sermon.

Consecration Address by Secretary Baer.

After reading from Galatians v. 16–25, Mr. Baer said : —

That is the reason why, going away from this meeting to-night, if we do go in that condition, we fight the spirit of God, that has been invited into our presence in every word that has been spoken to you ; aye, that is present in the hearts of many. O God, that all could say it was in theirs. In the few words that I shall say I bid you think of these things, — the flesh, with its crimes and deviltry ; the spirit, with its fruits and blessings. Choose, choose, for eternity. This is what I mean. O God, make it plain ! Listen.

A little fellow placed his hands in a very valuable vase to get a penny, but he could not draw his hand back. The father's attention was called to the predicament; every effort was made to release the boy's hand, but without success, and it seemed as if that valuable vase must be destroyed. But as a last resort the father said, " George, straighten out your fingers, lower your thumb as you see me do, and see if your hand will not come out." " Why, if I do that, father, I will drop the penny." God bids you drop the copper and reach for gold. I do not know how far your hand is in the vase, but I bid you before God to drop the penny, friends, and have gold. Holy Spirit, Spirit of God, come unto Christian Endeavor, and be to Christian Endeavor what thou wouldst be to it, even if we must be revolutionized and turned upside down.

Oh, as I see these great meetings, with their wonderful spiritual power, as I see the great throngs year after year traveling to our Conventions, as each year we are able to report increasing numbers, I tell you that with a mighty shout of gladness I am thankful for it all. But, O God, if this young life could at the same time be so full of the Spirit of God that it would overflow in each individual life, the Kingdom of God would come in the foreign field and at home. And what I ask for myself I ask for you to-night, that we may be kept so close to the heart of the Master that we shall always feel that he is with us.

That dear sainted man, Dr. Gordon, in many of his books has helped me. There are some present who knew him; indeed, on this platform are friends who were in his church, and there is another in the gallery. Listen! Dr. Gordon, I believe, before God, and I am reverent, knows what is going on. He has left these lines, and they help me; and I will repeat them, just to emphasize what Dr. Chapman has been telling you:—

" The mighty make-weight in the scale of success is the baptism of the invisible spirit of life. Science has perfected its balances, and made them so delicate and susceptible, that when two pieces of paper hold the scales in perfect equipoise, the writing of your name upon one will instantly tip the beam and bear it under. So it is when the signature of the Spirit is put upon the heart with the heavenly sealing. It is a transaction so hidden and so delicate that its subject may be quite unconscious of it as it is passing, but it has often changed the poise of one's life, transforming a weakling into a spiritual giant, so that he who utterly failed by the energy of the flesh has gone forth victorious in the power of the Spirit."

Oh for that I pray to-night; for that, Christian Endeavorers, I ask to-night. Will you? You have heard my voice in this Convention all too much, and I will not detain you any longer than to give you in substance seven suggestions that I prepared as a sort of farewell message, if you will allow me to make it, and then I am going to ask you in a very definite way if you care for it also.

I hope, as a result of this Convention, first, *that we will feed upon God's Word more.* Dr. Chapman has quoted Dr. Meyer. Dear man, he has recently, under God's guidance, sort of turned me upside down; and when we talked together the last time, when he was over in this country, he took my Bible and wrote this in it: " Thou shalt see greater things than these. The Lord Jesus said it, and he waits to reveal them, dear friend, in spirit, soul, and body, and in sphere of service. May it even be so." And I say it, too, for you. May it even be so. May we, this year, as never before, study and feed upon this Word daily; have the daily, quiet hour at the beginning of the day. It will make the day, all through, a sweeter and happier day. " What fire is to invisible ink, bringing it out clear and black, so the power of the Holy Spirit is to the Word of God, giving us his message for service, and for the guidance of our life." So says Mr. Meyer, and he is right. I would make secondly this suggestion: *let us get ourselves thoroughly right with God by abundoning every known sin or doubtful indulgence.* Those who will join me in that covenant with Jesus Christ, raise your right hand before God. (A large number raised their right hands.) O God, what a testimony!

Do you mean it? That you will abandon *every known sin and doubtful indulgence?* Let us bow our heads in prayer just a moment. There are some, Lord Jesus, who do not dare do that; they wanted to, but they could not honestly do it; something is keeping them back. O God, we will wait, we will wait; speak to them, speak to them now.

Third. *Trust absolutely to the Gospel as the power of God and the wisdom of God unto salvation, and expect that God's Word faithfully studied will not return void in a single instance.* Who will do this for the coming year? Those who will, raise your hands.

A large response was made to this request.

Fourth. *We will give ourselves to prayer, giving time enough to get the sense of God, in the closet, and never leaving the place of supplication until a divine vision is received, a new impartation of life and power.* Will you seek that? Will you join me? Those who will, raise your hands to God.

Fifth. It seems to me this one is very important. Who will go — go ourselves — and seek individuals, remembering that souls are won by individual approach? How many here will promise to seek at least one whose life they know is not in touch with Jesus Christ? Let them please rise.

Responded to by hundreds standing upon their feet.

Remain standing just a moment. This is a definite covenant with Jesus Christ. Let us bow our heads in prayer. O God, help us, help us to do this. Oh, may we taste the blessing that will come with it! Help us to show others that they must taste and see that the Lord is good. O God, many have in mind now their own brothers and sisters, father and mother, near ones and dear ones — God help us to answer our own prayers.

Sixth. *Keep from all direct or indirect dependence on man. Avoid seeking men's applause. Let us do for Christ what we are willing to do to please men.* Are you willing to do that? Oh, it is so easy to do things for men sometimes.

And now the last: *Live a life of faith, depending on God for strength, wisdom, and guidance, and cultivate in our associates the same spirit of direct leaning upon God.* All those who will do that, please stand. (Hundreds stand.) Just remain standing. There are some, you see, who are not on their feet, and we will wait for them just a moment. If there is any one who is not on his feet, and would like to have God encourage them, as we may ask him to do so, if they will stand I would like to pray for them. Yes, there are some. That is right. Oh, come! More. Do not allow this invitation to go by. We are going to ask God to encourage you to take this step and trust him. Yes, there are more. We will still wait for more. Dr. Chapman, will you lead us in a word of prayer?

DR. CHAPMAN: Our Heavenly Father, we are very grateful to thee this evening for what our eyes have seen, for what our ears have heard, and best of all for that which has been given to us in our spirits. We do thank thee that thou hast given us the privilege of holding up Jesus Christ and seeking to exalt the Holy Ghost. We pray thee now that thou wouldst press home these suggestions made by our beloved secretary. We thank thee for his life; we thank thee that it bears out what he has taught us. We pray that from this day on every one in this great throng may seek to order his or her life according to the plan of God and the mind of Christ.

O God, our Father, bless those of us whose hands have been uplifted — it seems to me that we could, as we put up our hands in covenant, almost feel the clasp of the hand of the risen Christ. We believe that in the book on high these resolutions have been written down, and one day we shall meet them.

Command thy blessing upon those who stood and said, Pray for us. And oh, our Father, those who in their hearts have wanted the prayer, and yet have been unable to rise, we pray thee that thou wilt bless them in this closing service. Let the power of the Holy Ghost rest upon us all, and as we go out from this meeting, may it be to a new experience, to a better life, to a nobler purpose, and to be more like the Lord Jesus Christ, who loved us and gave himself for us. Bless all who have had any part in this Convention, for Jesus' sake.

MR. BAER: As we go away from this Convention, which has been so blessed, may we go rejoicing; but let us remember that it will only be successful by keeping close to Jesus Christ. To-morrow things are going to be very different for you and for me — entirely different. We have been on the Mount of Transfiguration, but to-morrow we will go home. The home may not look any brighter, it may not be any happier, if you have left dull and unhappy homes. But, friends, this Convention will not have been a success if you cannot carry into that home a new light that shall change it and send its inmates rejoicing to the foot of the cross. And unless people can see we have been somewhere and gotten a little different hold of things, all these meetings have been in vain. But, thank God, after having talked with many individuals, knowing and believing in the power of the Holy Ghost, I have only a forward look to-night, for we are going to conquer, or he is through us, if we will let him.

A little fellow in New York City, nine years of age, became separated from his mother way out in the outskirts and was picked up by a police officer. The little fellow was crying. The officer took him to his station, where he was reported. They found out from the little fellow where he lived, and one of the officers told him when he went off duty at twelve o'clock he would take him home. Then he stopped crying. He was taken into the Sergeant's office and was told to lie down and go to sleep, and in a little while they would take him home. There was a sort of couch in the corner with one or two coats on it. The little fellow went over to it, but soon he came back and stood in front of the Sergeant's desk. He said to him, "Go and lie down, my boy; it is all right. We will take you home in a little while." He went back, but he did not lie down. By and by he came back again, and he seemed so restless that the officer said, "Why, what is the matter with you?" The little fellow said, "Would you mind, sir, if I said my prayer, as I do at home?" The officer did not mind, but it was a little new to this particular man. The little fellow stepped over to the other side of the office, and kneeling down by the couch, he uttered that prayer that I learned at my mother's knee, and probably you learned at your mother's knee, and which, bless God, my wife teaches my two little boys to say every night:—

> "Now I lay me down to sleep,
> I pray the Lord my soul to keep."

Watch the officers. Their hats are off and tears are trickling down their cheeks.

> "If I should die before I wake
> I pray the Lord my soul to take."

And then a little jump on to the couch, and he is perfectly happy and content. There was quiet in that police-station then.

O friends, the power of the testimony of the love for Jesus Christ, whether it be from one nine years of age, or from one of ninety!

So I bid you, as we go away or remain in this great State, remember that this little badge signifies that we stand for certain principles. Yes, more than that: every single person out of Christ has a right to expect that we will be every day before God what we profess to be. And so I remind you of our covenants with Jesus Christ. Trust in him. I promise you I will do whatever he would like me to.

We will rise and sing two verses of "God Be With You Till We Meet Again," and Mr. Johnston will pronounce the benediction, and the Sixteenth Annual Convention will be adjourned — no; it will be just commenced in our lives.

BENEDICTION.

Now may the God of peace, who brought again from the dead our Lord Jesus Christ, that great shepherd of the sheep, make us perfect in every good work to do his will, working in us that which is pleasing in his sight. And may the grace of our Lord and Saviour Jesus Christ, the love of God the Father, and the communion and fellowship of the Holy Spirit be with us and with all thy people forever. Amen.

Overflow Meeting.

In Odd Fellows' Hall, Treasurer Wm. Shaw conducted an inspiring and profitable service. The building was crowded. Rev. Matt. S. Hughes, D.D., of Minneapolis, one of the favorite Convention speakers, preached the sermon, after which Mr. Shaw led the closing consecration meeting.

THE RALLYING OF THE DENOMINATIONS.

THURSDAY AFTERNOON.

ONE valuable feature of every International Christian Endeavor Convention is the bringing together of some of the flowers of the different denominations. It was certainly true of San Francisco. Leaders with the same faith and polity spoke upon one platform to large audiences of their own church branch. Loyalty to the denomination, the need of an *esprit de corps*, a spirit of remembrance for the belief of the Fathers — all these were impressed upon the warm, young hearts of the Endeavorers.

Space will not permit giving more than a brief picture of these very important gatherings of the clans.

AFRICAN METHODIST EPISCOPAL : — At the Starr King African Methodist Zion Church a rally was carried on under the direction of Senior Elder T. Brown. The address at the commencement of the exercises was made by Bishop A. Walters, D.D., trustee of the United Society. He was followed by Rev. G. L. Caldwell, of Philadelphia, and others.

AFRICAN METHODIST EPISCOPAL ZION : — Gold and royal purple were well in evidence in the decoration of the speakers' platform and the organ-loft of the Bethel African Methodist Episcopal Church for the Endeavor rally. Among those to greet the audience was Bishop W. J. Gaines, of Atlanta, Ga., Rev. H. B. Johnson, D.D., editor of the *Christian Recorder*, led in prayer, and Rev. W. B. Anderson made the welcome address. Among the other speakers were Bishop B. W. Arnett, D.D., of Ohio, and Rev. R. C. Ransom, of Chicago.

BAPTIST : — " Bring Forth the Royal Diadem and Crown Him Lord of All " was the greeting over the speakers' stand that met the gaze of the vast assembly congregated at the First Baptist Church. Every pew in the auditorium and gallery was filled by attentive listeners. The program was introduced with solemn services, in which a number of Christian Endeavor songs, under the direction of Professor R. B. Evans, were enthusiastically rendered. The edifice was tastefully decorated, a feature being the full sheaves of ripened wheat that stood prominently forward at each end of the speakers' platform. Rev. Howard B. Grose had charge of the meeting, and as a result the Baptist rally has never been excelled.

CONGREGATIONAL : — The members of this denomination met in the First Congregational Church. Rev. G. C. Adams, the pastor, presided. The theme was " The Missionary Spirit in Congregationalism." It was considered in five addresses, as follows : " In the Voyage of the *Mayflower*," Rev. R. W. Brokaw ; " In Fellowship with Other Denominations," Rev. W. H. G. Temple ; " In Foreign Lands," Selah Merrill, LL.D. : " In Adaptation to Growth in Cities," Rev. C. A. Dickinson, D.D. : " The Value of the Spirit," Rev. Nehemiah Boynton, D.D. Each speaker dwelt upon the gifts of the denomination to the country and to the world.

CUMBERLAND PRESBYTERIAN : — At the Cumberland Presbyterian Church, Dr. W. J. Darby, trustee of the United Society of Christian Endeavor, presided. After musical selections and a short devotional exercise by Dr. F. P. Gray, of San Francisco, the Rev. E. L. B. McClellan, of Crow's Landing, Rev. L. E. Thompson, of Macminnville, Oregon, Rev. G. A. Blair, pastor of First Christian Endeavor Church, Cumberland Presbyterian denomination, Portland, Oregon, and Mrs. N. B. Sitton, superintendent Cumberland Presbyterian Chinese Mission, of San Francisco, described work in their various fields. The sense of the meeting was in favor of building a Christian Endeavor church of this denom-

ination each year. The subject of " Denominational Endeavor " was handled
by Dr. Eds. G. McLean.

CANADIAN PRESBYTERIAN: — One of the most enthusiastic and best
attended rally was that of the Canadian Presbyterians at the Howard Church.
This was conducted by Rev. J. S. Conning, of Caledonia, Ontario, who made
a very eloquent opening address. Rev. Dr. Patterson, of Cooke's Church,
Toronto, Ontario, and trustee of the United Society, spoke at some length
upon the Junior work of the church, being followed by Rev. James Cormack, of
Maxwell, Ontario. The latter chose for his subject, "The Extension of the
Christian Endeavor." Rev. John Chisen, of Dunbarton, Ontario, spoke upon
" Denominational Study," while the concluding address was made by Rev.
Robert Johnston, of London, Ontario, on " How To Reach Young Men."

DISCIPLES OF CHRIST: — The rally of the Disciples of Christ in the auditorium of the Young Men's Christian Association Building was attended by a
large congregation. The Rev. A. C. Smithers, of Los Angeles, presided. The
hall was adorned with flags and bunting. The program called for the following: vocal solo, by Mrs. Princess Long, of Alameda; report of the Senior
Society of Christian Endeavor of the Disciples in the United States, by the
secretary, Rev. J. Z. Tyler, D.D., of Cleveland, Ohio; report of the Junior
Society, by Rev. B. B. Tyler, D.D., of New York; report of the Bethany
Reading Circle, by Rev. J. Z. Tyler, D.D.; address by the Rev. Mr. Downing,
of Pomona, Cal.; talk by the Rev. James Small, formerly of Oakland; address
by Miss Thompson, national lecturer for the Christian Woman's Board of Mis-
sions; song by Mrs. Long; address on " Church Extension," R. L. McHatton,
State evangelist; address by Professor H. L. Willett, of the University of
Chicago; address by Rev. B. B. Tyler, D.D., of New York.

LUTHERAN: — This rally was well attended and inspiring. The First English Lutheran Church, which entertained the Eastern friends, gave them a most
cordial welcome. Abundance of fruit and flowers were distributed. Dr. M.
Rhodes, of St. Louis, spoke upon the value of the educational features of
Christian Endeavor. Dr. Bushnell rejoiced in the Convention as an opportunity for re-unions. Dr. Kapp, of Indiana, summoned the young people to be
aggressive. The chairman was Rev. W. S. Hoskinson, D.D., of Sacramento.
He desired the Lutheran Christian Endeavorers to take just pride in belonging
to the Church of Protestantism, — " the maternal home and field of Christian
Endeavor."

FREE BAPTIST: — The Union Square Baptist Church was well filled when
Rev. J. M. Lowden was introduced to the assembled Endeavorers. The prayer
was offered by Rev. Philip Graif, of Oakland. Rev. Philip Meserve welcomed
the visitors in hearty fashion, and surrendered the pulpit to Miss Fenner, of
Rhode Island. "The Grand Work of the Christian Endeavorers" was her theme.
and she applied it to the advancement and progress of spiritual affairs in her
own State. An address was made by Miss Cora B. Bickford, of Maine.

FRIENDS: — Central Methodist Episcopal Church was the meeting-place for
the Friends' denominational rally. Rev. Thomas Newlin, of Newberg, Oregon.
presided. Rev. C. E. Tibbetts, of Pasadena, read a paper on " The Mission."
He was followed by Prof. Robert B. Warder, of Howard University, Washington, D. C., in a talk entitled " Every Man a Missionary." Miss Ella F.
Macey, of Newberg, Oregon, Rev. C. C. Reynolds, of Pasadena, and Prof.
C. E. Lewis, of the Pacific College, Newberg, Oregon, made addresses.

GERMAN: — The German rally took place in the German Evangelical Church.
The attendance was large. Secretary Horner, of the German Branch Y. M. C.
A. of San Francisco, presided. Mr. Emil Pohl spoke of the positive influence
for good which the Convention would leave behind it. Prof. Allein Putzker, of
the University of California, emphasized the great need of noble ideals in the
choices of men. Rev. F. W. Fischer welcomed the delegates in behalf of the
German churches. Responses for the delegates were made by Allein Bartl, of
Rochester, N. Y., and Miss A. Schneider, of Chicago.

METHODIST EPISCOPAL, METHODIST EPISCOPAL SOUTH, AND METHODIST OF CANADA, IN JOINT RALLY: — This joint rally was held at the Howard Street Methodist Church. The spacious auditorium was filled, almost every State in the Union being represented, as well as Canada. Rev. Chas. W. Roads, of Chester, Pa., presided in the absence of Dr. G. C. Kelly, of Birmingham, Ala. The service was interspersed with music by a splendid choir under the direction of Prof. Martin Schultz. Addresses were delivered by W. H. Waste, of Berkeley, Oakland, on behalf of the Epworth League of the M. E. Church South; by Rev. F. D. Bovard, D.D., president of the Conference Epworth League of the Methodist Episcopal Church; by Rev. Ezra Tinker, of Wilmington, Del., representing the visiting Endeavorers; and a warm address of greeting was given by Rev Dr. Case, pastor of the church where the meeting was held, and by Dr. E. R. Dille. The speakers all emphasized the blessing Christian Endeavor was proving in uniting sections and sects, and especially in bringing into closer fellowship the members of the Methodist family. The speakers who represented the Epworth League were hearty in their expressions of fraternal good feeling for the Christian Endeavor Society, and their gratitude that this great Convention — the greatest religious gathering California has ever had — had been brought to our shores. Dr. Roads, the chairman, reported that there were 80 Methodist Christian Endeavor Societies in Pennsylvania, 60 of which were in the city of Philadelphia, and that largely because of the Methodist fire and fervor which those societies brought into the union, the Philadelphia C. E. Union was the greatest city union in the world.

The meeting was pronounced by many to have been the most successful Methodist rally ever held at a Christian Endeavor Convention.

After the set addresses, a genuine Methodist love feast was held, in which a very large number participated, and the enthusiasm reached shouting point before the meeting closed.

METHODIST PROTESTANT: — Dr. J. F. Cowan, a trustee of the United Society, presided at the rally of this denomination. Miss Mary E. Moall, secretary of the union, gave a report of the recent denominational convention at Adrian, Mich. Rev. Chas. D. Sinkinson, of Atlantic City, Rev. Eugenia F. St. John, of Kansas City, and Rev. L. R. Dyott, of Newark, spoke. The chairman referred to the fact that the Methodist Protestant Church now stood sixth in the denominations in number of Christian Endeavor Societies. Ten States were represented in the rally.

MORAVIAN: — A rally of the members of the Moravian Church, was held in the German lecture hall of the Y. M. C. A. Building to report progress made in missionary work. Among the prominent clergymen present were Bishop Edward Rondthaler, D.D., of North Carolina, Rev. W. H. Vogler, of Indianapolis, Rev. W. H. Rice, of North Carolina, and Rev. W. H. Weinland, and Rev. D. J. Woolsey, both of Riverside County, Cal.

PRESBYTERIAN: — The proceedings at this rally were opened with an address by the chairman, Rev. J. W. Cochran, of Madison, Wis., John Willis Baer made an interesting address and was followed by Dr. G. F. Pentecost, of Yonkers, N. Y. Dr. W. J. McKittrick, of Calvary Church, Buffalo, N. Y., followed with a stirring address. Dr. Hemphill, the pastor of Calvary Church, made a few remarks, after which Rev. Mr. Palmer, of Oakland, was called upon and spoke most interestingly on Presbyterianism on the Pacific Coast. William T. Ellis, the editor of *Forward*, Dr. D. K. Wilbur, of Sitka, and Dr. John R. Davis, of New York, and Rev. J. Miller Chapman, D.D., of Philadelphia, also spoke.

One of the pleasant features of the rally was the receipt of greetings from prominent men who could not be present. The messages were from John Wanamaker, Dr. Parkhurst, Dr. Samuel Nichols, of St. Louis, Dr. Herrick Johnson, Dr. John Hall, and others.

PROTESTANT EPISCOPAL IN CANADA AND THE UNITED STATES: — Rev. Canon J. B. Richardson presided. In a convincing way he pointed out the adaptability of Christian Endeavor to the Church. The pledge, Bible study, and consecration meeting were in harmony with church institutions. Archdeacon Emery was greatly impressed with the magnitude of the Convention. Mr. C. R. Wilkes found his church attachments promoted by the Y. P. S. C. E. Mr. Charles Harper, of Eureka, Cal., felt that if the society was known and understood, it would easily grow within the denomination. Lyle A. Dickey, of Hawaii, was especially interested in the spread of Endeavor in the Anglican Church. Short reports were heard from several others, each testifying to the value of Christian Endeavor.

REFORMED CHURCH IN AMERICA: — Rev. James M. Dickson, D.D., presided. Dr. Dickson alluded to the fact that the rally was the first public meeting ever held by his denomination west of the Rockies. He also referred to the Providence of God in the extent and possessions of our country. Addresses were made upon " The Secret of Strength for Service," " Some Kinds of Endeavorers," " Junior Work," " The Personal Element in Christian Endeavor Work," " Missionary Work."

REFORMED CHURCH IN THE UNITED STATES: — The rally of the Reformed Church in the United States took place at the Third Baptist Church. Rev. J. W. Meininger, of Lancaster, Pa., presided. Among the speakers were the Rev. J. H. Bomberger, of Heidelberg University, Ohio, Rev. Dr. Mosser, of Reading, Pa., and F. G. Hobson, of Norristown, Pa.

SOUTHERN PRESBYTERIAN: — The arrival of the Southern Presbyterians was expected early in the day, but the delay of the train was the cause of their non-appearance at the rally prepared for them. However, the few who were there to meet the visitors were entertained by speakers in the fore rank of the association. The meeting was conducted by Dr. Wm. T. Taylor, of Birmingham, Ala., who told of the progress of the work of the Endeavorers in his section of the country. Dr. N. Moore of Sherman, Tex., next addressed the meeting.

UNITED BRETHREN: — The United Brethren held their rally in the lecture-room of the Howard Street Methodist Church. It was presided over by Rev. H. F. Shupe, the editor of the *Watchword*. An address of welcome was delivered by Rev. F. E. Coulter, of Selma, Cal., and he was followed by Senator Edmonds, of Kansas, who spoke enthusiastically of his journey across the mountains. Rev. J. P. Landis, D.D., the president of the Young People's Christian Union, and professor of Hebrew in the Union Biblical Seminary at Dayton, O., was the closing speaker.

UNITED EVANGELICAL: — This rally was directed by Prof. D. M. Metzger, of Oregon. Miss Carrie Neitz, of Reading, Pa., gave an address upon " The Relation of the K. L. C. E. to the Sunday School." Miss Mohn, of Reading, Pa., spoke upon "Junior K. L. C. E. Extension." "The K. L. C. E. and Missions " was the topic of Rev. C. C. Poling. Rev. M. T. Maze, of Kearney, Neb., gave an address upon " Systematic and Proportionate Giving to God's Cause." A general discussion followed. A committee was appointed to present resolutions to the managing board, K. L. C. E. As a result of the rally a Keystone League of Christian Endeavor was organized.

UNITED PRESBYTERIAN: — About three hundred persons attended the rally. The pastor of the church, Dr. Gibson, welcomed the delegates. Rev. E. S. McKittrick, of Pasadena, Cal., was chairman. Rev. W. J. Buchanan, of Columbus, O., spoke upon " Witnessing for Christ." Rev. George M. Cormick, D.D., took as his topic, " Church Loyalty." " The Young Woman for the Times " was the subject of an able paper by Helen G. French, of Oakland. It was properly complemented by an address upon " The Young Man for the Times," by Dr. McMillan, of Pittsburg. The Eastern pastors rejoiced in the Christian fellowship to be enjoyed the world over.

WELSH RALLY: — Rev. David Davies, D.D., of Oshkosh, Wis., presided at the meeting. The motto was "The Lord our God be with us as he was with our fathers." Words of welcome were spoken by Rev. Moses Williams, Evan Watts, and others. Dr. Davies and Professor Lloyd made the responses.

After discussing the motto, the hour was taken in reminiscences of great gatherings. especially in connection with Christian Endeavor. Prayers for paricular objects were offered, and then the national song of Wales was sung.

CARRYING THE EVANGEL.

"THE future historian will recall this as the 'Pentecostal Convention'." So prophesied one of the pastors of the city. Assuredly the presence of the Spirit was manifest. — in overflow meetings, in the early morning prayer services, but in particular in the noonday and other evangelistic meetings.

In the Y M. C. A. auditorium. the Chamber of Commerce, and in the Emporium, services were held each day. These were addressed by the best Convention speakers, and were well attended by the business men.

Services were held in the public squares, at the water-front, Builders' exchange, in gospel wagons, in railway-cars,— in short, everywhere throughout the city where men could be gathered. The music was a feature of each service. The audiences were always serious and deeply interested. So long as their hour of rest lasted they remained within sound of the speakers and the songs. Many gave up their dinners to attend. Many desires for prayer were expressed ; many desired to begin the Christian life ; many a cold-grown Christian sought to know how he might find peace and life once more.

COMMITTEE CONFERENCES.

FRIDAY AFTERNOON.

TO obtain the benefit of the plans and successes of eminent workers throughout the country is an opportunity. So far as the delayed trains would permit, this is just what the Endeavorers sought in their conferences. From all over the land came leaders in Christian Endeavor work, and they were brimful of enthusiasm and suggestion.

LOOKOUT COMMITTEE CONFERENCE.

Five to six hundred delegates gathered Friday afternoon in the main auditorium of the First Congregational Church, for the Lookout Committee Conference. Chairman, W. E. Sweet, of Denver, Col. For two hours the work of the committees was earnestly discussed. The importance of special prayer-meetings by the Lookout Committee was emphasized first of all, and many societies reported union prayer-meetings with the Prayer-meeting Committee.

The discussion was divided into three heads: viz., looking up, an earnest desire for the Holy Spirit in our work ; looking out, seeking to enlarge our membership and spread the influence of the Society; looking in, the emphasis of faithfulness to the pledge. Most earnestly were these subjects discussed. The characteristics of a good Lookout Committee were emphasized as being spirituality, tactful love to God and love to men, faithfulness, and patience. The emphasis of the pledge, care in dealing with new applicants, a simple, brief reception service, dropping the unfaithful, were all subjects under discussion. Especially was emphasis laid upon the thought that no church-member should be allowed to join as an associate member. Raise the standard, no letting down, no compromise of our Christian Endeavor pledge, was the almost unanimous opinion of those present.

Many experiences were given of plans tried and found successful, and no one went away without a feeling of having been helped and inspired to more effective service on the Lookout Committee.

MISSIONARY COMMITTEE CONFERENCE.

The Missionary Committee Conference was held in Calvary Presbyterian Church, Mrs. George W. Coleman, of Boston, presiding. The subject considered was the methods of missionary work. Under this were discussed the organizing of the mission meetings, the raising of missionary money, the conduct of the meetings, work in the field, and the motive of missionary work.

Among the speakers were Prof. Amos R. Wells, of *The Golden Rule;* Miss Katherine M. Jones, Young People's secretary of the Presbyterian Board of Missions in New York; Dr. Kin Eca da Silva, of Alameda; Charles T. Studd, prominent in missionary work in China; M. N. Shand, of Washington, D.C., and Rev. J. R. Davies, D.D., of New York City.

The question of raising missionary money was discussed at some length by Amos R. Wells.

"I want to add a word," he said, "about The Tenth Legion. This is a body of those who have promised to give to the Lord at least one-tenth of what he gives them; this is the minimum."

Being asked how many belonged already to this legion, over one-half the listeners raised their hands.

Dr. Silva gave an interesting talk on the peculiar customs of the Chinese, and urged upon her hearers the necessity of missionary work in that country.

The conference was concluded by the whole congregation reciting "The Lord watch between thee and me, when we are absent one from another."

PRAYER-MEETING COMMITTEE CONFERENCE.

The Prayer-meeting Committee Conference was held in the First Presbyterian Church, San Francisco. Leader, Wm. G. Alexander, of San Jose, Cal.

The conference was a decided success. Nearly all of the 400 people present took part. The value and importance of the pledge was emphasized. All agreed that a ten-minute prayer conference by the committee with the leader, just before the regular meeting, was most helpful.

Have plenty of *prayer* in the meeting,— silent prayer, sentence prayer, fervent prayer. Be prompt in opening and closing the meeting. Avoid long speeches. Pauses may be seasons of blessing, and not as dreadful as we imagine.

Let the committee, as well as the leader, make careful preparation of the subject. Choose the leaders best qualified for the topic. Let the songs, as well as the chapters and remarks, be carefully selected. Let there be a definite aim and object to the meeting, and everything work up to the saving of souls.

Have your best and most consecrated leaders lead the consecration meeting. Make it a meeting of great spiritual uplift. Hold memory meetings. Have the different committees lead the meeting. Have concert exercises. Help the more timid by preparing something for them. Be present yourself.

SOCIAL COMMITTEE CONFERENCE.

The conference of members of Social Committees in the Sunday-school room of the First Congregational Church was delayed by the non-arrival of Angus

G. Brades, of Minneapolis, the chairman, who was kept away by illness. F. P. Ryall, of New Hampshire, was asked to preside. The meeting was well attended, though largely by ladies, as the chairman remarked. The discussion of social schemes tried in various societies was participated in by delegates representing States from New York to California.

SUNDAY-SCHOOL COMMITTEE CONFERENCE.

A large company of Endeavorers greeted Mr. W. L. Noell, of Huntingdon, Tenn., as he rose to preside over the Sunday-school Committee Conference in the Calvary Presbyterian Church. The chief points brought out in the discussion were: a committee holds a meeting every other Sunday, keeps account of absentees from the school, and visits them; one society makes its committee-chairman a permanent officer, or for a term of years, giving opportunity to gain acquaintance with church-members and parents; one society visits new families through this committee; absentees are remembered with flowers and Sunday-school papers by this committee; committees report visiting homes of the poor with clothing for the children that they may attend the school.

The answer to the important question, "What kind of persons should compose the committee?" was this, "Persons who are deeply interested in Sunday-school work, and who are consecrated, in the full sense of that word."

The meeting closed with a sweet consecration service. With bowed heads many asked God to make them what they ought to be; and then all who could say "I will be what he wants me to be, I'll do what he wants me to do, I'll go where he wants me to go" were asked to stand, — nearly all stood, — and sang one verse of "I'll live for him." Then all who would say "I am willing to be made willing" were asked to stand, and nearly all stood, closing with the last verse.

TEMPERANCE COMMITTEE CONFERENCE.

The Temperance Committee met, at 2 P.M. in the First Presbyterian Church. The session opened with the singing of several hymns, followed by a brief season of prayer. The leader, James A. Floyd, of Boston, Mass., introduced the discussion by dividing it into the following topics: "Pledge-Signing," "Rescue and Reform Work," "Educational," "Meetings."

A pledge was prepared, with stub append, that would enable the society to follow up the signer. This was endorsed by proposing a pledge-album that would have the same result. Rev. Frank E. Coulter, of the United Brethren Church, then made a stirring address, attacking the license system and maintaining that the basis of all work in this matter must be made with this end in view.

A San Francisco delegate gave his experience in school-work, and hoped that the presence of the Convention would bring about a more healthy public sentiment. He deprecated the side entrances of the saloon and grocery. A delegate from Hawaii told of the signers' pledge used in that country. There was a general feeling manifest that the Temperance Committee should be composed of the most enthusiastic and capable members of the Society.

CHRISTIAN-CITIZENSHIP COMMITTEE.

The Conference on Christian Citizenship was conducted by the leader, Rev. Wm. E. Davis, Lebanon, N. J., superintendent of the Christian-Citizenship Department of the New Jersey State Union.

The first speaker was Rev. A. A. Murphy, of the Second Presbyterian Church of New Brunswick, N. J.

His theme was "The Rights and Privileges of Citizenship." He emphasized the thought that loyalty to God embraced loyalty to Government, basing his declaration on the words of inspiration, "Render unto God the things that are God's, and unto Cæsar the things that are Cæsar's."

The next speaker was Rev. G. R. W. Scott, D.D., of Massachusetts.

His theme was "The American Spirit." It was a brilliant and forcible presentation of the spirit that animated our fathers and must be perpetuated by us to preserve our American institutions. Unrestricted emigration, Bossism, and Indifferentism are the foes most to be feared.

The third speaker was The Rev. Samuel Fallows, of Chicago, Bishop of the Reformed Episcopal Church.

His theme was "The Loyalty of the Adopted Sons of America." He spoke of the sacrifices and the devotion of those who had learned to love our American institutions.

Then came the general conference. The leader, the Rev. Wm. E. Davis, opened the discussion by saying that the hope of the nation was the enthronement of Christ in the nation. Salvation must come to the nation as it comes to the individual, from without and not from within. Civic righteousness must be the issue. To this end create public opinion, unite all the forces of righteousness, work on the principle that "the earth is the Lord's," — that he will and does claim his own. The downfall of iniquity is sure, from the Christian standpoint.

The general conference was spirited, showing that in various parts of our land much had been done in the way of suppressing vice in every form. Sunday baseball, immoral literature, unlicensed saloons, Sunday theatre-going, and the like were the evils at which efforts had been directed, and in many instances had prevailed.

GOOD-LITERATURE COMMITTEE CONFERENCE.

The leader of the conference was Rev. B. M. Price, of Dennison, O. There was a very pleasant company gathered in the Third Congregational Church. The importance of possessing the literature, and the best methods of distribution, outlined the conference. The employment of Good-Literature Committees in hospital and Sabbath-school work was strongly urged. To assign the members of the committees to various parts of the parish, that all the families of the church may be reached with religious papers, was advocated. The suggestions meeting with the most favor were, to supply religious papers to bootblack-stands, in order to counteract the baneful effects of the lurid publications with which they were, as a rule, supplied; to distribute tracts at racetracks as the patrons were leaving the grounds; to supply public hospitals, jails, and other corrective institutions with religious publications.

Miss Mary E. Drown, of Washington, D.C., gave the experiences of the Washington Endeavorers in distributing good literature, and suggested that one helpful plan was to cultivate a taste for good literature in the young by recommending good books to be read by them, and to suggest to others to read that book which in one's own reading had been found to be the most helpful.

LORD'S DAY COMMITTEE.

The Lord's Day committee meeting held in the Central Methodist Episcopal Church was largely attended, Francis W. Reid, State secretary of the California Union, presiding. After prayer by Dr. Briggs, the chairman spoke on the best means of securing Sabbath reform, and described how the California Union had won the banner given by Rev. Wilbur F. Crafts for the greatest amount of Lord's Day committee work done.

Remarks were made by Rev. D. Davies, of Oshkosh, Wis., who said that the best lawyers agreed that Sunday observance could be enforced by common law, whether there was a local statute or not.

Miss M. Kay, secretary of the Woman's National Sabbath Alliance, described that organization and its work, and read the pledge, which, on the resolution of Mr. Rich, of Watsonville, Cal., was adopted for recommendation to the Resolution Committee of the Convention. It is as follows: —

"We, women of America, recognizing the American Christian Sabbath as our rightful inheritance, bequeathed to us by our forefathers; as the foundation of our national prosperity; as the safeguard of our social, civil, and religious blessings; as the conservator of the rights of the wage-earner, do hereby pledge ourselves to resist by precept and example whatever tends to undermine Sunday as a day of rest and worship, such as the Sunday secular newspaper,

Sunday social entertainment, and Sunday driving and traveling for gain or pleasure ; and we further pledge ourselves to use our influence to create a right sentiment on all aspects of the Sunday question, especially in reference to traffic of every kind on that day."

Delegate Craig, of Santa Fé, N. M., said he did n't believe in boycotting, but he would boycott every man who kept his shop open on Sunday.

After some remarks by Mr. Reid and others on Sunday bicycling, Dr. Bentley, of Berkeley, pleaded with San Franciscans not to make a practice of coming over the bay on Sunday, thus breaking the Sabbath themselves and compelling their friends to do so.

INFORMATION AND PRESS COMMITTEES.

This conference, owing to the small attendance, was a very informal one. The appointed chairman, Rev. Warren P. Landers, press superintendent for the Massachusetts Christian Endeavor Union, was present. Special emphasis was laid upon the systematic publication of Christian Endeavor departments in the secular press. Ways and means for carrying on such work were considered. The use of *The Golden Rule* and other religious periodicals and papers by Information Committees, and the circulation of these papers by the societies, was also discussed. The conference was held in the Central Methodist Episcopal Church.

OFFICERS' CONFERENCES.

CORRESPONDING SECRETARIES' CONFERENCE.

A meeting of the corresponding secretaries from all parts of the Union was held in the First Baptist Church for the purpose of agreeing upon a system of general correspondence. Miss Carrie A. Holbrook, of St. Paul, presided.

A paper was read on " City and District Union Secretaries." After a general discussion upon " Interdependence of State and Local Societies," the meeting adjourned.

JUNIOR SUPERINTENDENTS'.

Miss Belle P. Nason, of San Diego, presided over the meeting of the Junior Superintendents at the First United Presbyterian Church. J. N. Dolph, of Portland, delivered an address upon " Superintendents' Responsibility and Soul-Saving Opportunities." Following was the program of the meeting : —

"Reception of Juniors Into Societies," Miss Ella J. Newton, Foochow, China ; " Temperance Work," Miss Minnie Ellingson, Minnesota ; " Missions," Miss Hall, Caldwell, Idaho ; " Band of Mercy Work," Miss E. Oney, Chicago ; " Committee Work," Miss Alice Wythe, Oakland ; " Our Consecration Meeting," Miss Helen Smith. Litchfield, O. ; " Social Work," Mrs. James Hill, Massachusetts ; " Parents' Work," Mrs. Clark, San Francisco ; " Shall Junior Work Be Under Pastor and Superintendent or Senior and Superintendent ? " Mrs. Greenweld, Deer Lodge, Mont. ; " Graduation," Miss Le Baron, Chicago ; " Best Time for Rallies," R. C. Burkes, Eugene, Oregon ; " Need of Junior City Officers," Miss C. Parsons, of Kalamazoo, Mich.

LOCAL UNION OFFICERS' CONFERENCE.

The Conference of the Local City Union Officers was attended by about fifty persons, among them representatives from Chicago, New York, Rochester, Cleveland, St. Louis, Virginia, Grand Rapids, St. Paul, Portland, Ore., Alameda City Union, Newark, N. J., and Worcester, Mass. The questions that were discussed were : —

How to meet the expenses of the Union? By collections.

How long should local societies' officers be elected for? One year. The best work was done when there were not so many changes.

How interest pastois in Union work? One pertinent inquiry was whether the co-operation of the pastors was really essential to success; but it was a question no one seemed to want to answer directly, though all agreed that the pastor's interest and aid were a great inspiration; how to get it was the problem.

One delegate from Richmond, Va., said the interest of his pastor had been secured by convincing him that the society was doing the Lord's work; and from a New Hampshire man came the idea that you could not invite the pastor's interest, but must compel it; while from New York came the suggestion that if the young people would act as the pastor's assistants in building up the church, and not try to do the pastor's work, there would be more cordiality between them. A lady from Alameda said she had given much consideration to the matter, and had thought of many ways, and had finally come to the conclusion that the best way to secure the pastor's interest in the work was for each society to appoint a member whose duty it should be to pray for the pastor, and all pray on the same day. A pastor who was present said that it would be better if all the members would pray for the pastor, as the pastors needed it.

Best program for a Union meeting? A good speaker on live open parliament. This would also get the societies to attend.

It was unanimously conceded that the best work the union could do was that which would help each local society to uphold its pastor, broaden the influence of the Church, and make the Society a power in its own immediate circle to bring the coming of the Lord's Kingdom.

Many features of special work by various unions owned blessed by the Master were mentioned, such as evangelistic effort, Bible study, missionary work, and, especially, a drinking-fountain erected by the Cleveland Union.

State Union Officers' Conference.

The State Union officers of the Christian Endeavor Association held a called meeting in the German lecture-hall of the Young Men's Christian Association Building, with H. H. Grotthouse, of Texas, as chairman, and Miss Tyler Wilkinson, of Temple, Tex., as secretary. The value of conventions in Endeavor work was the subject first considered. It was concluded that calling too many county and district rallies was not commendable. The means of securing statistics was also canvassed, as were the raising of money, the editing of a State Endeavor-paper, the selection of a Nominating Committee, the advantage of consecutive conventions in adjoining States, federating with other societies, and the best plan for extension work. The question, "Should the Christian Endeavor engage, as such, in work apart from its own?" was answered in the negative, the opinion being that the association was to be regarded in the light of an inspiration and not an institution. Regret and annoyance were expressed over the card-playing, dancing, and beer-drinking in which some of the excursionists on the Endeavor trains indulged, to the detriment of the association, for some of the culprits wore Endeavor badges, though not entitled to do so.

Special Workers' Conference. — Floating Society.

An eager, earnest band of about seventy-five workers were gathered at Simpson Memorial M. E. Church on Friday afternoon, with M. C. Turner, of San Diego, State Superintendent of California F. S. C. E., in the chair. After song and devotional exercise, the workers were addressed by Miss Annette Jones, of Falmouth, Mass., on "The Past, Present, and Prospective of F. S. C. E." Miss Jones gave a brief history of the seven years' life of this branch of Endeavor work, and described some of the plans for the future. She dwelt upon the best methods of reaching the sailor's heart, and advocated the use of the comfort-bag. She said, "Some people think the comfort-bags are things that are made, and thrown at the sailors. and that is all, but this is not so.

The Testament is the chief content of the bag, and the other contents and kindly notes are just to make the gift of the book more precious. But be careful in the making. Be sure your *drawstrings* draw! Four-fifths of the bags sent out are made badly, and are an incentive to profanity rather than a *comfort*." Miss Jones called for consecrated workers, and closed with the sentence, "One is your Master, even Christ, and all the seamen are our brethren."

Miss Jones was followed by an address on "The Use of the Pledge-Card," by that consecrated worker, Mrs. B. B. Goss (*née* Esther Rossier), of San Diego, Cal., who said : "WHEN to present the pledge-card is the chief thing. Careless or indifferent signing of the pledge is dangerous. Never force the pledge upon one. Prayer only can bring an answer to the question *how* to present the pledge ; the Spirit only can answer. May our Lord help us to forget ourselves in our work."

In the discussion that followed Mr. H. F. Eden, of San Francisco, thought the pledge should not be presented until the sailor shows a scriptural evidence of conversion. Other speakers were Miss M. L. Bowen, of Oakland, on "Formation of Societies " and " Prayer Circle ; " Miss Hoffman, of San Francisco, on " Socials." In the discussion that followed, " Home Socials " and " Correspondence with Sailors " seemed the all-absorbing themes. Mrs. Emma M. Livermore, of Santa Barbara, gave an interesting talk on work with the coasting schooners. Mr. Geo. E. Duncan, Jr., of San Francisco, Giles Kellogg, of San Diego, H. F. Eden, of San Francisco. spoke briefly on "Rooms for Seamen," " Limitation of Visitors," and " The Relation of Work in F. S. C. E. to the Seamen's Mission."

Mr. John Makin, of Tacoma, Wash., who goes soon to the home at Nagasaki, Japan. and Mrs. Emma T. Read, of San Diego, on " Financiering the Society," were the last speakers, on a very full and very instructive program.

TRUSTEES' AND OFFICERS' COUNCIL.

ONE of the most pleasant and most profitable features of the international conventions is the annual meeting of the Trustees and Officers of the United Society, with the presidents of the various State and Provincial Unions. Although the meeting this year came after the Convention closed, through force of circumstances, it was none the less enjoyable.

After a business session in which matters of mutual interest were discussed with perfect freedom, the company adjourned to the conservatory hall of the Palace Hotel. After the banquet Dr. Clark paid a high tribute to the genius and faithfulness of the Committee of '97. Continuing, he said : —

"We are more than grateful to all of you who have contributed to the success of the Convention, and we are thankful to Almighty God for the abundant blessings that he showered upon our big gathering. The numbers exceeded our expectations, and the spirit of all who came to deliberate with us in the Convention, during its quiet and still moments as well as during its enthusiastic moments, makes me feel that God has been with us. We are grateful for the spirit of goodness and hospitality of the people of San Francisco. We are grateful to all of you for what you have done. We appreciate the task that has been yours, and we rejoice that God has crowned all·your labors with unlimited success."

President Clark then announced that on behalf of the United Society he desired to present those who had managed the affairs of the Convention so ably with a little token of regard. On the lapel of Chairman Watt's coat he pinned a pretty gold pin, the emblem of the Christian Endeavor Society, the letters of which were studded with pearls and garnets. Attached to it was a gold guard pin and chain. After Mr. Watt had been decorated, President Clark distributed similar pins to each member of the Committee of '97.

Mr. Watt made a most felicitous response for himself and his co-laborers. He also referred in strong terms of approbation to those who had borne with him the burden of the great Convention.

Rev. Howard B. Grose, of Boston, member of the Board of Trustees, then presented the report of the committee on resolutions that should have been made to the meeting of the council in the morning. The resolutions were as follows:

Resolved, That the council composed of the trustees of the United Society and the presidents of the State Unions of Christian Endeavor, voicing the sentiments of the entire Convention, and gratefully recognizing the overwhelming kindness with which we have met on all sides, desires most heartily to record its profound appreciation of the service rendered by the Committee of '97, whose masterly grasp of details and splendid efficiency left nothing lacking for our comfort and the success of the great Convention; the cities of San Francisco, Oakland, and Sacramento, for characteristic Western welcome and hospitality, and the State of California, for legislative welcome; the railway officials, for their diligent efforts to conquer overwhelming difficulties of transportation, due in part to their own lack of faith in Christian Endeavor probabilities; the police, the conductors, and motormen, the railway employees and all public servants, for the thoughtful and patient courtesy everywhere extended; the press, for the insight and the sympathetic spirit of the editorials and the full and accurate reports of the meetings, by which the influence of the Convention has been spread throughout the country; the Convention choir, for its constant service and leadership in song; the churches and pastors whose doors were thrown open in fraternal welcome and broadcast interdenominational fellowship; and the community at large for an unsurpassed manifestation of cordiality and interest.

The resolutions were adopted by a rising vote, and the gathering then adjourned with a prayer by Secretary Baer.

THROUGH THE EYE TO THE SOUL.

THE church was crowded to the doors! The daily "Chalk-talks" given in the First United Presbyterian Church at 8.30 A. M. proved of great interest. The "hand-preacher" was Rev. Robert F. V. Pierce, of Philadelphia. Prefacing each exhibition of skill, he spoke of the methods and principles pursued in this important work. The place became a daily Normal Art School, for the time being. Every hour spent there was profitable.

Mr. Pierce strikingly illustrated the meanness of giving to God only the worthless last fragment of our life by imagining a man who had promised the gift of a canary, but put it off till, one morning, the bird was found fluttering on the bottom of the cage, and striking its bill feebly against the wires, its mouth gaping open. Mr. Pierce represented the man with the dying bird in his hands toddling over to his friend and exclaiming, "See, I promised you a canary. Here it is. Accept it, my dear friend!"

Mr. Pierce urged that chalk-talkers should always give the bad side first, and talk about the good last. To illustrate, he drew a heart, and transformed it with a few touches into a laughing face. But the devil of evil passions comes along, and, in an instant, if we let him into our hearts, can change them to anger and ugliness. A few strokes of the crayon, and the smiling face was distorted in a horrible frown. "Now *that* picture," said Mr. Pierce, "is not the one you want to leave with the children for them to draw on their slates all the week."

To illustrate the proper mode of treatment, Mr. Pierce drew the curved outline of the New York harbor, Brooklyn on one side, New York on the other. He told about Hell Gate, the ugly rocks in the harbor, and of how General Newton's little daughter, Mary, only twelve years old, by a touch of her finger upon an electric button applied the spark to the carefully prepared mine that blew the great obstructions out of the harbor. A few lines crossing one another stood for the streets of New York where Mary was, and a curved line for the electric wire running down to the big, black rocks in the harbor. A few strokes, and the heart-shaped harbor becomes a human heart, the heart harbor, in which are the great rocks of sin, our Hell Gate. The crossed streets of New York above the heart harbor become a red cross. From it, where the wire had run, flows a red stream. It widens, it spreads over the entire heart, it blots out the ugly rocks of sin. "The blood of Jesus Christ, his Son, cleanseth us from all sin." Now you have the bright thought last.

These were workers' conferences, and many note-books were used. It was pleasant, also, to see the number of children present.

A thin candle, only a fraction of an inch thick, stood for a life rapidly going out. It burned down while Mr. Pierce was talking. Yet its last flicker could light a young candle that had many hours to burn.

"The place of all others," said Mr. Pierce, "to make missionaries and workers for missions is in our Sunday-schools and young people's societies."

Mr. Pierce told the story of a Sunday-school superintendent that said one Sunday he wanted some boy to make a locomotive of himself. hitch on to some other boy, and bring him to the school. Next Sunday Sammy burst in right in the middle of the opening exercises. shuffled up the aisle, puffing, "Choo-choo-choo-choo," and after him thirteen new boys, holding on to one another's coats. Stopping before the astonished superintendent, Sammy, said, "There's my train of cars, sir!"

"'Don't' — that's the worst thing in the wide world to say to a child. What children want is the word 'Do.'"

A temperance rhyme Mr. Pierce would have the children learn : —

"Drink no cider. brandy, wine, or rum,
Nor anything else that makes drunk come."

"My cup runneth over," Mr. Pierce would illustrate with a glass which he fills with water from a lot of little cups. One addition stands for health, another for friends, another for food, for home, for clothes, etc. All being poured in, the cup is exactly full. But our cup of blessing should run over on to others. Moody shows how by taking a pitcher of water and pouring it all boldly into a glass tumbler.

"Thou preparest a table before me," Mr. Pierce illustrated once in his church by setting in his pulpit a table with the nicest linen and dishes, and having a long succession of Sunday scholars bring on, one at a time, plates heaped high with all kinds of good things to eat,— first a plate of what grows in the ground, then one of what grows on the ground, then a little above the ground, and so on. After enforcing the lesson of gratitude, he had the good things carried to this and that needy person.

"A life built on Christ." The chalk-talker told how sin comes down over our lives like a great box, darkening them. He drew the box. But Christ lets in the light, the light of Bethlehem's star. He drew a window. And Christ himself enters, being the Door. He drew a door. Then came a roof and a chimney, and behold, there was a pretty little house, the "home of the soul." Two crossing walks were put in rapidly, shaded, and lo! the house was seen to be founded on a crimson cross. "Underneath are the everlasting arms." "My hope is built on nothing less than Jesus' blood and righteousness." "All other ground is sinking sand." "Other foundation can no man lay."

These "Chalk-talks" were a new departure in convention proceedings, and are sure to be perpetuated.

STUDYING TO BE QUIET.

AT Washington, after the sermons of the opening night an impressive season followed which was called the "Quiet Hour." In this Convention, beginning on Thursday, such an hour was held each afternoon, excepting Saturday.

In the Calvary Presbyterian Church large numbers gathered at 4.30 to review the day and to prepare for the evening's feast.

These meetings, save that on Monday afternoon, were under the especial direction of Mr. Charles T. Studd, of London, England. The first of these "Hours" had for its topic "Deepening the Spiritual

Life." Secretary Baer presided. The church was filled. After a hymn Mr. Studd spoke.

Mr. Studd dwelt particularly upon the laxity of many so-called Christians, who seemed to be satisfied with their own salvation and were lukewarm when it came to the question of saving the millions to whom the name of Christ was unknown.

"There are millions and millions of these unhappy people in the world." he said, "to whom the name of God is unknown. If the Christians of to-day could only realize that lamentable fact it would help them to be better Christians, and it would bring them to a better state of mind and body to receive the spiritual life.

"Many are asking, 'What is the spiritual life?' Opinions differ on the matter. Some say one thing, some say another, and the result is that there is no consensus of opinion. The people to-day have not got the gospel of Christ. Many persons feel satisfied with their work as Christians. but God puts no limit on his work. We can never know how great his salvation is. We want to know all that he can do with us. We sing so often of crowning Christ as King of kings! The crown of England's Queen or the Presidential appointment of McKinley would be as a thimble for a crown for Christ. The only crown which will fit the head of Christ is the one of all nations. While we are crowning individuals, and making history and nations, we are forgetting that we are citizens of heaven. And as citizens of heaven, how lukewarm we are in the cause!

"As citizens of England or America, I care not which, how many of you would give your blood and money in defence of your country or flag? You would cheerfully do so. You would not spare your blood or money. Would you fight that way for Christ? We are more patriotic for our country than we are for Christ. Have we fought for Christ as we should? Unless we are prepared to do so. we had better quit being Christians. A soldier is useless if he has any other greater love than the one for his flag and country. He cannot give up his life for his country if he is thinking of his family or his worldly possessions. How, then, can we be soldiers of Christ if we are not prepared to sacrifice everything for the cause? If a General says to a regiment, 'Go and charge,' they do so like good soldiers; but when Christ, the General, says to us 'Go and charge; go into all the world and preach the gospel,' we skulk away and hide ourselves. Even as Christ said to his disciples, 'Unless a man renounceth all he hath, he cannot be my disciple.'"

On Friday a still larger number sought the church to hear the magnetic speaker. Hundreds failed to gain admittance.

Mr. Studd spoke pointedly upon "The Chinese and Their Needs." He depicted the terrible condition of the people in China, and the depths of degradation and darkness in which they existed. He told his hearers of some of his experiences in China, where he labored in the missionary field for ten years. "The Chinese," he said, "2,000 years ago had the best religion the time afforded ; but it has not led them on. They tell you that they are believers in Confucius, the oldest philosopher of the world ; but it is different to have a dead philosopher to believe in than a living Saviour. Two thousand years ago we were naked savages, but the Word of God has made us the most prosperous nation in the world. It is because we are so prosperous that it is our duty to send the gospel around the world, or God will take away from us all we have. There are brothers and sisters in foreign lands who are in need of help. In China things are very different to what they are here, and we ought to thank God that he has allowed us to be born in this land. Here we have faith and love ; in China they do not know of these things. Where there is no faith in God there can be none in man or woman. In China they build high walls around their cities and villages, and their houses have no windows, because they have no faith in any one and fear they will be robbed of all they have. There is no knowledge of confidence there because they have no knowledge of confidence in God."

Mr. Studd then described to his audience the awful extent of infanticide which exists in all parts of China, where the female babes are killed by their mothers. He told how he had seen towers built for the purpose of placing the babies that they might be eaten by wolves and dogs, and said that it was a common occurrence for the little ones to be thrown into ditches and left to die. It was not a crime in China for a mother to kill her girl babies. There was no such thing as love in married life. A man never made love to a girl there; he just went to a marriage-broker and told him that he was willing to pay so much for a wife, and he bought her the same as he would a horse, and she became the slave of her mother-in-law. The cruel system of binding the feet of the girls was graphically told, and a thrill of horror went through the audience when he detailed the horrible cruelty of drawing the nails from the feet.

" If these things took place in this country," said the speaker, "you would probably lynch the monsters who were the cause. Don't you think that it is your duty as Christians to help lynch the devil in China, who is the cause of all these horrors? Remember the word of the Master, ' Go ye into all the world and preach the gospel to every creature.' If you can't go in the body, go in the spirit, and do all in your power as Christians to help the gospel eradicate these awful things."

The meeting on Sunday was also crowded, and Mr. Studd spoke with greater power than ever.

Certainly the words of Rev. Robert Johnston, of London, Ont., are true : " The Quiet Hours, and noonday evangelistic services have been to many the most helpful parts of the Convention. I am inclined to think that greater prominence might be given to both of these in coming conventions."

PASTORS' CONFERENCE.

SOME three hundred ministers, with a sprinkling of laymen, were present at the special meeting of pastors at Odd Fellows' Hall, which was conducted by Dr. Francis E. Clark, president of the society. The principal theme discussed was "The Society as an Adjunct of the Church," and twenty-five speakers gave briefly their views and experiences. Dr. Clark, in his opening remarks, showed that the only mission of the organization was to help the church, and that when the first society was founded, in Portland, Me., its sole object then was as an auxiliary to the local church. No thought was then given of extending the society to its present proportions, but it had grown gradually and normally. In England, Australia, and India, which countries the speaker had recently visited, the movement was conducted on the same lines and with the same purposes as in this country. That the society had been of positive benefit in promoting church work was demonstrated by statistics which had been lately compiled.

They showed that 57 per cent of the active members of the society attended the mid-week services, while in the same churches only 27 per cent of the membership were participants in that meeting. As to the Sunday evening service, 86 per cent of the active members of the Christian Endeavor Society were represented, as against 58 per cent of the regular church membership, including both old and young. This comparison was not intended to reflect upon the usefulness of the church, or to indicate a decline in its strength, but served to illustrate the spirit of earnestness, sincerity, and fidelity that was inculcated by the methods of the society.

After President Clark's address the speaking was of an inspirational nature. Rev. Silas Mead, LL.D., of Adelaide, South Australia, and Rev. Barton W. Perry, Ph.D., of California, advocated the extension of the Senior Endeavor Society, with the object of doing for the mid-week service what had been accomplished for it by the young people's organization. This plan met with the approbation of the succeeding speakers, and a number instanced the benefits of the Senior Society where its operations had come under their notice.

SUNRISE DEVOTIONS.

WHEN Dr. Clark planned for the first sunrise prayer-meeting at one of the earliest International Conventions, held in Saratoga, the young man who had been assigned to lead it, and had never before even dreamed of such an idea, thought some one had blundered, and in his heart feared a dismal failure. When, a little later, he found the auditorium in which this early morning prayer-meeting was to be held crowded to its utmost capacity, with a great company filling the entrance, he saw his own mistake. From that time to this, through all these years, not only at International, but also at State and local conventions, the sunrise services have been most popular with the young people, and most blessed in the influence which they have exerted, and which goes to sweeten and brighten and heighten every event of the crowded Convention days.

In spite of all the attractions of the Convention, of the city, and of the warm welcome which greeted the delegates, all of which drew heavily upon the physical and mental powers, these early morning meetings were well attended and full of power, as was plainly manifested at the close of one of them, when a young man succeeded in getting around him quite a company for the express purpose of carrying on prayer-meetings in the liquor-saloons of the city. These evil institutions, by the way, joined with all the city in displaying the Convention colors and extending a hearty welcome.

Each morning opened with nine services, conducted by prominent workers from all parts of the country. The topics were especially adapted to the day, often leading out in their thought to the themes to be considered in the pavilions, — "The Christian Endeavor Pledge," "Committee Work—Service," and "Our Associate Members." On Sunday the topic was appropriately "Prayer for Church Services and Pastors."

LEARNING OF THE BOOK.

THE Convention was fortunate in securing as lecturer for its daily Bible study, Prof. Herbert L. Willett, of Chicago.

Large audiences greeted Mr. Willett at each session, and much interest was manifested in the addresses. They were four in number and were delivered in the Central M. E. Church, at 8.30 A.M. The topics were, "Micah : a Message of Warning and of Hope ;" "Philippians : a Message of Joy in the Midst of Adversity ;" "Habakkuk : a Message of Endurance and Hope ;" "John : a Message of Light and Love."

The lectures began on Friday morning. At that session Professor Willett said :—

"Preliminary to the study of our topic, I invite your thought to a consideration of prophets in general. What was a prophet? Not a foreteller of future events—that was not his prime business—but to speak a message of divine truth that was in his heart."

The following syllabi will show the ground covered by the studies each day : —

Micah : A Message of Warning and of Hope.

Friday, July 9.

I. INTRODUCTORY.

    1. The Bible the record of a divine revelation to humanity.
    2. This revelation made through the lives of specially chosen men.
    3. The prophets were the religious teachers of Israel to prepare for the final revelation in Christ.
    4. The essentially prophetic character and purpose of all Scripture.

5. The place of Micah among the prophets :
   - (*a*) His date, and the political situation in his time.
   - (*b*) The moral and religious condition of the people.
   - (*c*) Personality of Micah; comparison with (1) Amos, (2) Isaiah.
6. Sources and helps for the study of Micah.

II. THE MATERIAL OF THE BOOK OF MICAH.

1. The calamity impending over Samaria, in which Jerusalem will be involved, Chap. 1.
   - (*a*) The title, a statement regarding the author and his date, 1 : 1.
   - (*b*) The Lord is about to visit terrible judgments upon the land, 1 . 2-4.
   - (*c*) The cause of this visitation is the sin of Samaria and Jerusalem, 1 : 5-7.
   - (*d*) The prophet's distress in view of the coming trouble, 1 : 8.
   - (*e*) The fall of Samaria will involve Judah in disaster, 1 : 9.
   - (*f*) Graphic picture of the fate of towns in the path of the invading Assyrian, 1 : 10-16.
2. Sins that have brought on this calamity. Chaps. 2, 3.
   - (*a*) The nobles are greedy and oppressive; they shall be spoiled, 2 : 1-5.
   - (*b*) Angry protests against the rebukes of the prophet, 2: 6.
   - (*c*) Reply of Micah that *they* are responsible. 2 : 7-10.
   - (*d*) False prophets the only ones to whom they will listen, 2 : 11.
   - (*e*) An abrupt transition ; Israel united and victorious under the leadership of God. 2 : 12, 13.
   - (*f*) The heartless selfishness of the popular leaders. 3 : 1-4.
   - (*g*) In contrast with false prophets, Micah has a divine message, 3 : 5-8.
   - (*h*) Crimes of selfish priests and prophets are bringing Jerusalem to ruin, 3 : 9-12.
3. The promise of restoration and blessing. Chaps. 4, 5.
   - (*a*) The future exaltation of Mt. Zion, 4 : 1-5.
   - (*b*) In that time God will restore the scattered nation to its home, 4 : 6-8.
   - (*c*) But there will be first a period of distress and exile, 4 : 9. 10.
   - (*d*) Then Zion in might will thresh her enemies as sheaves, 4 : 11-13.
   - (*e*) To Israel, insulted by foes, Bethlehem will give the Messianic King, 5 : 1-4.
   - (*f*) Leaders will be found, and Assyria shall be punished, 5 : 5, 6.
   - (*g*) The remnant of Jacob, beneficent as dew, strong as a lion, 5 : 7-9.
   - (*h*) The nation transformed; war and idolatry banished, 5, 10-15.
4. God's controversy with Israel, Chaps. 6, 7.
   [NOTE.— The tone of these last two chapters is in striking contrast with the earlier portion of the book. A considerable interval has elapsed, and the prophet describes conditions less hopeful than before.]
   - (*a*) Israel commanded to meet God in judgment ; the mountains witnesses, 6 : 1, 2
   - (*b*) Jehovah's case stated; his constant care for Israel, 6 : 3-5.
   - (*c*) Israel's awe-stricken question, " What offering will atone? " 6 : 6, 7.
   - (*d*) The answer: " Justice, mercy, humility," 6 : 8.
   - (*e*) Divine denunciation of fraud, oppression, lies, and idolatry, 6 9-16.
   - (*f*) Lament of the righteous over the degenerate times, 7 : 1-6.
   - (*g*) In sadness he must wait for better days, 7 : 7-10.
   - (*h*) Prosperity can only come at a distant day, 7 : 11-13.
   - (*i*) The prophets prayer for the return of the divine presence as in the old time. This alone can bring victory and blessing, 7 . 14-20.

III. LEADING IDEAS OF THE PROPHET MICAH.

1. The sins of the city, as viewed by a countryman.
2. The sins of the rulers, as viewed by a tribune of the people.
3. The sins of religious leaders, as viewed by a prophet of God.
4. Judgments in the form of Assyrian invasion and Babylonian exile.
5. The hope of a better day to come; the Messianic King.
6. Applications of Micah's teaching to the present time.

Philippians; A Message of Joy in the Midst of Adversity.

Saturday, July 10.

I. INTRODUCTION.

1. The place of Paul in the New Testament church.
2. His earlier labors and writings.
3. The church of Philippi, and Paul's relations to it.
4. Date and occasion of the Epistle to the Philippians.
5. Sources and helps for the study of the Epistle.

II. THE MATERIAL OF THE BOOK OF PHILIPPIANS.

1. Paul's statements regarding himself, Chap 1.
   - (*a*) Salutation to the church, in which Timothy joins, 1 : 1, 2.
   - (*b*) Thankfulness for their unselfishness, confidence in them, 1 : 3-6.
   - (*c*) Paul's great love for them, 1 : 7, 8.

(*d*) His prayer for their spiritual well-being, 1 : 9-11.
(*e*) His imprisonment has benefited the cause of Christianity, 1 : 12-14.
(*f*) He rejoices in whatever good is done even by bad men, 1 : 15-20.
(*g*) Life and death equally blessed; which shall he chose? 1 : 21-24.
(*h*) Their need of him convinces him he will be spared, 1 : 25, 26.
(*i*) Exhorts them to continue faithful and fearless, 1 : 27-30.
2 The imitation of Christ, 2 : 1-18.
(*a*) They should be unselfish and mutually appreciative, 2 : 1-4.
(*b*) The divine example of self-renunciation. 2 : 5-8.
(*c*) The exaltation of the Christ, following his humiliation, 2 : 9-11.
(*d*) Their attainment of salvation the ground of Paul's glorying, 2 : 12-18.
3. Paul is about to send them helpers, 2 : 19-30.
(*a*) Timothy to go soon, Paul hoping to follow later, 2 : 19-24.
(*b*) Epaphroditus, just recovered from illness, will go at once, 2 : 25-30.
4. Warnings against false teachers, Chap. 3.
(*a*) Circumcision a mere fleshly rite, and of no value, 3 : 1-3.
(*b*) If birth or legalism could benefit, Paul is amply provided, 3 : 4-6.
(*c*) Yet he counts these as nothing, and trusts in Christ alone, 3 : 7-11.
(*d*) He has not attained perfection, but presses toward it, 3 : 12-14.
(*e*) Walking in the light, new light will come, 3 : 15, 16.
(*f*) Paul's grief at the conduct of worldly Christians, 3 : 17-19.
(*g*) Our citizenship is heavenly, for whose full disclosure we wait, 3 : 20, 21.
5. Admonitions to proper conduct, and acknowledgment of gifts, Chap. 4.
(*a*) Two women in the church urged to friendship, 4 : 1-3.
(*b*) Self-control and confidence should characterize them all, 4 : 4-7.
(*c*) The true standard of thought and conduct set forth, 4 : 8, 9.
(*d*) Paul's gratitude for the gifts brought by Epaphroditus, 4 : 10-20.
(*e*) Salutation and benediction, 4 : 21-23.

III. LEADING IDEAS AND TEACHINGS.

1. The Christian has constant cause for rejoicing.
2. The humiliation of Christ; his law of service.
3. Confidence in the gospel, no matter who may preach it.
4. The equal blessedness of life and death to the Christian.
5. Hints regarding Paul's character afforded by the Epistle.

Habakkuk: A Message of Endurance and Hope.

Sunday, July 11.

I. INTRODUCTION.

1. The prophet as a writer *vs.* the prophet as a preacher.
2. Absence of data regarding Habakkuk.
3. The date, shortly before the battle of Carchemish, in 604 B. C.
4. The political and religious situation in the reign of Jehoiakim.
5. Character of the Book of Habakkuk; beauty and strength of its style.
6. Sources and helps for the study of the book.

II. THE MATERIAL OF THE BOOK OF HABAKKUK.

A. A dialogue between the prophet and God; sin, punishment, and deliverance, Chaps. 1, 2.
1. The prophet's cry of despair; violence and injustice, 1 : 2-4.
2. The divine response; judgment is near. 1 : 5-11.
(*a*) A wonderful thing is about to occur, 1 : 5.
(*b*) God will raise up the proud and conquering Chaldeans, 1 : 6, 7.
(*c*) Fierce and swift, they plunder and capture, 1 : 8, 9.
(*d*) Kings and fortresses are powerless before them, 1 : 10.
(*e*) Resistless, wicked, and impious, they will sweep on, 1 : 11.
3. The prophet's anxious question, "Will God permit this?" 1 : 12-17.
(*a*) God has chosen the Chaldean as a corrector of Israel, 1 : 12.
(*b*) But how can God approve his ruthless career? 1 : 13, 14.
(*c*) He catches the nations like fish, and exults, 1 : 15.
(*d*) He worships, not God, but the instruments of destruction, 1 : 16.
(*e*) Is he to continue in this blood-thirsty career? 1 : 17.
4. A pause. The prophet, like a watchman, waits to see how God will justify his use of the Chaldean, 2 : 1.
5. The divine response in the form of an oracle, 2 : 2-4.
(*a*) Something important is to be spoken; write it plainly, 2 : 2.
(*b*) Its fulfilment not immediate; yet wait for it, 2 : 3.
(*c*) The oracle is this:
"The Chaldean is puffed up with pride;
But the just shall be preserved by his faithfulness." 2 : 4.
6. The prophet's comment on the oracle regarding the Chaldean, 2 : 5-20.
(*a*) Yes, like drunkenness, his pride and rapacity are insatiable, 2 : 5.
(*b*) The nations he is oppressing will taunt him for his
(1) Violence to conquered peoples, who will plunder him, 2 : 6-8.
(2) Utter selfishness in building his dominion on ruins, 2 : 9-11.

(3) Cruelty by which cities were built; God only is great, 2: 12-14.
(4) Barbarous degradation and destruction of subjects, 2: 15-17.
(5) Senseless adoration of dumb idols, 2: 18, 19.
(c) Jehovah is in his temple; let the earth keep silence, 2: 20.
B. An ode. Confidence in God.
  1. The title: a prayer of the prophet in dithyrambics, 3: 1.
  2. He is disquieted by the oracle, 2: 4; a plea-for mercy, 3: 2.
  3. A vision; God's majestic manifestation, and an explanation of the divine purpose in it, 3: 3-15.
    (a) The dazzling descent of God, preceded by terrors, 3: 3-5.
    (b) Nature and men in consternation at his presence, 3: 6, 7.
    (c) Was Jehovah angry with rivers and seas? (No), 3: 8.
    (d) Yet all nature was in terror before him, 3: 9-11.
    (e) God's indignation not against nature, but against the foes of his people, whom he destroys, 3: 12-15.
  4. The vision does not relieve the prophet; he must wait in silence for a future deliverance, while the Chaldeans devastate and the drought consumes, 3: 16,17.
  5. But he rouses his soul from depression and utters his supreme confidence in God, who is his strength and his salvation, 3: 18, 19.

III. LEADING CHARACTERISTICS AND IDEAS.
  1. General absence of predictive and Messianic elements.
  2. The perplexity; suffering without seeming cause or immediate relief.
  3. Refuge found in three thoughts:
    (a) The Chaldean will meet just retribution.
    (b) Jehovah is supreme; even the Chaldeans are his instruments.
    (c) The righteous man finds salvation in fidelity to God.
  4. The use of the "Oracle" in the New Testament, Rom. 1 : 17; Gal. 3 : 11; Heb. 10: 38.
  5. Application of the teaching of Habakkuk to the present time.

John : A Message of Light and Love.

Monday, July 12.

I. INTRODUCTION.
  1. The three periods in the life of the Apostle John.
  2. Relation of the First Epistle to the Fourth Gospel.
  3. Conditions prevailing among the churches in John's closing years.
  4. Sources and helps for the study of the Epistle.

II. THE MATERIAL OF FIRST JOHN.
  1. Fellowship with the Father is the secret of life and love, 1 : 1-2 : 17.
    (a) Actual facts, tested and approved, are being set forth, 1 : 1, 2.
    (b) The purpose of the writing is to widen the fellowship, 1 : 3, 4.
    (c) God is light, 1 : 5.
    (d) To walk in the light is to have fellowship and pardon, 1 : 6, 7.
    (e) The disclaimer of sin is self-deception, but pardon waits confession, 1 : 8-10.
    (f) The remedy for sin and the sign that it is effectual, 2 : 1-6.
      (1) Christians should not sin; but sinning, they have an advocate, 2 : 1, 2.
      (2) Obedience to the will of Christ indicates that one knows him, 2 : 3-6.
    (g) A commandment already given reapplied, 2 : 7-11.
      (1) The old commandment to love one another is enough, 2 : 7.
      (2) It needs only a new statement for the new time, 2 : 8.
      (3) Love and hate, darkness and light, 2 : 9-11.
    (h) A striking summons, and an impressive contrast, 2 : 12-17.
      (1) The challenge to the attention of the various classes in the church, 2 : 12-14.
      (2) The appeal not to love the world, 2 : 15.
      (3) Things that pass and things that abide, 2, 16, 17.
  2. The conflict of truth and falsehood, 2 : 18-4 : 6.
    (a) Disclosure of truth and falsehood, 2 : 18-29.
      (1) The last hour, as proved by rise of antagonists, 2 : 18, 19.
      (2) Believers anointed from above know the truth, 2 : 20, 21.
      (3) The antichrist defined as a denier of the Christ, 2 : 22, 23.
      (4) Necessity of holding fast the original teaching, 2 : 24-29.
    (b) Children of God, and the children of the devil, 3 : 1-12.
      (1) The immeasurable love of God to his children, leading to hope and purity, 3 : 1-3.
      (2) The inconsistency of sin in the life of a child of God, 3 : 4-9.
      (3) The life of sonship issues in love, not hatred, 3 : 10-12.
    (c) Fellowship in Christ, and hatred by the world, 3 : 13-24.
      (1) The two realms, Christianity and the world, love and hatred, 3 : 13-15.

        (2) We know the meaning of love through the example of Christ, 3: 16.
        (3) False and true exhibitions of love, 3: 17-22.
        (4) The twofold commandment and its reward, 3: 23, 24.
    (*d*) The rival spirits of truth and error, 4: 1-6.
        (1) The true test is belief in the reality of Christ's life, 4: 1-3.
        (2) These false voices are of the world, 4: 4-6.
3. The life of love and the victory of faith, 4: 7-5: 21.
    (*a*) The greatest message of the Bible — God is love, 4: 7-21.
        (1) Love is the secret of the life of God, and must be of ours, 4: 7-13.
        (2) The great declaration, God is love, proved by his love manifested, 4: 14-16.
        (3) Love creates boldness and casts out fear, 4: 17, 18.
        (4) Our love to God must issue in love to our fellowmen, 4: 19-21.
    (*b*) The victory and witness of faith, 5: 1-12.
        (1) Sonship to God comes by faith in Christ, and is expressed in love, 5: 1-3.
        (2) Faith is the victory that overcomes the world, 5: 4, 5.
        (3) The witnesses to Christ, 5: 6-9.
        (4) The highest witness is in the believer, 5: 10.
        (5) Eternal life is in Christ, 5: 11, 12.
    (*c*) The confidence of the Christian life, 5: 13-21.
        (1) We may have boldness for ourselves and in prayer for others, 5: 13-17.
        (2) A final word of confidence and exhortation, 5: 18-21.

III. LEADING IDEAS.

1. Not arguments and doctrines so much as watchwords: Truth, Light, Life, Love.
2. Love the essential characteristic of God, and therefore of his children.
3. Sin is not yet conquered in the Christian, but is being overcome.
4. The essence of sin is the denial of the reality of the life and work of Christ.
5. The impressiveness of the last voice of the apostolic age.

NUMBER OF SOCIETIES, JULY, 1897.

UNITED STATES.

	Young People's.	Junior.	Intermediate.	Mothers'.	Senior.	Total.
Alabama	120	41	2			163
Alaska Territory	6					6
Arizona	18	3				21
Arkansas	131	34	2			167
California	758	551	51		3	1,363
Colorado	203	120	6	1		330
Connecticut	532	217	6		2	757
Delaware	74	31	1			106
District of Columbia	80	61	5			146
Florida	178	50				228
Georgia	162	27	1			190
Idaho	49	16				65
Illinois	2,013	993	44	30		3,080
Indiana	1,387	549	21			1,957
Indian Territory	44	14				58
Iowa	1,336	518	8	1	1	1,864
Kansas	980	378	6	11		1,375
Kentucky	354	91	5	1		451
Louisiana	62	16				78
Maine	647	193	8			848
Maryland	375	118	1	1	1	496
Massachusetts	943	517	23	2	1	1,486
Michigan	1,071	468	16	1		1,556
Minnesota	540	266	15		1	822
Mississippi	57	9		1		67
Missouri	877	453	8		1	1,339
Montana	52	27	1			80
Nebraska	577	236	8	1	1	823
Nevada	10	6				16
New Hampshire	320	119	1		3	443
New Jersey	798	405	6			1,209
New Mexico Territory	32	9				41
New York	3,049	1,288	18		1	4,356
North Carolina	202	56	1			259
North Dakota	114	34				148
Ohio	2,384	970	32	3	1	3,390
Oklahoma Territory	156	28	1			185
Oregon	309	138	2		1	450
Pennsylvania	3,443	1,396	27	20	3	4,889
Rhode Island	146	74		2		222
South Carolina	69	11	1			81
South Dakota	210	74	2	1		287
Tennessee	389	150	1			540
Texas	438	232	10			680
Utah	39	27			1	67
Vermont	346	136	3	1		486
Virginia	201	34				235
Washington	273	97	5			375
West Virginia	231	55				286
Wisconsin	535	252	8			795
Wyoming	20	6				26
Total	27,340	11,594	358	67	21	39,380

CANADA.

	Young People's.	Junior.	Intermediate.	Mothers'.	Parents'.	Total.
Alberta	12	2				14
Assiniboia	47	7				54
British Columbia	45	7				52
Manitoba	118	24				142
New Brunswick	199	17				216
Newfoundland	6					6
Nova Scotia	405	49				454
Ontario	1,788	291	4	1		2,084
Prince Edward Island . .	67	2				69
Quebec	227	64	1		2	204
Saskatchewan	5					5
Total	2,919	463	5	1	2	3,390

FOREIGN.

	Young People's.	Junior.	Intermediate.	Mothers'.	Senior.	Total.
Africa	47	5				53
Asiatic Turkey	1	1				2
Australia	1,960	160			4	2,124
Austria	2	2				4
Belgium	1					1
Bermuda	6					6
Brazil	2	1				3
British Guiana	10					10
Burmah	14					14
Chili	6					6
Colombia	1					1
China	49	4				53
Denmark	2					2
Egypt	3					3
England	3,470	448	3	2	2	3,925
France	68					68
Germany	32					32
Guatemala	1					1
Hawaiian Islands . . .	7	3				10
Holland	1					1
India	238	12				250
Ireland	156	13				169
Italy	3					3
Japan	63	3				66
Labrador	1					1
Laos	10					10
Madagascar	93					93
Mexico	72	28				100
Norway	4					4
Persia	3	1				4
Samoa	10					10
Scotland	402	31				433
South Sea Islands . .	2					2
Spain	7					7
Switzerland . . .	1					1
Sweden	3					3
Syria	3	1				4
Turkey	33	8				41
Upper Hebrides . .	1					1
Wales	311					311
West Indies . . .	73	3				76
Total	7,179	729	3	2	6	7,919

RECAPITULATION.

	Young People's.	Junior	Interm'diate.	Mothers'	Senior.	Parents'.	Total.
United States	27,340	11,594	358	67	21		39,380
Canada	2,919	463	5	1		2	3,390
Foreign	7,179	729	3	2	6		7,919
Floating Societies							91
							50,780

COMPLETE INDEX OF THE REPORT.

Topics of Services. — Themes of Addresses, Sermons, and Lectures. — Christian Endeavor in Societies and Committees. — Rallies, Conferences, Studies, and All Special Meetings. — Presentations, Receptions, Greetings, Resolutions, Etc., Etc. — Reports and Statistics. — Poems and Special Songs. — Personnel.

www.ingramcontent.com/pod-product-compliance
Lightning Source LLC
Chambersburg PA
CBHW051748040426
42446CB00007B/267